1,50

THE NEW TESTAMENT
Its Making and Meaning

THE NEW TESTAMENT

Its Making and Meaning

By

ALBERT E. BARNETT

Professor of New Testament Interpretation
Garrett Biblical Institute

ABINGDON PRESS
New York • Nashville

THE NEW TESTAMENT: ITS MAKING AND MEANING

Copyright MCMXLVI by Stone & Pierce

Library of Congress Catalog Card Number: 46-5640

E

SET UP, PRINTED, AND BOUND BY THE
PARTHENON PRESS, AT NASHVILLE,
TENNESSEE, UNITED STATES OF AMERICA

TO

Students who have been introduced to the
study of the New Testament in my classes

PREFACE

AT THE TIME of his death on March 16, 1939, Dr. Andrew W. Sledd, of the faculty of the Candler School of Theology, Emory University, was engaged in writing a book with the same title as this volume. In June of the preceding year I sat with Dr. Sledd in his home at Decatur, Georgia, and discussed with him his treatment of the epistles of James and Second Peter. Knowing the order of his treatment of the materials, I received the impression that the book was nearing completion. Accordingly, a few months after Dr. Sledd's death, I inquired about the manuscript and offered to do whatever editorial work might be necessary to prepare it for publication. Mrs. Sledd and the agents of Abingdon-Cokesbury Press approved the suggestion. When, however, the manuscript was sought, only a few pages could be found. The conclusion was that Dr. Sledd had not been entirely satisfied with what he had done and, as was his custom, had destroyed the larger portion of the manuscript, intending to rewrite it *de novo*. All who knew Dr. Sledd must share my disappointment that he did not have the opportunity to bring his work to completion.

This volume, then, had its origin in the plans of Dr. Sledd and the publishers, but of necessity it represents an entirely new study. It is different in its arrangement of the materials, and the conclusions that it embodies are not infrequently other than those Dr. Sledd would have drawn. Anyone, however, who has studied with Dr. Sledd will be conscious of my deep indebtedness to him, an indebtedness that is gratefully acknowledged.

The numerous footnotes, it is hoped, will lead readers to acquaint themselves with the source materials on the basis of which conclusions have been drawn. The book will have failed of its purpose if it does not stimulate a careful reading especially of the New Testament. The conclusions are candidly expressed, but with the thought that they may stimulate independent study which may lead others to different judgments. No considerable degree of

7

originality is claimed for them, and in the main they are sufficiently representative of the judgments of competent scholarship in the field to deserve the attention of students.

The public which the publishers intended when Dr. Sledd originally undertook the preparation of his book has been carefully kept in mind. The book has been written with the needs of college and seminary students in view but at the same time with the thought that it should be both interesting and profitable to the general reader with a background of liberal education. As largely as possible, references have been restricted .to standard works in English, and quotations of source materials are in translations that can be consulted in almost any good library.

Acknowledgment is made:

To the University of Chicago Press for permission to quote the biblical passages used throughout the book from J. M. P. Smith and Edgar J. Goodspeed, *The Bible: An American Translation.*

To the President and Fellows of Harvard College, owners of the "Loeb Classical Library," for permission to quote the translation of selected passages from the following works in that series: *The Apostolic Fathers,* translated by Kirsopp Lake (1925) ; Tacitus, *The Annals,* translated by John Jackson (1937) ; Tacitus, *The Histories,* translated by Clifford H. Moore (1937) ; Pliny, *Letters,* translated by William Melmoth (1940).

To The Macmillan Company for permission to quote Eusebius, *The Ecclesiastical History,* translated by H. J. Lawlor and J. E. L. Oulton (1927) ; and to reproduce a diagram from B. H. Streeter, *The Four Gospels* (1925).

To Abingdon-Cokesbury Press for permission to reproduce a diagram from Frederick C. Grant, *The Growth of the Gospels* (1933).

Quotations from other early Christian literature are from *The Ante-Nicene Fathers,* edited by Alexander Roberts and James Donaldson (Edinburgh, 1867), American edition re-edited by A. Cleveland Coxe (Buffalo, 1885), and *The Nicene and Post-Nicene Fathers,* First and Second Series, edited by Philip Schaff and H. Wace (New York, 1886-1900).

The bibliography appended at the back of the book is not intended as an exhaustive list of relevant materials. Its primary function is to give the publication data regarding books actually consulted in the preparation of this volume and thus make possible an abbreviation of footnotes. It constitutes, however, a fairly adequate library of reference for readers who may desire to explore more fully a variety of lines of inquiry.

To my colleague Dr. J. Minton Batten for his careful reading of the proof and to the staff of Abingdon-Cokesbury Press for helpful editorial suggestions I desire to express my appreciation and thanks.

ALBERT E. BARNETT

CONTENTS

INTRODUCTION

JESUS, although the central figure of the New Testament, himself wrote nothing. His message was delivered orally, and for twenty years after the close of his earthly ministry the memory of his followers constituted the only record of its content. Much that he taught was forgotten, but he remained unforgettable. Confidence in him, fidelity to him, the hopes aroused by him, the values to which he gave contagious reality, the conviction that his life and leadership did not end with his death, combined to create the primitive Christian community.

However highly and deservedly Christians have valued and continue to value the New Testament, the fact is that instead of producing Christianity the New Testament was itself the product of the developing Christian movement. The collection of writings that became the New Testament and the individual books that found a place in that collection came into existence as phases of the growth of the church.

Yet from the outset Christians had a Bible. The Old Testament was the scripture of the primitive church, and its proper interpretation rather than its supplementation by the addition of new books was the preference of Christian leaders for more than a century. In no instance were the books that now make up the New Testament written for inclusion in a Bible. The practical needs of the first readers of these books caused them to be written. Only when the church found its religious and evangelistic needs inadequately met by the Hebrew Scriptures were these Christian writings recognized as co-ordinate in authority with the Old Testament. Their relationship to the life of the developing Christian community being of this sort, the books of the New Testament, individually and as a collection, shed indispensable light on the origin and nature of Christianity and constitute the classical literature for the understanding and cultivation of Christian experience.

An evaluation of these books by the methods of literary and historical criticism contributes to a discovery of the message they were originally intended to convey. By this means it becomes more nearly possible for their authors to speak for themselves. By undertaking to re-create the historical setting of each New Testament book and by exploring the possible solutions of the critical problems which these books severally present, the present study attempts to recover for the modern reader the message intended for those who were the reading public to whose needs and interests the books were first addressed.

The effort is made to arrive at such answers as the available evidence warrants to five principal questions about each of the twenty-seven New Testament books: (1) Who was its author? (2) Who were its original readers? (3) When was it written? (4) Where was it written? (5) What kind of situation occasioned its writing, and what, in view of that situation, did its author intend to accomplish? (6) Finally, in the light of the historically probable answers to these questions, what is the author's message?

The spirit in which these questions are asked and answered does not differ from that in which similar inquiries about any body of literature would be made. There is a careful ascertainment of the relevant facts, a candid—though in instances tentative—acceptance of these facts, and an effort to deduce from the facts conclusions that are unprejudiced by preconceived notions or apologetic interests. Where alternative possibilities exist, each with sound warrant in the evidence, preference is given the conclusion that contributes most naturally to an understanding of the content of the book.

Two types of evidence are taken into account in answering the literary and historical questions: (1) External evidence consists of testimony derived from literature other than the document under consideration. Certain of the books of the New Testament yield information about members of the collection that were written earlier. Then the noncanonical Christian literature of the first four centuries is an invaluable source of data. (2) Internal evidence consists of data supplied by the books themselves. Where such evidence is entirely clear, it is decisive. External evidence must always be treated as secondary to the data which a document itself affords.

External evidence that antedates A.D. 200 is especially valuable because it is less apt to be affected by the theological and institutional interests that developed with Catholic Christianity. The principal sources of evidence from this period and their probable dates are:

1. The First Epistle of Clement to the Corinthians—95
2. The seven epistles of Ignatius of Antioch to the Ephesians, the Magnesians, the Trallians, the Romans, the Philadelphians, the Smyrnaeans, and Polycarp—110-15
3. The Epistle to the Philippians of Polycarp, Bishop of Smyrna—115 [1]
4. The Epistle of Barnabas—130-35
5. The Shepherd of Hermas—130-40
6. The Didache—150
7. The Second Epistle of Clement to the Corinthians—150
8. The *Apology* and the *Dialogue with Trypho* by Justin Martyr—150-60
9. Excerpts preserved in the *Church History* of Eusebius (325) from the no longer extant writings of such men as Papias of Hierapolis (140), Hegesippus (180), Melito of Sardis (180), Pantaenus (180), etc.
10. Irenaeus' *Against Heresies*—175-89
11. Clement of Alexandria's *Miscellanies, Address, Tutor,* and *Outlines*—190-202
12. The two earliest lists of New Testament books regarded as canonical: (*a*) that of Marcion (144), consisting of an edited version of Luke's Gospel and ten letters of Paul; and (*b*) the Muratorian list, representing the sentiment of the Roman church in 185-200, and consisting of the four Gospels, Acts, thirteen letters of Paul (Marcion's ten plus the Pastorals), Jude, First and Second John, the Wisdom of Solomon, the Revelation of John, and the Revelation of Peter, with a favorable recommendation of Hermas for private reading.

Data supplied by the writings themselves require careful evaluation. Many of the books, such as the Gospels, Acts, Hebrews, are anonymous, and judgments regarding their authorship are inferences from allusions which are frequently indecisive. In certain

---

[1] P. N. Harrison undertakes to show that Polycarp wrote two letters to Philippi: (1) the earlier written about 115 as an introduction to the collected letters of Ignatius and consisting of chapters 13–14; (2) the second written about 135 in refutation of the views of Marcion and consisting of chapters 1–12. He identifies Marcion as the heretical teacher whom Polycarp describes as "the first-born of Satan" (7:1; cf. Iren. *Her.* III. 3. 4) on the ground that he "perverts the oracles of the Lord for his own lusts." See his *Polycarp's Two Epistles to the Philippians.* Edgar J. Goodspeed points out the serious weaknesses of this view (*History of Early Christian Literature,* p. 25).

instances, such as Ephesians, the Petrine epistles, the Pastoral epistles, explicit affirmations of authorship in the text of the writing are unconvincing. They appear to have the character of a literary device for acknowledging indebtedness or for securing a hearing for the author's message which his own name would not command. It has to be remembered, however, that authorship in antiquity did not involve property rights and that the message of a book took precedence over any credit that might be involved in authorship. Consequently the ethical problem involved in pseudonymity lacked the acuteness which it has for the modern author.[2] Titles, which are a part of extant manuscripts but not of the text of the books, are a phase of the process of canonization and are properly considered as external evidence.

The readers who determined the author's emphases are in some instances clearly designated, as in the Thessalonian and Corinthian letters. Elsewhere, as in Galatians and Philemon, the identification of the addressees leaves the modern reader with uncertainties that seriously affect his understanding of the author's meaning and purpose. In the instances of the epistles to Timothy and Titus, pseudonymity has apparently been employed in the designation of both the recipients and the author and is best interpreted as an aspect of the message of the epistles. Such books as Mark, Matthew, John, and Hebrews give no explicit information about the identity and location of their readers. Ephesians, Jude, and Second Peter are distinctive in that they clearly indicate Christians in general as their reading public.

The books of the New Testament never plainly specify when or where they were written. Reasonable probability in these matters can be reached by inference from allusions to events that can be dated, such as the period of Gallio's official residence at Corinth, and on the basis of acquaintance with the geography of the Mediterranean world and the history of the church during the first two centuries.

A brief preview of conclusions regarding the literary and historical problems examined in detail in the body of the present volume illustrates what has been said. The original disciples of Jesus appear to have written nothing, although the names of three of them are traditionally associated with certain New Testament

---

[2] Goodspeed, *New Chapters in New Testament Study*, pp. 169-88.

books: (1) Matthew with the first Gospel; (2) John with the fourth Gospel, the three Johannine epistles, and Revelation; (3) Peter with the Petrine epistles. No sound defense can be made of the Matthaean authorship of the Gospel that bears the disciple's name, although there is the probability that he contributed to the formulation of the oral tradition of Jesus' teaching that was incorporated in the documentary source which B. H. Streeter designates as "M." The same hand could hardly have been responsible for Revelation and the Fourth Gospel, and it is improbable that the Johannine epistles and the Fourth Gospel had the same author. On the basis of the representation of him in the Synoptic Gospels, the disciple John was more probably the author of Revelation than of the Fourth Gospel, although a stronger case can be made for the latter on the basis of the external evidence. The probabilities weigh heavily and all but decisively, however, against the assignment of any of the five books traditionally associated with the name of John to that disciple. Similarly, it is incredible that the same hand wrote First and Second Peter. External evidence supplies a foundation for a defense of the Petrine authorship of First Peter, but the content of the epistle itself greatly reduces the confidence which this evidence might otherwise warrant. All available evidence combines to discredit the ascription of Second Peter to the disciple. These results are not surprising. The first Christians lived in the momentary expectation of the return of Jesus to inaugurate the Kingdom. This expectation, together with the numerical and geographical smallness of the church, made writing unnecessary. Only when Christianity overflowed its original geographical and cultural boundaries was the impulse to write born. That this was the case is shown by the fact that the New Testament books and the written sources on which they drew were written in Greek. Their quotations of the Old Testament were, similarly, from the Greek translation known as the Septuagint.

The books of the New Testament were written between A.D. 49 and 175, Galatians being the earliest and the epistles to Timothy and Titus the latest of them. Arranged in chronological sequence, they are:

Galatians—49
The Thessalonian letters—50
The correspondence with Corinth—53-55
Romans—56

Philippians— (55?) 60
Colossians and Philemon— (55?) 51-62
Mark—65-67
Matthew—75-80
Luke-Acts—90-95
Ephesians—95
Hebrews—95
Revelation—95
First Peter—95-100
The Fourth Gospel—95-115
The Johannine epistles—110-15
James—125-50
Jude—125-50
Second Peter—150
The epistles to Timothy and Titus—160-75

This order differs (1) from that in the English Bible, where the order is, the four Gospels, Acts, Paul's letters, including the Pastorals and Hebrews, the seven Catholic epistles, and Revelation; and (2) from that of the manuscripts, where the usual order is, the four Gospels, Acts and the seven-letter Catholic corpus, the fourteen-letter Pauline corpus, and Revelation. These more familiar arrangements, however, reflect the history of the canon and of the text rather than the history of the literature itself. Since the history of the literature is the primary interest in this study, the chronological arrangement of the books is preferred. The books are treated in the order of their origin that they may shed light on the development of the Christian movement and that the growth of the church may in turn contribute to an understanding of the meaning of the books.

The first readers of these books were members of Christian groups located in the great cities of the Roman Empire. In the earlier phases of its expansion, the membership of the church represented a mixture of Jewish and non-Jewish Christians. After the Jewish War of A.D. 66-70, however, Christianity made few converts from Judaism, and by the close of the first century the church was largely non-Jewish in membership. The cities where Christians so largely lived were the localities where the New Testament books were written: Galatians and the Gospel according to Matthew at Syrian Antioch; the Thessalonian letters and Romans at Corinth; the Corinthian letters, Luke-Acts, Ephesians, Revelation, the Fourth Gospel, the Johannine epistles at Ephesus; Philippians, Colossians, Philemon, Mark, First and Second Peter, Jude, the epistles to Timothy and Titus at Rome; James at Caesarea; Hebrews at some point outside Italy, conceivably at Alexandria.

It was clearly not the purpose of those who wrote the books of the New Testament to create a body of literature that would supplement or compete with the Old Testament. What they wrote had to do with the needs of local groups of Christians or with crises of one sort or another that threatened the church. The exigencies of Christian missions, the destruction of Jerusalem, the hostility of the Roman government, which periodically expressed itself in persecution, as under Nero, Domitian, and Trajan, and the emergence of heretical sects constituted the general historical background of the literature. The common concern was in all instances with religious truth and its values for Christian living. The authors were missionaries, evangelists, apologists for the Christian faith. The stimulation and maintenance of faith was their chief interest. The Fourth Evangelist's description of his own purpose in John 20:31 suggests the motivation of every New Testament writer: "There were many other signs that Jesus showed . . . which are not recorded in this book. But these have been recorded so that you may believe that Jesus is the Christ, the Son of God, and through believing you may have life as his followers."

I

THE LETTER TO THE GALATIANS

Authorship.—As with other books of the New Testament, traces of the influence of Galatians on other Christian writings appear much earlier than an explicit mention of it by title and author.[1] During the last decade of the first century and the first quarter of the second century, indications of acquaintance with Galatians are clearest and most numerous in Ephesians, the Fourth Gospel, and the letter of Polycarp to the Philippians. Somewhat less clearly, but with a high degree of probability, Galatians appears to have been known to the authors of Revelation, First Peter, Hebrews, First Clement, and the letters of Ignatius. It shared the unpopularity of Paul's letters during the second quarter of the second century, with the result that no suggestion of acquaintance with it appears in the Shepherd of Hermas, Barnabas, the Didache, Second Clement, the Martrydom of Polycarp, or the Apology of Aristides. The Epistle of James alone during this period evidences a knowledge of it. Acquaintance with Galatians appears during the latter half of the second century, though without formal citation, in Second Peter, the writings of Justin and Athenagoras, and the Pastorals, with the greatest clarity and volume of use by Justin.

The earliest reference to Galatians by title is its inclusion in the canon of Marcion (*ca.* 144), where it stands first in the list of Paul's letters. In the Muratorian canon (*ca.* 185) it is attributed to Paul and is listed as the sixth of his letters. Thereafter it is quoted formally and is definitely assigned to Paul.

The letter itself claims to have been written by Paul.[2] No set of circumstances is anywhere implied that violates the scheme of Paul's life as it is sketched in the New Testament. The situation reflected in the letter is too complex to have been imagined, and all of the

---

[1] The data showing the early circulation of Paul's letters as a collection are exhaustively examined in my *Paul Becomes a Literary Influence.* There is no evidence for the circulation of the letters singly.

[2] 1:1.

21

data of the letter indicate that it was the product of that situation. If Paul wrote any letter ascribed to him, he wrote Galatians. No other letter has claims to authenticity that are sufficiently clearer to supply sounder criteria of genuineness than Galatians itself supplies. The available evidence warrants the conclusion that the letter as it stands is a unity and that it was written by Paul.

The First Readers.—The letter is addressed not to a single church but "to the churches of Galatia."[3] They were churches that owed their establishment to Paul's missionary activity.[4] His original stay in their midst was accidental. He was on his way elsewhere but was forced by illness to alter his plans, and the result was the evangelization of the territory included in the salutation.[5] These churches had been founded on the same general occasion, and Paul had visited them twice at the time he wrote.[6] The people who composed their membership seem to have accepted Christianity quite recently[7] and to have been largely non-Jewish.[8] The relationship between Paul and the readers of his letter was one of deep affection. He speaks of them as "my children," and his message to them has the warmth of parental love in its eagerness to deter the Galatians from accepting privileges less adequate than those to which he had introduced them.[9] This much the letter tells of its first readers.

Any further identification of them depends on the judgment formed of the geographical location of "the churches of Galatia."[10] A certain amount of uncertainty exists because "Galatia" had an ethnographical and also a political connotation in Paul's time. Behind this double meaning of the term lies a story which can only be sketched in bare outline.

Beginning in the fourth century B.C., and at one time threatening to capture Rome itself (390), migrating hordes of Gauls moved eastward and between 281 and 239 overran the peninsula of Asia Minor. They were decisively defeated by Attalus of Pergamum in 239, and were settled in a district north and east of the center of the peninsula. Bithynia and Paphlagonia lay to the north of the territory allotted to them, Cappadocia and Lycaonia to the south, and Phrygia to the west. This restricted section took the name "Galatia" from its new inhabitants.

[3] 1:2.	[4] 3:2-3; 4:12-14, 19, 20.	[5] 4:13.	[6] 3:1-3; 4:13-20.
[7] 1:6.	[8] 4:8; 5:2; 6:12.	[9] 4:16-20.	[10] 1:2; I Cor. 16:2.

In 189 B.C. Asia Minor was brought under Roman rule. Thereafter the area designated as Galatia was enlarged and so ceased to correspond to the geographical lines within which the Gauls had settled. In 40 B.C. Antony added a contiguous section of Paphlagonia to Galatia, with Kastor as king of the enlarged territory, and at the same time made Amyntas king of Pisidia and Phrygia. Four years later, when Kastor died, his kingdom, with part of Paphlagonia and most of Lycaonia added, was joined with that of Amyntas and placed under the latter's rule. The kingdom of Amyntas was further expanded under Augustus. After the death of Amyntas in 25 B.C. the major portion of his kingdom was organized into the Roman province of Galatia. The political meaning of the term did not completely take the place of the older sense, with the result that room for debate remains whether or not Paul employed it in its distinctly Roman and political sense when he directed the present letter.

If the churches addressed were located in the restricted territory to which the Gauls were confined in 239 B.C., they were founded on Paul's second missionary journey on the occasion suggested by Acts 16:6, and Luke's two references to the situation behind our letter are Acts 16:6 and 18:23. The principal cities in this area were Tavium, Ancyra, and Pessinus, and the churches addressed would normally be regarded as located in those cities.

If, however, Paul founded no churches in northern Galatia, and if he customarily used geographical terms in their Roman sense, the churches addressed in Gal. 1:2 were those established on the first missionary tour and were located at "Perga in Pamphylia," "Antioch in Pisidia," "Iconium," and the "Lycaonian towns of Lystra and Derbe and the country around." [11]

Those who urge the former possibility insist that it is unlikely that Paul designated the districts of Pisidia and Lycaonia by the Roman name of the province, and that it is still less likely that he would address the people living in those districts by the ethnic title "Galatians." [12] It is urged, furthermore, that Luke's failure to speak of the localities mentioned in Acts 13 and 14 as Galatia shows that his employment of the term in Acts 16:6 was definitely

[11] Acts 13:13, 14, 51; 14:6, 20-22.
[12] 3:1. Otto Staehlin, *Die altchristliche griechische Literatur* (München: C. H. Becksche, 1924), p. 1139; Jülicher, *Introduction*, p. 75.

ethnographic, and that Acts, therefore, supports the north Galatian location of the churches addressed.[13]

Without minimizing the weight of opinion favoring the north Galatian destination of the letter, the reasons for regarding it as addressed to Christian groups in the cities mentioned in Acts 13 and 14 are both more numerous and more convincing.

In the first place, there is no record in Acts that Paul did any missionary work in northern Galatia. Granted that Luke is hurrying him toward Europe at the point in the narrative where he might have given an account of such work, his silence loses the weight it might otherwise have by the absence elsewhere of any record of ancient Christian groups at Tavium, Ancyra, and Pessinus.

When Paul addressed his readers as "Galatians,"[14] it is as unlikely that he gave the term a definitely racial significance as when he referred to the Thessalonians and Philippians as "Macedonians."[15] Not only so, but there are other instances in which Paul clearly designates churches by the Roman province in which they were located.[16] It may even be maintained with sound warrant that Paul customarily employed geographical terms in their Roman sense.[17] Significantly, also, the author of First Peter, himself thoroughly acquainted with Paul's collected letters, names Galatia in his list of Roman provinces.[18]

On the first missionary journey Paul and Barnabas visited towns that had been in the Roman province of Galatia since the death of Amyntas in 25 B.C. On the second journey Paul and Silas revisited some of these churches.[19] Instead of a departure into different territory, Acts 16:6 describes the lap of the trip just completed, which had taken Paul and Silas through "Galatic Phrygia" as distinguished from Asian Phrygia and Galatic Lycaonia.[20] It would seem, therefore, that established usage of seventy-five years is supported rather than contradicted by Luke and that the recipients of Paul's letter were the communities mentioned in Acts 13 and 14. This conclusion is strengthened by the fact that the readers of the

[13] Moffatt, *Introduction*, p. 93.   [14] 3:1.   [15] II Cor. 9:2, 4.

[16] I Cor. 16:19; II Cor. 1:1; 8:1.

[17] Burton, *The Epistle to the Galatians*, p. xxv.   [18] I Pet. 1:1.

[19] Acts 16:1-5.

[20] Greek geographical names ending in ια normally had an adjectival sense. In Acts 16:6 τὴν Φρυγίαν καὶ Γαλατικὴν χώραν probably meant "the Phrygian-and-Galatic region," or "Galatic Phrygia." (McNeile, *Introduction*, p. 129.)

letter are well acquainted with Barnabas,[21] who had accompanied Paul on the first but not on the second journey. It may be significant, also, that the list of those who started with Paul to Jerusalem to deliver the collection gathered among the churches contains no names that represent churches in northern Galatia but does contain the names of Gaius of Derbe and Timothy of Lystra.[22]

Date.—The writing of Galatians may be located at any one of several junctures in Paul's career. The available evidence does not decisively fix the time. At the time the letter was written Paul had apparently visited the Galatian churches twice.[23] The two visits may have taken place during the first missionary journey.[24] If this is true, Galatians was the earliest of Paul's letters and was written upon his return to Syrian Antioch and prior to the visit to Jerusalem of Acts 15:2 f. This also requires that the visit to Jerusalem described in Gal. 2:1-10 be equated with that of Acts 11:30.

It is possible, however, to regard the two visits to the churches mentioned in Acts 13 and 14 as a single visit, and to identify the second distinct visit as that of Acts 16:1-6. This requires that the trip to Jerusalem of Gal. 2:1-10 be identified with that of Acts 15:2 ff., and that the trip of Acts 11:30 be viewed as not having occurred, its representation as a separate visit being due to Luke's confusion of the twofold purpose of a single visit with two separate occasions. Such a construction of the data means that Galatians was written at least four years after the churches were founded. Presumably Paul arrived at Syrian Antioch after the close of the second missionary journey, found bad news from Galatia, and at that time wrote his letter.[25] On this basis Galatians was his third letter.

If, however, the visits to the Galatian churches were those of Acts 16:1-6 and 18:23, the letter belongs to the period of the third tour. It has strong thought affinities with Romans and discusses issues resembling certain concerns of the Corinthian letters. Conceivably Galatians was written during Paul's long stay at Ephesus,[26] either

---

[21] 2:1, 9, 13.   [22] Acts 20:4; 24:17; cf. I Cor. 16:1-4; II Cor. 8:5-7; 9:1-2.

[23] Tὸ πρότερον in 4:13 may mean either "formerly" or "the former of two times." It probably means the latter in this context.

[24] Acts 14:21-26.   [25] Goodspeed, *Introduction*, p. 26.

[26] Acts 19:1, 10. J. H. Ropes sees no "sufficient reason for assigning the epistle to a . . . date . . . before the arrival at Ephesus" (Acts 19:1), except that the words "so quickly" of Gal. 1:6 remain problematical. See his *The Singular Problem of the Epistle to the Galatians*, p. 46.

between First and Second Corinthians [27] as his fourth letter, or after completion of the correspondence with Corinth [28] as his fifth.

The available data are best satisfied by the first of these three possibilities. The letter was written soon after the conversion of the readers.[29] Paul had visited the churches twice.[30] The second visit had been quite recently made, and the Judaizing agitation had followed this second visit. Paul shows no awareness that the disturbing tendencies had made their appearance during his second visit. The news that evoked his letter had taken him completely by surprise.[31]

Again, Paul had visited Jerusalem twice, and only twice, between the time of his conversion and the writing of Galatians.[32] The question of the number of his visits to Jerusalem is crucial and not incidental. The visits are mentioned as evidence that Paul was only slightly acquainted with the leaders of the Jerusalem church and was not indebted to them for his message in a sense that would make him in the slightest degree subordinate to them. He would not, under the circumstances, overlook a visit.

There is general agreement that the Jerusalem visit of Gal. 1:18 corresponds to that of Acts 9:19-26. Debate centers about the second visit. The visit of Gal. 2:1-10 more probably corresponds with that of Acts 11:30 than with the visit of Acts 15. On that second visit Paul had laid his understanding of the Christian message before the leaders "privately," [33] whereas in Acts 15 he seems to have made a public presentation. The pledge of co-operation given Barnabas and Paul [34] was probably a hesitant approval of their first missionary journey. In Gal. 2:10, Paul modifies his statement of 2:6 to the extent of mentioning the plea of the leaders that Barnabas and he "remember the poor," and he adds, "That I have taken pains to do." The purpose of the visit of Acts 11:30 was to take a contribution "to the brothers who lived in Judea," [35] whereas the central interest of the visit of Acts 15 was the settlement of a doctrinal question. The conclusive consideration that identifies the visit of Gal. 2:1-10 with that of Acts 11:30 instead of that of Acts 15 is the absence from Galatians of any citation of the favorable de-

[27] John Knox, "The Pauline Chronology," *Journal of Biblical Literature,* LVIII (1939), 15-29.

[28] McNeile, *Introduction,* pp. 133-36.   [29] 1:6.   [30] 4:13.

[31] 1:6; 4:16-20.   [32] 1:18; 2:1.   [33] 2:2.   [34] 2:9.

[35] Cf. Gal. 2:10.

cision of the Jerusalem leaders. Paul argues the issue on its merits, because the favorable decision at Jerusalem had not been made when he wrote Galatians.

If the narrative of Acts is at all relevant and correct, the letter to the Galatians was written after the visit of Acts 11 and before that of Acts 15. Paul visited the communities addressed twice during the journey of Acts 13 and 14. Several months intervened between the two visits, since modes of travel were slow, and the two visits were quite distinct. The return from Perga was by boat rather than by the shorter overland route, and when he reached Syrian Antioch messengers who had taken the shorter route were awaiting him with disturbing news. His first inclination was to return to Galatia, but it appeared imperative that he go to Jerusalem, where the agitation had originated. Faced with that dilemma, he dispatched his letter and hastened to Jerusalem [36] to fight the issues through with the responsible leaders.

Approximate accuracy is the best that can be hoped for in the matter of a calendar date for Galatians. The occasions of Paul's conversion and of his arraignment before Gallio are the points that afford a basis for reckoning. Of twenty-three representative opinions regarding the date of Paul's conversion which Moffatt cites,[37] ten suggest 31-33, nine 35 or 36, three 34, and one 38. The nearest to a consensus would appear to be 33.

On that basis, the first visit to Jerusalem after Paul's conversion [38] took place in 36. Treating the "fourteen years" of Gal. 2:1 as dating from the conversion occasion rather than from the first visit to Jerusalem,[39] and equating the visit which Paul describes as his second with that indicated as second by Luke,[40] the date of that visit is 47.[41] Allowing the usual two years for the first missionary

---

[36] Acts 15:2 ff.   [37] *Introduction*, p. 62.   [38] Gal. 1:18; Acts 9:19-26.

[39] Knox assumes (*op. cit.*) that II Cor. 12:2, written in the midst of Paul's stay at Ephesus during the third missionary tour, refers to the fourteen-year period of Gal. 2:1. He rules out the visit to Jerusalem mentioned in Acts 11:30 and locates Paul's conversion in the period 35-40. He overlooks that the context of II Cor. 12:2 places the emphases on a multiplicity of "visions and revelations," which tends to reduce the mention of a fourteen-year period in the two passages to an interesting coincidence instead of assigning it the decisive significance involved in his conclusions.

[40] Acts 11:30.

[41] C. J. Cadoux, "A Tentative Synthetic Chronology of the Apostolic Age," *Journal of Biblical Literature*, LVI (1937), 186.

journey, Paul returned to Syrian Antioch late in 49. If, as is here maintained, Galatians was written at this juncture, its date is 49.

A check on the approximate correctness of this chronology is furnished by the fairly certain date of the incumbency of Gallio as proconsul. After writing the letter Paul hurried on to Jerusalem for conference with the leaders, and shortly afterward began the second missionary tour,[42] which reached its consummation in the apostle's long residence at Corinth.[43] Paul's arraignment before Gallio[44] seems to have occurred when his own stay at Corinth was nearly over and shortly after Gallio assumed office. A letter from the emperor Claudius (41-54), the substance of which is preserved in an inscription unearthed at Delphi, indicates that Gallio assumed office in June, 51, which makes the year of his incumbency extend to June, 52.[45] Thus Paul reached Corinth early in 50, shortly after the Jerusalem conference.

Of course the location of Galatians at a different juncture would affect its date. The acceptance of 49 as the date is predicated on the judgment that the letter was written at Antioch at the close of the first tour. If it was written during the second tour, while Paul was at Corinth, the date was late in 51 or early in 52. If written from Antioch upon his return from the second journey, the letter falls about the middle of 52. Conceivably it was written at Ephesus during the third missionary campaign and belonged to the context of the correspondence with Corinth, and thus should be located within the period 53-55. A final possibility is that it was written at Corinth during the winter of 56.[46]

Place of Composition.—Galatians could have been written at any of the several places already suggested—Antioch, Ephesus, Corinth. A decision favoring a given city will be determined by judgments regarding the destination and date of the letter. The reasons for preferring Syrian Antioch have been made clear.

Antioch was an appropriate setting for the earliest book of the New Testament. The church there antedated Paul's contact with it and may have been founded by refugees from the persecution in which Stephen died.[47] At Antioch Barnabas brought Paul into the main current of the Christian movement.[48] There Paul urged

---

[42] Acts 15:36.   [43] Acts 18:11.   [44] Acts 18:12-17.
[45] Foakes-Jackson and Lake, *The Beginnings of Christianity*, I, v, 460-64.
[46] Acts 20:3.   [47] Acts 6:5; 11:19.   [48] Acts 11:26.

upon Peter the completely nonracial character of Christianity,[49]
and from Antioch as a base of operations the evangelization of
Asia Minor and the first phase of missions in Europe proceeded.
At Antioch "the disciples first came to be known as Christians." [50]
There, during the last quarter of the century, Matthew, favorite of
the four Gospels throughout Christian history and the Gospel that
reaches its climax in the "Great Commission," [51] was written.

Occasion and Purpose.—Paul had visited the Galatian churches
twice,[52] both visits, according to the judgment expressed above,
having occurred during the tour when the churches were established.[53] Paul had not sensed the presence during these visits of
the trends that had now developed. Instead he had been impressed
by the wholeheartedness with which the Galatians had accepted his
message and by the fervor of their piety.[54]

Shortly after his second visit, and presumably during the time required for the trip by boat from Attalia "back to Antioch," [55] certain
anti-Pauline missionaries, among them some persons of prominence,
visited the Christian communities in Galatia.[56] Paul questioned the
integrity of their motivation [57] and in the heat of his first reaction
to the confusion they had wrought even invoked a curse upon
them.[58] Actually they were simply Christians of conservative tem-
perament, whose background was Jewish and who retained as
Christians a rigorously Jewish point of view. They were convinced
that righteousness required obedience to the Mosaic law [59] and that
there could be no participation in the salvation promised Abraham
except on the basis of such obedience.[60] The popular symbols of
this obedience were circumcision, the observance of feasts,[61] and a
meticulous keeping of the Sabbath.[62] They wanted to protect the
Galatians against an uncritical acceptance of Paul's representation
of Christianity, which they regarded as basically defective because
it minimized legal obedience and, in their judgment, tended toward
antinomianism.[63] They supported their attack on Paul's message

[49] Gal. 2:12.   [50] Acts 11:26.   [51] Mat. 28:18-20.   [52] Gal. 4:13.
[53] Acts 14:21-26.   [54] Gal. 3:1-5; 4:6; 5:7.   [55] Acts 14:26.
[56] Gal. 5:10.   [57] 1:7; 4:17; 6:12-13.   [58] 1:8; 5:12.
[59] 2:16, 21; 3:2, 8, 11; 5:4.   [60] 3:7-9; 6:16.
[61] 4:21; 5:1, 3; 6:12-13.   [62] 4:10.

[63] 4:10; 5:11; 6:16. Ropes does not regard the Judaizers as Jewish Christian
emissaries from Jerusalem. They were instead a small group of "judaizing gentile
Christians" who exaggerated Paul's own emphasis on "the importance of the

with a denial of the validity of his apostleship and of the originality of his interpretation of Christian truth.

By an appeal to the naturally conservative tendency implicit in all religion, these visiting missionaries disturbed the inexperienced Galatian Christians.[64] Their abandonment of Pauline Christianity was not complete but seems rather to have been in process,[65] and Paul wrote to arrest and reverse the process. He would have preferred to return and think the issues through with them personally; but since the disturbance owed its origin to an antagonistic point of view within the Jerusalem church, he was impelled to go straight to Jerusalem for conference with the leaders. In the dilemma [66] he wrote the Galatians a hurried letter.

As a means of accrediting his message, Paul vigorously affirmed his own apostleship and the inspired character of his gospel.[67] He insisted that law and faith are so inherently different as to involve mutually exclusive principles,[68] and therefore that those who accepted the conservative viewpoint of the Judaizing Christians actually endangered their salvation.[69] He urged the Galatians to choose between the gospel he had presented and the "counterfeit" gospel of his opponents,[70] and his purpose in writing was to make them see the momentous character of their decision.

Message.—Paul's exposition of Christianity in Galatians and elsewhere was the outgrowth of his own experience. He had been a strict legalist, and "by the law's standard of uprightness, no fault could be found" with him.[71] Religion as legal obedience, however, instead of creating spiritual repose and moral effectiveness, had burdened him. He felt as though the last vestige of spontaneity had been excluded from life. The assumption of the attitude and relationship which he described as "faith" brought Paul joy in place of despair, inner composure where he had known only tension, the experience of an access of moral energy instead of fatigue of spirit. He concluded that the satisfaction he possessed as the sequel to his unqualified self-entrustment to a Christlike God could never have come to him on an achievement basis. The attitude of faith which Christ inspired set Paul free to live out the radical

---

Hebrew tradition for Christians" as represented in his references to Christians as Abraham's true children (3:26-29; 4:21-31). They made no attack on Paul, but looked upon him as authority for their point of view. (*Op. cit.*, pp. 43-45.)

[64] 3:1; 5:7.   [65] 1:6.   [66] 4:20.   [67] 1:15–2:21.
[68] 3:10 ff.; 5:3-4.   [69] 5:4.   [70] 5:7, 9.   [71] Phil. 3:6.

implications of love and gave him a sense of newness of life.[72]

Because the effort has been made to nullify his message by a denial of the validity of his apostleship, Paul begins by declaring that he is no self-appointed pretender, but a bona fide apostle sent "by Jesus Christ and God the Father." [73] Because opposition to his message centers in a denial of his personal fitness, he insists at great length that his apostleship is not "a human affair" in the sense of its having been bestowed by any sort of human mediation, but instead that it came to him "through a revelation of Jesus Christ." [74] By his preconversion persecution of the church,[75] by his independence of the Jerusalem leaders immediately following his conversion,[76] by the infrequency and informality of his relations with those leaders over a period of fourteen years following his acceptance of Christ,[77] by his public rebuke of Peter at Antioch,[78] by his unvarying insistence on the adequacy of faith, whether preaching to Jews or non-Jews,[79] Paul supports the contention that his exposition of Christianity has the character of revelation and that his call to be an apostle is as valid as that of any of the Twelve.

Having thus established his right to speak, Paul proceeds to set forth his basic message that acceptance with God rests on the twin bases of man's faith and God's grace.[80] Faith like Abraham's rather than physical descent from Abraham makes men heirs of God's promises. In the following variety of ways he undertakes to show that sound reasoning and the weight of available evidence combine to disclose the ineffectiveness of legal conformity and the adequacy of faith for the achievement of God's approval: (1) The possession of the Spirit by the Galatians has no connection with "doing what the Law commands," but antedates their acquaintance with the Law.[81] (2) The Old Testament implicitly teaches the necessity of faith in that the Law leaves men under a curse of spiritual impotence from which the faith aroused and justified by Christ's atoning death releases them.[82] (3) Since the covenant with Abraham preceded by some centuries God's gift of the Law through Moses, Abraham's faith rather than his conformity to legal prescriptions moved God to make the promises that constituted the covenant.[83] (4) A sound philosophy of history argues for the sufficiency of faith;

[72] Gal. 5:1, 6.	[73] 1:1-5.	[74] 1:6–2:21.	[75] 1:13-14.
[76] 1:15-17.	[77] 1:18–2:10.	[78] 2:11-14.	[79] 2:15-21.
[80] 3:1–5:12.	[81] 3:1-5.	[82] 3:7-14.	[83] 3:15-22.

for man's status under the Law was manifestly temporary and represents slavery, and the drift of history has been toward his emancipation. The logic of history thus makes the Law only an "attendant" whose function was to bring humanity to its true Master; and so, "now that faith has come," men remain "no longer in the charge of the attendant." [84] (5) The response aroused in the hearts of the Galatians by Paul's personal example and influence suggests the soundness of the faith principle.[85] (6) Legalism and racism are natural corollaries, and faith alone affords a basis for universalistic religion. The allegory of Abraham's sons shows that spiritual affinity transcends race in importance, which means that faith takes precedence over law as a religious principle.[86] (7) Because the possession of the Spirit is conditioned on faith, the achievement of true righteousness is implicit in faith rather than legal obedience.[87]

Paul makes it clear, however, that freedom from the demands of the Law involves no approval of license.[88] Instead of lowering the standard of behavior, he undertakes to show that faith furnishes the only adequate motivation for true righteousness. By interpreting faith to mean "acting through love," he fills it with rich moral connotation and discloses the sense in which he conceives of faith as opening the way to fruitful collaboration between man and God. This gives intelligibility to the position that faith is the condition of man's possession of the Spirt,[89] and it makes guidance by the Spirit morally significant.[90] The "new creation" which represents the outcome of what God does for man when man exercises faith is the supremely important religious achievement for Paul, and is appropriately the final emphasis in his message to the Galatians.[91]

[84] 3:23–4:11.   [85] 4:12-20.   [86] 4:21-31.   [87] 5:1-12.
[88] 5:13–6:18.   [89] 5:13-24.   [90] 5:25–6:10.

[91] 6:11-18. Ropes thinks Paul's real opponents in Galatia were a group of "spiritualistic radicals" whose point of view was substantially that of "the opponents who called out Paul's invective in II Corinthians and who were at the bottom of many of the difficulties dealt with in I Corinthians." They exaggerated Paul's teaching that the Holy Spirit caused believers "to be in Christ a new creation," and correspondingly minimized the importance of moral discipline. (*Op. cit.*, pp. 25-26.) Between these *pneumatici* on the one hand and the Judaizers on the other were the main body of Galatian Christians. Ropes interprets Galatians as a middle-of-the-road statement of the meaning of Christianity that corrected the errors of the extremist parties and undertook to correlate "the various interests included in his comprehensive system." (*Ibid.*, pp. 28-42.) Although he does not convincingly establish his critical positions at every point, his discussion is an extremely valuable contribution to the understanding of Paul's message.

II

THE FIRST LETTER TO THE THESSALONIANS

Authorship.—Evidence for the early existence of First Thessalonians is by no means as strong as for Galatians. There is no instance in the later books of the New Testament nor in the writings of the Apostolic Fathers where acquaintance with the letter can be conclusively shown. A limited use of it is reasonably clear, however, in Ephesians, Revelation, Hebrews, the Fourth Gospel, the Johannine letters, the letters of Ignatius, the letter of Polycarp, Second Peter, and the Pastorals. No trace of acquaintance with it appears in First Peter, First Clement, James, Hermas, Barnabas, the Didache, Second Clement, or the Martyrdom of Polycarp; and apparently no use of it was made by Justin. This silence is most serious in the instances of First Peter, First Clement, and Justin, who belong to periods when Paul's letters were popular. First Thessalonians was, however, certainly included in the earliest collection of Paul's letters, and its inclusion reflected opinion favorable to its authenticity around the close of the first century. It was included in Marcion's canon as the fifth of Paul's letters and in the Muratorian list as the seventh. There are definite quotations of it as a letter of Paul by Irenaeus, Tertullian, Clement of Alexandria, Origen, and Dionysius of Corinth. From the second century onward it was everywhere accepted as Pauline and as canonical.

Certain data within the letter itself suggest doubt of its authenticity to some scholars. If Galatians, the Corinthian letters, and Romans are made the exclusive sources of valid criteria for estimating the genuineness of Pauline letters, the vocabulary, style, and thought content of First Thessalonians create a problem. The letter makes no use of the Old Testament and is silent on such characteristic themes as justification and the Law. Certain allusions are interpreted as showing a knowledge of the destruction of Jerusalem[1] or an acquaintance with the Acts account of the origin of the Thessalonian church.[2] References to the progress of the Thessa-

[1] 2:14-16.　　　[2] 2:1-3.

lonian group are taken to involve a longer period than Paul's residence at Corinth during the second missionary tour would allow.

These criticisms have less actual weight than a cursory glance at them might suggest. The criterion by which First Thessalonians is adversely judged is itself the arbitrary creation of those who employ it. Very probably the nonuse of the Old Testament in the letter is explained by the omission of a discussion of the themes of justification and the Law, which argues for genuineness rather than spuriousness. The situation at Thessalonica involved its own problems, and a later Paulinist would be much more apt than Paul himself to inject a discussion of themes that were irrelevant. The letters in which the emphases omitted from First Thessalonians are most prominent were addressed to communities where opposition to Paul stemmed from a type of Christianity which he regarded as either false or inferior. At Thessalonica the problem was anti-Christian opposition. The conception that Christ as the indwelling Spirit empowers the individual to attain actual righteousness and creates the hope of future salvation is elemental in Pauline Christianity. Its prominence in First Thessalonians argues for the authenticity of the letter. Agreements between the survey of the history of the Thessalonian group in I Thess. 1–3 and the Acts account testify to the genuineness of First Thessalonians, and points of difference [3] establish its literary independence of Acts. Furthermore, allusions to the progress of Thessalonian Christians [4] testify to the warmth and loyalty rather than the maturity of their piety.

If there is really a reminiscence of the destruction of Jerusalem in I Thess. 2:14-16, the passage would more normally be treated as a later addition than as fixing the date of the original letter.[5] The passage is very probably genuine and expresses the vehemence of Paul's feeling that Jewish opposition to his work at Thessalonica had its background in the kind of opposition Jesus met and that it could only presage doom.[6]

The letter loses its problematical character when taken for what it was originally intended to be—an informal, friendly letter of advice to a recently established group, largely Gentile in member-

---

[3] 3:1; cf. Acts 17:14-16; 18:5.   [4] 1:7-8; 2:18; 3:10; 4:10-12.

[5] Moffatt, *Introduction*, p. 73.

[6] Jülicher, *Introduction*, p. 60; Frame, *The Epistles of Paul to the Thessalonians*, pp. 10, 39.

ship, whose faith, however sound, was in rather a rudimentary stage. Paul's letters were not theological treatises. He was a busy missionary, and the present letter was a practical handling of the actual needs of a Christian community.

The First Readers.—The letter is addressed "to the Thessalonian church in union with God the Father and the Lord Jesus Christ." [7] Its first readers were the Christians of Thessalonica, the provincial capital of Macedonia. Thessalonica was an important commercial center on the Aegean Sea with a teeming population made up of many nationalities. Named for the sister of Alexander the Great, the city was nearly four hundred years old when Paul first visited it, and had for practically a century enjoyed the status of a free city.

With Silas and Timothy, Paul had come to Thessalonica from Philippi.[8] The Lukan account of the establishment of the Thessalonian church [9] suggests that Paul and his associates were in the community for only three weeks, but other evidence indicates a period of as many months. Paul established himself in his trade and made his own living according to his custom.[10] "More than once" while he was there the Philippians sent him money.[11] Again, the widespread reputation that the church had developed when Paul addressed this first letter to them would indicate that his ministry among them had been a matter of months rather than weeks.[12] His departure was apparently due to opposition aroused by Jewish leaders,[13] who charged him with seditious utterances and actions [14] and with being avaricious.[15]

The Thessalonian Christians are described as having "turned from idols to God," [16] and they are contrasted so objectively with the Jews [17] as to create the impression that they were an entirely non-Jewish group. However, the Lukan account [18] suggests that many of them were proselytes from Judaism.

The relationship between Paul and his readers seems to have been one of warm affection. He compares it to that of "a mother nursing her children" and of "a father with his children." [19] He speaks with pride of their exemplary behavior in the midst of

[7] 1:1.   [8] Acts 16:1, 4, 12, 19, 40; 17:1,4; I Thess. 1:1; 2:2; 3:1.
[9] Acts 17:1-9.   [10] I Thess. 2:9; II Thess. 3.8; cf. Acts 18:3; 20:34.
[11] Phil. 4:16.   [12] I Thess. 1:8.   [13] Acts 17:5-10.
[14] Acts 17:7; cf. I Thes. 2:12.   [15] 2:5, 9.   [16] 1:9.
[17] 2:14.   [18] Acts 17:4.   [19] 2:7, 11.

trouble,[20] but he is conscious of their continuing need for his guidance.

Date.—From Athens Paul had sent Timothy back to Thessalonica to encourage and guide the young church and to report their situation to him.[21] He had gone on to Corinth, which was to be his headquarters for eighteen months;[22] and after a reasonable time Timothy joined him there with "good news." Paul wrote at once to express his joy at knowing that the Thessalonians were "standing firm in the Lord."[23] This suggests that the letter was written during the first several months of Paul's residence at Corinth.

The letter of Claudius to Delphi, mentioned in the discussion of the date of Galatians, fixes the term of Gallio's proconsulship as June, 51, to June, 52. He had recently assumed office when Paul was arraigned before him at Corinth,[24] and Paul left Corinth shortly thereafter.[25] It would seem, then, that Paul arrived at Corinth early in 50 and wrote First Thessalonians in the spring of that year.

Place of Composition.—Timothy is not mentioned in the Acts account [26] as having worked with Paul at Thessalonica. Silas accompanied him to Berea when trouble arose.[27] From Athens, however, Paul sent instructions back to Berea for Silas and Timothy,[28] and the two younger men did not rejoin him until he was well into his work at Corinth.[29]

Paul's own testimony is that Timothy was with him at Athens and that he sent him thence to Thessalonica.[30] He tells of Timothy's return with "good news" as though considerable time had been required for the round trip.[31] The fact that "again and again" since his departure he had planned to return to Thessalonica is a further indication of a period of some months since he had been with them.[32] These data together with indications that his stay at Athens was brief and unsatisfactory make Corinth rather than Athens the more probable setting of First Thessalonians.[33]

Occasion and Purpose.—Paul had left Thessalonica because his presence there endangered his followers. Unable for this and other reasons not specified to return and see how they fared,[34] and anxious lest suffering had weakened their loyalty,[35] he sent Timothy to

[20] 1:7: ff.	[21] 3:1; cf. Acts 17:14-16.	[22] Acts 18:1, 11.	[23] 3:6-8.
[24] Acts 18:12-17.	[25] Acts 18:18.	[26] Acts 17:1-9.	[27] Acts 17:10.
[28] Acts 17:15.	[29] Acts 18:5.	[30] 3:1-5.	[31] 3:6.
[32] 2:18.	[33] 3:1; Acts 17:16-18:1.	[34] 2:18.	[35] 2:14.

them.[36] Paul's concern looked beyond the Thessalonian situation itself. The enterprise there had made a widespread impression,[37] and its success or failure had implications for the missionary undertaking generally.

The occasion of First Thessalonians was the return of Timothy with "good news." [38] In addition to his own appraisal of the situation, Timothy may also have brought Paul a letter from the Christians at Thessalonica. At times in First Thessalonians Paul writes as though he were discussing questions they had themselves raised.[39] He wrote to express his joy and sense of relief at the "good news" Timothy had brought, and to give advice on the problems they had presented. There had been interpretations of Paul's motivation that were designed to undercut his message.[40] In the interest of his larger objectives, he dealt with these personal thrusts.

The main problem was the outgrowth of confusion regarding the second coming of Christ. The Thessalonians had gathered from Paul's preaching that the Parousia was so near that they would all live to witness it. During the ensuing months, however, some members of the group had died. This disturbed the rest, not so much with reference to their final resurrection but lest they miss some of the initial blessings of the new age. In writing them Paul himself apparently felt that he and a majority of his readers would enter the Kingdom without experiencing death, and his effort was merely to give assurance that those who had died unexpectedly would miss none of the blessings of the messianic era.[41]

Message.—Paul's exhortation to the Thessalonian leaders provides an excellent summary of the message of the entire letter: "We beg you, brothers, warn the idlers, cheer up the despondent, keep hold of the weak, be patient with everybody." [42] He has three classifications of Christians in mind, and with their respective problems vividly before him he counsels the responsible leaders of the Thessalonian church.

Certain Thessalonian Christians were idle because they thought the return of Jesus was imminent. The new age was so near that no compelling reason remained for their continuation at their accustomed tasks. The unhappy result was poverty on the one hand and meddlesomeness on the other. These idling adventists became

36 3:1.   37 1:7 ff.   38 3:6.   39 4:9, 13; 5:1; 12; cf. I Cor. 7:1; 8:1; 12:1.
40 2:5-6.   41 4:13-18.   42 5:14.

so problematical that Paul devoted his second letter almost entirely to a correction of their errors.[43] Here Paul's message concerning them [44] is briefer, but it is the same in substance.

The "despondent" seem to have been persons who were anxious about their own salvation and about that of their fellow believers who had unexpectedly died. They were apprehensive lest the return of the Messiah take place so soon and so suddenly as to find them unprepared. Paul meets this phase of their problem by reminding them that the presence of Christ as the Spirit in their hearts is a resource for the achievement of moral victory day by day and is also the guarantee of their future acceptance with God.[45] Regarding those members of the church who had died, he expresses the confidence that they will share with the living all of the eschatological blessings.[46]

The "weak" were apparently Christians whose severance of relations with paganism had not been sufficiently radical. They had been brought into the church as adults, and the attraction of established interests and habits remained. The allurements of crasser pagan practices, especially sex immorality, were a constant source of temptation, and their relapse from higher Christian standards was viewed by Paul as serious both for the individuals involved and for the Christian community.[47]

[43] II Thess. 3:1-17.   [44] 4:9-12.   [45] 5:1-11.   [46] 4:13-18.   [47] 4:3-8.

III

THE SECOND LETTER TO THE THESSALONIANS

Authorship.—The use made of Second Thessalonians by other Christian writers of the pre-Catholic period was extremely limited. The character of the letter was probably responsible for this. There are traces of acquaintance with it of sufficient clarity to indicate that it was included in the original Pauline letter collection, but the number of such instances is small. They involve a high degree of probability of literary indebtedness in Ephesians, the letter of Polycarp, the writings of Justin, and the Pastorals, and reasonable probability of such indebtedness in Revelation and the Fourth Gospel. From the remainder of the later books of the New Testament, the Apostolic Fathers, and the early Apologists, the reader would know nothing of Second Thessalonians.

As early as Christian writings were formally quoted, Second Thessalonians was treated as a letter of Paul. It was listed in Marcion's canon as the sixth of Paul's letters and in the Muratorian canon as the eighth. It was quoted by Tertullian, Irenaeus, and Clement of Alexandria, and from their time onward it was accepted as Pauline throughout the church.

The situation which the letter itself reflects seems to be entirely natural. Only an overemphasis on certain easily explainable details creates the impression of artificiality. In the main the contents of the letter substantiate the tradition of Pauline authorship that dates from the middle of the second century. It must be admitted, however, that certain data within the letter create difficulties. These difficulties are chiefly four: (1) apparent divergencies between the eschatology of I Thess. 5:1-11 and of II Thess. 2:1-12; (2) literary resemblance between the two letters that some regard as so close and continuous as to make Second Thessalonians hardly more than a paraphrase of First Thessalonians; (3) an emphasis on Paul's apostolic authority in terms of officiality; (4) the suggestion that pseudonymous letters under the name of Paul are in circulation.

Several considerations require careful attention in the matter of the apparent contradiction in Second Thessalonians of the escha-

39

tology of First Thessalonians. Paul's primary concern was always practical rather than theoretical. He assumed the traditional eschatology of Judaism as modified by the first Christian leaders and employed it homiletically. Dramatic and emotional effectiveness rather than logical consistency were the qualities of this apocalyptic eschatology, and conceptions that the Day of the Lord would come suddenly and that there would be premonitory signs of its approach could easily exist side by side. The Thessalonian letters complement rather than contradict each other. They were written with different purposes but not, necessarily, by different authors. They reveal a variation of emphasis but not a difference in point of view. In I Thess. 5:1-11 the characteristic of the Parousia is unexpectedness because this was the feature that troubled the "despondent." In II Thess. 2:1-12 the effort is made to refute teaching that has been disseminated in Paul's name to the effect that the Day of the Lord has already dawned. For the correction of this misrepresentation Paul reviews what he has previously taught them about premonitory signs of the end.[1] The "embodiment of disobedience"[2] is not an allusion that necessarily looks back to the times of either Nero or Domitian; it is adequately satisfied by the imagery that developed around the historical events of the times of Antiochus Epiphanes.

Contrary to the representation that the second of the letters is largely a repetition of the first, a considerable proportion of Second Thessalonians is new material.[3] This amount of new material is doubly impressive when it is noted that the distinctly personal contents of I Thess. 1-3 do not reappear in Second Thessalonians. Apart from the close adherence of the second letter to the epistolary outline of the first, the indebtedness of the one to the other lies in the area of chapters 4 and 5 of First Thessalonians. The utilization of materials there is hardly that of the slavish imitator, as the introduction of so large a proportion of new content in a space so brief shows. Too, the knowledge of the Thessalonian situation is direct and detailed in the briefer letter. The clear grasp of the inner life of the church in II Thess. 3:6-15 would not have been gained merely by the reading of I Thess. 4:11-12 and 5:14.

Such assertions of authority as the letter contains have a personal

---

[1] 2:5; cf. I Thess. 5:2.   [2] 2:8.

[3] 1:5-12; 2:2-12, 15; 3:1-5, 10, 13-14, 17.

rather than an official tone.[4] There is no such effort as appears in the writings of a later period to make Paul the sponsor for a system of disciplinary regulation. Except for their greater mildness, the directions Paul gives his Thessalonian readers have the character of his similar admonitions in the Corinthian letters.[5] His name has been used in the promotion of teaching with which he disagrees, and he employs his customary vigor of speech in clarifying the confused situation.

The statements interpreted as indicating the circulation of pseudonymous letters under Paul's name,[6] and therefore as indicating a late date for the letter, are closely related to the matter of his authority. Paul can recall having made no such statements as are being attributed to him, and he employs all possible emphasis to put an end to misrepresentation.

The difficulties involved in the letter are thoroughly real. Only their undue exaggeration, however, can make them a sufficient basis for the denial of the authenticity of Second Thessalonians. They can, in fact, be so interpreted as to give support to Pauline authorship.

The First Readers.—The second letter, like the first, is addressed "to the Thessalonian church in union with God our Father and the Lord Jesus Christ." The same persons join in the salutation—Paul, Silvanus, and Timothy. This address to a specific church is an argument for authenticity, the pseudonymous letters of a later period being ordinarily addressed to the church as a whole. Two of the problem groups of First Thessalonians reappear in the present letter—the "despondent" and the "idlers." The somewhat altered and aggravated character of the problems these groups present gives the situation the appearance of reality. The detailed acquaintance with local conditions is thoroughly lifelike and tends to confirm the historicity of the address.[7]

Both letters become more intelligible if they are regarded as written to the same group with a brief intervening interval of time. The supposition that the second letter was pseudonymous and its situation hypothetic creates confusion.

Date.—Critical judgments about Second Thessalonians are all related to the interpretation of its second chapter. That chapter is

---

[4] 2:15; 3:4, 6, 9, 14.

[5] I Cor. 4:21; 5:3-5; 7:18; II Cor. 10:6; 12:20; 13:10.

[6] 2:2; 3:17.   [7] 3:6-16; cf. I Thess. 4:11-12.

an integral part of the letter, and whoever wrote it wrote the entire document. If the writing was pseudonymous, its function was to gain Pauline authority for eschatological views that were in keeping with the thought of some later period. That period may have been the latter part of the seventh decade of the first century, although there is no reason to relate it to the milieu of Revelation. Either a revived Nero or Domitian may be regarded as "the embodiment of disobedience." [8] In support of the second possibility resemblances between the eschatological ideas of Second Thessalonians and Revelation [9] may be stressed, and the two writings viewed as having the same general historical background.

Certain evidence, however, makes a late dating of the letter difficult. At the time it was written the temple in Jerusalem seems to have been standing.[10] The address of the letter to a local church instead of to the church as a whole accords more normally with an early than with a late date. The view of the empire in Revelation lies entirely beyond the horizon of Paul's lifetime, and that view does not make its appearance in Second Thessalonians. Paul regarded Rome as friendly to Christianity and as the political agency by which God restrained lawlessness. In Revelation, however, the empire has itself become the agency of the anti-Christian forces of the universe. Resemblances in eschatological detail between the two writings are adequately explained on the basis of their common indebtedness to the book of Daniel and do not require their contemporary origin.

As a genuine letter of Paul, Second Thessalonians must have been separated from First Thessalonians only a few months. If it is dated in the late spring or early summer of 50, sufficient time is allowed for the bearer of the earlier letter to reach Thessalonica, counsel with the leaders, make an appraisal of the new elements in the situation, and report back to Paul at Corinth. The reduction of the time interval between the two letters to a minimum is suggested by the similarity in the general outlines of the Thessalonian situation reflected in them and by the appearance in more advanced form in the second letter of problems that are visible in the first.

Place of Composition.—Silvanus and Timothy, who are associated with Paul in the salutation,[11] were with him during his long

[8] 2:8.   [9] II Thess. 1:6 (cf. Rev. 6:10) ; 2:4 (cf. Rev. 13:2) ; 2:8 (cf. Rev. 20:10).
[10] 2:4.   [11] 1:1.

residence at Corinth on the second journey.[12] They were not located together elsewhere during the period when the letter must have been written if Paul was its author. Silvanus thereafter drops out of sight, and when Timothy reappears his associate is Erastus.[13] This letter was the sequel to First Thessalonians,[14] and was written a few months afterward when information reached Paul that the Thessalonians were confused regarding the dawning of the Day of the Lord.[15] Corinth is the only locality that satisfies the relevant evidence and is accordingly to be regarded as the place where Second Thessalonians was written.

Occasion and Purpose.—The letter itself supplies the only data available for the visualization of the situation to which it belonged. Paul's earlier letter had been only partially successful, and may even have contributed to the new turn of events.[16] The idling adventists had precipitated a crisis involving serious moral implications and vexing administrative difficulties. They had exhausted the patience of local Christian leaders[17] and had increased the bewildment of the "despondent."[18] Paul had been aware of this state of affairs in its incipiency,[19] and he was now called on to deal with it in a more mature and complicated stage.

The Thessalonian leaders probably described the existing condition of things to Paul in a letter,[20] to which our Second Thessalonians was a reply.[21] Whether by letter or oral report, two interrelated sets of facts were laid before Paul: (1) The "idlers" were convinced that the final period of which the Day of the Lord would be the consummation had actually begun. They therefore saw no necessity for continuing the performance of ordinary work and had given themselves wholly to watching for the spectacular coming of the Messiah on the clouds. They expected that their economic needs would be supplied from the resources of members of the local Christian community. (2) The outlook that brought a sort of ecstatic peace to the "idlers" struck consternation into the hearts of the "despondent." These sensitive souls had all along feared that the end would find them unprepared;[22] and now, with the Day of the Lord imminent, they would lack time for the development of those spiritual qualities requisite for divine approval.

---

[12] II Cor. 1:19; Acts 18:5.   [13] Acts 19:22.   [14] 2:15.   [15] 2:2, 5; 3:11.
[16] 2:2.   [17] 3:15.   [18] 2:1-5.   [19] I Thess. 4:11-12; 5:14.
[20] Cf. I Thess. 5:12-13.   [21] 2:1; 3:1, 3, 6, 11.   [22] I Thess. 3:13; 5:8.

They were "unsettled" and "wrought up" because they were too realistic to spend their days with the cloud-watchers and yet lacked the confidence they deserved as they did their daily work because the "idlers" claimed Paul's authorization for their absurdities.[23]

Paul addressed his letter to this situation with a threefold purpose in mind: (1) the encouragement of the "despondent," [24] (2) the issuance of a pointed warning to the "idlers," [25] (3) the reinforcement of the patience of the Thessalonian leaders.[26] He wrote in the spirit of a troubled pastor. His interest was exclusively practical. He had not the slightest intention of composing a systematic treatise on eschatology. The subjects treated in the letter were discussed at the request of the Thessalonian leaders, and they were already somewhat familiar to the Thessalonians from earlier oral and written treatment.[27] The apostle's effort was so to correlate disjointed impressions with the basic values he had emphasized as to restore social sanity and wholesome spiritual poise where chaos and panic threatened.

Message.—Paul exemplified the qualities of a missionary statesman in his clear realization of the importance of indigenous leadership. His procedure was to seek out and train local leaders and by revisitation and correspondence work co-operatively with them as problems arose. The two Thessalonian letters were written largely for the benefit of the responsible leaders of the Thessalonian church. The difficulties discussed did not belong to the leaders as persons, but the leaders required Paul's guidance in dealing constructively with them.

The patience of these local leaders had been taxed about equally by the "despondent" and the "idlers." The fearfulness of the former was as problematical as the cocksureness of the latter. The keynote of Paul's counsel in both letters is, "Be patient with everybody." [28] In his own careful treatment of every question that came to him he illustrates the meaning and the redemptiveness of Christian patience.

For the sake of the encouragement of the "despondent" he discusses in chapter 2 the premonitory signs that show that the Day of the Lord is still future. In chapter 3 he warns the "idlers" and deprives them of the approval they had claimed from him. In dealing with both groups his spirit is that of the patience he has urged.

---

[23] II Thess. 2:1-5.   [24] 2:1-17.   [25] 3:6-12.   [26] 3:14-16.
[27] 2:5; cf. I Thess. 5:1-11.   [28] I Thess. 5:14; II Thess. 3:14-15.

This comes out in the first chapter, which serves as a sort of preface. There he recognizes the problematical element in the Thessalonian picture, but at the same time he refuses to permit a question mark to symbolize the situation as a whole. He fixes on their positive virtues as overbalancing failure and their achievements as more significant than their debates. He speaks with pride of their "steadfastness and faith in the face of all the persecutions and troubles" they have undergone, and he dignifies them by including them as fellow sufferers with himself for the sake of the Kingdom of God.

IV.

THE CORINTHIAN CORRESPONDENCE

PAUL's letters were not originally designed for publication. They were addressed to local groups and in many instances were not kept beyond the immediate occasion that evoked them. Those that were preserved in the chests of local churches had no general circulation as separate letters. It was as members of a published collection that these letters became known in Christian history. The two letters known in their published form as First and Second Corinthians contain the remains of an extensive correspondence.

First Corinthians is a more elaborate discussion of a problem or problems treated in a previous communication.[1] Another letter, which evidently is to be distinguished from the one where the allusions occur, and with which First Corinthians can hardly be identified, is described in II Cor. 2:4 and 7:8. Here, then, are indications of at least four letters to Corinth.

Data in the published letters assist in the identification of the possible remains of the original letters. The theme treated in II Cor. 6:14–7:1 corresponds with that of the letter mentioned in I Cor. 5:9. The possibility that a fragment of the earlier letter is there preserved becomes highly probable in view of the perfect sense connection between II Cor. 6:3-13 and 7:2-4. The omission of 6:14–7:1 causes no break in the thought sequence, whereas its inclusion completely confuses the sense of the context.

Just as definitely, II Cor. 10–13 violates the spirit and import of II Cor. 1–9. If, in these four chapters, a portion of the letter mentioned in II Cor. 2:4 and 7:8 is preserved, Paul's "trouble and distress of mind" and his "many tears" become entirely intelligible. Granted that Paul's intention had not been to "hurt anybody's feelings," the modern reader has no difficulty in imagining the mixed emotions with which members of the church at Corinth listened to the public reading of this letter, and how Paul himself properly questioned the wisdom of having sent it.

[1] 5:9.

46

There are also indications that the correspondence was two-sided. The members of the church at Corinth communicated with Paul by letter and messenger. Persons in the employ of Chloe, perhaps while on a business mission, told Paul that "quarrels" were dividing the Christian group into competing cliques, each organized about the name of its favorite leader.[2] Others wrote Paul about a variety of matters and asked his written counsel.[3] In the interest of better understanding, Stephanas, Fortunatus, and Achaicus came for conference with Paul.[4] At different times, Paul sent Timothy[5] and Titus[6] to Corinth, and he himself made a visit to the church that is not mentioned in Acts.[7] These are the data out of which one may attempt the reconstruction of the sequence of the correspondence.

The published form of these letters was the work of the collector, who, with the accounts of Paul's journeys in Acts as his guide, visited a number of the communities where the apostle had worked and gathered together the extant remains of what he had written. There was frequently no account of the circumstances that lay back of the separate written bits available to this early editor. Even if there had been, the space limitations imposed by his writing materials would have made the separate recording of small sections of correspondence difficult. The composite character of the published letters makes it preferable to discuss the questions about them jointly.

Authorship.—Both of the Corinthian letters in substantially the form in which the modern reader knows them were included in the Pauline letter collection as originally published. Doubt regarding the inclusion of Second Corinthians[8] was due to the more copious use made of First Corinthians in Hebrews, First Clement, the Fourth Gospel, the letters of Ignatius and Polycarp, the writings of Justin, and the Pastorals.[9] However, the authors of Revelation, First Peter, and Second Peter were rather clearly acquainted with Second Corinthians but appear to have made no use of First Corinthians at all, while in Ephesians the number of instances showing acquaintance with the two letters is exactly the same but with a greater

---

[2] I Cor. 1:11-12.   [3] I Cor. 7:1.   [4] I Cor. 16:17.

[5] I Cor. 4:17; 16:10.   [6] II Cor. 7:6.   [7] II Cor. 12:14; 13:1.

[8] Goodspeed, *Formation of the New Testament*, p. 27.

[9] I Clem. 47:1 is the earliest citation of a Christian writing by author. The succeeding context shows that he had I Cor. 1:10 ff. in mind.

degree of clarity in the case of Second Corinthians.[10] Except for the writings of Justin and Second Clement, which seem to have made no use of Second Corinthians, all Christian writings between 95 and 175 that manifest a knowledge of First Corinthians also show some acquaintance with Second Corinthians.

The letters stand second and third respectively in Marcion's Pauline list, immediately following Galatians. In the Muratorian canon they introduce the Pauline list as the first and second letters. Both letters enjoyed a wide popularity after the middle of the second century and were regularly attributed to Paul.

With the case for authenticity established by external testimony only half as strong as it is, the letters themselves would require their assignment to Paul. Both assert their Pauline authorship, and these claims are borne out by the contents of the letters.

The author of Luke-Acts knew Paul as a pioneer missionary leader, either through personal acquaintance or by tradition, but he did not know him as a writer of letters. The agreements between the Corinthian letters and Acts, therefore, have the character of corroborative testimony and at the same time argue for the primary value of the data in the letters. Many details that could have had no general interest and that would naturally not be included in a secondary work are vividly emphasized in the letters. The critical character of certain situations and the intensity of emotion with which they were approached lie on the surface in the letters without any evidence of the retouching that is inevitable in secondary writings. Except on the hypothesis of authenticity, no sufficient motives for these letters are discoverable. There remains no sound basis for any question of the genuineness of the component elements of these letters in their published form.

The First Readers.—First Corinthians is addressed "to the church of God at Corinth, to those who are consecrated by union with Christ Jesus, and called as God's people." Similarly, the address of the second letter is "to the church of God that is at Corinth, and all God's people all over Greece."

The Corinth of Paul's day was the relatively new city founded as a military colony by Julius Caesar in 46 B.C. and largely settled at the time by Caesar's veterans. The original Greek city had been destroyed by the Roman consul L. Mummius Achaicus in 146 B.C.

---

[10] For a complete display of the data, see my *Paul Becomes a Literary Influence.*

By New Testament times, however, Greek had become the common
language, and all elements in the population, Roman, Greek, Orien-
tal, and Jewish, shared a common Hellenistic culture.

An advantageous geographical situation brought commercial
prosperity to the new as it had done to the ancient city. Corinth
was important also as the political capital of the Roman province
of Achaia and the residence of the proconsul.

The ancient city had been a great religious center, and its
reputation for licentiousness was largely due to the excesses encouraged by the Astarte-Aphrodite worship. This cult flourished in
the new Corinth, but with somewhat less glaring immorality. More
important in Paul's time were the mystery cults, with their emphases
on individualism, mysticism, and universalism.

The establishment of the church at Corinth and Paul's long residence there are described in Acts 18:1-17. The continuing character
of his relationship with the group is suggested in Acts 18:28; 19:1;
and 20:3-6. The sense of "weakness" and of "fear and trembling"
with which Paul began his work at Corinth [11] had probably been
due to his anxiety about the Thessalonians, the unsatisfactory character of his visit at Athens,[12] and the magnitude of both the problems and the opportunity at Corinth. His work there was, nevertheless, attended by great success.[13]

Paul claims to have been the first to bring Christianity to
Corinth.[14] Aquila and Priscilla were at Corinth when Paul arrived, but they were probably converted under his ministry. His
associates in the establishment of the church were Silas and Timothy,[15] but Paul was of course the real founder.

Except for such assistance as came from Philippi, Paul financed
his stay at Corinth by working at his trade.[16] He got the first hearing
for his message in the local synagogue,[17] and when opposition arose
"he moved to the house of a devout proselyte named Titus Justus." [18]

The membership of this first house-church was recruited largely
from among humble people,[19] although some differences in social
status probably existed.[20] There were a few Jewish converts in the

---

[11] I Cor. 2:3.   [12] Acts 17:18, 32; I Thess. 3:1.   [13] I Cor. 1:4-7.
[14] I Cor. 3:6-10; 4:15; 9:1-2; II Cor.3:3.   [15] Acts 18:5; II Cor. 1:19.
[16] I Cor. 4:12; 9:6, 11-15, 18; II Cor. 11:7-12; Acts 18:3.
[17] Acts 18:4.   [18] Acts 18:7.   [19] I Cor. 1:26-29.
[20] I Cor. 11:20.

group,[21] but the majority had been "heathen" prior to their conversion.[22] They brought with them the weaknesses inherent in their background, but the number and variety of their problems were an indirect blessing in that they made necessary the revealing correspondence gathered into the letters known to the modern reader as First and Second Corinthians.

Date.—The relative order of the Corinthian letters can be fixed with reasonable assurance. Calendar dates are at best only estimates. Paul's stay of eighteen months at Corinth fell within the years 50-51. Leaving Corinth late in 51, he crossed with Priscilla and Aquila to Ephesus, where he left his companions and went on to Jerusalem alone.[23] From Jerusalem he returned to Syrian Antioch; and "after spending some time there, he started out again, and traveled systematically through Galatia and Phrygia,"[24] and thence on to Ephesus.[25]

The events of the interim between his departure from Corinth[26] and his return to Ephesus[27] probably required the whole of the year 52. The two-and-a-half-year residence at Ephesus can be regarded, then, as having commenced early in 53 and extended somewhat beyond the middle of 55.[28] The four letters to Corinth thus fall between the winter of 53 and the autumn of 55.[29]

During the first year or early in the second of his stay in Ephesus news reached Paul that the Corinthians were troubled about the proper relations of Christians with their unconverted "heathen" neighbors. Paul responded with the letter mentioned in I Cor. 5:9, a fragment of which is almost surely preserved in II Cor. 6:14–7:1.

Corinthian Christians, in Ephesus on business or specially sent for conference with Paul,[30] kept him informed about the church. In the interest of keeping his counsel and his oversight of the churches more personal, Paul sent Timothy by way of Macedonia to Corinth.[31] Hardly had Timothy started by this longer route when a letter requiring an immediate answer arrived from Corinth.[32] Paul at once wrote the letter known as First Corinthians and dis-

---

[21] I Cor. 7:18; 9:20; Acts 18:8.   [22] I Cor. 12:2.   [23] Acts 18:18-21.
[24] Acts 18:22-23.   [25] Acts 19:1.   [26] Acts 18:18.   [27] Acts 19:1.
[28] Acts 19:10, 22.

[29] It is possible that the letter mentioned in I Cor. 5:9 was written during the stop at Ephesus of Acts 18:19-21. More probably it belongs with the other letters to the period indicated in Acts 19:1–20:1.

[30] I Cor. 1:11; 16:17-18.   [31] I Cor. 4:17; Acts 19:22.   [32] I Cor. 7:1.

patched it with the expectation that it would reach Corinth before Timothy arrived.

He states that he wrote this letter just before Pentecost,[33] which means in May or earlier. In the same context there is the indication that the collection for the poor Christians of Jerusalem had not been taken at Corinth at the time.[34] In the last of his letters to Corinth, when his long stay at Ephesus had ended, and when he was somewhere in Macedonia on his way to Corinth, he speaks of this collection as having been begun "last year."[35] The probabilities are that Paul was reckoning by the Roman calendar, which would suggest that something like eighteen months intervened between the second and the fourth of the letters and that First Corinthians was written in the spring of 54 and the first nine chapters of Second Corinthians in the autumn of 55.

Neither Timothy's visit nor our First Corinthians achieved the results for which Paul had hoped. In fact, the affairs of the church at Corinth seem to have gone from bad to worse. Paul had for a long time desired to revisit the church himself,[36] and in the autumn of 54 he probably made the "painful" visit from which he returned with a sense of complete defeat.[37]

He could not surrender to the intolerable condition that existed, however, and he decided to attempt by letter a change that he had been unable to bring about by his personal presence. Sometime during the spring of 55 he wrote what is known as the "harsh" letter,[38] which he sent by Titus.[39] The body of this letter is probably preserved in II Cor. 10–13.

The final letter to Corinth was written during the period suggested by Acts 20:2, when Paul had left Ephesus and was en route to Corinth by way of Macedonia. Titus met him with the news that the "harsh" letter had accomplished its purpose and that a welcome awaited him, whereupon Paul wrote a conciliatory message and sent it on ahead by Titus and two companions,[40] while he and certain Macedonian friends followed at a more leisurely pace.[41] This letter is represented in the first nine chapters of Second Corinthians, excepting 6:14–7:1.

[33] I Cor. 16:9.   [34] I Cor. 16:1.   [35] II Cor. 8:10; 9:2.
[36] I Cor. 4:19-21; 11:34; 16:7.   [37] II Cor. 2:1-5; 12:14; 13:1.
[38] II Cor. 2:4; 7:8.   [39] II Cor. 2:13; 7:6, 13-14.
[40] II Cor. 8:16-23.   [41] II Cor. 9:4-5.

Place of Composition.—The available data combine most naturally to create the probability that the first three of the letters to Corinth were written at Ephesus. The second of these letters, our First Corinthians, specifically indicates Ephesus as the place of its composition.[42] Priscilla and Aquila, who had worked with Paul at Corinth and later made their home at Ephesus, are included with Paul in the closing salutations of the letter.[43] The last of the letters was written from somewhere in Macedonia, when Paul was en route to Corinth for his third and last visit.[44] Notations in some manuscripts suggest that the letter was written at Philippi, but there can be no certainty that this was the case.

Occasion and Purpose.—Paul's first letter to the Corinthians dealt with the single problem of association with "immoral people."[45] He had not desired that the members of the church isolate themselves, but that they avoid relationships of such character and intimacy as might involve a lowering of ethical standards. His advice may have been sought in the matter, or he may have written entirely on his own initiative.

Subsequently, disquieting accounts of conditions in the Corinthian group reached Paul. Employees of Chloe probably brought him these reports.[46] The news they brought included such items as (a) the increasing tendency among members of the church to divide into cliques based on their preferences of leaders,[47] (b) the marriage of a member of the group to his widowed stepmother,[48] (c) the complete misunderstanding of what he had written them earlier about their association with "immoral people,"[49] (d) the resort of Christians to civil courts for the settlement of disputes among themselves,[50] and (e) widespread misapprehension of proper standards of sex morality.[51]

As though these matters were not enough, leaders in the church wrote Paul a letter in which they laid additional problems before him and asked his advice on definite questions.[52] The main items on which they desired his counsel seem to have been (a) the desirability of marriage for Christians,[53] (b) whether or not Christians endangered themselves by eating meat purchased in temple

[42] I Cor. 16:8-9.   [43] Acts 18:18-19; I Cor. 16:19.
[44] II Cor. 2:13; 7:5; 8:1; 9: 2 ff.   [45] I Cor. 5:9.   [46] I Cor. 1:11.
[47] I Cor. 1:10–4:21.   [48] I Cor. 5:1-8.   [49] I Cor. 5:9-13.
[50] I Cor. 6:1-11.   [51] I Cor. 6:12-20.   [52] I Cor. 7:1.   [53] I Cor. 7.

markets,[54] (c) the behavior of women in the public services of the church,[55] (d) the significance and proper employment of "spiritual gifts,"[56] (e) the resurrection of Christ and its meaning for the future life of believers,[57] and (f) how they should make the collection for the poor Christians of Jerusalem.[58]

Paul would have preferred to go to Corinth and deal with these difficult matters in person, but this was not possible at the time.[59] In the same spirit of pastoral helpfulness and concern in which he had previously written them [60] he wrote a second letter, our First Corinthians.

Apparently there followed an increase of factiousness and an aggravation of certain other of their difficulties. One of the more determined of those who differed with Paul undertook to wrest leadership from him and destroy his influence. Paul made a visit to Corinth, only to be insulted and driven out. Personally humiliated and burdened with a sense of complete defeat, he returned to Ephesus. The militancy of his affection asserted itself, however, when the passage of time restored perspective, and he determined not to permit the situation to continue out of hand without doing the one last thing within his power. He wrote them a letter for which few if any parallels exist for intensity of emotion, stinging accusation, threat of dire penalty, biting sarcasm, yet tempered throughout with a genuine tenderness that could not be mistaken, and that was calculated to conciliate the bitterest enemy. This is the letter which he says he wrote "in great trouble and distress of mind" but the only purpose of which was to make his readers "realize the extraordinary affection" he had for them.[61] The letter is preserved in large part in II Cor. 10–13.

Titus took this third letter to Corinth. Paul remained for a time at Ephesus; but his misgivings got the better of him, and he started for Corinth, by the longest route. He was welcomed at Troas; but because Titus did not arrive with news from Corinth, his "mind could not rest," and he left Troas for Macedonia.[62] He required more than a change of scene, however, for he says his "poor human nature could get no relief—there was trouble at every turn; fighting without, and fear within." [63]

[54] I Cor. 8:1 ff. [55] I Cor. 11:4 ff. [56] I Cor. 12–14. [57] I Cor. 15.
[58] I Cor. 16:1 ff. [59] I Cor. 4:18. [60] I Cor. 5:9. [61] II Cor. 2:4.
[62] II Cor. 2:12-13. [63] II Cor. 7:5.

The world took on a new aspect when Titus finally came with news of how the Corinthians "longed to see" him, and how "sorry" they were, and how they took Paul's part.[64] Paul immediately wrote them and sent the letter by Titus, while he followed more slowly. His purpose in this letter was threefold: (1) to say how glad he was that he could again "feel perfect confidence" in them; [65] (2) to express his own unqualified forgiveness of the individual who had insulted him, and to ask the church to restore him to its fellowship lest he be "overwhelmed by his remorse"; [66] and (3) to urge the generous completion of the collection for the poor Christians of Jerusalem.[67]

Message.—The emergence of the problems that are discussed in the Corinthian letters was the natural outcome of Paul's understanding of the Christian message and the acceptance of that message by Corinthian believers. These problems and the apostle's counsel regarding them were the corollaries of his insistence that devotion to Christ implied a type of morality that was radically new. Christian morality was new in the sense that the faith-approved life was viewed as lived under the daily tutelage of "the Spirit of the living God." [68] Its qualities were "spiritual gifts." It involved the proposal to live by the criteria of the Kingdom of God in advance of the inauguration of that Kingdom on earth. It mattered little that those criteria were the antithesis of the whole scheme of life in Hellenistic society.

In reviewing his original presentation of the gospel at Corinth, Paul says that when there he had resolved "to forget everything but Jesus Christ and his crucifixion." [69] His letters were of a piece with his spoken message. They constitute a sort of running commentary on the implications of the total sweep of the life of Christ for human relations. They interpret morality as a phase of man's duty to God and so make the way to God a way of holiness and obedience, of which Christ is both author and exemplar.

The earliest of the letters is fragmentarily preserved in II Cor. 6:14–7:1. As indicated in I Cor. 5:9, the letter dealt with the single problem of association with "immoral people." "Unbelievers" and "immoral people" are synonymous designations. Because of the moral implications of faith, a "believer" can have little "in com-

---

[64] II Cor. 7:6-7.   [65] II Cor. 7:16.   [66] II Cor. 2:6-8.
[67] II Cor. 8:6.   [68] II Cor. 3:3.   [69] I Cor. 2:2.

mon with an unbeliever." [70] The vocation of all Christians is complete "consecration," and to this end Paul exhorts the Corinthians to cleanse themselves "of everything that can defile body or spirit." [71]

First Corinthians begins with a discussion of the matters of which "Chloe's people" had brought Paul news.[72] The most serious of these and the one treated at greatest length is factionalism.[73] "For the sake of our Lord Jesus Christ" Paul urges the Corinthians "not to allow factions" among them, "but to be perfectly united in mind and judgment." He says that their organization into cliques around the personalities of favorite preachers creates the totally false impression that "Christ has been divided up!" The partisans of Paul, Apollos, Cephas must remember that it was Christ who was crucified for them. These leaders ought to be regarded as simply "Christ's servants and managers authorized to distribute the secret truths of God." [74]

A second matter of which Chole's people told Paul was a case of incest.[75] A member of the church had married his widowed stepmother, and his fellow church members showed no evidence of "being overwhelmed with grief" either at the moral lapse itself or at the necessity of expelling the guilty man. They had actually been able to "put on airs" about the secondary phases of religious attainment, thereby indicating a failure to realize the primacy of moral values. Had they understood the point of Paul's earlier letter about association with "immoral people," they would now perceive that redemptive concern rather than complacency should govern fellowship.

Litigation between Christians in courts where judges and the criteria of judgment were "heathen" is next discussed.[76] Paul shames his readers with the reminder that instead of being so involved they ought themselves to qualify "to be judges of the world." At least "trivial cases" ought not to have their importance magnified so as to prevent amicable settlement within the Christian community. "Having lawsuits with one another at all" discloses to the world a lamentable breakdown of brotherhood. Christians should prefer to "be wronged" rather than permit an estrangement between themselves over "ordinary matters."

In concluding his treatment of the matters of which Chloe's

[70] II Cor. 6:15.   [71] II Cor. 7:1.   [72] 1:1–6:20.   [73] 1:10–4:21.
[74] 4:1.   [75] 5:1-13.   [76] 6:1-11.

people had told him, Paul discusses the religious significance of the body.[77] He insists that the body is not morally separable from the inner life, but that what defiles one also defiles the other. Man's life in its entirety has been "bought and paid for," which means that "the body is not meant for immorality, but for the service of the Lord." [78]

The main body of First Corinthians [79] is a discussion of problems regarding which the Corinthians had made written request for Paul's counsel:

Regarding the propriety of marriage for Christians,[80] Paul expresses the judgment that wholly "in view of the present distress . . . it is an excellent thing" for single men, widows, and single women to avoid marriage. That this opinion is predicated solely on the basis of the imminence of the end of the existing world order and not on an ascetic view of marriage as evil or wholly physical appears in the assurance that if an individual does marry "there is no sin in that," and that married couples are not to separate.

The sacramental view of religion widely prevalent in antiquity required the elaborate discussion of the use of meat purchased from markets that were connected with pagan temples.[81] Certain portions of the animals used as sacrifices were consumed in the liturgical rites themselves, and others were eaten by communicants in temple feasts. Participation in these feasts was supposed to have sacramental effectiveness in the sense that persons became mystically united with the deity of the temple. Cuts not used for temple purposes were sold to the public for food. Extremely devout pagans might count meat in this third category as also "holy," and so a Corinthian Christian with a "heathen" background might with poignant seriousness debate whether eating such meat endangered his relationship to Christ.[82] The gist of Paul's counsel was that Christians were under no circumstances to eat meat sacramentally in a temple. To do so would be the equivalent of abandoning Christ in their preference for a rival lord.[83] In a private home, however, they might ask Christ's blessing on whatever food was served.[84] Only if someone made a point of the sacramental character of the food need a Christian abstain from eating under these circumstances, but

[77] 6:12-20.   [78] 6:13.   [79] 7:1–16:4.   [80] 7:1-40.
[81] 8:1–11:1.   [82] 8:7.   [83] 10:14-22.   [84] 10:25-28.

then his abstention would be a matter of respect for a brother's conscience.[85]

The proper conduct of corporate worship involved certain problems that were inherent in pagan life at Corinth. The participation of women [86] and the proper administration of the Lord's Supper [87] could be discussed with relative brevity, but the exercise of gifts of the Spirit required elaborate discussion.[88] Paul makes it clear that women along with men "come from God," but he recognizes that certain proprieties had been established in Hellenistic society that should be observed in Christian meetings. As an instance he grants that although a woman may "explain the will of God" and "offer prayer to God" she must do neither bareheaded. In the observance of the Lord's Supper the solemnity of the occasion of its origin ought to determine the atmosphere of its observance, so that neither clannishness nor a spirit of carousel can be tolerated on these occasions. Gifts of the Spirit were becoming a hindrance rather than an asset to public worship because ecstatic utterance tended to be unduly emphasized. Paul takes the position that corporate worship ought not to be exploited by exhibitionists and that since the needs of the group are primary the "inspired preacher" deserves higher recognition than the person who merely "speaks ecstatically." While admitting that he speaks "in an ecstasy more than any," Paul urges a proper sense of proportion in public worship in his statement, "I would rather say five words with my understanding so as to instruct others also than ten thousand words in an ecstasy." [89]

Resurrection was a conception that belonged to Judaism and primitive Christianity. Greek-thinking people conceived of the future life in ways of their own. The Corinthians, therefore, had difficulty in understanding Paul's preaching on this subject.[90] Paul first insists that Christians possess a factual basis for their eschatological hopes in the resurrection of Jesus.[91] The new meaning given life and the superior quality of the behavior of believers are spiritual corollaries of the historical fact of the Resurrection and shed light on its meaning.[92] Speculation about the character of the resurrection body has created a needless difficulty. However it may be conceived, the basic faith of Christians is that God, who has furnished man with a mechanism admirably adapted to earthly relationships, can be

[85] 8:12; 10:29.   [86] 11:2-16.   [87] 11:17-34.   [88] 12:1–14:40.
[89] 14:19.   [90] 15:1-58.   [91] 15:1-28.   [92] 15:29-34.

trusted to make similarly appropriate provision "when this mortal nature puts on immortality." [93]

Finally, the plan for raising money for aiding the poor Christians of Jerusalem that had worked nicely in Galatia is urged for Corinth. It is a plan based on saving a reasonable part of weekly earnings. Churches that contribute to the fund have the privilege of selecting representatives to accompany the gift to Jerusalem.[94] The letter closes with a brief discussion of administrative and personal matters.[95]

The "severe" letter mentioned in II Cor. 2:4 and 7:8 is preserved in major part in II Cor. 10–13. It has the character of a vigorous apologia in which Paul defends himself against slanderous statements designed to wrest leadership from his hands. The charges of cowardice,[96] hyperbolical overstatement,[97] officiousness,[98] boasting [99] are shown to be absurd, and then Paul impressively presents his apostolic credentials.[100] On the basis of his service and suffering,[101] the revelations and visions that have come to him,[102] the heroic ethical standards to which he has consistently held,[103] none possess apostolic credentials of superior merit. In his role as apostle, without thought of courting social approval but speaking as "in the sight of God and as a follower of Christ," Paul urges drastic reformation at Corinth and threatens severe disciplinary measures if this is unduly delayed.[104]

When Paul learned from Titus that this "severe" letter had wrought the desired changes at Corinth, he immediately wrote to express his joy. This letter of conciliation appears in II Cor. 1–9, omitting 6:14–7:1. Comfort and harmony are its emphases throughout. The body of the letter [105] consists of a review and reinterpretation of Paul's recent relations with the Christian community at Corinth and closes with a fervent plea for mutual confidence. As a test of the reality of their reconciliation Paul urges the Corinthians to contribute generously to the church-wide collection for the Jerusalem poor.[106]

[93] 15:35-38.   [94] 16:1-4.   [95] 16:5-24.   [96] 10:1-6.
[97] 10:7-11.   [98] 10:12-18.   [99] 11:1-15.   [100] 11:16–12:18.
[101] 11:16-33.   [102] 12:1-10.   [103] 12:11-18.   [104] 12:19–13:14.
[105] 1:1–7:16, omitting 6:14–7:1.   [106] 8:1–9:15.

V

THE LETTER TO THE ROMANS

Authorship.—Romans is approached only by Ephesians, among the letters of the first Pauline letter collection, in the widespread popularity it enjoyed during the early stages of the development of Christian literature. Only those writings that show little or no literary indebtedness [1] appear to have made no use of the letter. Acquaintance with it is certain in the instances of Ephesians, First Peter, First Clement, the Fourth Gospel, Justin's writings, and the Pastoral epistles; highly probable in Hebrews, the Johannine epistles, the letters of Ignatius, Polycarp to the Philippians, James, and Second Peter; and reasonably probable in Revelation and the Epistle of Barnabas.

As with the rest of Paul's letters, Marcion makes the earliest direct mention of Romans. It is the fourth in his list of Pauline letters. In the Muratorian canon it stands ninth in the list of Paul's letters.[2] From the time of Irenaeus on, the letter is formally quoted as a letter of Paul.

In the case of Romans, as with Galatians, no sources exist that afford better criteria for authenticity than the letter itself supplies. The vocabulary, literary style, religious point of view are as definitely Pauline as the historical student knows. The situation reflected in the letter is entirely understandable in the light of the career of Paul as known in the earliest tradition. If any letters are ascribed to Paul, Romans must be included as authentic.

The First Readers.—The letter is addressed "to all those in Rome whom God loves, who are called to be his people." [3] The residence of these Christians was the Rome of the time of Nero. Nero was a man of ability and courage and during the earlier part of his career was a wise and vigorous administrator. Justice was within

---

[1] Jude, the Didache, Second Clement, Martyrdom of Polycarp.

[2] From the fourth century onward, Romans regularly stands at the head of the list of Paul's letters in the Greek manuscripts and in the manuscripts of the versions.

[3] 1:7.

reach for most of the people, and there existed a degree of security
and prosperity that approximated that of the reign of Augustus.

Paul's own attitude toward the Roman state was one of admiring
loyalty.[4] The order it created enabled him to do his work as a missionary. In complete disagreement with the author of Revelation,
for whom Rome was the agent and embodiment of cosmic evil,
Paul regarded the authority of Rome as thoroughly beneficent and
as God's agency for the restraint of forces hostile to Christianity.[5]
He looked forward eagerly to an opportunity of visiting the church
at Rome both because of the needs and character of the church
itself and because of the advantageous setting that this particular
Christian group enjoyed.[6] As he had used Syrian Antioch and
Ephesus as bases of operation for his missionary campaigns in the
eastern end of the Mediterranean world, he hoped to use Rome
as a center for his further work in more distant western regions.[7]

How this church began or who its founders were, nobody knows.
Clearly Paul did not establish it, although he knew of its existence
and desired to be understood by it. The effort to connect Peter
with its early years lacks historical foundation. Probably Christian
travelers who came to Rome for the variety of reasons that created
constant intercourse between East and West brought Christianity
with them and rooted it there. They would be people from such
centers as Syrian Antioch, Corinth, Ephesus, and Jerusalem. From
returning travelers Paul learned what he knew about western
Christianity.[8]

The membership of the Roman church was probably predominantly non-Jewish,[9] although there are indications of some
Jewish Christians among the first readers of this letter.[10] Unfor-
tunately there is no reliable historical source other than the letter
itself by which to check these data. There was probably an original
Jewish-Christian nucleus, but the recent growth in membership
had created a Gentile majority in the Roman church.

There are certain textual data that suggest the possibility that
Romans was meant for a circle of churches. The chapter headings
of the codex Fuldensis and of the codex Amiatinus reflect a form
of the letter which lacked chapters 15 and 16 and from which the

---

[4] 13:1-7.   [5] Cf. II Thess. 2:7.   [6] 1:8-15; cf. Acts 19:21; 23:11.
[7] 15:28-29.   [8] Cf. Acts 18:2.   [9] 1:5-6, 13; 11:13; 15:15-16.
[10] 3:9; 4:1; 7:1-6; 9:10.

name of Rome was omitted in 1:7, 15. Clement of Alexandria and
Origen alone among the Ante-Nicene Fathers quote Romans 15 and
16, but the manuscript they used seems to have omitted the name of
Rome. Chapter 16 was hardly addressed to Rome but seems to have
been a letter of introduction for "our sister Phoebe" to the church
at Ephesus.[11] The probabilities are that the original letter consisted of the first fifteen chapters and that its first readers were
members of the Christian community at Rome. The deletion of
local allusions and emphases is best understood as a phase of its
later circulation.

Date.—The letter to the Romans bears the marks of having been
written late in Paul's missionary career. He thinks of the area he
has covered and the people he has reached in comprehensive
terms.[12] He regards his work in the East as about finished,[13] and
he feels free to plan similar campaigns in the West.[14] Before he can
undertake the execution of such plans, however, he must go to
Jerusalem "to take help to God's people." [15] He explains the nature
of this "help" by saying that "Macedonia and Greece have determined to make a contribution for the poor among God's people in
Jerusalem."

In Acts 24:17 the delivery of this gift has been accomplished, and
the visit of which the purpose had been "to bring charitable dona-
tions . . . and to offer sacrifice" has become the occasion of Paul's
arrest. This is clearly the collection that figures prominently in the
letters to Corinth.[16] The allusions to it in Romans determine the
location of that letter with reference to the Corinthian correspondence and suggest that if that correspondence falls between winter
of 53 and autumn of 55 the letter to the Romans was written during the winter or early spring of 56.

Place of Composition.—According to the Lukan narrative, Paul
left Ephesus at the close of the third missionary campaign, traveled
through Macedonia, and then "went on to Greece where he stayed
for three months." [17] Corinth was probably the place where he de-

---

[11] For a highly ingenious argument that chap. 16 was an "integral part" of
Paul's letter to Rome see C. H. Dodd, *The Epistle of Paul to the Romans,* pp.
xiv-xxiv. After an elaborate effort to show the possibility that the numerous
addresses in this chapter resided in Rome, he admits that the arguments for a
Roman destination come "far short of proof."

[12] 1:13.   [13] 15:18-23.   [14] 15:24, 28.   [15] 15:25.
[16] I Cor. 16; II Cor. 8-9.   [17] Acts 20:2-3.

bated the advisability of embarking at Lecheum for Rome or at Cenchreae for Jerusalem. His decision was to accompany the collection gathered in Galatia, Asia, Macedonia, and Achaia to Jerusalem.[18] The delay required by that long journey caused him to write the Roman Christians about his ultimate intentions,[19] and assure them that it was neither a lack of interest in the West nor any lack of confidence in the efficacy of his gospel that explained the further delay of his visit.[20]

Occasion and Purpose.—Paul had long been eager to visit the church at Rome.[21] Just when the demands of his work in the East left him free to carry out this desire it became necessary for him further to defer his plans.[22] He explains that he is just "starting for Jerusalem, to take help to God's people" in the form of "a contribution" gathered in Macedonia and Greece.[23]

The letter to the Romans, then, was a temporary substitute for a personal visit. That much of its purpose lies on the surface. Difference of opinion begins when the inquiry is made as to the reasons for having written this particular kind of letter. Some hold that this letter, like the others Paul wrote, had its content determined solely by the circumstances and needs of the local Christian group addressed. Others see practically no reference to the circumstances of the readers and view the letter as a statement of the system of thought of which the Roman church became custodian for the future needs of the Christian cause.

Each of these views involves serious difficulties. The issues discussed are much the same as those that figure prominently in the letter to the Galatians. They are more dispassionately stated and are discussed at greater length, but they are the same issues. Yet Paul knew the Roman situation by hearsay, whereas in Galatians he addressed a group he had established and had known intimately. That the letter is not a compendium of theology is shown by its failure to treat many emphases that other letters show mattered vitally in Paul's thought, such as "spiritual gifts," eschatology, the the resurrection of believers, the Lord's Supper.

A fruitful clue is supplied by statements of the twofold objective of Paul's proposed visit to Rome: (1) he feels that he is qualified "to produce some results" among the Romans of the sort that have

[18] Acts 20:3.   [19] 15:24-29.   [20] 1:16-17.   [21] 1:10-15.
[22] 15:19.   [23] 15:24-26.

attended his ministry "among the rest of the heathen," [24] and (2) he is looking toward missionary activities in Spain and desires to enlist the co-operation of the Roman community in those endeavors.[25] Both of these interests figured in his eagerness to make a personal visit to Rome. They are the proper starting point for the discovery of the purpose of the letter that was intended to serve as the temporary substitute for that visit.

The blessing that Paul felt pre-eminently qualified to share is described as a "spiritual gift." [26] Conceivably the readers might miss this endowment if they remained personally unacquainted with Paul.[27] The character of this "gift" is best understood from the extensive and detailed descriptions found in other Pauline letters.[28] Paul probably felt that Roman Christianity lacked the "charismatic" quality which for him was so highly significant. The bestowal of this "gift" would be the chief interest of his visit, but hardly of a letter.

The enlistment of his readers' support for missionary plans in the "far West" was, however, a matter that could be handled by correspondence. In exactly that connection the meaning of the letter becomes thoroughly clear. Paul understood Christianity in terms of inclusiveness and universalism. This point of view explains his emphasis on the efficacy and adequacy of "faith" as the basis of acceptance with God. The leaders of the Jerusalem church, however, lacked the insight that "in Christ" racialism and nationalism had been abolished. They were inclined to make the synagogue the way of entry into the church, and to exalt legal obedience as complementary to faith obedience.

At every crucial turn of his career in the East, Paul had been involved in time-consuming controversy over this issue. At Antioch he had publicly opposed Peter for compromising this principle of universalism because of "fear of the party of circumcision." [29] The letter to the Galatians had been written to refute the racism of conservative Christians by showing that "the real descendants of Abraham are the men of faith." [30] The deferment of his missionary plans in order that he might attend the Jerusalem council represented Paul's effort to deal with this vital issue at the point of its

[24] 1:13. [25] 15:24. [26] 1:11 (χάρισμα πνευματικόν).
[27] Acts 19:2-6. [28] Gal. 5:16, 22-25; I Cor. 12:1–14:40.
[29] Gal. 2:11-12. [30] Gal. 3:7.

origin.[31] The parties of Cephas and of "Christ" at Corinth,[32] in one way or another, were probably protagonists of the restrictive principle of legalism.

As Paul turned his face to the West, he hoped that he might be spared the necessity of fighting this old battle all over again. If he could avoid the dissipation of time and limited strength in controversy, he could be doubly effective in the actual task of missions in Spain. More than that, if the Roman church understood his point of view sympathetically, their co-operation, which was so vital to his maximum success, would be forthcoming from the outset. The purpose in writing Romans, then, was to create that understanding. Its principal intention was to clarify and win assent to those phases of Paul's exposition of Christianity that had been most frequently misunderstood. The letter was thus as definitely "occasional" as any of Paul's letters, although less local in that its discussion of problems was hypothetical so far as its readers were concerned.

Message.—The original form of the letter to the Romans consisted of the first fifteen chapters. The prayer of 15:33, with or without the "Amen," ended the letter as Paul wrote it. The contents of the sixteenth chapter are best understood as a note of introduction for Phoebe addressed to the church at Ephesus.[33] When Paul's letters

---

[31] Acts 15:1-29.   [32] I Cor. 1:12.

[33] There are certain textual data that raise a question about chaps. 15 and 16. Although extant Greek manuscripts contain these chapters, the variety of ways in which the doxologies appear indicates that a shorter recension of the epistle was known in the early church. So far as numerical count goes, the majority of Greek manuscripts have a doxology after 14:23, although the best give it after 16:24. Some manuscripts have a doxology only after 14:23; others, such as the fifth-century codex Alexandrinus, have doxologies after 14:23 and 16:24; and a few dispense with the doxology entirely. There are also Greek manuscripts from which the phrase "in Rome" is omitted from 1:7, 15. There appears also to have been a Latin version of Romans older than the Vulgate that circulated in North Africa and Italy during the third century which lacked chaps. 15 and 16 and in which the doxology of 16:25-27 followed 14:23. It is unlikely that Paul himself prepared two forms of the letter, but it is entirely understandable that at a later time church leaders reduced it to the form of a theological tract for general circulation by deleting its place name and the two final chapters. For a detailed description of the textual data see Lake, *The Earlier Epistles of St. Paul*, pp. 324-70. On the basis of its thought content, the fifteenth chapter is logically viewed as an integral part of the original letter. The course of the thought of 14:13-23 requires 15:1-6 for completion, just as the letter as a whole needs some such conclusion as 15:7-33 supplies without any appearance of artificiality. This can hardly be said of chap. 16. The

were collected and edited for publication around A.D. 95, the brief note or collection of fragments from several letters [34] was appended to the longer letter and became textually a part of that letter. The sixteenth chapter is therefore not taken into account in the present summary of the message of Romans.

The thought of the letter centers about the basic inquiry into what God expects of men. Paul felt that the uniqueness of Christianity lay in the answer it gave to this profound and perennial question. This answer was not to be viewed as an appendix to older answers. It neither required nor permitted supplementation. It possessed the character of adequacy and finality. It was as universal in its effectiveness as the religious quest itself.

The bases of man's acceptance by God are viewed as implicit in certain provisions God has himself made, which are effective from God's own point of view. Because of the ethical satisfactoriness of these provisions, the possibility of gracious forgiveness is opened for men. As the corollary of his self-involvement with man's sin in the vicarious death of Christ, God accepts man's attitude of complete and utterly sincere self-surrender as preferable to legal conformity.

Paul represents faith as making God's gracious forgiveness actually operative for the individual person. God treats the wholly surrendered life as though it were actually righteous, when as yet

---

numerous salutations of this chapter are hardly appropriate for Rome, where Paul had never been, but are entirely intelligible for Ephesus, where he resided for better than two years (Acts 19:10; 20:17-38). Certain of the persons mentioned were clearly residents of Ephesus. Epaenetus (16:5) is said to have been "the first man in Asia to turn to Christ." Prisca and Aquila (16:3), similarly, were residents of Ephesus during the period of Paul's correspondence with Corinth, and the Ephesian church convened in their house (I Cor. 16:19; cf. Acts 18:2, 26). The Roman author of the Pastoral epistles, writing around the middle of the second century, represents Prisca and Aquila as residents of Ephesus (II Tim. 1:18; 4:12, 19), which suggests that tradition in the Roman church associated them with Ephesus rather than Rome. It is worthy of note also that the warnings of 16:17-20 can more normally be interpreted as intended for Ephesus than for Rome (Col. 2:4, 8, 19; Acts 20:29-32).

[34] It is possible that chap. 16 is a compilation of several fragments. The longest of them (vss. 1-16) appears to have been a note introducing Phoebe to the Ephesian church. The salutations of vss. 21-23, however, could have belonged to a letter to Corinth, Erastus having been associated with Corinth in early tradition (II Tim. 4:20). Ephesus and not Corinth, however, could have been Erastus' home (Acts 19:22). The warnings against schism in vss. 17-20 could have been intended for Corinth or Ephesus. The doxology of vss. 25-27 was probably the formulation of an editor who wanted to round off this collection of bits. Its style, ideas, and vocabulary are notably un-Pauline.

it only aspires to be righteous. He does this without compromising moral values because the Cross discloses the seriousness of his concern with sin and because faith as a life attitude contains the promise of a superior quality of goodness. Paul thinks of faith also as making available an access of spiritual energy that gives the individual a sense of moral victory and security. Growth in actual righteousness thus becomes the consequence of fellowship between the forgiven man and the Spirit of God, who is none other than the glorified Lord himself.[35]

Paul introduces his letter with an impressive statement of his apostolic credentials,[36] an explanation of the nature of his interest in the Roman church,[37] and a summary description of Christianity as the revelation of the only effective way of securing God's approval.[38] The remainder of the letter is an amplification of this summary.

Because he has been so generally misunderstood, Paul gives an elaborate exposition of the meaning of justification.[39] He contends that, instead of being the unworthy thing his critics have represented it to be, his gospel of the sufficiency of faith actually sets forth the only effective means of securing God's approval.[40] He finds in the universal sway exercised by sin prima facie evidence of the ineffectiveness of all different approaches. Gentiles [41] and Jews [42] stand on common ground in that both are without hope. Without fresh insight humanity's plight is hopeless. This representation of universal failure to win God's approval by traditional procedures is then examined critically and is found to be realistic by the tests of the revelation contained in the Old Testament itself.[43] Having established humanity's need for some better way of seeking God's approval, Paul next describes the gospel as a disclosure of precisely that new and effective way into God's forgiveness.[44] The propitiatory death of Christ is its basis, and it is independent of the Law in the sense that it involves a radically different principle. The Cross leaves man in no doubt about the costliness of sin, and it effectively dispels the misconception that divine forgiveness indicates moral indifference. Because of this God can freely forgive any person who unreservedly commits his life to him, whatever the level of his

[35] Cf. II. Cor. 3:17-18.   [36] 1:1-7.   [37] 1:8-15.   [38] 1:16-17.
[39] 1:18-5:21.   [40] 1:18-3:20.   [41] 1:18-32.   [42] 2:1-29.
[43] 3:1-20.   [44] 3:21-31.

moral attainment at the time. Although new in the sense of being adequately set forth in the Christian revelation, the sufficiency of faith is illustrated in the Old Testament in the instances of such heroic figures as Abraham and David.[45] The case for faith being so clear, believers are urged to forget their misgivings and actually appropriate the blessings inherent in the state of approval made accessible by their faith.[46]

Down to this point Paul has employed juridical analogies for the illustration of his thought. He now turns to the more intelligible conceptions of mysticism.[47] His view of Christianity has been suspected of minimizing righteousness; and he undertakes to show that, although the ethic of the gospel is not legalistic, it is nonetheless real and central. He does this in three ways: (1) He shows that a right understanding of faith leaves no place for the continuation of sinfulness.[48] It involves a mystical union with Christ, and this presupposes a severance of any vital relationship to sin and brings about spiritual resurrection into "a new life." (2) He shows that Christianity, although independent of the Law, does not encourage antinomianism.[49] The Law itself is held to be "holy," and its commands are described as "holy, just, and good." The trouble is with the moral deficiency of human nature and a misconception of the function of the Law. Instead of enabling man to achieve righteousness the Law merely brought the character of sin to light and thereby precipitated the moral struggle in which man was consistently the loser. (3) He shows that the basis of moral triumph is the alliance of man's better self with the Spirit, who is conceived as being the risen and exalted Christ.[50] Although God's approval is instantaneous at the point of man's self-surrender, the achievement of actual righteousness through fellowship with Christ involves gradual growth. The indwelling Spirit assists man's better self to master the whole life and the resulting growth in Christlikeness is "a foretaste of the future."

At this point Paul is impelled more by emotion than by logic to give an account of Israel's unbelief.[51] In the midst of his exultation at the prospect of the final triumph of those whom God approves on the basis of their faith, he is stung by the poignant recollection of the limited success of the gospel within Judaism.

---

[45] 4:1-25.   [46] 5:1-21.   [47] 6:1–8:39.   [48] 6:1-14.
[49] 6:15–7:25.   [50] 8:1-39; cf. II Cor. 3:17-18.   [51] 9:1–11:36.

What he says is determined by a tender love for his own race, an intense eagerness to heal the widening breach between church and synagogue and between Jewish and non-Jewish Christians, perplexity with reference to the promises contained in the Old Testament, and a recognition of the necessity of warning Hellenistic Christians against spiritual complacency. He begins by reminding his readers that God's historic way of working has been by selection. He has repeatedly weeded out a single generation in order that later generations might avoid the folly of disobedience. Israel's rejection of Christ, therefore, is actually God's rejection of Israel; and since God possesses the right to do whatever he pleases, man has no right to find fault.[52] Nevertheless Israel is guilty because she ignored the truth embodied in Old Testament revelation.[53] Israel's failure, however, has been partial and temporary rather than absolute and permanent.[54] There has always been a righteous minority, as the experience of Elijah demonstrated. Had the Jews immediately accepted Christ, opportunity might have been denied the heathen; and, conversely, the enthusiastic acceptance of the gospel by non-Jews is God's way of opening Jewish eyes to their own glorious heritage in Christ.

In conclusion Paul points out the ethical and social implications of faith.[55] Fundamentally it involves the "new attitude of mind" that makes the discovery of God's will man's sole concern.[56] It finds concrete expression in the relationship which the individual sustains within the Christian community itself,[57] in his social contacts generally,[58] in his discharge of civic duty,[59] in his enthronement of love as the regulative principle in his life,[60] in considerateness for the overscrupulous person,[61] and in his resolute denial of the significance of race among Christians.[62]

[52] 9:1-33.   [53] 10:1-21.   [54] 11:1-36.   [55] 12:1-15:33.
[56] 12:1-2.   [57] 12:3-8.   [58] 12:9-21.   [59] 13:1-7.
[60] 13:8-14.   [61] 14:1-15:6.   [62] 15:7-13.

VI

THE LETTERS TO THE PHILIPPIANS

WHEN Paul says to the Philippians that he does not "mind writing the same thing over and over" to them,[1] the natural inference is that he has written them previously and repeatedly.[2] That two such letters are preserved, in large part at least, in canonical Philippians is highly probable.

This probability is strengthened by other data in the letter. When in 3:1 Paul says, "Now, my brother, goodbye, and the Lord be with you," he is clearly bringing the letter to a close.[3] Serenity is the mood of the preceding context. Between verses 1 and 2, however, there is a complete break in the sequence of the thought, and in 3:2 Paul lashes at Jewish Christian critics with an emotional intensity that has its only counterpart in II Cor. 9–13 and addresses himself to a situation closely resembling that which inspired Galatians. These data seem to mean that in 1:1–3:1 and 3:2–4:23 there are two letters, written for entirely different occasions and probably brought into their traditional form when Paul's letters were edited for publication during the last decade of the first century.

Authorship.—Philippians does not appear to have been among the most popular of Paul's published letters. Until the last quarter

---

[1] 3:1.

[2] Neither the contents of Philippians taken as a whole nor the immediate context in 3:1 afford a satisfactory explanation of τὰ αὐτά. The phrase seems to imply letters previously written. It is possible that Polycarp, writing to the Philippians sixty years later, understood Paul here as referring to many letters: ὃς καὶ ἀπὼν ὑμῖν ἔγραψεν ἐπιστολάς (3:2). Walter Bauer so understands Polycarp (*Die Briefe des Ignatius von Antiochia und der Polykarpbrief* [Tübingen: J. C. B. Mohr, 1920], p. 287). Just as probably, however, Adolph Harnack is right in holding that Polycarp was thinking of the published corpus of Paul's letters as having a message for each local church ("*Patristische Miscellen,*" *Texte und Untersuchungen zur Geschichte der altchristlichen Litteratur* [Leipzig: J. C. Hinrichs, 1900], XX, ii, 89).

[3] The introductory τὸ λοιπόν may mean "as to what remains," and be intended to introduce a new subject within a single letter. So understood it serves to reduce the impression of abruptness as the reader passes from 3:1 to 3:2. Much more probably it means "finally" or "now" and indicates that the letter has been completed.

of the second century certainty of acquaintance with it can be predicated only in the instances of Polycarp, Marcion, and the author
of the Pastoral letters. Its use by the author of Hebrews is reasonably
clear, and acquaintance with it is probable in Ephesians, Revelation,
First Clement, the Fourth Gospel, the Johannine letters, the letters
of Ignatius, and James. It is especially noteworthy, in view of their
liberal use of literary sources, that First Peter and the writings of
Justin are wholly without traces of the influence of Philippians.
Early in the last quarter of the second century it is quoted with
exactness in the letter from the churches of Lyons and Vienne,[4] but
without any allusion to its authorship.

Polycarp, of course, specifically refers to the "letters" Paul wrote
the Philippians,[5] and there can be no doubt that the canonical letter
was at least included in the allusion. Marcion regarded Paul as its
author and listed it as the ninth of the letters in his canon, placing
it between Colossians and Philemon. It is fourth among the letters
ascribed to Paul in the Muratorian canon, where it is located between Ephesians and Colossians. Irenaeus, Clement of Alexandria,
and Tertullian quote it as by Paul, and from their time onward
it was generally so regarded.

The letter itself claims to have been written by Paul. Its
language and style create no suspicion of this representation. The
allusions to the author's circumstances and to persons associated
with him in his work fit intelligibly into the scheme of Paul's life
as it can be pieced together from the available sources. The situations that appear to lie back of the correspondence seem to be the
real situations that inspired the letters. The personality of the
author is too lifelike, wherever it comes to the surface, to be regarded as a fiction. The portrayal of religion in the letter is
warmly and profoundly experiential, and the terminology employed entirely lacks the sound of stereotyped formulae.

Insofar as the content of Philippians is theological, it is of a
character that is attributable to Paul. Its Christology,[6] its doctrine
of faith,[7] its eschatology [8] are of a piece with the similar emphases
of the recognized letters. The mention of "the superintendents and
assistants" creates some difficulty,[9] but the conception involved is
probably no more formal than is contemplated in the allusion

---

4 Euseb. *Hist.* V. 2. 2; cf. Phil. 2:6.   5 Polyc. Phil. 3:2.   6 2:6-11.
7 3:5-11.   8 4:5.   9 1:1.

in First Thessalonians to "those . . . who lead you in the service of the Lord, and teach you." [10] It certainly points to no such concern with polity as appears in the letters to Timothy and Titus.

The First Readers.—The letter in its canonical form is addressed to "all the devoted adherents of Christ Jesus who are in Philippi." It has been suggested that the two halves of the published letter were originally intended for different sets of readers.[11] It is argued that no such problems as are introduced in 3:2 ff. ever troubled the church at Philippi. Where information about Paul's relations with his churches is so disconnected, however, certainty in such a matter is unwarranted. The allusion to "those mischief-makers, with their amputation" is itself evidence of the existence of the problem.

The content of the letters involves no inherent necessity for two sets of readers. The data rather weigh in favor of a single group. A similarly warm and personal relationship between author and readers is reflected in both letters.[12] The designation of the readers as "you at Philippi" [13] quite clearly identifies them with the group described in the salutation as "the devoted adherents of Christ Jesus . . . in Philippi." [14] In both halves of the published letter Epaphroditus is mentioned as having been the agent of the readers in bringing assistance to Paul.[15]

Philippi, although an inland town, was conveniently located within eight miles of Neapolis, a good port.[16] It was the scene of the defeat of the forces of Brutus and Cassius by Antony and Octavius in 42 B.C. and thereafter was favored in many ways by the imperial government. Octavius recognized its strategic value and made it a military colony. Although Thessalonica was the political capital of Macedonia, Philippi was made an administrative center of almost equal importance. Its favored status was probably the point of the description of it as "a Roman garrison town, and the principal place in that part of Macedonia." [17]

The Lukan account of Paul's ministry at Philippi [18] leaves untold much that the modern reader would like to know. Its primary interests were evangelistic and apologetic rather than historical. Its emphases were the miraculous accompaniments of Paul's preaching and his complete exoneration before the Roman magistrates.

[10] I Thess. 5:12.   [11] McNeile, *Introduction,* p. 172.
[12] 2:12; 3:17; 4:1, 10.   [13] 4:15.   [14] 1:1.   [15] 2:25; 4:18.
[16] Cf. Acts 20:6.   [17] Acts 16:12.   [18] Acts 16:10-40.

Instead, therefore, of an informative narrative of the establishment and character of the Philippian church, incidents are told that establish the political inoffensiveness of Christianty and that reveal the supernatural auspices under which the missionary enterprise proceeded.

The chronological hints in the account are so general as to give no indication of the length of Paul's stay.[19] The inference from the turbulent termination of the visit is that he remained there for a rather short time.[20] The hostility that shortened this first sojourn did not, however, prevent later contacts with Philippi. Toward the close of the third missionary journey Paul went from Ephesus to Corinth by way of Macedonia,[21] and it is likely that he wrote his final letter to Corinth while at Philippi.[22] After the winter at Corinth, Paul again took the long way around "by way of Macedonia" because of the discovery of a plot against him. It was in connection with this roundabout journey to a port of embarkation that the final allusion to his relations with the Philippian church prior to his imprisonment at Rome occurs.[23]

The membership of the Philippian church may have been entirely Gentile. Paul did his first preaching there not in a synagogue[24] but "outside the gates . . . where . . . there was a praying place."[25] Subsequently his headquarters was the home of a certain Lydia, who had been divinely led "to accept Paul's teaching."[26] The "mischief-makers, with their amputation" were propagandists from the outside rather than a Jewish-Christian element within the church.[27] That they had less success at Philippi than in Galatia and at Corinth may have been due to the completely non-Jewish character of the local group.

Paul's relations with this church seem to have been peculiarly happy. The people were warmly attached to him personally and were in a sense without parallel elsewhere his partners.[28] At Thessalonica and at Corinth they sent him financial assistance,[29] and on two other occasions Epaphroditus was sent from Philippi to look after Paul's needs.[30]

Date.—Of the two letters that were combined to make canonical

[19] Acts 16:12, 18, 40.   [20] I Thess. 2:2.   [21] Acts 20:12; II Cor. 2.12.
[22] II Cor. 7:6-7.   [23] Acts 20:6.   [24] Acts 13:15; 14:1; 17:1.
[25] Acts 16:13.   [26] Acts 16:14.   [27] 3:2-3.   [28] 2:12; 3:17.
[29] 4:15-17; cf. II Cor. 11:9.   [30] 2:25; 4:18.

Philippians, the earlier seems to have been 3:2–4:23 and the later 1:1–3:1. The differences in the tone of the two letters and in the descriptions of Paul's circumstances create this impression.

The main body of this earlier letter consists of a denunciation of Jewish-Christian opponents that belongs to the atmosphere of II Cor. 11:22 ff. It is ordinarily supposed that Paul went from Ephesus to Corinth by way of Macedonia [31] for the purpose of delaying his arrival at Corinth until he had ascertained the effect of the "harsh" letter.[32] This end might better have been accomplished by simply waiting at Ephesus. The detour through Macedonia was probably due to the development there of some such situation as that described in Phil. 3:2-21. It is not unlikely that Paul wrote to Philippi at about the time he wrote so severely to Corinth. The tone of the letter in the one instance is milder than in the other because Paul was more confident of the loyalty of his Philippian readers, but the mood of belligerency is common to the two messages. The irenic tone of the final letter to Corinth [33] may be partly due to success at Philippi as well as to the good news Titus brought from Corinth.[34]

Paul's allusions to his imprisonment [35] belong to the first half of the published form of Philippians, which is here regarded as a second letter. There is nothing in 3:2–4:23 that requires imprisonment for its explanation. Paul is represented as having a hard time but not as being a prisoner. In the letter that he probably wrote the Corinthians from Philippi he describes an experience belonging to his stay at Ephesus that left him "utterly and unendurably crushed," so much so that he "actually despaired of life itself." [36] This or any one of a series of bad situations [37] belonging to the same general period would be a sufficient explanation of the "difficulties" which the Philippians had thoughtfully tried to "share." [38] Epaphroditus, who on a later occasion when Paul was in prison was sent to be with him but became ill and had to leave without completing his mission, brought Paul assistance in this earlier instance. He shows none of the symptoms here that later made it necessary for him to return to Philippi. "Those who belong to the emperor's household" [39]

[31] II Cor. 2:12-14; Acts 20:1-2.   [32] II Cor. 10-13.
[33] II Cor. 1–9 except 6:14–7:1.   [34] II Cor. 7:5-7.   [35] 1:7, 13, 17.
[36] II Cor. 1:8.   [37] I Cor. 4:9-13; 15:32; II Cor. 4:8-12; 11:23-27.
[38] 4:12-18.   [39] 4:22.

may denote an entirely different group from "the Imperial Guard." [40] Neither allusion requires Paul's presence in Rome, although the latter suggests it more strongly than the former.

These data combine to locate Paul at Ephesus at the time he wrote this earlier letter. The spring of 55, when he wrote his third letter to Corinth, is a thoroughly intelligible date for the message to Philippi.

Judgment regarding the place of composition is decisive in any effort to date the second letter to Philippi. Paul was a prisoner at the time he wrote,[41] but this was his status several times during the period within which the letter conceivably belongs. The allusions were hardly to the imprisonment at Caesarea,[42] because the prospect of going to Rome would make an early visit to Philippi unlikely.[43] The other possibilites are Ephesus [44] and Rome.[45]

There are no insuperable obstacles to locating the letter at Ephesus. The allusions to "the Imperial Guard" [46] and "those who belong to the emperor's household" [47] are not identical in meaning, and both can refer to groups at Ephesus. The former, however, points more naturally to Rome. The absence from Acts of a mention of an Ephesian imprisonment weighs in favor of Rome but is not decisive against Ephesus, since Acts is not an exhaustive narrative. The homesickness of Epaphroditus [48] is more easily explicable at Rome than at Ephesus. The inclusion of Timothy in the salutation tends to link the letter with Colossians and Philemon, but it must be remembered that Timothy was with Paul at Ephesus [49] and that Colossians and Philemon may have been written there.

In favor of a Roman setting for the letter it has been argued that Paul was hopeful as long as he looked forward to an appeal of his case to the emperor. The supposed spirit of depression pervading Philippians is interpreted as disillusionment at the failure of Roman justice and therefore as an indication of the latter part of the period of imprisonment at Rome.[50] Actually, however, joy-

---

[40] 1:13.   [41] 1:7, 13, 17.   [42] Acts 23:33; 24:27.   [43] 1:26; 2:24.
[44] II Cor. 11:23.   [45] Acts 28:30.

[46] Phil. 1:13: ὥστε τοὺς δεσμούς μου φανεροὺς ἐν Χριστῷ λενέσθαι ἐν ὅλῳ τῷ πραιτωρίῳ καὶ τοῖς λοιποῖς πᾶσιν; cf. John 18:33: εἰς τὸ πραιτώριον ὁ Πειλᾶτος; Acts 23:35: κελεύσας ἐν τῷ πραιτωρίῳ τοῦ Ἡρῴδου φυλάσσεσθαι αὐτόν. It is evident that the reference in Philippians is to a group rather than, as in the other passages, to a place.

[47] 4:22.   [48] 2:25 ff.   [49] I Cor. 16:10; II Cor. 1:1.   [50] Acts 28:30.

ousness and hope are the pervasive notes, and the tone of the letter is that of radiant freshness. These qualities suggest that if the letter belongs at Rome it was written shortly after Paul's arrival.

Some who locate the letter at Rome argue that it belongs late in the period of imprisonment because time must be allowed for news of Paul's arrival at Rome to reach Philippi, and for the raising and dispatch of funds for his use. The abandonment of Paul by his friends [51] is also interpreted as meaning that he had been in custody a long time. More probably those friends would have remained had they imagined that he would be detained as long as two years. As likely as not, also, the Philippians kept up with Paul's affairs, knew when he began the voyage to Rome, and had Epaphroditus on hand with aid when Paul reached Puteoli. It could have been Epaphroditus who notified the Christians at Rome of Paul's coming and suggested that a group go "as far as Appius' Forum and Three Taverns" to meet him.[52]

The data are indecisive as between Ephesus and Rome. Insofar as they incline one way or the other, however, they favor Rome as the place where the second letter was written. If it was written there during the earlier part of the two years of confinement, the probable calendar date for the letter is 60.

Place of Composition.—The data that shed light on Paul's location when he wrote to Philippi have been examined in connection with the effort to date the letters. They are at best inconclusive. The probabilities, however, favor Ephesus for the earlier and Rome for the later letter.

Occasion and Purpose.—The circumstances of Paul's long stay at Ephesus [53] had made self-support difficult. Since "the early days of the good news" his friends at Philippi had assumed responsibility for helping bear the expense of his undertakings.[54] This had become such a settled policy that Paul thought of them as having gone "into partnership and opened an account" with him. Now Epaphroditus had arrived with another such gift. Paul speaks of it as the final payment on their investment account and trusts that they will be pleased with the profits that may accumulate to their credit. He likens the gift to "fragrant incense, just such a

[51] 2:20.   [52] Acts 28:15.
[53] Phil. 4:10-20; I Cor. 4:9-13; 15:32; II Cor. 4:8-12; 11:23-27.
[54] Phil. 4:16; II Cor. 11:9.

sacrifice as God welcomes and approves." [55] However well he may have "learned the secret, in any and all conditions, of being well-fed and of going hungry, of having plenty and of going without," he is deeply moved at their desire to share his difficulties. He accordingly writes to express his gratitude.

Epaphroditus brought news as well as money, and the news was disconcerting. As in Galatia and at Corinth, conservative Jewish Christians were attempting to commend to the Philippian church a type of Christianity that Paul felt was inferior and fallacious. Their effort had apparently met with little success, but their temerity in attempting to estrange those to whom he felt so close gave heat to his denunciation of them as intruders. This is the explanation of the introductory exclamation, "Look out for those dogs, those mischief-makers, with their amputation!" [56]

The twofold purpose of this first letter, then, was to warn the Philippians of the unsoundness of the propaganda of those missionaries who represented the viewpoint of the leaders of the Jerusalem church [57] and to thank them for the generous gift brought by Epaphroditus.

The thoughtfulness of these friends followed Paul to Rome. They sent Epaphroditus ahead to be on hand when he reached his destination. They provided funds with which to secure the necessities for his comfort and health and directed Epaphroditus to remain as long as he might be useful as a personal assistant. But Rome was a long way from Philippi, and Epaphroditus became ill and unhappy.[58] Nothing would suffice but that he return home. Yet his return was apt to be humiliating, and Paul knew how deeply severe blame might injure his miserable companion. He desired that the membership of the church credit the poor fellow with having done his best, even though he was leaving without completing his mission. He therefore sent a letter by Epaphroditus, the primary objective of which was to ensure the bearer a comfortable homecoming. The letter is preserved in 1:1–3:1 of canonical Philippians.

Message.—The thought of Paul's earlier letter to the Philippians centers in the differentiation of Christianity as a way of life from legalism on the one hand and antinomianism on the other. It describes a "better way" that avoids both formalism and sensualism.

[55] 4:18.   [56] 3:2.   [57] Cf. Gal. 2:6, 11.   [58] 2:26 ff.

The distinctiveness of that "better way" inheres in the conception of religion as the worship of God "by his Spirit." [59] The outcome is an uprightness "not based on law but coming through faith in Christ—the uprightness that comes from God through faith." [60] An active preference for "everything that is excellent or praiseworthy" represents the inner meaning of faith and constitutes the condition for a personal enjoyment of "the peace of God." [61] The superiority of Christianity as here described grows out of its understanding of spiritual maturity as growth rather than as final, static achievement. He is mature who is always "straining toward what lies ahead," because the man who has been "captured by Jesus Christ" knows no goal short of "the prize to which God through Christ calls us upward." [62]

Paul's gracious acknowledgment of the gift from Philippi [63] affords an insight into his personal religion. Faith has set him free from the tyranny of things. By means of it he has discovered a source of strength that enables him to transcend circumstance, whether it involves "going hungry" or "having plenty." He is nonetheless deeply moved when the habitual kindness of the Philippians causes them to share his immediate "difficulties" by sending a generous gift. That gift is regarded as a token of their partnership with him in spreading the gospel. It is also a symbol of the generosity of God, who through their "union with Christ" will "with his wealth" supply their deepest spiritual needs.

The second letter [64] was occasioned by the necessity of sending Epaphroditus home.[65] Paul desired that the homecoming be joyous rather than humiliating, and so he wrote a cheerful, newsy letter urging that the unhappy man be given "a hearty Christian welcome." He told the Philippians the things they most wanted to know about his personal condition and plans: that he was in prison,[66] but had found in his imprisonment a challenging evangelistic opportunity;[67] that his associates in Christian service were men of varying motivation;[68] that his trial was impending and ought to turn out favorably;[69] that he planned to visit Philippi;[70] that he would soon send Timothy to bring him news of them.[71]

For a letter so brief and so largely occupied with miscellaneous,

[59] 3:3.   [60] 3:9.   [61] 4:2-9.   [62] 3:2-16.   [63] 4:10-20.
[64] 1:1-3:1.   [65] 2:25-30.   [66] 1:7, 13, 17. [67] 1:12-14.   [68] 1:15-20.
[69] 2:23.   [70] 2:24.   [71] 2:19-23.

personal matters, there is here a surprisingly stimulating religious message. Its central theme is contained in the exhortation, "Whatever happens, show yourselves citizens worthy of the good news of the Christ." [72] Christ is himself made the norm of this "worthiness," and human salvation consists in the development of "the same attitude that Christ Jesus had." [73] If resolved into its elements, this attitude is shown to be a compound of modesty, brotherliness, sympathy, humility, and filial obedience to God. This attitude is crucially significant because Christ has shown it to be an ultimate insight into God's character and therefore the criterion by which all men will be judged.[74]

[72] 1:27.   [73] 2:1-11.   [74] 2:5-11.

VII

THE LETTER TO THE COLOSSIANS

Authorship.—The heavy indebtedness of Ephesians to Colossians is convincing evidence of the inclusion of the latter in the earliest published collection of Paul's letters. It enjoyed a more limited popularity than certain others of the letters, but it was by no means the least known of them.

There are few parallels in early Christian literature for the liberal use of Colossians in Ephesians. Only the writings of Justin approximate the clarity of its use in Ephesians prior to 160. Literary acquaintance with it is highly probable, however, in Revelation, the Fourth Gospel, the letters of Ignatius, and the Pastoral letters, and reasonably probable in Hebrews and the Johannine letters. Among the writings whose literary indebtedness to Paul's published letters is clear, First Peter, First Clement, and Polycarp to the Philippians seem to have made no use of Colossians.

Marcion regarded the letter as genuine and included it as the eighth in his Pauline list, placing it between Laodiceans (our Ephesians) and Philippians. In the Muratorian canon it appears between Philippians and Galatians as the fifth of Paul's letters. It was used as a letter of Paul by Irenaeus, Clement of Alexandria, and Tertullian. From their time until the middle of the ninteenth century its authenticity was not questioned.

This tradition of genuineness has been called in question in modern times on the basis of such internal data as vocabulary, style, and thought content. These data are interpreted as indicating the hand of a Paulinist who addressed his message in Paul's name to a later situation. The tacit assumption is that Paul was widely known as a letter writer and that the pseudonymous employment of his name was natural. It can be shown, however, that Paul was not generally known as a writer of letters prior to the collection and publication of the extant remains of his correspondence during the final decade of the first century, so that the inclusion of Colossians in this original corpus becomes an impressive credential of its genuineness.

The internal data themselves are not as unfavorable to authenticity as has been imagined. The Christology of Colossians bears stronger marks of resemblance to the Fourth Gospel than to Romans, Corinthians, and Galatians, which might be taken to mean that it belongs to the end of the first century. Speculative elements are present, however, in the christological statements of unquestionably genuine letters,[1] and the problem that had arisen at Colossae could have given Paul's thought the particular turn revealed in this letter. Paul was a practical missionary whose thought centered about the needs of situations. What he said on a particular occasion was determined not so much by the principle of consistency with things previously said as by the immediate circumstances.

Furthermore these resemblances may be due in a measure to indebtedness to Colossians on the part of the Fourth Gospel. The Christianity of the latter is built around emphases that originated with Paul. The Fourth Evangelist knew Paul through his published letters, and his intention was apparently to demonstrate a basis for the apostle's message in the message of Jesus himself.

Traces of Gnosticism appearing in Colossians may be interpreted as requiring a date later than the period of Paul's life. Gnosticism in Colossians, however, lacks the maturity of the forms in which it appears in the second century. Such tendencies were widespread during the earlier half of the first century and probably became a problem for Paul toward the latter part of his career. His discussion of them only in Colossians merely indicates that they constituted a problem for the addressees of this letter. Similarly, such differences of vocabulary and style as are involved can be accounted for on the basis of the subject, the indirectness of Paul's acquaintance with his readers, and the conditions of the Colossian situation.

The letter specifically claims to have been written by Paul.[2] Timothy, Luke, and Mark are his companions. Epaphras, a member of the Colossian church, has brought Paul the information on which the letter was based. The agreement of these personal allusions with those of Philemon contributes to the lifelikeness of the situation. The concreteness and emotional quality of Col. 3-18–4:1, in contrast with the stereotyped tone of Eph. 5:22–6:9, and the naturalness with which the circumstances reflected in the letter can

[1] Rom. 8:19-22; II Cor. 3:17-18; Phil. 2:6-11.   [2] 1:1, 23; 4:18.

be fitted into the narrative framework of Acts strengthen the case for Pauline authorship. These data, coupled with the inclusion of Colossians in the first collection of Paul's letters, leave little room for doubt of its authenticity.

The First Readers.—The letter is addressed "to the devoted and steadfast Christian brothers in Colossae." Colossae was a Phrygian town of secondary importance located on the left bank of the Lycus River. The neighboring cities of Laodicea and Hierapolis[3] overshadowed it, and the Christian groups in those localities were apparently more significant. The Colossian church is notably absent from the list of groups addressed in Rev. 1:11.

The narrative of Acts never locates Paul at Colossae. He passed through Phrygia on his second and third journeys,[4] but he seems not to have gone by way of Colossae. When he passed "through the interior" to Ephesus on the third journey,[5] he apparently followed a route other than the main road through the Lycus Valley. In agreement with this representation, the data of the letter show that Paul and his readers were not personally acquainted.[6]

Nevertheless there is a certain warmth of understanding between Paul and his readers, and he writes with complete assurance that they will admit his right to counsel them.[7] This atmosphere of mutuality is probably explained by Paul's description of Epaphras, the founder of the church, as "my faithful representative as a servant of Christ."[8] Very probably Epaphras came under Paul's influence during the latter's residence at Ephesus and undertook evangelistic work at Colossae with his knowledge and encouragement.[9]

Date.—Paul was in prison when he wrote Colossians.[10] This in itself has little chronological import, since it was frequently his plight.[11] The representation of this particular experience, however, sets it apart. It was more than just another in a series of difficulties. Paul describes it as involving the cause of the gospel. He feels that he faces trial as a representative Christian and that in some sense Christianity is on trial in his person. This is also the view expressed in Philemon,[12] where the general situation and the personal allusions are additional ties that bind the two letters together. These

[3] 4:13. [4] Acts 16:6; 18:23. [5] Acts 19:1. [6] 1:4, 8, 9; 2:1.
[7] 4:2-18. [8] 1:7. [9] Acts 19:10. [10] 4:18.
[11] II Cor. 11:23. [12] Col. 1:24, 29; 2:1; 4:3-4; Philem. 1, 9, 13.

letters were manifestly written at the same time and sent by the same messenger.[13]

Conceivably they were written while Paul was at Ephesus, in which event they should be dated in 54 or 55. More probably they were written at Rome. The view of his trial as crucial in importance and representative in character suggests not merely that Paul was writing from Rome but that these letters were later than the second letter to Philippi. If so, 61 or 62 is their approximate calendar date.

Place of Composition.—Colossians supplies no information about Paul's location other than that he was in prison. Its picture of the seriousness of his situation and of the representative character of his case agrees with that in Philemon. The two letters manifest a common interest in Onesimus. These points of resemblance, together with numerous coincidences in personal allusions, conclusively show the letters had the same setting.

Ephesus or Rome with almost equal probability could have supplied that setting. Acts has no account of an Ephesian imprisonment, but it does indicate that Paul was involved in difficulties there.[14] The letters written from Ephesus refer to a series of experiences possibly involving confinement in prison while Paul was at Ephesus,[15] but they leave the matter doubtful. Either place was a logical refuge for Onesimus. Ephesus was more accessible when Epaphras desired to confer with Paul, but Rome is not thereby removed as a possibility.

The seriousness with which Paul viewed his case appears, however, to be a development upon the optimistic outlook of Phil. 1:1–3:1. This final letter to Philippi was more probably written from Rome than elsewhere, and the considerations that locate it there strengthen the likelihood that Colossians was written there at a somewhat later date.

Occasion and Purpose.—Two factors of about equal importance occasioned the writing of Colossians: (1) the arrival of Epaphras to confer with Paul about the progress of Gnosticism at Colossae,[16] and (2) Paul's decision to use the return of Onesimus to his master as an opportunity to seek his emancipation in order that he might give himself wholly to Christian service as his helper.[17]

---

[13] Col. 4:7-9.   [14] Acts 19:23–20:1.
[15] I Cor. 15:32; II Cor. 1:8-10; 4:7-15; 11:23; Phil. 4:10-20.
[16] 1:8; 4:12-13.   [17] 4:9, 16-17; Philem. 10, 13-14,20.

The sharing of values between groups of varying cultural heritage always involves the adaptation of forms of thought as well as the translation of language. The Gentile mission required that Christian missionaries think in Hellenistic terms. Even with leaders of the exceptional abilities of those who wrote the books of the New Testament, complete success was not achieved. Recipients of their message saw meanings in what they heard and read that had not been intended and that were the outgrowth of their own reflection. Gnosticism is the inclusive term applied to the effort of Greek speculative thought to fit the content of the Christian message into its own categories. It was more a tendency than a clearly defined movement and was characterized by variation in stages of development and concrete emphasis.

The Gnosticism reflected in Colossians is elemental by comparison with the elaborate systems of the late second century. It involved the general principles, however, of God's remoteness and the possibility of human access to him only by means of a gradation or series of qualities or beings. Christ was apparently viewed as a member of some such series, a sort of bottom round in the spiritual ladder whereby the properly disciplined soul might make its ascent to the realm of pure spirit where God dwelt. Such a point of view involved an implicit denial of the uniqueness of Christ and of the adequacy of the reconciliation he effected between man and God. Christ became merely one of many intermediaries rather than "a likeness of the unseen God, born before any creature" and alone qualified "to reconcile to God all things on earth or in heaven, making this peace through his blood shed on the cross." [18] Moreover, by equating spirituality with esoteric rather than with ethical interests, this understanding of the gospel threatened the moral values that gave Christianity its distinctive character.

Epaphras saw the dangerous implications of this point of view. Feeling his own inadequacy for checking it, he sought the aid of the man to whom Asian Christianity largely owed its origin.[19] The letter to the Colossians was Paul's response. In it he undertook to show the completeness of the gospel as Epaphras had learned it from him and interpreted it at Colossae. Neither was it an appendix to existing systems nor did it require supplementation by them. It was a disclosure of truth "without any reference to law," and

[18] 1:15, 20.   [19] 1:7-8; 4:12-13.

just as certainly without any reference to such theosophical speculations as were popular in the communities of the Lycus Valley.
Believers are members of a spiritual body whose head is Christ.
Union with him through faith is sufficient, because as author and
end of creation he is Lord of all imaginable angelic beings.

The letter to the Colossians was as definitely concerned with the
case of Onesimus as with the refutation of heresy.[20] The fullness
and concreteness with which the letter treats the relation of masters
and slaves reflect this concern. [21] The desire that it be "read to the
church at Laodicea also" [22] probably means not only that the two
churches had similar theological problems but also that Paul
desired their joint support for the request he was making regarding
Onesimus. He hoped to secure the reinforcement of a considerable
body of public sentiment for his insistence that Archippus "perform
the Christian service" assigned him.[23] If Archippus was the owner
of the runaway slave, the "service" Paul practically demanded
involved more than a kindly reception of Onesimus. It contemplated
both his forgiveness and his emancipation in order that he might
devote himself to Christian work as Paul's assistant.[24] As a means
of adding force to such a plan, Paul laid the matter before the
Colossian church in two letters and arranged also for the public
reading of both to the church at Laodicea.

Message.—Paul was eager that the recipients of this letter possess
a proper understanding of the office and person of Christ and,
equally, that they grasp its implications for Christian living. Colossians is as definitely religious and as concretely practical as any other
letter Paul wrote. The theological problems discussed derive their
interest from the bearing Paul felt they had on Christian character
and social relations.

Christ is described as "a likeness of the unseen God, born before
any creature," the agent through whom "everything was created
in heaven and on earth, the seen and the unseen, angelic thrones,
dominions, principalities, authorities." [25] By comparison with him
the "principalities and dominions" whom heretical teachers were

---

[20] Scott, *Literature of the New Testament,* p. 176.
[21] 3:22–4:1.   [22] 4:16.   [23] 4:17.
[24] Knox, *Philemon Among the Letters of Paul,* pp. 26-27.
[25] 1:15-16.

exalting fade into their proper insignificance.[26] Perfect access to God can be had through Christ alone.

This view of Christ supplied the basis for Paul's exhortation to the Colossians: "That the lives you live may be worthy of your Master and wholly pleasing to him, and you may be fruitful in all kinds of good deeds, and may grow into fuller knowledge of God." [27] Their status as "followers of the Lord Jesus" [28] should determine whatever they say or do. All distinctions of race and class and status must lose primary importance by comparison with the one thing of real significance, that Christ be "everything and in us all." [29]

Paul interprets God's judgment as requiring that men's lives be "wholly pleasing" to Christ.[30] Advancement in "spiritual wisdom and insight" must take the practical direction illustrated by Epaphras rather than the speculative and essentially idolatrous turn of his heretical rivals. A "fuller knowledge of God" for believers will be the outcome of lives "fruitful in all kinds of good deeds." Such living derives its inspiration and justification from a proper recognition of the true character of Christ. Pre-eminent by nature and office, superior to all other authorities, Christ alone is qualified to "reconcile to God all things on earth or in heaven"; and this he has done, "making this peace through his blood shed on the cross." [31]

Having thus represented Christ, Paul makes a spiritual repetition of the Incarnation the vocation of the believer. Especially the Christian teacher worthy of being followed must accredit himself as a believer in this vital sense.[32] Paul unhesitatingly applies this test to himself. He insists on his "divine appointment" as an apostle and on his having made up in his own person "what is lacking in Christ's sufferings for the church." Paul does not regard the knowledge of Christ as an aristocratic privilege, and so he urges the Colossians to "live in vital union" with Christ and be "rooted and built up in him and made strong in faith"—a relationship in which are inherent "all treasures of wisdom and knowledge."

The "pretensions of philosophy" are contrasted with following Christ and are characterized as "material ways of looking at things," which the Colossians will do well to avoid.[33] Because "all of the fullness of God's nature lives embodied" in Christ, believers become "filled" with that "fullness" through union with Christ, and

---

[26] 2:10.   [27] 1:10.   [28] 3:17.   [29] 3:11.
[30] 1:3-23.   [31] 1:15-23.   [32] 1:24–2:7.   [33] 2:8–3:4.

no function remains for those "principalities and dominions" of whom heretical teachers have made so much.

This "vital union" with Christ is conclusively evidenced by its profoundly significant ethical fruitage.[34] Sins of passion and greed cannot continue where this "vital union" exists because self-identification with Christ involves a stripping off of the "old self with its ways." [35] The characteristic virtues of the "new self newly made in the likeness of its Creator" are "tenderness of heart, kindness, humility, gentleness, forbearance." Giving unity to these qualities is "love, which completes them and fastens them all together." [36] The relationships of the Christian household reflect this love in concrete ways that must eventually type human society.[37] The treatment of the master-slave relation is disproportionately full because of Paul's immediate concern for Onesimus. He appears eager to exert the maximum moral suasion on Archippus, the probable owner of Onesimus. Persistent prayer sustains the vitality of union with Christ and gives the good life the spiritual nourishment it continually requires.[38]

[34] 3:5–4:6.   [35] 3:5-11.   [36] 3:12-17.   [37] 3:18–4:1.   [38] 4:2-6.

VIII

THE LETTER TO PHILEMON

Authorship.—The inclusion of Philemon in the original collection of Paul's letters is indicated by convincing evidence of its use by the author of Ephesians.[1] Ignatius' acquaintance with it is equally certain.[2] Thereafter no clear evidence of a knowledge of the letter appears until Marcion mentions it. In Marcion's canon it follows Philippians as the tenth of Paul's letters. It was clearly known to the author of the letters to Timothy and Titus, and a few years later was included among Paul's letters in the Muratorian canon, where it stands between Romans and Titus as the tenth letter. Tertullian and Origen, who was the first to write a commentary on it, both attributed Philemon to Paul.

The surprising thing about Philemon is not its comparatively limited use but its preservation. It could hardly have survived except as a member of the published collection of Paul's letters, and its inclusion in that collection is a strong testimonial to its authenticity. This is especially true if the author of Ephesians and publisher of the letters of Paul was Onesimus.

The intricacy of the relationship between Philemon and Colossians is a further and conclusive proof of genuineness. The ascription of Colossians to Paul requires that he be also regarded as the author of Philemon. The character of the contents of the letter is its final credential. Only the actual circumstances which the letter reflects can explain a document so homely, so historically revealing, so ethically instructive.

The First Readers.—The letter is addressed to "our dear fellow-worker Philemon, and our sister Apphia, and our fellow-soldier Archippus, and the church that meets in your house." Almost uniformly since the second century the assumption has been that the letter to Philemon was entirely private in character, a letter from one Christian to another about a personal matter. The inclusion of

[1] See my *Paul Becomes a Literary Influence*, pp. 7, 17, 23, 25.
[2] Knox, *Philemon Among the Letters of Paul*, pp. 37, 50-53.

others in the address, like the mention of "brother Timothy" as though he were co-author, was interpreted as wholly a matter of courtesy. That view has deprived later readers of a valuable clue to the proper understanding of both Philemon and Colossians and has considerably reduced the historical and religious import of the two letters.

The salutation lends itself to a much more illuminating explanation. The data it supplies, taken in connection with relevant information from Colossians, suggest that the letter was intended for the attention of the churches at Laodicea and Colossae and that Paul hoped the membership of those churches might induce Archippus to carry out "the Christian service" he had "assigned" him.[3]

Epaphras, who had come to Paul's place of imprisonment for counsel regarding theological problems, and whose arrival probably precipitated a crisis in the affairs of Onesimus, sustained a similarly responsible relationship to the churches at Laodicea, Colossae, and Hierapolis.[4] These churches formed a sort of triangle, Laodicea and Colossae being situated about eleven miles apart on the highway that ran eastward from Ephesus up the Lycus Valley, with Hierapolis six miles across the valley to the north of Colossae. Intercourse between these communities was easy, and the common concern Epaphras had in them probably reflected a very real community of interests among them. The principal characters in the letters to Philemon and to the Colossians were members of the church at Colossae, but the matters jointly treated in those letters were of interest to the churches as a group. This is shown in the directions that Colossians be "read to the church at Laodicea also" and that a letter coming from Laodicea be read at Colossae.[5]

Onesimus is described in Col. 4:9 as "one of your own number." He is further identified as a Colossian by the fact that Paul made him jointly responsible with Tychicus for the delivery of the Colossian letter.[6] The considerations that caused Paul to send Onesimus would require him to go directly to the place of his master's residence. Thus Onesimus and his master, whether Philemon or Archippus, were residents of Colossae.

Archippus, like Onesimus, is prominently mentioned in Colossians and Philemon. In Colossians there seems to be a connection between "the Christian service" Paul "assigned" Archippus and

---

[3] Col. 4:17.   [4] Col. 4:13.   [5] Col. 4:16.   [6] Col. 4:7-8.

the directions that two letters, one of them certainly Colossians, be publicly read at Colossae and at Laodicea.[7] Presumably one of the letters, clearly not Colossians, specified what that "service" was. In Philemon, Archippus is the third in the series of three persons who, with the Colossian church, are the addressees of the letter. The thoroughly natural conclusion is that the letter to Philemon is the second of the two intended for the attention of the churches at Colossae and Laodicea, that its chief concern is with "the Christian service" Paul expected of Archippus, and that it is the letter which was to come to Colossae from Laodicea.[8]

Philemon has ordinarily been regarded as the owner of Onesimus, as the person in whose home the Colossian church met, and as the principal recipient of the letter bearing his name. That, however, leaves unexplained the impressive allusions to Archippus in Col. 4:17 and Philem. 3, and it leaves the nature of the "service" expected of him a complete enigma. As Knox has shown,[9] all of the data ordinarily associated with Philemon apply equally well to Archippus. No grammatical problem is created if "your" in Philem. 3 is construed as referring to the house of Archippus, and only the accustomed understanding that the house of Philemon was intended creates any hesitancy in so interpreting the allusion. To assume that Archippus was the master of Onesimus, that the Colossian church met in his home, that Philemon was minister to that church and Apphia his wife, that our letter was the letter to be read first at Laodicea and then sent on to Colossae and was thus the letter "from" Laodicea[10] so illuminates the meaning of the letter to Philemon and its companion letter to the Colossians as well nigh to guarantee the correctness of the assumption.

Date.—The letter was written from prison.[11] That it was the same imprisonment which formed the background of Colossians is shown by the fact that Onesimus is sent home in the company of Tychicus, the bearer of the Colossian letter.[12] The same considerations, therefore, that operate to fix the calendar date of Colossians as 61 or 62 suggest an identical date for Philemon.

Place of Composition.—Caesarea, Ephesus, and Rome are the possible places for the composition of Philemon. Personal allusions in the letter suggest its setting was the same as for Colossians and

[7] 4:16-17.   [8] Knox, *op. cit.*, pp. 13-27.   [9] *Ibid.*
[10] Col. 4:17.   [11] Vss. 9, 13.   [12] Col. 4:9.

the second letter to the Philippians.[13] References to Paul's imprisonment further indicate an identical background for the three letters.
Onesimus, the bearer of the letter, was also joint bearer of the letter
to Colossae. From very early times these three letters have been
associated with Paul's Roman imprisonment. Rome was surely the
most secure refuge for a runaway slave. The same considerations that
relate Philippians and Colossians to Rome create a similar connection for Philemon. Rome is accordingly to be regarded as the
place where the letter was written.

   Occasion and Purpose.—Onesimus was a slave of Archippus, a
Colossian Christian in whose house the local church met. The fact
that Archippus was an active churchman did not mean, however,
that he was a kind and considerate master. He may have made no
connection between his acceptance of Christ and his treatment of
other people, least of all his treatment of slaves. Under Roman law
a slave was simply a piece of property and as such was entirely in
the power of his master. Quite understandably Archippus' conscience might not disturb him as long as he conformed to current
social practice in his treatment of his slaves. Centuries had to pass
before Christians generally grasped the challenge to slavery implicit
in the spirit and message of Jesus. Iniquities comparable to slavery
in their violation of the dignity and welfare of persons enjoy legal
sanction in the modern world and are taken for granted by many
people in the churches.

   Oppressive or abusive treatment possibly caused Onesimus to run
away and to feel justified in stealing from Archippus what he
needed to defray his expenses.[14] He had, at least, not been won to
his master's Christianity. The interests of the Colossian church, as
Epaphras interpreted them to Paul,[15] were speculative rather than
ethical; and Archippus conceivably typified that interest in being
more concerned with theology than with social duty.

   At Rome, Onesimus made the acquaintance of Paul, and his
conversion to Christianity resulted.[16] The new convert greatly
endeared himself to his benefactor.[17] He probably took responsibility for the duties which the Philippians had intended that
Epaphroditus assume.[18]

   Epaphras had probably known Onesimus and the circumstances

[13] Col. 1:1; 4:10ff.; Phil. 1:1.   [14] Vs. 18.   [15] Col. 1:7.
[16] Vs. 10.   [17] Vss. 10-13, 16-17; Col. 4:9.   [18] Phil. 2:25-30.

under which he left Colossae. His arrival at Rome required Onesimus to give Paul a complete statement about himself. Under the circumstances Paul was unwilling to keep Onesimus as his helper without the knowledge and consent of his master.[19] He also felt he should repay Archippus what the runaway had stolen. It would be wholesome for Onesimus also to acknowledge his moral obligation in the matter. Paul was not personally acquainted with Archippus, on whose will he was wholly dependent, and he could not be sure of the latter's reaction. Even if he were personally inclined to be kindly, he might feel under the necessity of supporting the contemporary slave economy by dealing severely with Onesimus.

Accordingly, when Tychicus was ready to go to Asia, Paul sent Onesimus with him and by them both sent two letters, Colossians and Philemon, each dealing with "the Christian service" expected of Archippus, and each to be publicly read at Laodicea and Colossae.[20] Our letter to Philemon was the letter mentioned in Col. 4:17 which would come "from" Laodicea to Colossae. Thus Colossians and Philemon were both concerned with the case of Onesimus, and both were directed to the attention of two churches and an influential individual, Archippus. The shorter letter specifies the precise nature of the "service" which is mentioned in Col. 4:17 and with which Colossians is itself so largely concerned.

The discussion of the relationships of the Christian household in Col. 3:18–4:1 really begins with 3:12. The master-slave relation occupies the center of attention in the catalogue of duties and seems to explain the section as a whole. In 3:12-17 the cardinal Christian virtues are listed as "tenderness of heart, kindness, humility, gentleness, forbearance"—the qualities Paul hoped for in Archippus. The final plea "Whatever you have to say or do, do it all as followers of the Lord Jesus," was the equivalent of an exhortation that Archippus act as a Christian rather than as a Roman in dealing with Onesimus.

The concern that Onesimus be kindly treated was the secondary and implied purpose of the letter to Philemon. Its major and expressly stated objective was to secure the freedom of Onesimus in order that he might return to Paul's place of imprisonment as his assistant.[21] To accomplish such an end, Paul appealed to Archippus on the basis both of Archippus' duty to serve the Christian cause

[19] Vs. 14.　　[20] Vs. 3; Col. 4:17.　　[21] Vs. 13; Knox, *op. cit.*, pp. 4-11.

and of the fact that Paul as Onesimus' spiritual father was actually the owner of the "new man in Christ" that Onesimus had become. In the interest of his request he also undertook to enlist the support of the churches of Colossae and Laodicea, thus, in effect, counteracting the pressure of the standards of Roman society with that of a Christian social pattern. This desire to enlist the Christian sentiment of two communities explains the directions that our two letters be publicly read in Laodicea and Colossae.

Message.—The letter was an appeal to the master of Onesimus that he be set free to return to Rome as Paul's helper. This was the "Christian service" that Paul "assigned" to Archippus, and the letter to Philemon was the assignment. Paul made it clear that the appeal might legitimately have been a demand, both in view of his own relationship to Onesimus and in view of the relationship that he himself and Archippus sustained to the Christian cause. His preference was that Archippus voluntarily relinquish his lower claims on Onesimus in the interest of the higher claim that Paul could assert as "an envoy of Christ Jesus" and the spiritual "father" of Onesimus. Onesimus' freedom to devote himself to Christian work is what Paul hoped to "make" out of Archippus "in a Christian sense!" [22]

[22] Vs. 20.

IX

THE ORIGIN OF THE GOSPELS

ACCORDING to tradition that reaches back into the closing decades of the second century, the earliest of the Gospels was written after the deaths of Peter and Paul.[1] This means that large numbers of Christians lived out their lives without having seen a Gospel or heard one publicly read.

Oral proclamation was the original method by which the Christian message was disseminated, and memory preserved the only record of the words and deeds of Jesus. The needs of the churches in such practical matters as evangelism, worship, the creation and maintenance of moral standards, and defense against hostile criticism supplied the bases on which the original gospel materials were preserved and utilized. These same needs determined the forms of statement with which the narratives of Jesus' life and the accounts of his teaching were invested before Christian teachers began to create the first written records.

Paul is an early witness to the currency of an oral tradition of Jesus' life and message,[2] and at the time he wrote this tradition appears to have been rather thoroughly conventionalized. Similarly, the author of Luke-Acts indicates in his preface [3] that the testimony of "eye-witnesses" supplied early preachers with the basic content of their messages. Their preaching in large measure consisted in stories about Jesus and reports of his teaching.[4]

The transition from oral tradition to written gospels did not take place abruptly. There were many in-between steps. The preface to Luke-Acts clearly states that oral and written accounts were utilized in the compilation of this two-volume work. There is equally good warrant for assuming that Mark, Matthew, and John were also indebted to oral and documentary sources. All four of the canonical

[1] Iren. *Her.* III. 1. 1; cf. Euseb. *Hist.* V. 8. 3.
[2] I Cor. 11:23; 15:3-7; cf. Acts 10:36-42; 20:35.   [3] Luke 1:4.
[4] See the excellent discussion of Frederick C. Grant, *The Earliest Gospel,* pp. 15-33.

93

Gospels were built about earlier documents and involved the use of materials the effectiveness of which in both oral and written forms had been proved in such principal Christian centers as Antioch, Caesarea, Rome, and Ephesus. The newness of these Gospels consisted in their comprehensiveness rather than in the materials they incorporated or in the presentation of those materials in writing.

The Gospels yield their meaning most reliably when there is an understanding of the processes of development of which they were the culmination. For such an understanding one may begin with the factors involved in the process and trace them in their operation until they eventuate in the finished Gospels, or one may work backward through the several intermediate stages to a discovery of the original factors and the vital character of the development. The latter is the preferable procedure.

The data of the Gospels themselves afford sufficient guidance for the isolation of the written sources immediately underlying them and for a clear perception of how the evangelists used these sources. There is the further and more difficult task of forming a historically probable conception of the tradition lying back of the written sources.

The Fourth Gospel was in a sense the culmination of the gospel-making process. As the latest of the canonical Gospels it is the natural starting point for an examination of the process. To regard it, however, as typical and as related to the earlier three Gospels in a succession the character of which is exhibited in Mark, Matthew, and Luke is misleading. The Fourth Gospel does not simply illustrate such a succession in a more advanced form. So to represent it suggests that all of the Gospels were historical in appearance only, their actual character being in the nature of ideal creations whereby the church gave authority to its own positions by attributing them to Jesus.

The men who wrote the Gospels were missionary preachers and not scientific biographers. Their books were forms of preaching rather than history for its own sake. Each of the four Gospels was in a thoroughly real sense an expression of the religious insights and convictions of its author as he addressed himself to the needs of the Christian community in the locality where he worked. Each evangelist might have given what he wrote the title "What Christianity Means to Me." [5] Mark, Matthew, and Luke were no different from the Fourth Gospel in this respect. All four were gospels.

The three earlier Gospels resemble one another and differ from the Fourth Gospel, however, in that they were compilations of materials from older documents, which in their own turn were crystallizations of oral tradition that achieved a considerable degree of fixity during the two decades immediately following the Crucifixion. The author of the Fourth Gospel, by contrast, made use of sources without reproducing them. What he wrote represented meditation on materials gleaned from other gospels and from oral tradition and involved practically no report of the materials themselves. Events were significant for him chiefly as disclosures of divine light and power. The inner meaning of history was his primary concern. This distinction is illustrated by the fact that if we compare the contents of the four Gospels, only 8 per cent of the materials of the Fourth Gospel are found to be coincident with materials in one or more of the other three, whereas the coincidence of contents for the other Gospels amounts to 93 per cent for Mark, 58 per cent for Matthew, and 41 per cent for Luke.[6]

The extreme individuality of the Fourth Gospel is apparent both in its representation of Jesus' teaching and in the account it gives of his life and ministry. Jesus' own person rather than the Kingdom of God becomes the principal theme of the teaching. The apocalypticism of the older tradition almost entirely disappears, and where its terminology is retained new meanings are usually implied. The universal availability of Christ in the Comforter takes the place of the Parousia, and the Judgment, which turns upon present belief or disbelief in Christ, is a present and continuous mystical process rather than a future and catastrophic event. This transformation of the apocalyptic framework of an earlier period into the thought forms of Hellenistic mysticism is evident throughout the Gospel. It is especially impressive in the elaborate supper discourses,[7] which are the Johannine equivalent for the eschatological discourses that precede the supper in the earlier Gospels.[8] Differences in theme and world view are accompanied by differences in teaching forms. Allegory supplants the parable and the beatitude, and the

---

[5] Cf. Rom. 2:16; I Cor. 15:1-2; Gal. 1:6, 9.

[6] Bacon, *Introduction*, p. 176.   [7] John 13-17.

[8] Mark 13=Matt. 24-25=Luke 21.

discourses are those of the philosopher rather than the prophet and wise man.

In the account of Jesus' life and ministry there is a complete omission from the Fourth Gospel of such familiar items as the genealogies and birth stories, the baptism, the temptation, the transfiguration, the agony in Gethsemane. There are miracles, but they are presented as "signs" instead of as deeds of mercy, and only one miracle is described that has a parallel in the other Gospels.[9] The miracle of the raising of Lazarus, which is peculiar to the Fourth Gospel, is made the basis on which the Jews determined to put Jesus to death. The representation elsewhere is that the cleansing of the temple precipitated this decision. The exorcism of demons, which is the character of most of the miracles of healing in the older Gospels, is entirely absent from the Fourth Gospel.

The scene of Jesus' ministry and the social circumstances of his life are considerably different in the Johannine picture. Judea is the location of Jesus' principal activity, and there are brief interludes of retirement to Galilee, whereas in the older Gospels Jesus is principally active in Galilee and the vicinity until the beginning of Passion Week. Not only so, but the groups within Jewish society— the scribes, the Pharisees, the Sadducees—tend to disappear, and the Jews as such become Jesus' opponents. Sixty times in the Gospel the Jews are thus indiscriminately mentioned.

The events of Jesus' ministry extend over two and a half or three and a half years in this Gospel,[10] whereas they fall within the limits of a single year in the older accounts. The inherent probabilities favor the longer period, but the reliability of the Johannine chronology cannot be otherwise urged. In fact the sequence of events within the ministry is so exploited in the interest of teaching emphases as to suggest the characterization of the narrative in its entirety as "one whole anachronism." [11] From chapter 18 onward the story approximates that of Mark, but prior to that point such transpositions as the following occur:

1. Jesus is publicly proclaimed by John the Baptist as Savior of the world and is so recognized from the outset by the disciples, in contrast

[9] Mark 6:30-46=Matt. 14:13-23a=Luke 9:10-17=John 6:1-13.
[10] Three Passovers are specifically mentioned in 2:13; 6:4; 11:55. If the Greek definite article was intended in 5:1, a fourth Passover is involved.
[11] Riddle, *The Gospels*, p. 232.

with the representation in the older Gospels that his identity dawned upon his associates gradually and that only as late as the confession at Caesarea Philippi did the inner circle of disciples perceive that he was Messiah.

2. The incident of the cleansing of the temple occurs at the outset of Jesus' ministry instead of during Passion Week.

3. The institution of the Eucharist is moved backward from the supper occasion during Passion Week and is identified with the incident of the miraculous feeding.[12]

4. The church is treated as having been already established and as possessing the Paraclete as its teacher.[13]

5. Instead of Jesus' eating the Passover with his disciples, as in the older Gospels, the Passover is still future when Jesus is arraigned before Pilate,[14] and the Crucifixion occurs on the day when the Passover victim was killed.[15]

Such handling of chronology had the didactic purpose of lifting Christian truth out of the localism of circumstance and creating for it the setting of the universal and the ultimate.[16] It is typical of this evangelist's whole approach to history and sheds light upon the relationship of the Fourth Gospel to older written sources. He stood at the confluence of the streams of historical Christian tradition, as embodied in the earlier Gospels, and of Hellenistic piety with its tendencies to Docetism and Gnosticism.[17] He was critical of the older accounts as being too Jewish and too external, but he found the speculative extravagances to which Hellenistic piety tended equally distasteful. Instead, therefore, of reproducing the materials of his sources, as Mark, Matthew, and Luke had done, he transmuted them and intentionally created out of them a new and independent exposition of the significance of Christ for faith.

The literary independence of the Fourth Gospel, however, is more apparent than real. In language, religious point of view, and thought content there is an evident indebtedness to Paul's collected letters.[18] For the gospel form and for such historical substratum as is present in the book there is an equally clear indebtedness to the earlier written Gospels.

---

[12] 6:49-58.   [13] Chaps. 14–17.   [14] 18:28.
[15] Cf. I Cor. 5:7-8; John 1:30, 36.   [16] Riddle, *loc. cit.*
[17] Grant, *Growth of the Gospels*, p. 17.
[18] See my *Paul Becomes a Literary Influence*, pp. 104-42.

The literary dependence of the Fourth Gospel on Mark is easily established. Because materials drawn from sources are transmuted rather than copied, the occasional reproduction of distinctly Marcan phraseology has convincing evidential value.[19] It is equally significant that where parallels between the Gospels occur, the adherence of the Fourth Gospel to Mark is regularly the closest.[20] Except in the single instance of John 13:16, which resembles Matt. 10:24 and Luke 6:40, sayings attributed to Jesus that have verbal parallels are all found in Mark. Such data, supplemented by others that are less impressive but have cumulative weight, leave little doubt that the author of the Fourth Gospel was thoroughly acquainted with Mark.

The indications that the author of the Fourth Gospel knew and used Luke, though somewhat less convincing than in the case of Mark, are sufficient to create a high degree of probability of such knowledge. They consist in the references to Mary and Martha that occur in these two Gospels only and in similarly significant points of contact in their accounts of the Passion.

Mary and Martha are known to readers of the New Testament exclusively from the stories of Luke 10:38-42 and John 11:1–12:3. Their introduction as entirely familiar characters in John 11:1 suggests that the evangelist and his readers knew them from Luke's story. Acquaintance with Luke as well as with Mark is further indicated by the identification of the "certain village" of Luke 10:38 as Bethany and of the woman who anointed Jesus in Mark 14:3-9 as Mary. That Luke's story was in mind is made practically certain by the statement, "And Martha waited on them." [21] The introduction of details from Luke's story of the anointing of Jesus leaves

[19] Streeter lists five instances of the reproduction of unusual Marcan phraseology that require the predication of literary relationship, as follows: John 6:7=Mark 6:37; John 12:3, 5=Mark 14:35, where the use of πιστική is unique in Greek literature; John 18:18=Mark 14:54; John 18:39=Mark 15:9; John 5:8-9 and Mark 2:11-12, where the use of τὸν κράβαττόν σου in the different stories is best accounted for as a recollection of Marcan vocabulary. The correspondence involved in these passages becomes doubly significant when it is noted that in Matthew and Luke the wording has been changed. (*The Four Gospels*, p. 397.)

[20] Typical instances are: John 1:19-34=Mark 1:7-10; John 2:13-22=Mark 11:15-19; John 6:1-15=Mark 6:31-34; John 13:21=Mark 14:18; John 13:38=Mark 14:30; John 18:33, 37=Mark 15:2. For a more complete list of instances see *ibid.*, pp. 398-99, note 2.

[21] John 12:2; cf. Luke 10:40-41.

little room for doubt that the story of John 12:2-8 is a conflation of the stories of Luke 7:36-39 and Mark 14:3-9.[22]

In his account of the Passion the author of the Fourth Gospel agrees with Luke that Jesus' first resurrection appearance to the disciples as a group took place at Jerusalem instead of in Galilee.[23] With Luke and against Mark he lists two disciples by the name of Judas.[24] He makes use of such peculiarly Lukan details as that Judas' offer to betray Jesus was due to the devil's suggestion,[25] that it was the *right* ear of the high priest's servant that was cut off,[26] that Pilate three times declared, "I can find nothing to charge him with," [27] that the tomb in which Jesus was buried was one "in which no one had yet been laid," [28] that two angels rather than one appeared to the women at the tomb.[29] These data carry the strong suggestion of literary indebtedness.

Definite traces of Matthaean influence are almost totally lacking in the Fourth Gospel. They are limited to a few coincidences of wording and detail for which literary acquaintance is not required.[30] Papias was acquainted with Matthew but apparently thought less well of it than he did of Mark.[31] The nonuse of Matthew by the author of the Fourth Gospel possibly signifies distaste rather than lack of acquaintance. This distaste may have been due to the Jewishness of some of the source materials incorporated in Matthew, which he mistook for the point of view of the author. Such distaste was probably increased by the exaggerated apocalypticism of Matthew. In view of the inherent probabilities of this evangelist's acquaintance with Matthew his silence may have positive rather than negative significance.

That the author of the Fourth Gospel knew our three earlier Gospels in substantially their present form and used them in his own distinctive way is a matter of reasonable certainty. That they

[22] John 12:3 agrees with Luke 7:38 that the woman anointed Jesus' feet and wiped them with her hair. Mark 14:3 says that she "poured the perfume on his head."

[23] John 20:19 ff.; Luke 24:33-39; cf. Mark 16:7, 15-18; Matt. 28:7, 9, 16-20.

[24] John 14:22; Luke 6:16; cf. Mark 3:16-19.

[25] John 13:2; cf. Luke 22:3.   [26] John 18:10; cf. Luke 22:50.

[27] John 18:38; 19:4, 6; cf. Luke 23:4, 14, 22.

[28] John 19:41; cf. Luke 23:53.

[29] John 20:12; Luke 24:4; cf. Mark 16:5; Matt. 28:5.

[30] Streeter, *op. cit.*, pp. 408-15.   [31] Euseb. *Hist*. III. 39. 15-16.

were his chief sources of information and among the most powerful
of the influences that affected him are equally reasonable cer-
tainties.[32] This is evident in such occasional verbal parallels as
have been mentioned and in such specific episodes as this Gospel
has in common with its predecessors as the Baptist's ministry, the
cleansing of the temple, the miraculous cure of the nobleman's son,
the feeding of the multitude, walking on the water, the entry into
Jerusalem, and the chief events of Passion Week. It is more subtly
evident in numerous instances where story and exposition that are
wholly this evangelist's composition owed their origin to the sug-
gestiveness of materials in the older Gospels. Such materials are
always adapted to the Johannine point of view and purpose, but
when closely examined turn out to be from the cycles of tradition
of which the other Gospels are composed rather than elements
drawn from an independent tradition. Thus Nicodemus not improbably "has his counterpart in the rich young ruler who inquired
of Jesus concerning eternal life," and the symbolical story of the
transformation of water into wine at Cana may have owed its
inception to the meaning this evangelist saw in the two sayings of
Mark 2:19, 22.[33]

Luke-Acts, Matthew, and Mark resemble the Fourth Gospel in
being built about older Greek documents of which their authors
were critical and which they were designed to supplant. They are
different in that they reproduce materials selected from their documentary sources, exercising freedom in the creation of new settings
and distinctive arrangements for these materials. Because the other
Gospels provide bases of comparison for the gospel half of Luke-
Acts, that half of the work is studied separately. This must not be
allowed to obscure the character of the two volumes as a single
work nor the relationship of the work in its entirety to the gospel-
making process.

The three earlier Gospels present a complex series of agreements
and differences, presenting episodes and teachings of which the
wording is approximately identical, and individually setting out
materials found nowhere else. They are too much alike to be
wholly independent, and they are too different for their data to

---

[32] Scott, *The Fourth Gospel*, pp. 32-45; Bacon, *The Gospel of the Hellenists*,
p. 114.

[33] Scott, *op. cit.*, p. 37.

be explained in many instances in terms of interdependence. The language in which they were originally written is Greek, and their agreements in vocabulary and phraseology suggest their common dependence on documentary sources also written in Greek. The isolation of these sources and a clear grasp of how the evangelists used them are essential to an understanding of the process out of which the Gospels originated. This is facilitated by a display of the relevant materials in proper groupings.

There is a body of material, mostly narrative but with a small amount of teaching, that is common to Mark, Matthew, and Luke. A comparative study of the three shows that this core which they have in common furnishes the basic character of a representation of Jesus from which no single one of the three radically departs. This basic representation is characteristically Marcan and would exist in its main outlines if Mark were the only Gospel extant. This is illustrated by the closeness with which Matthew and Luke adhere to the order of the Marcan narrative. There is no instance of an agreement of Matthew and Luke against Mark in the order of incidents. They vary from Mark singly but never jointly. Where one differs from the Marcan sequence, the other supports it. Within the area of Mark's account, Matthew and Luke support Mark generally in the sequence of sections, in subject matter, and in actual wording. Before Mark's story begins, however, and after it closes,[34] divergence rather than agreement becomes the rule. Not only so, but approximately eleven twelfths of the contents of Mark are incorporated in Matthew, and in excess of half in Luke, the Marcan element constituting respectively a half and a third of the two longer Gospels.[35]

Only seven of the Marcan stories are absent from Matthew. They are:

[34] Mark 16:8.

[35] Only about 7 per cent of the content of Mark is peculiar to that Gospel. The only complete episodes that are found in Mark alone are the healing of the man who was deaf and had an impediment of speech (7:32-36), the blind man of Bethsaida (8:22-26), and the young man who fled naked from Gethsemane (14:51-52). Briefer narrative touches that are found in Mark alone are: 1:1; 2:2, 13, 15b, 18a; 3:9, 14b-15, 17b, 19b-21; 6:52, 56; 7:2-4, 24b; 9:14b-16, 22b-24, 33; 10:32b; 11:11; 12:32-34. The parable of the fruit-bearing earth (4:26-29) is the only teaching material other than scattered statements of a verse or two in length that is exclusively Marcan. These brief sayings are: 2:27; 9:29, 39b, 48-49, 50b; 10:24; 13:33, 36-37.

1:23-28=Luke 4:33-37—the demoniac of Capernaum

3:20-21—the effort of Jesus' relatives to restrain him on the ground that he was "out of his mind"

7:32-36—the man who was deaf and had an impediment of speech

8:22-26—the blind man of Bethsaida

9:38-41=Luke 9:49-50—the rival exorcists

12:41-44=Luke 21:1-4—the widow's gift of "two little copper coins which make a cent"

14:51-52—the young man who fled naked from Gethsemane

The grand total of these omissions is only twenty-eight verses. The smallness of this amount is further reduced by the probability that only the second and the last two of the stories listed were actual omissions. The story of the demoniac of Gadara in Matt. 8:28-34 appears to be a conflation of the two stories of Mark 1:23-28 and 5:1-20.[36] Again, although the story of Mark 7:32-36 is not retold, Matt. 9:32-33 gives a story of the cure of dumbness, and in Matt. 15:29-31 Jesus is described as having healed "those who were lame, crippled, blind, or dumb, and many others." The story of the cure of blindness in Matt. 12:22 conceivably justified the omission of the more definite story of Mark 8:22-26. Finally, the story in Mark 9:38-41 may be a later addition to Mark from Luke 9:49-50. The sense of the Marcan context is improved by its complete omission, verse 42 making a natural sequence for verse 37.

A very much larger proportion of Marcan narrative material is without any equivalent in Luke. Luke's difference from Matthew in this matter is emphasized by noting the frequency of Matthaean parallels for Marcan sections that do not appear in Luke. There are instances also in which Luke has apparently discarded the Marcan version of a story and utilized a preferred version. In the following table the Lukan passages where these alternative versions appear are cited for comparison. The most impressive instance of nonuse of Marcan narrative materials by Luke is Mark 6:45–8:26—seventy-four consecutive verses, all but eleven verses of which are incorporated in Matthew. The Marcan stories not used by Luke are:

1:5-6=Matt. 3:5-6—description of John's audiences and of his appearance

1:16-20=Matt. 4:18-22 (cf. Luke 5:1-11) —call of the four disciples

[36] The cry of the demoniac in Matt. 8:29 is a combination of Mark 1:24 and 5:7.

3:22-27=Matt. 12:24-32 (cf. Luke 11:14-23)—Beelzebub controversy

4:33-34=Matt. 13:34—Jesus' use of parables

6:1-6=Matt. 13:54-58 (cf. Luke 4:16-24)—rejection at Nazareth

6:17-29=Matt. 14:4-12—John and Herod

6:45-46=Matt. 14:22-23a—trip across the lake to Bethsaida

6:47-52=Matt. 14:23b-33—Jesus walks on the water

6:53-56=Matt. 14:34-36—they cross the sea to Gennesaret

7:2-4—the purification customs of the Jews described

7:5-23=Matt. 15:2-20—eating with unwashed hands

7:24-30=Matt. 15:21-28—the Syrophoenician woman

7:31-36—the man who was deaf and had an impediment in speech

8:1-10=Matt. 15:32-39—feeding of the four thousand

8:11-21=Matt. 16:1-10—the Pharisees demand a sign

8:22-26—the blind man of Bethsaida

9:10-13=Matt. 17:10-12—discussion about Elijah

9:28=Matt. 17:19—disciples inquire about their inability to exorcise

10:2-10=Matt. 19:3-12—the Pharisees ask about divorce

10:35-41=Matt. 20:20-28—ambition of James and John

11:12-14, 20-21=Matt. 21:18-22—cursing of the fig tree

14:3-9=Matt. 26:6-13 (cf. Luke 7:36-50)—anointing of Jesus

In the area of the hundred verses composing the core of Mark's passion story [37] Luke interweaves Mark and an independent narrative, which makes it difficult to tabulate his nonuse of Mark's stories with complete accuracy. Approximately 60 per cent of the Marcan narrative, however, is clearly not used by Luke, as follows:

14:26-28=Matt. 26:30-32—retirement to Mount of Olives; promise to meet the disciples in Galilee

14:31=Matt. 26:35—Peter's confidence that he will be loyal

14:33-34=Matt. 26:37-38—the inner circle of disciples in Gethsemane

14:37b=Matt. 26:40b—Peter reprimanded for being asleep

14:38b-42=Matt. 26: 41b-46—twice again the disciples are found asleep

14:43b-44=Matt. 26:47b-48—the kiss as a sign of betrayal

14:46=Matt. 26:50b—the seizure of Jesus

14:49b-50=Matt. 26:56—the arrest a fulfillment of prophecy

14:51-52—flight of a youth from Gethsemane

14:55-61=Matt. 26:59-63—Jesus questioned; false testimony given

15:1=Matt. 27:1—conference of chief priests, elders, and scribes

15:3-5=Matt. 27:12-14—Jesus' silence when arraigned before Pilate

15:6-11a=Matt. 27:15-20a—Pilate's offer to release Barabbas

[37] Mark 14:17–16:8.

15:12b=Matt. 27:22—Pilate's question

15:16-20=Matt. 27:27-31—mockery of Jesus by the soldiers

15:23=Matt. 27:34—Jesus' refusal of drugged wine

15:25—Jesus was crucified at nine o'clock in the morning

15:27b-29=Matt. 27:38b-40—Jesus crucified between two robbers

15:34-36=Matt. 27:46-49—the cry from the cross; the Aramaic translated

15:40-41=Matt. 27:56—Galilean friends who watched at the cross

15:44-45—Pilate amazed at the quickness of Jesus' death; grants the body to Joseph of Arimathea

16:1=Matt. 28:1—names of the women who prepared to anoint Jesus' body

16:3—the question of who would roll the stone from the entrance of the tomb

16:5b—the young man in a white robe sitting in the tomb

16:7-8=Matt. 28:7-8—Jesus promises to meet the disciples in Galilee

Matthew and Luke each tells stories not found elsewhere. These are quite numerous in Luke, but in Matthew they are almost as few as the omissions of Marcan stories. The stories peculiar to Matthew are:

1:1–2:23—infancy narratives

9:27-31 (cf. 20:29-34) —two blind men healed

9:32-34 (cf. 12:22-45) —a dumb man cured

14:28-31—Peter's attempt to walk on the water

17:24-27—the temple tax

21:10-11—Jesus' appearance stirs Jerusalem

21:14-16—Jesus acclaimed in the temple

26:52-54—rebuke of the sword wielder

27:3-10—Judas' repentance

27:19—Pilate's wife sends word of her dream

27:24-25—Pilate disavows responsibility for the condemnation of Jesus

27:43—they taunt Jesus

27:52-53—the resurrection of the saints

27:62-66—the high priests and Pharisees ask Pilate to post a guard

28:2-4—the women find the stone rolled from the tomb and an angel seated upon it.

28:9b-10a—Jesus sends the disciples word that he will meet them in Galilee

28:11-15—the soldiers are bribed not to tell what happened

28:16-20—Jesus meets the disciples in Galilee and commissions them [38]

[38] Additional brief narrative touches in Matthew are: 3:14-15; 4:23b; 5:1-2; 14:33; 15:30-31; 16:22b; 17:6-7.

The stories peculiar to Luke are:

1:1–2:52—infancy stories
3:1-2—Christian events synchronized with the Roman calendar
3:10-15—various groups question John as to their proper conduct
3:23-38 (cf. Matt. 1:1-17) —genealogy of Jesus
4:28-30—the attempt to throw Jesus over a cliff
5:1-10—the miraculous catch of fish
7:3-6a—delegation of Jewish elders bring Jesus a Roman captain's request
7:11-17—the widow of Nain
7:20-21—Jesus demonstrates his messiahship to the messengers of John
7:29-30—the Pharisees refuse baptism by John
7:36-39, 43-50 (cf. Mark 14:3-9) —anointing of Jesus
9:51-56—inhospitable reception in a Samaritan village
10:1, 17-20—dispatch and return of the seventy
10:38-42—Mary and Martha
13:10-17—the woman who was bent double
13:31-33—the Pharisees warn Jesus against Herod
14:1-6—Jesus cures a man afflicted with dropsy
17:11-19—ten lepers cured, of whom only a Samaritan was grateful
19:1-10—Zacchaeus
23:4-16—Pilate and Herod
23:27-32—the crowds along the way to the cross
23:39-43—the penitent thief
24:13-35—the walk to Emmaus
24:36-43—Jesus appears to the disciples in Jerusalem
24:44-53—appearance and ascension in the vicinity of Bethany [39]

Certain narrative sections and a limited amount of discourse material in Mark appear in Matthew and Luke, usually in an expanded form, with details and emphases suggesting a different and independent version. These passages constitute a total of only thirty-six verses in Mark. They are:

1:7-8 (cf. Luke 3:7-9, 16-17; Matt. 3:7-10, 11-12) —John's message
1:12-13 (cf. Luke 4:1-13; Matt. 4:1-11) —temptation of Jesus
3:22-27 (cf. Luke 11:14-23; Matt. 12:22-27) —Beelzebub controversy
3:28-29 (cf. Luke 12:10; Matt. 12:32) —blasphemy against the Spirit
4:21 (cf. Luke 11:33; Matt. 5:15) —figure of the lighted lamp

[39] Additional brief narrative touches in Luke are: 4:23; 8:1-3; 9:32-33a, 43; 11:1, 27-28, 37-38, 45-46a; 12:41; 13:1; 15:1-2; 16:14-15; 17:20; 18:34; 21:38; 22:15-16, 31-32, 48-49, 51, 53b, 61a, 68; 23:2, 36a, 48, 51, 53b, 56b; 24:4, 6-7, 10-11.

4:22 (cf. 8:38; Luke 12:2-9; Matt. 10:26-33) —revelation of the hidden

4:30-32 (cf. Luke 13:18-19; Matt. 13:31-32) —parable of the mustard seed

6:6-11 (cf. Luke 10:3-12; Matt. 10:16, 9, 10a, 11-13, 10b, 7-8, 14-15) —instructions to missionaries

8:12 (cf. Luke 11:29-32; Matt. 12:38-42) —sign of Jonah

8:34 (cf. Luke 14:26-27; Matt. 10:37-38) —counting the cost

9:42 (cf. Luke 17:1-2; Matt. 18:6-7) —respect for humble believers

9:50 (cf. Luke 14:34-35; Matt. 5:13) —savorless salt

10:11-12 (cf. Luke 16:18; Matt. 5:32) —divorce and adultery

11:22-23 (cf. Luke 17:6; Matt. 17:20) —faith

12:38-40 (cf. Luke 11:39-44, 46-48; Matt. 23:25-26, 23, 6-7a, 27, 4, 29-31) — inside and outside of cup and platter.

13:21 (cf. Luke 17:23-24; Matt. 21:26-27) —lightning flash as an analogy for the Day of the Son of Man

13:34 (cf. Luke 19:11-27, parable of the pounds; Matt. 25:14-30, talents) — entrusted wealth

There is a body of non-Marcan material, mostly discourse but with a minimum of narrative, present in Matthew and Luke.[40] The narrative episodes are:

LUKE   MATT.

3:7-9, 16-17=3:7-10, 11-12 (cf. Mark 1:7-8) —John the Baptist

4:1-13=4:1-11 (cf. Mark 1:12-13) —temptation of Jesus

7:1-10=8:5-10, 13—centurion's servant

7:18-20, 22-28, 31-35=11:2-11, 16-19—message from John

10:13-15=11:21-24—denunciation of Chorazin, Bethsaida, and Capernaum

11:14-23=12:22-27 (cf. Mark 3:22-27) —Beelzebub controversy

The remainder of this non-Marcan material has the character of discourse:

LUKE   MATT.

6:37-38, 41-42=7:1-2, 3-5—judging

6:43-45=7:16-18, 20; 12:33-35—a tree is known by its fruit

6:47-49=7:24-27—two builders

9:57-60=8:19-22—Jesus' demand for supreme loyalty

10:2=9:37-38—an abundant harvest but few reapers

10:3-12=10:16, 9, 10a, 11-13, 10b, 7-8, 14-15—instructions to missionaries

[40] The maximum of verbal identity among the passages cited is found in the following: Luke 3:7-9 and Matt. 3:7-10, 12 (cf. Mark 1:7-8) ; Luke 4:2-13 and Matt. 4:2-11 (cf. Mark 1:12-13) ; Luke 12:22-31 and Matt. 6:25-33; Luke 7:18-28, 31-35 and Matt. 11:2-11, 16-19.

LUKE   MATT.

10:23-24=13:16-17—rare privilege of the disciples
11:9-13=7:7-11—asking, searching, knocking
11:24-26=12:43-45—danger of spiritual emptiness
11:29-32=12:38-42—sign of Jonah
11:33=5:15—a lighted lamp belongs on its stand
11:34-35=6:22-23—a sound eye
11:42-43, 46-48=23:23, 6-7a, 4, 29-31—denunciation of the Pharisees
11:49-51=23:34-36, 13—the guilt of Jesus' contemporaries
12:2-9=10:26-33—faith and fearlessness
12:10=12:32—to revile the holy Spirit is unpardonable
12:22-32=6:25-33—the banishment of anxiety
12:33-34=6:19-21—heavenly treasure
12:39-46=24:43-51—unexpectedness of the coming of the Son of Man
12:51-53=10:34-36—Jesus brings discord, not peace
12:54-56=16:2-3—interpretation of signs
13:18-19=13:31-32 (cf. Mark 4:31-32)—parable of the mustard seed
13:20-21=13:33—yeast
13:26-27=7:22-23—acquaintances who are strangers
13:28-29=8:11-12—universalism of the Kingdom
13:34-35=23:37-39—lament over Jerusalem
14:11=23:12—humility the way to exaltation
14:26-27=10:37-38—loyalty to Christ comes first
14:34-35=5:13—salt that loses its strength is thrown away
16:13=6:24—no servant can belong to two masters
16:16=11:12-13—the Kingdom supersedes the Law and the Prophets
16:17=5:18—every "dotting of an i" in the Law to be fulfilled
16:18=5:32—divorce and adultery
17:1-2=18:6-7—hindrances to humble people
17:6=17:20—vital efficacy of faith
17:23-24=24:26-27—lightning as a symbol of the coming of the Son of Man
17:26-27=24:37-39—danger of engrossment in worldly interests
17:34-35=24:40-41—the days of the Son of Man
17:37=24:28—a dead body attracts the vultures

There are between fifty and sixty verses of discourse common to Matthew and Luke and without Marcan parallels where resemblances are sufficient to establish kinship of some sort, but in which differences are almost equally noteworthy. They are:

LUKE   MATT.

6:20-23; cf. 5:3-6, 11-12—Beatitudes
6:27-33, 35-36; cf. 5:44, 39-40, 42; 7:12; 5:46-47, 45, 48—love for enemies

LUKE　　　MATT.

6:39-40; cf. 15:14b; 10:24, 25a—disciple and teacher

6:46; cf. 7:21—ascription of lordship implies readiness to obey

11:2-4; cf. 6:9-13—model prayer for disciples

11:39-41, 44; cf. 23:25-26, 27—false emphasis on externals

12:58-59; cf. 5:25-26—reconciliation with adversaries should be prompt

13:23-24; cf. 7:13-14—entrance by the narrow door

14:15-24; cf. 22:1-10—parables of the great supper and the marriage feast

15:4-7; cf. 18:12-14—parable of the lost sheep

17:3-4; cf. 18:15, 21-22—forgiveness of an offending brother

19:11-27; cf. 25:14-30—parables of the pounds and the talents

22:30b; cf. 19:28b—the disciples will sit on thrones and judge Israel

In addition to these discourse materials common to Luke and Matthew, each has a considerable body of teaching matter peculiar to itself, amounting respectively to one fifth and one fourth of the length of the Gospel. These materials largely consist of parables, but each Gospel contains a body of peculiar teaching matter of other descriptions, this latter type occupying larger space in Matthew than in Luke.[41] The parables peculiar to Matthew are:

> 13:24-30, 36-43—the tares and the explanation
>
> 13:44—hidden treasure
>
> 13:45-46—the pearl of great price
>
> 13:47-50—the drag net
>
> 13:51-53—the scribe who has become a disciple
> of the Kingdom of Heaven
>
> 18:23-35—the unmerciful servant
>
> 20:1-16—the laborers and the hours
>
> 21:28-32—the two sons
>
> 22:1-14—the marriage feast of the king's son
>
> 25:1-13—the wise and foolish bridesmaids
>
> 25:14-30—the talents
>
> 25:31-46—the judgment of the Son of Man

[41] Nonparabolic teaching peculiar to Matthew: 4:13-16; 5:5, 7-10, 13a-16, 17-38, 41, 43; 6:1-7, 16-18, 34; 7:6, 15, 19; 8:17; 10:5-8, 16b, 23, 25b, 36, 41; 11:14, 20, 23b, 28-30; 12:5-7, 11-12a, 17-21, 36-37, 40; 13:14-15, 35; 15:12-13, 23-25; 16:2b-3, 11-12, 17-19, 17:3; 18:4, 10, 14, 16-20; 19:9a, 10-12, 28; 21:4-5; 23:1-3, 5, 7-10, 15-22, 24, 28, 32; 24:10-12, 14, 30. Nonparabolic teaching peculiar to Luke: 3:5-6; 4:17-22; 6:24-26, 34; 9:51-56, 61-62; 11:12, 36, 40, 52-54; 12:32-33, 35-38, 47-49, 52, 57; 13:1-5, 22-23, 25a-26; 15:6-7; 17:28-31; 19:39-44; 21:22, 24, 25a-26, 28, 34-36; 22:28-30a, 35-38; 23:34a-46b.

Parables that are preserved only in Luke are:

> 5:39—old wine
> 7:40-42—the two debtors
> 10:25-37—the good Samaritan
> 11:5-8—the friend at midnight
> 12:13-21—the rich fool
> 13:6-9—the barren fig tree
> 14:7-10—the chief seats
> 14:15-22—the great supper
> 14:28-30—the uncompleted tower
> 14:31-32—the king's rash warfare
> 15:8-10—the lost coin
> 15:11-32—the lost son and the elder brother
> 16:1-12—the unjust steward
> 16:19-31—the rich man and Lazarus
> 17:7-10—the unprofitable servant
> 18:1-8—the unjust judge
> 18:9-14—the Pharisee and the publican at
>   prayer in the temple
> 19:11-28—the pounds

These data are generally interpreted to mean two things at the minimum: (1) Mark is the oldest of the canonical Gospels and was used in substantially its present form as the primary source for the Matthaean narrative and as a highly important though supplementary source for the narrative of Luke; (2) Matthew and Luke both incorporated considerable sections of the content of a second documentary source composed chiefly of discourse and usually designated as "Q," from the German word *Quelle,* meaning "source." This was the essence of the old "two-document hypothesis."

Almost as widespread as the acceptance of the essential soundness of this hypothesis has been in recent years the increasing awareness of its inadequacies. These inadequacies are chiefly three: (1) it sheds insufficient light on the origin of Mark, which is assumed to incorporate the tradition received from Peter; (2) it gives no satisfactory account of the wealth of non-Marcan narrative in Luke nor of the considerable nonuse of Marcan narrative materials by Luke; (3) it tends so to expand Q or to multiply the variant versions of it in the effort to make it the source of all non-Marcan materials common to Matthew and Luke, however these may differ in wording and emphasis, as to destroy all actual identity for the document. It also leaves practically out of account the wealth of teaching matter peculiar to Matthew and to Luke.

The development of a "four-document hypothesis" by B. H. Streeter [42] marked a long step forward in the study of the Gospels. Accepting Mark and Q as important sources for both Matthew and Luke, Streeter conceived of the narrative and discourse peculiar to Luke—except chapters 1 and 2, which he attributed to a cognate source—as having been the contents of a written source designated as "L." The materials peculiar to Matthew—except chapters 1 and 2 and the few non-Marcan narrative sections—he regarded as having been the contents of a document which he calls "M." Almost equally fruitful with his identification of these four main sources was Streeter's conviction that the several sources represented crystallizations of Christian tradition in terms of the interests and needs of such important centers as Jerusalem, Antioch, Caesarea, and Rome. This insight facilitated the delimitation of the contents of the sources no longer extant and shed valuable light on the use made of them by the evangelists.

Mark is regarded by Streeter as having been written at Rome about A.D. 65 in response to the needs created by the passing of the original Christian leaders and the shock to faith administered by the Neronian persecution. Beyond suggesting that a well-defined older source was incorporated in chapter 13, Streeter gives no clear account of the derivation of Marcan materials other than to say that their primitive characteristics show the evangelist depended on "early and unsophisticated tradition." [43]

As early as A.D. 50, and reflecting the interests of the Christian group at Syrian Antioch, the document known as "Q," made up chiefly of teaching matter but containing a few bits of narrative, was written. Streeter allows for the possibility, now generally given up,[44] that Q was an expanded version in Greek of an account of Jesus' teaching which Papias said the disciple Matthew "compiled . . . in the Hebrew language." [45] He emphasizes what is entirely evident, that it is easier to establish the fact of the existence of Q than to determine its content with precision. The latter task involves more than the isolation of the non-Marcan materials common to Matthew

[42] *The Four Gospels.*
[44] Goodspeed, *Introduction,* p. 174.
[43] *Ibid.,* p. 495.
[45] Euseb. *Hist.* III. 39. 16.

and Luke.[46] Judging by the use the later evangelists made of Mark, neither Matthew nor Luke exhausted the contents of Q, but each utilized sections which the other omitted. Differences in judgment among equally competent scholars as to passages to be assigned to Q illustrate the difficulty of being precise in the matter.[47] Because of Luke's practice of incorporating his source materials in blocks instead of conflating a variety of sources as Matthew does, the most faithful report of Q probably appears in Luke.

The contents of the document Streeter calls "L" he regards as belonging to Christian tradition at Caesarea. He suggests that when Luke was there as Paul's companion he prepared a rather full account of this tradition, which he shortly thereafter, about A.D. 60, combined with Q to create "Proto-Luke." Proto-Luke is conceived to have been a complete gospel, entirely independent of and similar in length to Mark, its narrative beginning with Luke 3:1 and closing with an account of the Passion. Approximately a third of its content as reconstructed, represents an incorporation of a large proportion of Q, with the remaining two thirds from L, Luke's initial formulation of the Caesarean tradition. Some twenty years later Luke produced the final form of his Gospel by supplementing Proto-Luke with liberal blocks of material drawn from Mark and at that time prefixed chapters 1 and 2, representing a cognate Caesarean source.[48]

The source Streeter calls "M" is not regarded as having been a complete gospel. It was made up entirely of teaching matter. Its contents were the equivalent of the discourse materials peculiar to Matthew, consisting of twelve parables and a limited amount of teaching of other types.[49] The Jewishness of these passages is their

[46] These materials are tabulated on pp. 106-8.

[47] Streeter, op. cit., pp. 273-92; Easton, The Gospel According to St. Luke, pp. xviii-xxiii; Grant, Growth of the Gospels, pp. 74-81.

[48] Proto-Luke as Streeter reconstructs it contained the following Lukan passages: 3-1–4:30; 5:1-11; 6:14-16; 6:20–8:3; 9:51–18:14; 19:1-27; 19:37-44; 21:18, 34-36; 22:14–24:53 except 22:18, 22, 42, 46-47, 52-61, 71 and 23:3, 22, 25-26, 33-34, 38, 44-46, 52-53, these scattered verses having been drawn from Mark's passion narrative and, contrary to Luke's usual method of using his sources in blocks, conflated with his own non-Marcan account of the Passion (op. cit., p. 222). The blocks of Marcan material by which Proto-Luke was expanded are represented in the following passages in Luke: 4:31-44; 5:12–6:19; 8:4–9:50; 18:15-43; 19:28-36; 19:45–21:33; 21:37–22:13.

[49] Listed on p. 108. They correspond in the main to Streeter's list of passages peculiar to Matthew, the narrative passages excepted (op. cit., p. 196).

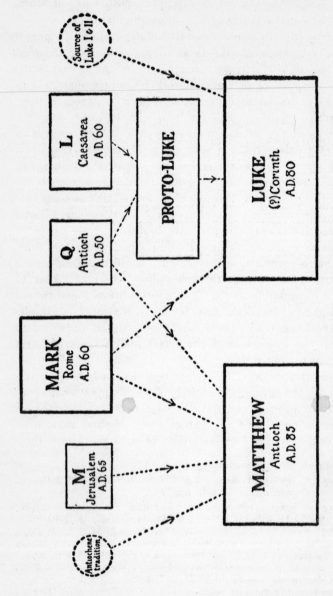

STREETER'S HYPOTHESIS OF THE SYNOPTICS AND THEIR SOURCES

The areas of the rectangles are in proportion to the number of verses in the respective documents according to Streeter's estimates, as follows: Mark 661, Matthew 1,068, Luke 1,149, Proto-Luke *ca.* 700, Q 270+, M 230+, L 400+. (From *The Four Gospels*, p. 150.)

distinguishing quality and constitutes the basis for the conception that they reflect the interests of Jerusalem Christianity of the type associated with the party of James. Supposedly the formulation of Christian tradition represented in M belonged to about A.D. 60, with Jerusalem the place of its origin. It was brought to Syrian Antioch at the outbreak of the Jewish War by Christians who fled from Jerusalem. In this way it became available to the author of Matthew. With Q and Mark and M at his disposal at Antioch, the author of Matthew wrote his finished Gospel about A.D. 85, introducing it with the stories of chapters 1 and 2, which were popularly current among Antiochene Christians.

The contents of these documentary sources, according to Streeter's conception of them, involved a certain amount of overlapping.[50] Parallel versions of the same original episode or teaching thus become the explanation of materials such as are listed on pages 105-6 rather than the prediction of indebtedness to Q on the part of Mark.[51] Similarly, other materials which evidently involve some kind of kinship but which are too different to have been derived from a common written source can be accounted for as representing the overlapping of Q and M, or of Mark and M or L.

There is a general recognition of the essential soundness of Streeter's investigations; but, as in the instances of the older two-document hypothesis, certain details of his conclusions are questioned, and the adequacy of the account given of the origin of the Gospels is challenged.[52] There are five principal criticisms of the four-document hypothesis: (1) there is too little advance beyond the older two-document hypothesis toward a discovery of Marcan sources; (2) while there is general agreement that there was a real document corresponding to L, the case for Proto-Luke remains highly debatable; (3) dissent is greatest in the matter of M, where the materials are held to be too heterogeneous to have been included in a single document; (4) the designation of four principal sources reduces to too few the abundance of documentary materials avail-

[50] *Op. cit.*, pp. 242 ff.

[51] Grant is inclined to differentiate the sources more sharply and to multiply their number to account for the phenomena that Streeter explains by overlapping. He is certain that Mark was indebted to Q to the extent of about 11 per cent of the total length of his account. (*Growth of the Gospels*, p. 130.)

[52] Rawlinson, *The Gospel According to Mark*, p. xxvi; Scott, *Literature of the New Testament*, p. 58; Riddle, *The Gospels*, pp. 112-31.

able to the evangelists; (5) the character of the process back of all written sources is left too largely unexplored.

There is an increasing tendency to predicate for Mark a process similar to that clearly implied in Luke 1:1-4 for Luke-Acts. Like the Gospels that made such large use of it, Mark is held to be composite in the sense of having incorporated and superseded earlier documents. These written sources must have been relatively brief and are conceived to have dealt with interests of the growing church. B. H. Branscomb has attempted to identify these sources and lists eight of which he feels fairly confident: (1) an account of controversies with Jewish leaders, 2:1–3:6 and 12:13-34; (2) the eschatological discourse of chapter 13; (3) parables concerning the Kingdom, with Christian missions as the focus of interest, chapter 4; (4) the passion narrative, 14:1–16:8; (5) a written list of the Twelve as the probable explanation of 3:16-19; (6) a summary of the Baptist's work, of which 1:4-8 was probably an abbreviation; (7) a collection of proof texts from which scripture citations were drawn; (8) possibly an account of Jesus' activity around the Sea of Galilee evidenced in the retention of place names and topographical allusions irrelevant to the teaching purpose of the evangelist such as are found in chapters 6 and 8.[53]

This number of written sources may be open to question,[54] and judgments as to the probability of the existence of a particular document will be found to vary,[55] but Branscomb's position represents a sounder principle than the oversimplified explanation of the origin of Mark in the statement of Papias.[56]

There is dissent from the predication of Proto-Luke as an intermediate step between the use of Q and L and the creation of the finished Gospel.[57] It is regarded sufficient simply to assume L as having embodied the bulk of the material peculiar to Luke, which with Q and Mark became a principal source for the completed third Gospel. However, Luke's nonuse of Mark is rendered much

---

[53] *The Gospel of Mark,* pp. xxii-xxvi.

[54] Filson, *Origins of the Gospels,* p. 142.

[55] Goodspeed thinks that chapter 13 may have been incorporated ready made and that a narrative of such length and detail as is found in 14:1–16:8, though not written, had been "substantially formed." He thinks it extremely unlikely that there existed at an early date a collection of Old Testament testimonies that served Christian leaders as an arsenal of proof texts. (*Introduction,* pp. 152, 162.)

[56] Euseb. *Hist.* III. 39. 15.   [57] Easton, *op. cit.,* pp. xxiii-xxx.

more intelligible on the assumption that the latter came into this evangelist's hands after he had already written a gospel that answered to the proportions and character of Proto-Luke. Instances in which Luke uses versions of episodes and teaching matter which he prefers to Marcan parallels in contexts other than those Mark provides argue cogently for the documentary existence of Proto-Luke.

Comparably strong reasons do not exist for confidence regarding the documentary character of M. Relevant considerations impress equally able scholars differently. To regard the characteristic interests of materials supposed to constitute M as simply a "flavor," [58] however, definitely affects the conception of the author of the Gospel and practically requires that those interests be regarded as his personal interests. Such a conclusion is difficult to reconcile with the character of this Gospel as a whole, the tendency and purpose of which are more anti-Jewish than Jewish.[59] The chief consideration commending Streeter's view of M is therefore its provision of an understandable explanation of the inclusion of the emphases represented in these materials. If they are conceived to embody the Christianity of persons newly arrived in Antioch from Jerusalem, their inclusion in Matthew reflects a concern for conciliation and unity on the part of the evangelist, whose own point of view is more nearly that of Q and Mark. Such a conception accords with the universalistic outlook of Matthew and explains the representative character that has made it the most popular of the Gospels.

The "multiple-source theory" of Frederick C. Grant has the value of emphasizing the abundance of materials at the disposal of the gospel writers and the many strands of tradition woven into the picture of Christian beginnings presented in the Gospels. It also opens to the student sound paths along which to explore the oral tradition necessarily presupposed in any conception of the written sources.

Streeter and Grant both emphasize the Palestinian and Syrian origin of the contents of the sources on which the authors of the canonical Gospels relied. Geographically and chronologically those sources belonged to circles where the leadership of the newer missionary churches had the opportunity of vital contact with Palestinian Christianity. They enshrined a tradition which reached

[58] Grant, *Growth of the Gospels,* pp. 189-99.
[59] Riddle, *op. cit.,* pp. 164-78.

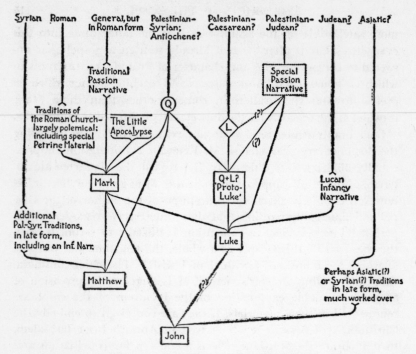

GRANT'S MULTIPLE-SOURCE THEORY OF GOSPEL ORIGINS
(From *The Growth of the Gospels*, p. 66)

back closer to the context of Jesus' earthly ministry than any Christian document. This tradition must have been formulated while "the original eye-witnesses who became teachers of the message" [60] lived. The view held of that tradition is highly important because the dependability of the completed Gospels is inextricably bound up with that of the tradition upon which they ultimately rested. Inquiry here focuses upon the two decades following the Crucifixion—A.D. 30-50.

The statement of Papias about the origin of Mark's Gospel [61] suggests that, even though the evangelist possessed a knowledge of the broad outlines of Jesus' ministry, the materials out of which he undertook to create an orderly story consisted in the main of fragments of teaching and self-contained stories. An essentially similar description would apply also to the materials with which the authors of such documents as Q, L, and M worked and in a modified

[60] Luke 1:2.   [61] Euseb. *Hist.* III. 39. 15.

sense to much that the authors of Matthew and Luke-Acts incorporated. The contents of the three earlier Gospels retain characteristics supporting the implications of Papias' statement that, before Christian teachers began to reduce their messages to writing, the materials later woven into extended narrative and discourse existed orally as short, self-contained units which were severally invested with standardized forms designed to facilitate retention in memory.

This quality of fragmentariness is illustrated in the complete absence of time and place connections in typical Marcan stories.[62] Such stories are complete within themselves and do not depend for their effectiveness on the context in which they appear. Where there is the appearance of an articulated sequence,[63] close examination discloses the arrangement is purely topical in character and the separate stories have qualities indicating their original circulation as separate stories. The similar character of the tradition incorporated in Luke's special source is indicated by the appearance of Jesus and his disciples in Luke 17:11 at the point of their supposed departure for Jerusalem although they had presumably been traveling toward Jerusalem since Luke 9:51. This impression of the fragmentariness of the narrative tradition in its oral form seems to require modification in the case of the account of the Passion. From a very early time this appears to have circulated as a continuous story. Here as elsewhere, however, the materials are resolvable into brief and relatively self-sufficient units.[64]

The tradition of Jesus' teaching antedating the earliest written

[62] Mark 1:16-20; 1:40-45; 3:13-19; 3:22-26; 4:1-8; etc.

[63] Mark 1:21-39; 2:1-3:6; 4:45-5:43; 6:31-8:26; 11:15-12:40.

[64] Mark 14 and 15 break up into such units as the anointing of Jesus (14:1-9); the perfidy of Judas (14:10-11); preparation of the Passover supper (14:12-16); Jesus' prediction of the betrayal (14:17-21); the establishment of the Lord's Supper (14:22-26); Jesus' prediction of desertion by the disciples (14:27-31); the agony in Gethsemane (14:32-42); the arrest of Jesus (14:43-50); the flight of a young man (14:51-52); the arraignment of Jesus before the Sanhedrin (14:53-65); Peter's denial (14:66-72); Pilate's judging of Jesus (15:1-15); Jesus mocked and scourged (15:16-20); the Crucifixion (15:21-32); Jesus' death (15:33-41); Jesus' burial (15:42-47); the Resurrection (16:1-8). Luke's special source contained a passion narrative representing an independent line of transmission. The materials composing it were of the same type as those of the Marcan story, and they are equally resolvable into brief units. The probabilities are, however, that although the passion narrative grew, there was from the beginning a nucleus of connected stories supplying a description of Jesus' death and resurrection.

sources appears likewise to have been composed of brief, self-contained units. This is illustrated in the different placement of sayings in the Sermon on the Mount, in the presentation of the same sayings in totally different settings, and in sayings retained apart from any sort of framework.[65] It is equally clear in certain highly artificial compilations of sayings [66] where unrelated materials have been editorially organized for the treatment of selected topics. In other sayings cycles [67] where the marks of naturalness suggest their origin with Jesus himself,[68] the paragraphs into which the materials are resolvable have the sound of summaries intended to serve as guides for Christian behavior.[69] Jesus would hardly have used such summaries in popular preaching, although he probably did reduce the gist of his thought to such forms to aid the memory of disciples. Collections of parables such as appear in Mark 4 and Matthew 13 are editorially organized for the treatment of themes and implicitly suggest an earlier circulation of the stories singly and in pairs. Rather extensive collections of parables seem to have been part of the Christian tradition treasured in given church centers,[70] but here as elsewhere these groupings point back to the existence of the materials as isolated units.

The detached oral units composing the tradition incorporated into the written sources on which the Synoptic Gospels depended were of two general classifications, narrative and discourse. The forms in which these materials were cast have been variously designated.[71] The nomenclature here preferred as most accurately de-

[65] Matt. 5:13=Luke 14:34b, 35a; Matt. 5:15=Luke 11:13; Matt. 5:18=Luke 16:17; Matt. 5:25-26=Luke 12:58-59; Matt. 5:29-30=Luke 9:47, 43; Matt. 6:9-13=Luke 11:2-4; Matt. 6:22-23=Luke 11:34-35; Luke 16:18; cf. Matt. 5:32.

[66] Mark 4:21-25; 8:34—9:1; 9:41-50; Luke 6:39-42; 16:16-17 (cf. Matt. 11:12; 5:18).

[67] Luke 6:27-38; Matt. 5:17-48.   [68] Easton, *Christ in the Gospels,* p. 41.

[69] Note how naturally Luke 6:27-38 breaks up into vss. 27-31, 32-35, 36-38.

[70] Matthew's special source contained twelve parables, and Luke's contained nineteen.

[71] Vincent Taylor: pronouncement stories, miracle stories, sayings of Jesus, and stories about Jesus (*The Formation of the Gospel Tradition*); Donald W. Riddle: paradigms, tales, exhortations, legends (*The Gospels*); Ernest F. Scott: paradigms, miracle stories, tales, aphorisms, controversies, apocalyptic utterances, legends (*The Validity of the Gospel Record*); Rudolf Bultmann: apothegms (described as dialogues introduced by enemies, dialogues introduced by friends, and dialogues introduced by incidents), miracle stories, sayings (more specifically designated as wisdom-words, prophetic and apocalyptic sayings, community rules, sayings in the first person singular, and parables), legends (*Die Geschichte der*

scriptive is: pronouncement stories, miracle stories, sayings, and narrative tradition.

The distinguishing characteristic of the *pronouncement story* is its climax in a saying of Jesus. The story as such is incidental. Its function is to preserve what Jesus said and to shed such light on the meaning of his statement as the narrative setting may provide. The story usually arises from a question suggested by an incident or put to Jesus by a friend or an opponent. Jesus ordinarily responds with a question or a precept or both, and the conclusion is a description of the effect of Jesus' saying on the hearers. The story of the effort of the Pharisees and Herodians to entrap Jesus [72] illustrates these several elements perfectly.[73] Jesus' statement is the significant item in all such stories. While germane to the immediate circumstances of his ministry, the things he said usually had significance for the problems which the Christian community confronted—Sabbath observance, church discipline, worship, marriage, divorce, taxes, obedience to civil authority, persecution, eschatology—and it was mainly for the sake of their value in the establishment and maintenance of Christian patterns of behavior that the sayings remained a part of early Christian tradition. Of the maximum of thirty-five pronouncement stories in the Synoptic Gospels, twenty occur in Mark and the remainder in Q and L. The Palestinian origin of the stories, as suggested by their contents, and their preservation in the cycles of tradition of the Christian communities at Antioch, Caesarea, and Rome establish the pronouncement story as one of the authentic forms with which the earliest Christian tradition was invested.

The *miracle story* differs from the pronouncement story as such

---

synoptischen Tradition [Göttingen: Vandenhoeck & Ruprecht, 1921]; also *Jesus and the Word,* tr. Louise P. Smith and Erminie Huntress [New York: Charles Scribner's Sons, 1934]) ; Martin Dibelius; paradigms, old stories, miracle tales, paraenese or sayings, parables, and legends or myths (*Die Formgeschichte des Evangeliums* [2nd ed.; Tübingen: J. C. B. Mohr, 1933]; Dibelius' pioneer work has been translated into English by Bertram Lee Woolf under the title *From Tradition to Gospel* [New York: Charles Scribner's Sons, 1935]; very illuminating for Dibelius' point of view also is his *The Message of Jesus Christ,* tr. Frederick C. Grant [New York: Charles Scribner's Sons, 1939]) .

[72] Mark 12:13-17.

[73] Other illustrations are: Mark 3:31-35; 10:13-15; 11:27-33; 12:18-27; 12:28-34; 12:41-44; Luke 9:57-62 (cf. Matt. 8:19-22) ; 11:27-28.

in its importance as a story.[74] The story itself carries the message and is therefore more detailed and circumstantial. It opens with a description of the situation or with the introduction of a sufferer. There follows a picture of human helplessness or of the failure of previous efforts to alleviate affliction. Then Jesus acts confidently and effectively to bring order out of chaos, whether in nature or in the life of a person. Finally the effect of what Jesus has done on those who have witnessed it is recorded as evidence of the reality of the result. The detailed and vivid story of the demoniac of Gadara [75] illustrates the principal features of the miracle story. Of the total of eighteen such stories in the Synoptic Gospels, fifteen are preserved in Mark. Thirteen of the eighteen describe miracles of healing, of which eleven have been transmitted by Mark. Five are accounts of "nature" miracles, and of them four belong to Mark.[76]

The philosophical considerations that make these stories prob- lematical for the modern reader of the Gospels did not exist for those who first heard the stories.[77] The ease or difficulty with which they are now believed is almost wholly a matter of "world view." The problem they constitute is essentially theological, and historical inquiry per se cannot solve it. Interest here is in the function of the stories and whether or not they belonged to the earliest Christian tradition. Miracle stories were an important part of the messages of early preachers.[78] They served to describe Jesus' sympathy, his high appraisal of individual worth, his divine adequacy for every exigency of man's existence. In him all spirits found their Lord and acknowledged him to be Messiah. Opinion varies with reference to the circles within which these stories were used. Their concen- tration so largely in Mark is interpreted by some to mean they

[74] Stories that involve miracle but in which the more important element is Jesus' teaching are more properly classified as pronouncement stories—for example Mark 3:1-6 = Matt. 12:9-14 = Luke 6:6-11; Luke 7:1-10 = Matt. 8:5-13; Mark 7:24-30 = Matt. 15:21-28; Luke 14:1-6; 17:11-19.

[75] Mark 5:1-20.

[76] The stories of miracles of healing are: Mark 1:23-27; 1:30-31; 1:40-45; 2:1-12; 5:1-20; 5:21-43; 5:25-34; 7:32-37; 8:22-26; 9:14-29; 10:46-52; Luke 7:11-17; 11:14 (cf. Matt. 12:22-24). The stories of "nature" miracles are: Mark 4:34-41; 6:34-44 (cf. 8:1-9); 6:45-52; 11:13-14, 20-21; Luke 5:1-11.

[77] Case, *Experience with the Supernatural in Early Christian Times;* Richard- son, *The Miracle-Stories of the Gospels.*

[78] Acts 2:22; 10:38.

grew up in Hellenistic Christian communities and were never a part of the earliest Palestinian tradition.[79] More probably such stories formed a part of Christian tradition from the outset [80] and were a popular and effective element in Palestinian Christian preaching. As with other types of materials, these stories were arranged in topical groupings and were combined with sayings and pronouncement stories to form more comprehensive cycles.[81]

Interest in Jesus' words antedated and from the outset paralleled interest in his death and resurrection. The conviction of the extreme importance of what Jesus said is one of several factors that help explain the limited extent of strictly biographical materials in the Gospels. Data for a connected account of Jesus' life are lacking; but there is little doubt about the values he exalted, the motives to which he appealed, the delineation of the way men must live who desired God's approval at the Judgment. The first preachers used Jesus' words as instruction for the guidance of all who desired admission to the messianic Kingdom immediately to be inaugurated. The passion narrative accentuated the authoritative character properly belonging to the instructions of a Messiah who had suffered and died vicariously, who had triumphed over death, and who would shortly return to inaugurate the Judgment, assign men their eternal destinies, and establish the Kingdom of God.

The needs of the Christian community stimulated the selective memory of Christian teachers and determined their pedagogical methods, but the actual teaching of Jesus was the source of the *sayings* tradition.[82] The care with which the judgments of Christian

[79] Bultmann and Riddle think of Christian tradition as growing with the Christian movement. As the movement developed it created materials appropriate to its needs. Thus the Synoptic tradition is viewed as made up of layers that can be identified and approximately dated, "form" being a valuable clue to date. Of stories about Jesus, the passion narrative is the earliest, and it alone had its content and form determined during the primitive period. Pronouncement stories, miracle stories, and legends or narrative tradition came later and in that order. Since most of the miracle stories involved exorcism, which was forbidden among Jews, these stories are held to have grown up in Hellenistic Christian communities. Applied to discourse materials, this principle means that sayings reflecting distinctly Palestinian color and interests are oldest, and that those are most apt to be genuine that urge repentance, commend nonviolence, emphasize eschatology.

[80] Easton, *Christ in the Gospels*, p. 43.

[81] Mark 4:35–5:43; 6:32–7:37, etc.

[82] Apocalypse and wisdom were the literary dress of postexilic Jewish prophecy. They also supplied the modes of thought employed by Jesus. Wisdom de-

leaders were distinguished from what Jesus said testifies to this fact.[83]

The tradition of Jesus' teaching existed in parables, in isolated sayings, and in groups of parables and sayings. In Mark the sayings are in the main preserved in pronouncement stories, but there are also a limited number of parables and clusters of sayings. It is reasonably certain that Jesus did not limit himself to sentence sermons. The crisp, epigrammatic sayings retained in the memory of the disciples represent the gist but not the complete statement of the Master's thought.[84] Jesus himself may have reduced much that he said to the multitudes to the form of compact summaries, and he probably originated for his first followers the practice of gathering these summaries into clusters treating the related phases of a theme.[85] Clusters of sayings and parables were organized into longer cycles of like materials and these into such expanded groupings as Q, M, and L. Traces of some such process are visible in sayings collections that were incorporated at varying stages of development in Mark, Q, and L.[86]

Materials in excess of editorial passages and the classifications already discussed consist of stories about Jesus and make up the *narrative tradition*. Because it consisted from the outset of at least a nucleus of connected stories, the passion narrative, which is a considerable part of the narrative tradition, is properly classified as itself a distinct "form" in which primitive Christian tradition clothed itself. Apart from the birth stories, which have a history distinctly their own, and the passion narrative, there are thirty-six

---

veloped a wide variety of types of expression, the chief of which were the similitude, the riddle, the fable, the parable, the proverb or epigram, the paradox, the gnomic essay—in which a number of units on the same subject were assembled, such as Prov. 26:1-12; 31:10-31, etc.—the didactic drama, the philosophical drama, and the philosophical homily. The groups of sayings and parables that composed the bulk of the sayings tradition were in principle like the gnomic essay.

[83] I Cor. 7:10, 12, 25, 39-40.

[84] Somewhat after the fashion of *Pirqe Aboth*.

[85] Such as Matt. 5:17-48; Luke 6:27-38. Sayings groups that are more artificial are Mark 4:21-25; 8:34–9:1; Luke 6:39-42; etc.

[86] Mark 1:7-8 (cf. Luke 3:7-9, 16-17; Matt. 3:7-10, 11-12); 3:22-29 (cf. Luke 11:14-23; Matt. 12:22-27, 32); 4:22; 8:38 (cf. Luke 12:2-9; Matt. 10:26-36); 6:6-11 (cf. Luke 10:3-12; Matt. 10:7-16); 12:38-40 (cf. Luke 11:39-44, 46-48; Matt. 23:4-31); 13:14-37 (cf. Luke 21:20-24; 17:23-24, 37; 21:25-33; 17:26, 27, 34-35; 19:12, 13; 12:39-40; Matt. 24:15-44; 25:14).

stories about Jesus in the Synoptic Gospels belonging to the period of his public ministry. These stories differ from the passion narrative in their completeness as isolated units and because they picture Jesus as vocal rather than largely silent. They resemble the birth stories and the passion narrative in the significance they had for the institutional and religious interests of the early church.

There is no standard form to which these stories conform, such as exists for the pronouncement and miracle stories. Certain general characteristics are, however, usually present. Jesus is regularly the focus of attention; and many of the stories have to do with turning points in his career, such as his baptism, temptation, the call of the disciples, Peter's confession, the transfiguration, the triumphal entry, and the cleansing of the temple. Conversation between Jesus and one or more persons or a group is usually an important feature of such stories, with the secondary characters in the situation rather indefinitely identified. Finally, the stories ordinarily leave the impression of having been told primarily for the sake of their practical implications rather than their content as history. Eighteen of these stories are preserved in Mark,[87] eleven in L,[88] five in Q,[89] and two in Matthew.[90]

The small number of these stories, their isolated character, their

[87] Mark 1:5-8; 1:9-11; 1:12-13; 1:16-20; 1:35-39; 3:13-19; 6:1-6a; 6:14-16; 7:24-30; 8:14-21; 8:27-30; 8:31-33; 9:2-10; 9:30-32; 9:33-37; 10:32-34; 11:1-11; 11:15-18 The more detailed among the stories probably owed their origin to the reminiscences of Peter. Vincent Taylor suggests that the following had such an origin: 1:16-20; 1:35-39; 3:13-19; 6:1-6a; 8:27-30; 8:31-33; 9:2-10; 9:30-32; 10:32-34; 11:1-11; 11:15-18 (op. cit., pp. 148-52). F. C. Grant includes a much more restricted list of stories of this variety in his catalogue of Petrine materials: 1:16-20; 1:23-26; 1:35-39; 8:27-30; 8:32-33; 9:2-8 (Growth of the Gospels, p. 133). Both lists estimate Peter's contribution to Mark at the minimum rather than the maximum. They are chiefly valuable as suggestive of the type of materials that have their foundation in the testimony of Peter.

[88] Luke 4:16-30; 5:1-11; 7:36-50; 9:52b-56; 10:1, 17-20; 10:38-42; 13:31-33; 17:11-19; 19:1-10; 19:39-40; 19:41-44. By comparison with Mark's stories, those drawn from Luke's special source are lacking in detail and vividness. They bear the marks of having been more widely used in Christian preaching and, as a result, of having a typical and symbolical character. Their limited number gives the impression of adequacy for the evangelist's purposes because they illustrate the kind of things Jesus was accustomed to do rather than everything that he did.

[89] Luke 3:7-9, 16-17=Matt. 3:7-10, 11-12; Luke 4:1-13=Matt. 4:1-11; Luke 7:1-10=Matt. 8:5-10, 13; Luke 7:18-20, 22-28, 31-35=Matt. 11:2-11, 16-19; Luke 10:13-15=Matt. 11:21-24.

[90] Matt.14:28-31; 17:24-27. Bacon says that these two stories were "seemingly gathered from floating legend" (Introduction, p. 182).

evidently practical interest combine to show that the preachers who used the stories during the oral period of Christian tradition, as well as the evangelists who later wrote the Gospels, were not interested in biography as such. Their absorbing concern was with the future rather than the past. The proclamation of a righteousness designed to gain for those who exemplified it entrance into the coming Kingdom was their task. The mission of these early "heralds" was to supply guidance for the creation of a pattern of life distinctively Christian and to stimulate believers to adopt that pattern. The words and the deeds of Jesus useful for such practical objectives survived. The passion narrative was no exception. Nowhere else do practical interests more clearly outweigh purely biographical considerations.

The investment of the materials constituting the substance of the earliest Christian tradition with the forms that have been described discloses the earliest Christian pedagogy. The process of standardization and selection extended throughout the two decades when the tradition was entirely oral. It involved the selection of the materials whose worth had been demonstrated in making converts and sustaining their faith. It was also a way whereby those materials were more easily remembered and were conserved in accepted versions. Reduction to writing would of course have served the latter objective better, but the motive for the creation of written records was lacking at the outset, and the development of oral forms was an effective substitute as a device for reducing variation to the minimum. The Gospels are seen in their true character when they are regarded as depositories of the evangelistic materials which the first-century church found most useful. They supply a typical but by no means exhaustive record of those materials.

There is widespread agreement among New Testament scholars that the tradition presupposed by the Gospels is resolvable into small, self-contained units which were invested with some such forms as have been described before they were reduced to writing. Crucial differences of judgment appear when the effort is made to determine whence the tradition took its rise and the precise character of its original element. By some the tradition is regarded as the outgrowth of the message of early "heralds." On this basis the Gospels afford almost no certain knowledge of the career and message of Jesus but are rather a disclosure of how the growth of the

Christian movement was paralleled by the growth of the Christian message. By others the tradition is itself held to have been the content of early Christian preaching, and the Gospels are assumed to supply a substantially historical representation of Jesus' life and message. A brief statement of the two positions will contribute to the formation of a sound judgment of the matter.

In the first case the basic element is held to have been experience rather than history. Vivid reports of visions of the risen Christ and revelations attributed to him were the content of the first preaching. People who listened to such stories reacted to them in ways determined by their cultural backgrounds. Jewish hearers with a background of acquaintance with the Old Testament and the ethical emphasis of scribal teaching would respond quite differently from non-Jews whose religious inheritance was from the Hellenistic cults. Preaching had as its objectives the winning of converts and the maintenance of the faith of believers. Responses to preaching and the institutional needs of the growing church determined the content of teaching attributed to Jesus and of stories about him. Such materials were less a matter of recollection than of immediate inspiration and in effect represent the technique of sermon building.

As the corollary of this view, the several "forms" into which the materials were cast represent successive layers of tradition. Origin in a Jewish or a Hellenistic situation is discoverable by the interests displayed in a story or a saying. Such a story as the plucking of grain on the Sabbath or eschatological sayings such as are found in Mark 13 reflect a Palestinian Jewish milieu. Similarly, accounts of healing that involved exorcism, the vice lists of Mark 7:21-23,[91] and the teaching regarding divorce in Mark 10 never enjoyed currency except in a Hellenistic setting. The primitive passion narrative, which was based on vision experiences of the risen Christ,[92] and which grew as additional stories were produced, became the earliest element in Christian tradition. Other stories and teachings were subsequent to it and were the creation of the Christian community. They were the kind of stories and teaching that would grow within a movement founded upon faith in a Savior like Jesus, who had suffered and died on man's behalf, had proved himself superior to death, and had been exalted to heaven, whence he would shortly return to judge the world.

[91] Cf. Matt. 15:19-20.   [92] I Cor. 15:1-9.

The alternative view makes allowance for the adaptation of the tradition of Jesus' words and deeds to the practical objectives of evangelistic preaching and catechetical instruction. Matthew and Luke reflect such adaptation in their use of Mark and Q and presumably the authors of Mark, Q, L, and M exercised similar freedom in the interest of pedagogical effectiveness. Adaptation rather than outright creation, however, more accurately describes the process, and there were checks on the extent to which adaptation could proceed unchallenged.[93] Much that Jesus had said and done remained latent in Christian memory until stirred to life by some concrete situation. Christians solved their problems less by abstract reasoning than by appeal to the authority of the example and message of Jesus. Memories of him survived that had meaning for the needs of believers. In the sense that selective memory determined the content of tradition, tradition owed its inception and growth to the Christian community.

The disproportionate space devoted to the passion narrative in each of the Gospels does not indicate that the account of Jesus' antecedent ministry was a secondary development. His death and resurrection were probably never the sole items of interest for the early church. The account of how Jesus did his work, what he taught, the ends for which he died, the reality of his triumph were all elements in the Christian message from the first. The various elements composed a unity for believers, and the tradition in its wholeness supplied the substance of early preaching. Jesus' victory over death and his exaltation to heaven made what he had done and said more significant, but Christian interest in his deeds and words existed prior to those final phases and had much to do with the meaning seen in the Passion.[94] The tradition of Jesus' words rather than the passion narrative was probably the original element in Christian tradition. The likelihood that Jesus himself trained his disciples to disseminate his message and provided such forms as the isolated saying, the sayings group, and the parable as aids to memory

[93] Early opposition to the Fourth Gospel grew out of its radical handling of the Synoptic tradition. The publication of the fourfold Gospel during the first quarter of the second century was designed to secure a more hospitable reception of that great work.

[94] Note the emphasis in Rom. 1:4 on "holiness of spirit" as the distinguishing characteristic of the divine sonship of Christ, which the Resurrection "decisively declared."

is strengthened by the fact that this was normal procedure for a rabbi.[95]

On this second view, vivid and abundant memories of Jesus were the warp and woof of the fabric of Christian tradition woven during the twenty years following the Crucifixion. The first "heralds" had known Jesus directly, and their preaching was largely the repetition of what he had said and done. These men did fragmentarily what the author of Luke-Acts undertook on a grand scale, and they supplied the source materials with which he worked.[96] Both he and they had evangelistic ends in view, but the materials they handled were substantially historical. The completed Gospel only had such validity as history as the source materials themselves warranted.

According to this view the Gospels, their written sources, and the antecedent oral tradition disclosed but did not originate an interest in Jesus. He never dropped out of the memory of believers. His first followers were active in the growing church; and while the influence of eye-witnesses must not be overstated, it should not be ignored in accounting for materials incorporated into the earliest documents used by the evangelists. Though relatively late, the Gospels were enlargements upon earlier documents, and these documents had a vital continuity with the earliest oral tradition. The Christian public guarded rather jealously the generally received versions of the materials. In line with this conservative disposition Papias as late as the first quarter of the second century evaluated the written Gospels by the criterion of the "old-fashioned" oral tradition.[97]

The sermonic sound that characterizes so many pericopes in the Gospels is reminiscent of the setting in which the tradition of Jesus' words and deeds took shape. The church meeting, whether for evangelistic preaching or corporate worship or catechetical instruction, was the agency for the conservation of the materials, and its thoroughly practical objectives were decisive in their selection and formulation. The oral repetition in such meetings of accounts of what Jesus had said and done was the method of instruction and became the process by which memories of Jesus were reduced to the forms that became generally current.

[95] Burton Scott Easton, "The First Evangelic Tradition," *Journal of Biblical Literature,* L (1931), 148-55; Goodspeed, *Formation of the New Testament,* p. 33.
[96] Luke 1:1-4; Acts 1:21-22; 10:37-43.   [97] Euseb. *Hist.* III. 39. 4.

The Old Testament was the first Bible of the church. For its most fruitful understanding by Christians, however, it required illumination from the events of Jesus' life and the wisdom of his words. The illustration of the import of the Scriptures was one of the earliest uses in church meetings to which "heralds" and "teachers" put the materials out of which the gospel tradition was wrought.[98] "Inspired preachers" also found in them a rich resource for clothing their own messages with vividness and authority. The induction of large numbers of people of divergent heritages into the church created a pedagogical task of prodigious proportions. Converts gave assent to more than a Christological formula. Faith became the portal of a new and lofty way of living for whose definition the example and words of Jesus were the authoritative guide.[99] The "teacher" was charged with the responsibility of making the Christian pattern effective in life situations and occupied a place second only in importance to that of the "apostle" and the "inspired preacher." [100] He had himself in the beginning been the beneficiary of "apostolic" instruction,[101] and his duty was to pass on and effectively apply the principal facts and emphases thus received in local life situations. The formation of the first evangelic tradition was thus the achievement of early Christian pedagogy.

A brief glance at the several stages of the process out of which the Gospels were produced in their approximately chronological sequence may be of assistance in understanding both the nature of that process and the true character of the Gospels. Competent scholarship no longer raises the question of the historicity of Jesus. That he lived and that his life and message were in some sense responsible for the Christian movement are not subjects of debate. Without him there would have been no church, no evangelic tradition, no Gospels, no New Testament.

Jesus himself wrote nothing. He employed the forms of expression of the prophet and the wise man and their oral method of teaching. Like them he also surrounded himself with disciples, whom he trained as assistants in extending his ministry. For their convenience he gave his thought the compact and picturesque statement that made it immediately intelligible and easily remembered. It is

---

[98] "As the Scriptures foretold." (I Cor. 15:3.)   [99] Luke 6:46-49.
[100] I Cor. 12:28; Matt. 13:52; Eph. 4:11.
[101] I Cor. 15:3; Luke 1:1-4; Acts 1:21-22.

a datum of utmost historical importance that Jesus was survived by a band of followers whom he had trained to transmit the substance of his message. The training thus received was vitalized by the resurrection faith, under whose spell these early "heralds" lived. His words possessed the authority not merely of their intrinsic beauty and truth but of the utterances of one who had been decisively demonstrated to be Messiah by the Resurrection and who would shortly return to judge the world on the basis of the delineation of the will of God contained in his historical message.

During the two decades following the Crucifixion, from 30 to 50, Christians wrote little.[102] They lived in expectation of the imminent return of Jesus, and their primary concern was to proclaim the gospel as widely as the intervening time permitted. The language employed in the first preaching was Aramaic; [103] but as Greek-speaking residents of Palestine were reached, and as missionaries went beyond the boundaries of Palestine into the Hellenistic world, Greek rapidly displaced Aramaic in Christian usage. The employment of writing by Christian leaders was a part of the adaptation of missionary activity to a non-Jewish public. Had Christianity remained a movement within Judaism, there would probably have been no gospels. The earliest documents of which any traces remain were composed in Greek, and there probably were never any Aramaic Christian writings.[104]

[102] Among the reasons that Christians began to write relatively late were: (1) the general prevalence of the expectancy of the Parousia; (2) the adequacy of the oral method for the limited geographical scope of the movement; (3) the superfluousness of writing as long as eye-witness testimony was available; (4) Palestinian preference for oral instruction; (5) the purely evangelistic motivation of the first missionaries; (6) the cost of writing materials; (7) the fact that although the Greek world was "a reading and writing world" the first Christians in that world were humble folk (I Cor. 1:26-30; Matt. 10:42; 11-:25).

[103] Jesus possibly knew Greek. Probably, however, he habitually taught in Aramaic.

[104] Grant thinks it wholly unnecessary to suppose that the Gospels were "originally composed in Aramaic and later translated into Greek." The idea that they were written at an early date as "personal memoirs" in his judgment violates the "canons of Semitic historiography." (*The Earliest Gospel*, pp. 27-28.) In his opinion "the best solution of the problem of the gospel tradition is . . . the form-critical one of stereotyped oral tradition . . . originally . . . in Aramaic and then translated . . . into Greek . . . by different persons at different times." He concedes the possibility that some "pericopes and sayings may . . . have been written down in Aramaic before translation into Greek," but he is sure that such a document as Q was never anything but "a Greek document." (*Ibid.*, pp. 123-24.)

Thoroughly practical interests dominated this entire period. Although there existed the kind of knowledge of the general course of events in Jesus' ministry disclosed in Mark and reproduced in Matthew and to a somewhat less degree in Luke, there was little concern to preserve an accurate ordering of historical data. The chief interest was in Jesus' message, and the lack of genuinely biographical predisposition denied to the evangelists the data required for real biography, if biography was a part of their purpose. Memories of Jesus were the materials of preaching; and the most serviceable forms to which they could be reduced were the self-contained story, the single saying, the sayings group, and the parable. The exception to the rule of "fragmentariness" during the major portion of this period was the passion story, which from the outset consisted of a nucleus of connected stories, and which was the oldest narrative element incorporated in Mark.[105]

Investment of units of material with these forms belonged to the oral period of the Christian tradition. The preachers and teachers who rendered this service were close to the original facts and were in vital contact with those who possessed first-hand information. Groups of sayings and cycles of stories were arranged by these early "teachers," but the purely topical character of their arrangements indicates the practical character of their objectives. Toward the close of the first two decades of Christian history, blocks of tradition, both sequences of narratives and groups of sayings and parables, may have been reduced to writing, although this more probably belonged to the ensuing period. The development of fixity in the materials, whether the isolated unit or cycles of such units, was the result of repetition in preaching and catechetical instruction. Versions of individual units of material and blocks of such units that were developed in such important centers as Antioch, Caesarea, Rome, and Ephesus tended to become standard and to reduce to a minimum the miscellaneousness that might otherwise have prevailed. Variety, however, was not wholly lost, as is shown by the divergencies existing between the narrative traditions incorporated in Proto-Luke and in Mark, and in the accounts of the teaching preserved in Q, L, M.

Between 50 and 65 the written sources about which the Synoptic Gospels were built were compiled. This is the period to which

---

[105] 14:1–16:8. For an excellent discussion see *ibid.*, pp. 76-88, 175-87.

Paul's letters belong; and the absence from those letters of the emphasis on Jesus' earthly life and message [106] characteristic of such documents as Q, L, and M suggests that the latter were produced in Hellenitic Christian communities where Paul's influence was not entirely predominant.[107] The organization of materials into elaborate subject groupings exceeding the passion narrative in length and their reduction to writing in Greek were the outstanding development of this period. Interest continued to be primarily in Jesus' teaching, as the preponderantly discourse character of Q, L, and M shows. This emphasis on the supreme importance of what Jesus said is largely the explanation of the scarcity of stories about Jesus during the three subsequent decades when Mark, Matthew, and Luke-Acts were written. The definition and enforcement of a characteristically Christian pattern of life appears to have been the interest served by these written collections of sayings. Writing was necessitated by the proportions to which the task of "teachers" grew with the rapid expansion of the Christian movement.

The canonical Gospels belong to the period from 65 to 100. The original leaders were gone,[108] and there had developed in Gentile Christian communities an interest in the beginnings of the movement originating in Palestine but now established in the principal cities of the Roman Empire. Practical objectives, though dominant, were less exclusively the interest of the authors of the Gospels than had been the case with their predecessors. They undertook on a more comprehensive scale the essential task to which earlier writers had addressed themselves, but they saw in the events of Jesus' career a significance previously minimized.

The rapid growth of the Christian movement during the last thirty years of the first century was attended by the development of a number of acute problems. The disastrous course of the Jewish War (66-70) left Christianity with little appeal for Jews. There was need among Gentiles for an explanation of the relative failure of the gospel among those to whom it had been originally pro-

---

[106] II Cor. 5:16.

[107] The tendency to make "experience" of the ecstatic and visionary types the sole foundation of Christian tradition fails to give sufficient weight to the fact that such churches as Damascus, Antioch, Caesarea, and Rome were not established by Paul and that Paul was profoundly distrusted by the leaders of Jerusalem Christianity.

[108] Iren. *Her.* III. 1. 1.

claimed. The destruction of Jerusalem gave new life to eschatological expectations. The delay of the Parousia dampened the ardor and shook the faith of many believers. The clearer self-differentiation of the church brought bitter competition and open hostility between itself and the synagogue. The Roman government became increasingly suspicious of the church, and there were forewarnings of repressive measures to come. Heretical movements within Christian circles arose as younger leaders undertook to express their faith in Hellenistic forms of thought.

The needs which such problems made apparent provided the motivation for the writing of the Gospels. They were designed to steady the faith of the persecuted, to relate the Christian movement more intelligently to the actual course of history, to satisfy the historical interests of younger generations of Christians who were largely non-Jewish, to disarm and divert governmental suspicion, to check the spread of heretical sects by the creation of ordered and comprehensive accounts of Christian beginnings.

X

THE GOSPEL OF MARK

Authorship.—Traces of acquaintance with Mark antedate by half a century specific references to it. It was the primary source for the Matthaean story of Jesus' ministry, and the author of Luke-Acts used it as an important supplementary source. It was clearly known to the authors of the Fourth Gospel,[1] the Preaching of Peter, the Gospel of Peter, Second Peter,[2] and to Justin Martyr.[3] It may also have been known to Hermas[4] and the author of the Didache.[5] The authorship is ascribed to Mark by Papias of Hierapolis,[6]

[1] See p. 98

[2] II Pet. 1:15-16 clearly reflects acquaintance with the tradition of the Petrine source of Mark's Gospel. Familiarity with the Gospel on the part of readers of the epistle is assumed.

[3] Justin knew Mark as part of the fourfold Gospel collection, passages from which were customarily read in the Sunday services of the church (*Apol.* 67:3). Justin's relatively limited use of Mark was due to his interest in Jesus' teaching, which he found more satisfactorily reported in Matthew and Luke. John Knox agrees that "Justin may possibly have known and made use of all the four Gospels," but Justin was not, in his opinion, a witness "for the existence of the fourfold Gospel of which Irenaeus speaks." (*Marcion and the New Testament*, p. 149.)

[4] In Herm. Sim. IX. xx. 3, in a context treating the difficulty with which the rich enter the Kingdom, the phraseology of Mark 10:24 is exactly reproduced. See also Vis. III. vii. 3 (cf. Mark 4:18); Mand. IV. ii. 1 (cf. Mark 6:52; 8:17).

[5] Although Matthew was probably the only Gospel used by the author of the Didache, the possibility of his acquaintance with Mark is suggested by the numbering of the commandments (Did. 1:2) as in Mark 12:29-31 (cf. Matt. 22:37-39).

[6] Papias' statement as reported by Eusebius (*Hist.* III. 39. 15) is a defense of Mark's Gospel against the criticism that it lacked "order." He accounts for this on the ground that its contents represent Mark's recollections of Peter's preaching and that the apostle himself had edification in mind rather than orderly arrangement. Papias names the "Presbyter" as his source of information, which means that, whether he refers to John of Ephesus or not, he is reporting a judgment that goes back to within approximately twenty-five years of the publication of Mark. Papias' statement has much that is problematical about it, but it is clear in its assignment of authorship to John Mark. Clement of Alexandria (Euseb. *Hist.* VI. 14. 5-7) and others after him exaggerate the degree of Peter's influence, but the essential fact of Mark's authorship is never obscured.

133

Irenaeus,[7] and the Muratorian fragment.[8] External evidence consistently identifies Mark, a companion of eye-witnesses but not himself one of the original followers of Jesus, as author of the Gospel. Allusions to Mark in the New Testament add to the weight of this external testimony.[9]

The Gospel itself is anonymous, but much can be gleaned from it about its author. He was a Christian Jew who viewed Christianity as a new world religion. He knew Aramaic and was familiar with the Old Testament, which, however, he used in its Septuagint version. Certain geographical inaccuracies [10] and an overstatement regarding Jewish purification practices [11] raise the question whether or not he was a Palestinian. Other data fit in with the possibility of his Palestinian origin. Although he lacked a detailed knowledge of Galilee, he was apparently well acquainted with Jerusalem and its environs and was familiar with the larger geographical divisions of Palestine. He knew Judea was ruled by Roman procurators, that Herod was tetrarch of Galilee, and that the Sanhedrin, though supreme in matters strictly Jewish was subordinate to Roman civil

[7] To the datum of Marcan authorship, for which he was probably indebted to Papias, Irenaeus adds the detail drawn from Roman tradition that Mark wrote after the deaths of Peter and Paul (*Her.* III. 1. 1).

[8] Evidently referring to Mark's attendance on occasions when Peter preached, the Muratorian fragment opens with the broken sentence, ". . . at some of which he was present, and so wrote them down." The second-century author of the Muratorian fragment was probably acquainted with Papias' statement and with independent Roman tradition to the same general effect that Mark had personally known Peter and had used reminiscences of the apostle's preaching in writing his Gospel.

[9] The Jerusalem church met in the home of Mark's mother (Acts 12:12). Mark was associated with Paul and Barnabas in their missionary undertakings (Acts 12:25; 13:13; 15:37-39) , and was with Paul at Rome (Col. 4:10; Philem. 24). He is located at Rome as the companion of Peter and Paul in I Pet. 5:13 and II Tim. 4:11. The statements of Irenaeus and the Muratorian fragment locate Mark at Rome in connection with the ministries of Peter and Paul. Grant, however, points out the difficulties of being entirely certain that the Mark to whom early tradition attributed the authorship of the Gospel was the John Mark who figures in the book of Acts (*The Earliest Gospel,* pp. 52-57) .

[10] Mark 5:1 seems to make the country of the Gerasenes immediately contiguous to the Sea of Galilee, whereas it was inland and to the south. In Mark 7:31 Jesus is made to pass from Tyre to the Sea of Galilee by way of "the district of the Ten Towns." The order of the villages seems to be confused in Mark 11:1, Bethphage being nearer to Jerusalem than Bethany.

[11] The statement of Mark 7:3-4 that all Jews practiced this and other rites is an exaggeration. The statement may be a later explanatory addition, however.

authority. Writing in Greek and reflecting emphases and interests of the church of his own time, he at the same time produced a work which is the most Aramaic of the four Gospels, and of which the reminiscences composing the contents bear the marks of primitiveness. Although his interest is clearly in the value of history for faith, and edification accordingly takes precedence over "order," his Gospel nevertheless creates the impression of having been written by one who possessed an acquaintance with the original facts at close range.

The data supplied by the Gospel itself receive their most natural interpretation in the external testimony designating John Mark as author. Mark was not prominent enough for his name to have sufficient weight to explain its unwarranted attachment to the Gospel. Foundation in fact becomes, therefore, the natural explanation of early assignment of authorship to him. The Gospel has come down virtually as he wrote it. It does not have the characteristics of editorial expansion from a more primitive edition.

The First Readers.—The Gospel was written originally in Greek. There is no sound basis for a view of the Gospels as translations from Aramaic originals. Had Christianity remained a Palestinian movement, there might have been no Gospels. The writing of gospels was a phase of the adjustment of the Christian message to Hellenistic forms and taste. That the first readers of Mark were Hellenistic Christians is borne out by the regularity with which explanations of customs,[12] phrases,[13] and names [14] are supplied. Such explanations would have been superfluous for Palestinian readers. Christians in general rather than a limited circle seem to have composed the public to which the evangelist addressed his message.

The relatively late tradition of an Alexandrian destination for this Gospel grew out of the legend making Mark the father of Egyptian Christianity and the first bishop of the church at Alexandria.[15] The earlier and more authentic tradition locates Peter and Mark at Rome shortly before the generally accepted date for the Gospel. Presumably Mark continued to work there for a time following Peter's death and had the needs of Roman Chris-

---

[12] 7:3-4, 11; 14:12; 15:42.   [13] 5:41; 7:34.   [14] 3:17; 10:46.

[15] Chrysostom so understood the statement of Eusebius (*Hist.* II. 16. 1).

tians in mind when he wrote. Conclusive evidence, however, is lacking.[16]

Date.—Information regarding the date of Mark is not sufficiently definite to make exactitude possible. The earliest explicit allusion is the statement of Irenaeus: "After their decease [the deaths of Peter and Paul] Mark, the disciple and interpreter of Peter, handed down to us in writing the things that Peter used to preach."[17] The opening phrase of this statement probably echoes Roman opinion with reference to the date of Mark's Gospel and suggests a proper *terminus a quo*. The *terminus ad quem* is the certain use of Mark by the authors of Matthew and Luke-Acts, which makes the limits of the period within which the Gospel was written 64 to 75.

There are no clear allusions to contemporary events in the book. Except for the implicit suggestion in 9:1 of the death of the majority of Jesus' original followers, all indications of date in the book itself are found in chapter 13. The fixing of a *terminus a quo* on the basis of internal evidence depends on the interpretation of the extremely indefinite allusions of this chapter. Inferences from these data vary in locating the Gospel either just before or shortly after the destruction of Jerusalem in A.D. 70. There is general agreement as to the relevancy of that catastrophe.

The thirteenth chapter of Mark is known as the "Little Apocalypse." It was one of the ready-made sources incorporated by Mark and may already have been reduced to written form at the time. It originally had nothing to do with the fall of Jerusalem and probably expressed the speculation of some Jewish Christian regarding the bearing of the eschatological program of Daniel on the events clouding the horizon of his own time. The figure of a personal Antichrist was a familiar feature of primitive Christian speculation[18] and a part of its heritage from later Judaism.

[16] Acquaintance with the gospel story in such writings of the Roman church as Hebrews, First Clement, and First Peter more probably reflects the influence of oral tradition than of the written Gospels. However, the survival of Mark in the face of the disappearance of the other sources used by Matthew and Luke and its subsequent inclusion in the fourfold Gospel, even though its general popularity waned, indicates some such powerful church as Rome sponsored it.

[17] *Her.* III. 1. 1; Euseb. *Hist.* V. 8. 3. The statement of Clement of Alexandria (Euseb. *Hist.* VI. 14. 5-7) to the effect that Mark wrote during Peter's lifetime and with his approval reflects the later tendency to make Peter the real author of the Gospel and Mark only his amanuensis, a tendency of which the interest was apologetic rather than historical.

[18] Cf. II Thess. 2:3-12.

If the connection established between verses 1 and 2 and the body of this chapter represents the evangelist's adaptation of his source to the explanation of the destruction of the temple, and if verses 14-20 specifically refer to the horrors of the sack of Jerusalem,[19] the destruction of the city in the year 70 becomes the *terminus a quo* for the estimation of date, and the Gospel can confidently be located in the period 70-75. However, the trials of such leaders as Peter and Paul and the sufferings involved in the Neronian persecution conceivably satisfy most of the allusions.[20] The opening events of the Jewish War supply the suggestion of more ominous events to come, which were as yet undefined, and the effects thus created may be adequately accounted for by supposing the book was written shortly before the destruction of Jerusalem.[21]

The absence of specific mention of the temple in 13:14 and the employment of the indefinite clause "where he has no right to stand" may mean the temple no longer stood. The retention of the figure of the personal Antichrist, however, more probably means this clause was synonymous with "God's sanctuary." [22] The imagery could thus be interpreted to show the temple had not been destroyed. The explicitness of Luke 21:20, where the "sign" is altered to read "Jerusalem being surrounded by armies" argues strongly for the traditional connotation of Mark's imagery and indicates the temple still stood when Mark was written. The recent martyrdoms of Peter and Paul, the horrors of the Neronian persecution, and the opening phases of the Jewish War supply sufficient explanation of the situation to which the evangelist adapted the source incorporated in chapter 13. This makes 65-67 the probable date.

Place of Composition.—Clement of Rome's description of the deaths of Peter and Paul implies the two apostles were martyred at Rome during the Neronian persecution.[23] The author of First Peter, a contemporary of Clement, assumed that Peter worked at Rome and Mark was associated with him there.[24] Ignatius of Antioch in his letter to Rome referred to the active participation

---

[19] Goodspeed, *Introduction* p. 147; Scott, *Literature of the New Testament*, p. 56; Branscomb, *The Gospel of Mark*, p. xxx.

[20] Such as vss. 9, 12.

[21] Rawlinson, *The Gospel According to Mark*, p. xxx; McNeile, *Introduction*, p. 30; Taylor, *The Gospels*, p. 59.

[22] Cf. II Thess. 2:4.   [23] I Clem. 5:4-7.

[24] I Pet. 5:13; cf. Col. 4:10; Philem. 24; II Tim. 4:11.

of Peter and Paul in the affairs of the Roman church as a vivid memory during the first decade of the second century.[25] The connection with Peter affirmed for Mark's Gospel by Papias of Hierapolis seems to mean the Gospel came to Asia from Rome.[26] Following his description of Peter and Paul as "preaching the Gospel in Rome and founding the Church," Irenaeus added that after their deaths Mark "handed down to us in writing the things that Peter used to preach."[27] Clement of Alexandria, though in error in dating the Gospel during Peter's lifetime, voiced the generally accepted tradition when he explicitly said it was written at Rome.[28] The later suggestion of the Egyptian origin of the Gospel can hardly offer an alternative to its consistent association with Rome in the earliest testimony. Rome has no serious competitor as the place where Mark was written, and although the origin of the Gospel at Rome cannot be demonstrated, it remains a matter of practical certainty.

Occasion and Purpose.—The Christian message first reached Rome in the form of missionary preaching. By their nonuse of any written Gospel such writings as Hebrews, First Clement, and First Peter indicate a continued preference for the oral tradition at Rome around the close of the first century.[29] A particular crisis rather than the normal needs of the local Christian group thus seems to have inspired the writing of Mark's Gospel. The situation best corresponding to the contents of the book itself and to the earliest testimony regarding it is the aftermath of the Neronian persecution. Tacitus describes the vicious character of the officially inspired attack on the Christian community during the latter part of the year 64 and gives in some detail the kind of indignities its members suffered.[30] The deaths of Peter and Paul were the most

[25] Ign. Rom. 4:3.   [26] Euseb. *Hist.* III. 39. 15.   [27] *Her.* III. 1. 1.

[28] Euseb. *Hist.* VI. 14. 5-7. This is the earliest explicit statement that the Gospel was written at Rome.

[29] See p. 136.

[30] "To scotch the rumor [that the burning of Rome was Nero's work], Nero substituted as culprits and punished with the utmost refinements of cruelty, a class of men, loathed for their vices, whom the crowd styled Christians. First, then, the confessed members of the sect were arrested; next, on their disclosures, vast numbers were convicted, not so much on the count of arson as for hatred of the human race. And derision accompanied their end: they were covered with wild beasts' skins and torn to death by dogs; or they were fastened on crosses, and when daylight failed were burned to serve as lamps by night." (*Annals* XV. 44.)

famous of a whole series of martyrdoms which deprived the Roman church of many of its ablest leaders.[31] The bitter antagonisms aroused and the prejudices to which appeal was made in justification of the outrages lived on. After the immediate outbreak had subsided, the possibility of a renewal of mistreatment continued to exist.

Rome during the closing years of the reign of Nero provided the situation to which Mark addressed his message. The course of events seemed to presage the end, but the Parousia was apparently being delayed. Worse calamities than those already undergone appeared to be in prospect with the outbreak of the Jewish War. The world situation accentuated the threatening character of the local circumstances of Roman Christians. The needs of those Christians in their distressing condition determined Mark's purpose. The contents of the Gospel supply an account of Jesus' words and deeds adapted to provide the maximum of inspiration for his hard-pressed followers in the midst of persecution. Attention is focused on Jesus' suffering as illustrating both what all Christians must be prepared to endure and the resources available to them in the midst of trial.

In two ways the author undertakes to interpret what has happened and to fortify believers for what seemed to be in prospect. He first tries to help them see their history in proper perspective. He shows his readers the distinct advantage they enjoy over Jesus' original associates, who either missed the meaning of his message and ministry entirely or else understood them inadequately. Jesus was not the helpless victim of circumstance but a divine Savior. He was the ideal martyr, and his death was a "ransom for many." The outcome of his earthly career was providentially determined.[32] The events surrounding the closing period of his life, far from suggesting defeat, were actually the truest demonstration of Christian claims for Jesus. During his lifetime, moreover, Jesus was shown to be the Son of God [33] by the effectiveness of his teaching [34] and by the authority with which he cast out demons.[35]

[31] I Clem. 5:4-6; cf. Ign. Rom. 4:2–5:3; Euseb. *Hist.* II. 25. 7; III. 39. 15.

[32] 8:31; 9:3, 9, 13, 31; 10:33-34, 39, 45.   [33] 1:11, 24; 3:12; 5:7; 13:32; 15:39.

[34] 1:16-20, 22, 27, 38; 2:2, 13-15; 4:1; 6:2, 31-33; 9:7; 10:1; 11:18; 12:17, 34.

[35] 1:23-27, 39; 3:11-12, 22 ff.; 5:2-19; 7:25-30; 9:14-27.

In the second place, Mark glorifies the Christian's vocation. The challenge of a great task is his antidote for skepticism. Suffering, whether past or future, is incidental to the privilege of sharing the saving mission of Christ. Terrible things have transpired, and others are in prospect,[36] but the matter of transcendent importance is the proclamation of the message of salvation to all nations.[37] Those who would share in the task of Jesus must see that discipleship may lead to the cross.[38] Peter, who has recently been martyred at Rome, was once blind to that insight,[39] but his final discovery of it transformed his life and became the basis of the high esteem in which the church holds him. The greatness of Peter illustrates what the weakest disciple may become by a sufficiently complete self-identification with Christ.

Mark had no thought of writing to meet the needs of posterity. He wrote to steady the faith of the average Roman Christian in a persecution situation. He undertook to present to the Christian community at Rome such a sketch of Jesus' life and death as would justify their faith, refute the calumnies of their enemies, make the suffering of Christ intelligible, and dignify their own by showing it was the technique of saviorhood.

Message.—Textually Mark's Gospel comes to an end with 16:8. Verses 9-20, which appear in a majority of extant manuscripts, seem to have been an appendix added early in the second century to relieve the impression of abruptness created by the ending of the authentic text with verse 8 and to bring Mark more nearly into conformity with the other Gospels. The passage was probably not written specifically for this purpose. Perhaps it was built up out of materials from Luke and Matthew as a catechetical summary of the events of the postresurrection period. It was certainly not the kind of ending Mark himself had planned.[40] Although the verses occur in a numerical majority of the extant

---

[36] 13:4, 14, 23, 25.   [37] 13:10.   [38] 8:34 ff.

[39] Peter's behavior was frequently such as to require severe rebuke. He had great difficulty in seeing that discipleship involved martyrdom. Most references to him in the Gospel illustrate this: 8:33; 9:5-6; 10:31; 14:29-31, 37, 66-72. No Roman Christian was more perplexed than Peter had been.

[40] Branscomb, *op. cit.*, pp. 305-11. The clue to the kind of ending Mark wrote or planned to write is supplied in Mark 14:28; 16:7 (cf. I Cor. 15:5 ff.).

manuscripts, the weight of textual evidence and of patristic testimony is against their authenticity.[41]

The variety of endings which manuscripts of the Gospel preserve constitutes the chief evidence of the editorial character of 16:9-20:

a) In the oldest and best manuscripts [42] the text ends with verse 8. A tenth-century Armenian manuscript contains verses 9-20 but separates them from the body of the text with a note that informs the reader that "the presbyter Ariston" wrote them. Eusebius and Jerome both testify that the "accurate copies" of the Gospel end with the words of 16:8, "for they feared."

b) Other early manuscripts and versions contain what is known as the "Shorter Ending":

But they reported briefly to Peter and his companions all they had been told. And afterward Jesus himself sent out by them from the east to the west the sacred and incorruptible message of eternal salvation.

This ending appears sometimes as a marginal note and sometimes as a part of the text. It is part of the text and the only ending in the African Latin manuscript k. Elsewhere it is introduced by the words, "This also is current," and is followed by verses 9-20. There are no patristic witnesses for the Shorter Ending.

c) Verses 9-20 are known as the "Longer Ending." As already noted, they are absent from the oldest and best manuscripts, and are preceded in others by the Shorter Ending. They are, however, a part of the text of the majority of extant manuscripts, were in the text of Mark included by Tatian in his *Diatessaron* about 170, and were familiar to Irenaeus some fifteen years later. The fifth-century Freer uncial manuscript of the Gospels, known as W, has the following between verses 14 and 15 of the Longer Ending:

But they excused themselves, saying, "This age of lawlessness and unbelief lies under the sway of Satan, who will not allow what lies under the unclean spirits to understand the truth and power of God; therefore," they said to Christ, "reveal your righteousness now." Christ answered

[41] Streeter, *The Four Gospels*, pp. 335-60; B. F. Westcott and F. A. Hort, *The New Testament in the Original Greek: Appendix* (2nd ed.; London: Macmillan Co., 1907), pp. 29-51.

[42] The codices Sinaiticus and Vaticanus (fourth century), the Syro-Sinaitic palimpset (fourth or fifth century), Theta and its allied group, the oldest manuscript of the Georgian version, and three of the four oldest Armenian manuscripts.

them, "The term of years for Satan's power has now expired, but other terrors are at hand. I was delivered to death on behalf of sinners, that they might return to the truth and sin no more, that they might inherit that glory of righteousness which is spiritual and imperishable in heaven."

Whether this section was an original part of the passage and, if so, when it dropped out are matters of uncertainty.

Why the Gospel ended as the manuscripts indicate is a matter of speculation. There are three possible explanations, each with something to be said in its favor: (1) The author stopped unexpectedly in the middle of a sentence and never had the chance to resume his work. Conceivably he was arrested and put to death, or left Rome hurriedly to avoid such an eventuality and never returned.[43] (2) The original ending was removed because it failed to harmonize with the accounts of postresurrection appearances in the other Gospels.[44] (3) Most probably, the original copy of the Gospel was accidently mutilated.[45]

Two types of analysis are required for an adequate display of the thought content of Mark's Gospel. It was in the intention of its author both a story and a religious message. Its character as a message of comfort and inspiration is obscured when it is treated solely as a narrative. Equally, its value as a source of information about the career of Jesus may drop out of sight if treated exclusively as an exposition of faith.[46]

Treated as a narrative of the career of Jesus, the contents of the Gospel fall into seven divisions:

[43] Rawlinson, op. cit., p. 270.   [44] Jülicher, Introduction, p. 328.

[45] McNeile, op. cit., p. 57. A fourth possibility is that the evangelist, expecting his readers to know from oral tradition the account of the postresurrection appearances of Jesus, intentionally closed with 16:8. Its extreme improbability is discussed by Bacon in The Beginnings of Gospel Story, pp. 234-35.

[46] Ernest W. Burch some years ago described Mark's Gospel as "a closet drama, that is, drama whose power is felt by the reader without stage presentation." ("Tragic Action in the Second Gospel: A Study of the Narrative of Mark," Journal of Religion, XI [1931], 346.) The suggestion has been an extremely fruitful one for the interpreter of the Gospel. It need not be regarded as requiring the view that the appearance of history is a literary fiction and that its imposition on the materials lacked justification in fact. It can as well mean that the essentially historical record of Christian beginnings, arranged with a rarity of skill and judgment not ordinarily credited to the author of the earliest Gospel, proved itself to be what the evangelist himself regarded it, an extremely effective exposition of certain profound phases of the Christian message. See Riddle, The Gospels, pp. 141-44.

I. Title—1:1. "The beginning of the good news of Jesus Christ."
II. Introduction—1:2-13.
    1. The ministry of John the Baptist—1:2-8.
    2. The baptism of Jesus—1:9-11.
    3. The temptation of Jesus—1:12-13.
III. Jesus' ministry in eastern Galilee—1:14-7:23.
    1. Jesus proclaims "the good news from God"—1:14-3:12. A group of disciples is recruited. Conflict with Jewish leaders begins.
    2. From the appointment of the Twelve, "whom he called apostles," to the rejection of Jesus at Nazareth—3:13-6:6.
    3. From the sending forth of the Twelve to their withdrawal with Jesus to the vicinity of Tyre and Sidon—6:7-7:23.
IV. Jesus' ministry in territory of which the population was predominantly non-Jewish—7:24-9:50.
    1. From the meeting with the Syrophoenician woman to the departure to the vicinity of Caesarea Philippi—7:24-8:26.
    2. From Peter's confession to the second passion announcement—8:27-9:50.
V. Jesus' journey through Perea and Judea toward Jerusalem—10:1-50.
VI. The events of the last week—11:1-15:47.
    1. The first day—11:1-11. The entry into Jerusalem. Jesus looks about the temple. With the Twelve he retires to Bethany for the night.
    2. The second day—11:12-19. The cursing of the fig tree. Cleansing of the temple.
    3. The third day—11:20-13:37. Discourse on the withered fig tree. Church leaders challenge Jesus' authority. Efforts of representatives of various groups to "entrap" him. He disavows claims to Messiahship on the basis of Davidic descent. The eschatological discourse.
    4. The fourth day—14:1-11. Jesus anointed in the house of Simon the leper. Judas agrees to betray Jesus.
    5. The fifth day—14:12-52. Jesus eats the Passover supper with his disciples. The agony in Gethsemane. The arrest of Jesus.
    6. The sixth day—14:53-15:47. Jesus arraigned first before Jewish leaders and then before Pilate. Pilate finds no basis on which a prosecution can be justified but finally yields to clamor of accusers. Jesus is mocked, then crucified. He is buried in the tomb of Joseph.
VII. The resurrection morning—16:1-8.
    1. The women go to the tomb "very early on the first day of the week"—16:1-3.
    2. The women find the entrance to the tomb open and the tomb empty; an angel announces Jesus' resurrection—16:4-7.
    3. The women flee, frightened, and keep what they have heard to themselves—16:8.

The key to the message of Mark's Gospel is the evangelist's doctrine of the Cross. As indicated in the discussion of purpose, the twin emphases of Mark are: (1) that Jesus deliberately chose the way of the Cross as God's will for him as Savior of the world, and (2) that discipleship to such a Lord may involve martyrdom, since it contemplates participation in Christ's saving task. Saviorhood and self-renunciation are inextricably bound up together. However, martyrdom in the interest of the Kingdom contains the promise of triumph more glorious than any satisfaction of the present age. The disciple may meet death, therefore, in the confidence of sharing Jesus' resurrection triumph.

In terms of its religious message for Roman Christians, the contents of Mark fall into two divisions of nearly equal length: 1:1–9:50 and 10:1–16:8. The evangelist himself starts with the assumption of Jesus' messiahship, as indicated in the title he gives his book;[47] but he lets Jesus' contemporaries achieve that insight by the two processes of prolonged personal association and divine revelation, the one leading naturally to the other. In contrast with demons, who know Jesus because they belong to the supernatural order, all human beings hear Jesus' words and observe his deeds with amazement without being able to explain what they hear and see. What the demon immediately perceives man confronts as "mystery." Understanding of the truth has to come to man by revelation.

The climax of the first general division of the Gospel is Peter's confession.[48] This has as its reverse side Jesus' first passion announcement.[49] The Transfiguration, momentarily revealing the truth fully disclosed in the Resurrection, divinely authenticates Peter's inspired confession and Jesus' own correlation of messiahship and martyrdom.[50]

In the second half, Mark represents Jesus as continuing the kind of ministry undertaken from the outset but as more specifically devoting himself to the instruction of the disciples in the full implications of Peter's and his own declarations regarding his identity and his mission. Enemies plot his destruction and to all practical purposes appear to accomplish it. But the actualities contradict this surface appearance, and what seems a story of defeat turns out to be a record of triumph. The passion narrative pictures the climax of the struggle between the opposing forces and is itself

---

[47] 1:1.   [48] 8:27-30.   [49] 8:31-33.   [50] 9:2-8.

the climax of the entire Gospel. The Resurrection functions in the development of the story in its entirety as the Transfiguration does for the earlier half.

Three basic questions occupy the author's mind throughout his exposition: (1) Who was Jesus? (2) Why was he crucified? (3) What did he expect of his followers? A threefold answer is given each of the questions, and these answers largely constitute the evangelist's message for his first readers. Jesus is decisively shown to be Messiah [51] by the "authority" with which he taught, by his mastery over demons and over nature as demonstrated in his miracles, and by his resurrection. He is described as having been crucified because of the "envy" of Jewish leaders,[52] because of his own complete self-renunciation,[53] and because the way of the Cross was somehow God's will for him.[54] The duties and characteristics of disciples are set forth in the discourse sections that follow the three passion announcements: (1) 8:34–9-1, following the passion announcement of 8:31, stresses the obligation of disciples to be unashamed of the Son of Man and his teaching "in this unfaithful and sinful age." Courage will involve them in suffering, but the suffering will be brief, and many will "live to see the reign of God come in its might." (2) 9:33-50 and 10:13-31, following the passion announcement of 9:30-32, exalt humble service as the pathway to true greatness. (3) 10:33-45, following the passion announcement of 10:32-34, makes self-renunciation, even to the sacrifice of life itself the final test of discipleship.

[51] Mark's usual designation of Jesus as Messiah is "Son of Man." It more nearly accorded with a nonnationalistic conception of the nature of Jesus' mission as Savior. The specific repudiation of "Son of David" as an appropriate designation (12:36-37) has the effect of a disavowal of the essentially political eschatology it connoted. This rejection of nationalism from the messianic conception was made doubly significant for Mark's immediate situation by the immediately preceding direction (12:17) that payment of Roman taxes was no violation of duty to God.

[52] 15:10. No charge of lawlessness was sustained against Jesus (15:14), nor should there ever be against any true disciple (12:13-17; cf. I Pet. 4:15-16).

[53] 10:45; 14:24.

[54] 8:31; 9:31; 10:33; 14:21, 36. Grant's discussion "The Theology of Mark" (The Earliest Gospel, pp. 148-74) is helpful.

XI

THE GOSPEL OF MATTHEW

Authorship.—Early traces of acquaintance with Matthew are neither as numerous nor as clear as for Mark and Luke. The probabilities favor a knowledge of Matthew by the author of the Fourth Gospel, but the evidence is not decisive.[1] Indications that the author of Revelation knew Matthew, however, are more numerous than for Mark and Luke,[2] a fact which somewhat strengthens the case for a use of Matthew by his Ephesian contemporary, the Fourth Evangelist. The author of Second Peter probably knew Matthew as a member of the fourfold Gospel.[3]

Numerous passages in the letters of Ignatius of Antioch establish his acquaintance with the Gospel and are the basic argument for its Antiochene provenance.[4] The letter of Polycarp to the Philippians probably reflects the oral tradition; but if a written Gospel

[1] See p. 99.

[2] Charles, *The Revelation of St. John,* I, lxvi. The principal parallels are: Rev. 1:3 (cf. Matt. 26:18); 1:7 (cf. Matt. 24:30); 1:16 (cf. Matt. 17:2); 2:7 (cf. Matt. 11:15); 3:3 (cf. Matt. 24:42-44; 25:13); 3:6 (apparently a conflation of Matt. 10:32 and Luke 12:8); 13:10 (cf. Matt. 26:52); 19:9 (cf. Matt. 22:1-14; 25:1-13), where "These are the true words of God" may be derived from the imagery of the Matthaean parables.

[3] The clearest specific instance of acquaintance is the reference to the Transfiguration in II Pet. 1:17-18, where the order of the words closely parallels Matt. 3:17 and 17:5. Knox regards Irenaeus the earliest witness for the fourfold Gospel. He grants Justin may have known the four Gospels separately but doubts his acquaintance with "the fourfold Gospel of which Irenaeus speaks." Similarly, he thinks Second Peter fails "even remotely to reflect Luke." See his *Marcion and the New Testament,* pp. 142, 149. Harnack, on the other hand, thought the publication of the four Gospels as "The Gospel" happened "before the middle of the second century" rather than "shortly before the year A.D. 200." In his opinion discussions in which John the presbyter "played an authoritative part" brought the four Gospels into a single compilation. (*Origin of the New Testament,* pp. 68-72.) Moffatt thought "the four gospels . . . had begun to be read together" by the time of Papias. (*Introduction,* pp. 187, 577.)

[4] The chief of these are: Ign. Eph. 18:2 (cf. Matt. 3:15); 19:2 (cf. Matt. 2:2); Smyrn. 1:1 (cf. 3:15); 6:1 (cf. Matt. 19:12); Polyc. 1:3 (cf. Matt. 8:1-17); 2:2 (cf. Matt. 10:16).

was used, Matthew was the Gospel.[5] The Didache is demonstrably saturated with Matthaean influence.[6] For its author Matthew was "The Gospel." He seems either to have known no other Gospel or else to have ignored other Gospels. The author of the Epistle of Barnabas seems to have known Matthew. Justin Martyr knew the four Gospels and was accustomed to hearing them read at Christian services on Sunday.[7] Justin's chief interest was in Jesus' teaching, and his largest use was of materials from Matthew and Luke.[8] Similarly, the author of Second Clement used Matthew and Luke most frequently, although he knew the four Gospels and quoted them as scripture.[9]

Eusebius quotes Papias, with "John the elder" as his authority, as having said, "Matthew compiled the sayings in the Hebrew language; but everyone translated them as he was able."[10] What the elder's authority was for whatever he said and whether or not Papias correctly interpreted him as referring to the Gospel of Matthew are matters of conjecture. Rather clearly, however, Papias was referring to the completed Gospel in Greek and not to one of its sources, and he regarded it as a translation of an Aramaic original written by Matthew the apostle.[11] He was so understood by Irenaeus,[12] Origen,[13] Eusebius,[14] and Jerome.[15] Conceivably the Fourth Gospel was regarded as normative by Papias, and his statements about Mark and Matthew may have involved the tacit criticism that in their Greek forms they were the work of "interpreters" rather

[5] The relevant passages are: Polyc. Phil. 2:3 (cf. Matt. 7:1, 2; 5:3, 10); 6:2 (cf. Matt 6:12); 7:2 (cf. Matt. 6:13; 26:41); 12:3 (cf. Matt. 5:44).

[6] Streeter, *The Four Gospels*, pp. 507-11. In Kirsopp Lake, *The Apostolic Fathers*, I, note the numerous marginal notations of indebtedness to Matthew.

[7] *Apol.* 67:3.

[8] Justin was acquainted with all four of the canonical Gospels. He quotes them at times as though he regarded them as scripture, but it was probably the words of Jesus rather than the books containing them that he so regarded. There are twenty-six instances in the *Apology* and fifty in the *Dialogue* in which Justin clearly shows he knew Matthew. He seems to have preferred the Matthaean to the Lukan record of Jesus' teaching, as he uses it about twice as frequently.

[9] II Clem. 2:4.   [10] *Hist.* III. 39. 16.

[11] Jülicher, *Introduction*, p. 302; Easton, *Christ in the Gospels*, p. 23.

[12] *Her.* III. 1, 1; cf. Euseb. *Hist.* V. 8. 2.

[13] Fragment of commentary on Matthew preserved in Euseb. *Hist.* VI. 25. 4.

[14] *Hist.* III. 24. 6.

[15] *Lives of Illustrious Men* III; preface to the Vulgate version.

than apostles and so had only a secondary authority.[16] Such an interest on the part of Papias could have created a misunderstanding on his part of the tradition to which he gave currency. However that may be, his statement is the earliest specific reference to the authorship of this Gospel, and it is almost certainly erroneous in both of its particulars.

The Greek of the Gospel reveals none of the qualities of a translation. Its uniformity of language and style rather indicate it was written originally in Greek, as do its agreements in Greek with Mark and with the Greek documentary source used by its author in common with Luke. There is, furthermore, no evidence showing even an acquaintance with Hebrew on the part of the author of this Gospel. He makes no independent use of the Old Testament in Hebrew, but customarily quotes the Septuagint version. Nor is it understandable for one of the Twelve to have relied, as this evangelist demonstrably did, on secondary accounts of the life and the message of Jesus.

Christians probably wrote nothing in Aramaic. The extant documents from the earliest period are all in Greek, as were the documentary sources they presuppose. Christian leaders first reduced their messages to writing probably as a phase of the Gentile mission. If there is a residuum of solid historical fact, then, in the Papias tradition, it amounts to no more than that the disciple Matthew was influential in the organization of Jesus' sayings in oral form for the purposes of catechetical instruction, with the result that the association of his name with the oral formulation continued when it was put into written form in Greek at Antioch approximately a quarter of a century before the author of our Greek Gospel made use of it there.

The Gospel itself does not claim to have been written by Matthew,[17] nor does it supply a hint of the identity of the author. It does, however, reveal items of interest about him more important than his name. The remoteness of many of his allusions and his dependence on secondary sources show clearly that he did not

[16] Moffatt, *loc. cit.;* Harnack, *loc. cit.*

[17] In Matt. 9:9 the tax collector, who in Mark 2:14 and Luke 5:27 is known as Levi, is given the name of Matthew. It is possible that the man had two names; but it is also possible, as E. F. Scott suggests, that a later hand altered Levi's name as a means of establishing this slight connection of Matthew with the Gospel attributed to him by tradition (*Literature of the New Testament*, p. 66).

write as an eye-witness. He resembled Paul in his conception of Christianity as destined for all nations,[18] but in his formulation of religion as normative teaching he was basically different from Paul. His rejection of the legalism of Judaism [19] was by no means a rejection of the legalistic principle but rather the repudiation of an inferior and outmoded system of teaching for a new and authoritative message the validity of which was beyond question.[20]

The evangelist is ordinarly assumed to have been a Hellenistic Jew, and certain qualities of the Gospel carry that suggestion. His formulation of religion as law, like the style and subject sequence of the teaching sections, suggests a Jewish turn of mind. Respect for the scribal office, however unworthy the behavior of particular scribes,[21] lends itself to such a conception of the author. His sympathy for Israel, despite his interpretation of her woes as divine penalties for the rejection of Jesus,[22] might identify him as a Jew.

Characteristics more directly related to the writer's personality make it difficult to regard him as a Jew. Paul was optimistic about his "natural kindred," [23] but no vestige of such optimism remains for the author of Matthew. He never bases religious status on Jewishness.[24] He knows no Jewish parallel for such faith as a Roman captain demonstrated.[25] The representation of the original mission of Jesus as restricted to the Jews [26] emphasizes the justness of their subsequent and final abandonment [27] in the interest of the evangelization of "all the heathen." [28] Where the author's own point of view appears, it is characteristically un-Jewish and even anti-Jewish. Scribes and Pharisees cease to be groups within Judaism and become typical of Judaism as such. The startling bitterness and hostility apparent in the twenty-third chapter seem to be elements in an indictment of Judaism as Christianity's irreconcilable rival.

[18] 24:14; 28:19. [19] 5:20. [20] 5:21-48. [21] 14:18; 23:1-3.
[22] 23:37-39; 27:35. [23] Rom. 9:4-6; 11:25-32. [24] 3:9-10.

[25] 8:5-13; cf. Luke 7:1-10. The friendly delegation of Jews who in Luke plead that Jesus assist the Roman captain do not figure in Matthew's story. Instead the Matthaean emphasis is that "the heirs" will be deprived of their heritage and be "driven into the darkness outside," and non-Jews will be shown to be Abraham's true descendants.

[26] 10:5-7; but even this original restriction can be overstated, as the incident of 15:21-28 shows.

[27] This is the point for the evangelist of the parables of 20:1-16; 21:23-46; 22:1-14. The specific statement of 21:43 that Gentiles will displace Jews as heirs of the Kingdom summarizes the teaching of the entire series.

[28] 28:15, 19.

Jesus is represented as consciously creating a movement which could never come to terms with Judaism and must therefore supplant it. The appearances of Jewishness in the Gospel probably belong to the traditional materials utilized by the author and testify to the historicity of the materials rather than the Jewishness of the author.[29]

The First Readers.—Patristic witnesses responsible for the tradition that this Gospel was written by Matthew "in the Hebrew language" are also responsible for the tradition that its first reading public was Jewish. The total weight of the evidence supplied by the book itself shows it was written originally in Greek for non-Jewish readers.

Its author never makes the slightest effort to win Jews over to Christianity, nor does he appear to have entertained an idea of the likelihood of their future conversion. He thought Christian missionaries should devote their undivided attention and energy to the evangelization of Gentiles, God himself having completely abandoned the Jews because of their rejection and crucifixion of Jesus.[30] That a Gospel so un-Jewish and even anti-Jewish in its basic point of view should have been written primarily for Jewish readers is wholly improbable. True, the evangelist claims the Old Testament for the church, but for the anti-Jewish purpose of proving from it God's utter rejection of the Jews and in their stead the election of the Christian community as the channel through which his continuing purposes will come to fruition.

The identification of a particular group of Gentile Christians for whose benefit this book was originally produced can be only approximately accurate. As will be seen, all evidence points to Syrian Antioch as the place of its composition, and the predication of the Antiochene Christian community as the reading public the author had in mind best fits the contents of the book.

Date.—According to tradition Matthew was the earliest of the Gospels and might even have antedated the Gentile mission.[31] Irenaeus, Clement of Alexandria, Origen, and Eusebius apparently subscribed to this view. Their testimony is rendered valueless for

[29] The reference of 13:52 is more probably due to the creativeness with which the author handles his traditional materials than to his own scribal background and training.

[30] 21:43; 22:8, 14; 23:14, 35-39; 27:25.

[31] Iren. *Her.* III. 1. 1; Euseb. *Hist.* III. 24. 6; VI. 14. 5; VI. 25. 4-6.

the determination of the *terminus a quo* of the Gospel because the data of the documents themselves establish the priority of Mark and the composition of Matthew in Greek for Hellenistic readers.

Other external evidence dependably establishes a *terminus ad quem*. Ignatius and the author of the Didache both knew Matthew. Almost as certainly the author of Revelation was influenced by it. Moreover, in the localities and literature where the earliest traces of acquaintance with Matthew are found there exist almost equally abundant indications of acquaintance with the collected letters of Paul.[32] The total absence from Matthew of any consciousness of the existence of Paul's published letters argues that the Gospel was written before the letters were collected and published. These data combine to fix 95 as a later limit for the period to which Matthew belongs.

The use of Mark in approximately its extant form by the author of Matthew and his view of the destruction of Jerusalem as an accomplished event[33] establish 70 as the earlier limit of the the period. When the effort is made to establish the date more narrowly within the limits of 70-95, differences of opinion appear. Certain considerations tend to identify the book with the decade immediately following the destruction of Jerusalem. Other equally relevant data point to the closing five years of the period. The respective judgments depend on whether the heightened apocalypticism of the book[34] or its pronouncedly ecclesiastical interests[35]

[32] See my *Paul Becomes a Literary Influence.*

[33] In 22:7 the detail about the burning of the city of those who "proved unworthy" of the king's invitation violates the imagery of the parable. It is not a part of the story as Luke tells it (14:16-24) and is best accounted for in Matthew as a reminiscence of the burning of Jerusalem. Similarly, the terrible indictment of the Jewish people in 23:35-36 indicates that the destruction of Jerusalem was a vivid memory and was regarded by the author as a fulfillment of this pronouncement of doom.

[34] Harnack, *Chronologie*, I, 653-54; Goodspeed, *Introduction*, pp. 159, 176-77. The lament of 23:37-39 following immediately upon the indictment of 23:35-36 suggests that the destruction of Jerusalem is recent. Note the very different contexts of the parallels in Luke 11:49-51; 13:34-35. The addition of "immediately" in Matt. 24:39 (cf. Mark 13:24) and of "soon" in 26:64 (cf. Mark 14:62) indicates the author's expectation that the Parousia would follow shortly upon the fall of Jerusalem. The avoidance of a resort to violence enjoined in 26:52 is better satisfied by the conditions that pertained just prior to the Jewish War of 66-70 when Christians withdrew to Pella (Euseb. *Hist.* III. 5. 3) than by those forming the prelude to the revolt of Bar Kochba when Jewish neighbors urged Christians to take up arms (Just. *Apol.* 31:6). Indications of time separation from the original events and of an awareness of the problem of the delay of

are regarded as central and determinative. Probably the data are best satisfied by a date of 75-80.

Place of Composition.—Patristic opinion suggesting a Palestinian origin for Matthew grew out of Irenaeus' understanding of Papias' statement that "Matthew compiled the sayings in the Hebrew language." As Streeter pointed out,[36] the statement has only the negative value of identifying the book with the East rather than with Rome. The exclusive use of Matthew by Ignatius and the author of the Didache strongly suggests Syrian Antioch as the place where it was written. Such a conclusion fits the data of the Gospel.

Rome maintained close contact with Antioch, and the arrival of Mark in Syria shortly after its publication in the West and its almost immediate incorporation in an Antiochene Gospel are entirely understandable. Antioch with its enormous Jewish population would naturally require the establishment of those distinctions between Christianity and Judaism on which the author of Matthew insists. Antioch would also naturally welcome a formulation of Christianity as authoritative teaching. Antioch was, furthermore, the natural refuge for Christian fugitives from Palestine,[37] whose interests are reflected in the Matthaean source known as "M."[38] The heightened apocalypticism of Matthew probably made an effective appeal in Antioch at about the time the Gospel was written.[39] Its universalism and strong institutional consciousness were most ap-

the Parousia (24:48; 25:5; 27:8; 28:15) need mean no more than such a lapse of time since the days of Jesus as would be involved between 30 and 75.

[35] McNeile, *Introduction,* pp. 31-33; Grant, *Growth of the Gospels,* p. 183; Riddle, *The Gospels,* pp. 164-78. The eschatology of Matthew is held to be didactic rather than realistic. The atmosphere of imminence is gone, and the traditional expectation of the Parousia is used merely as motivation for joining the church and being governed by its teaching. The threat of conflict with civil authority (10:18) and an eagerness to establish the political harmlessness of Christianity (17:27; 27:11-24, 58) suggest the reign of Domitian. Christian prophets who are renegades (7:15, 22), veneration of the apostles (8:26; cf. Eph. 3:5; Rev. 21:14), the church conceived as endowed with power to discipline and even excommunicate (16:18; 18:15-19), a conscious program of world evangelism with the expectation of a sufficiently long future for its realization (28:18-20) reflects developments that are held to belong to the closing decade of the first century.

[36] *Op. cit.,* p. 500.   [37] Acts 11:19.   [38] See pp. 111-13.

[39] Rev. 11:1-2 incorporates an earlier source written at about the time of the fall of Jerusalem and probably reflecting Syrian opinion. It expected the end of the age in about 74, three and one half years after September 4, 70. The Nero redivivus myth also had great vitality in Syria.

propriate for the community where the Greek mission originated [40] and where "the disciples first came to be known as Christians." [41] Although specific testimony identifying Matthew with Antioch is lacking, the great Syrian city has no competitor with equally strong credentials, and is accordingly the center where the Gospel of Matthew is usually located.

Occasion and Purpose.—The idea that the intention of the author of this Gospel was to supply the Jews with a written version of his message to compensate for his personal ministry "when he was about to go also to others" [42] hardly does justice to the real problems reflected in the Gospel. Christianity had ceased to be a movement within Judaism. Moreover, it had largely lost its appeal for Jews, and no further expenditure of evangelistic effort in their direction seemed warranted. Christianity had accordingly undertaken to distinguish itself completely from Judaism.

For some decades the chief growth of the Christian movement had been among non-Jews. The Jewish War of 66-70, which ended in the destruction of Jerusalem, accelerated the trends already tending to make the synagogue and the church bitter rivals. The relative failure of Christianity in its original environment required an explanation advantageous to the church.[43] It made doubly imperative an exposition of Christianity that distinguished it as a religion of redemption from its Hellenistic rivals and from Judaism. This definition of the distinctive character of Christianity was the primary objective of the author of Matthew. His representation of Jesus as the supremely authoritative teacher discloses his basic emphasis. He undertook above all else to give Jesus' message such compelling force as to induce believers actually to order their lives by the lofty ideals Jesus had proclaimed. For the enforcement of those ideals the author relied on the appeal which his elaborate and carefully wrought display of Jesus' teaching would make, on the enthusiasm generated by the heightened apocalyptic eschatology that served as a theological framework for the teaching, and on the disciplinary authority with which he invested the church.[44]

The relatively recent catastrophe of the destruction of Jerusalem supplied the author's theological and practical incentives. That fearful event became for him the convincing sign of the nearness

---

[40] Acts 11:20; 13:2 ff.   [41] Acts 11:26.   [42] Euseb. *Hist.* III. 24. 6.
[43] Cf. Rom. 9–11.   [44] 18:15-20.

of the Parousia hitherto unaccountably delayed. It served to demonstrate the blameworthiness of the Jews for their rejection of Jesus and to establish God's transference to the church of the destiny originally belonging to Israel. The atmosphere of imminence pervading Matthew cannot be accounted for entirely by the traditional character of the source materials incorporated. Nor is it a purely formal didactic device. It expresses the author's sincere conviction of the nearness of the end.

The motive of apocalyptic eschatology was always basically practical. It was the form prophecy took in times of crisis. It sought to persuade rather than forecast. It furnished ground for optimism in the midst of adversity. It aimed at the creation of emotional effects sufficiently profound to inspire heroic fidelity and make the immediate costs of righteousness appear irrelevant. The author of the Gospel of Matthew employed it in complete good faith to give effect to Jesus' teaching as the basis of God's impending judgment. The punishment of the Jews in the destruction of Jerusalem was symbolic of the eternal damnation in store for all who refused to obey Jesus' words as the revelation of God's law. The church as the new Israel was challenged to duplicate within its corporate life the pattern which Jesus' teaching described as normal in the coming Kingdom. As the corollary of that expectation the church was also charged to "make disciples of all the heathen, . . . and teach them to observe all the commands" Jesus had given.

Message.—The narrative framework of Matthew is substantially that of Mark. Following chapters 1 and 2, which function as a preamble, and for which Mark has no equivalent, the general course of the story is the same:

> Period of preparation—3:1–4:11=Mark 1:2-13
> Ministry in eastern Galilee—4:12–13:58=Mark 1:14–7:23
> Ministry in northern Galilee—14:1–18:35=Mark 7:24–9.50
> Journey through Perea and Judea—19:1–20:35=Mark 10:1-50
> Last week in Jerusalem—21:1–27:66=Mark 11:1–15:47
> The Resurrection—28:1-20=Mark 16:1-8

Throughout, however, Matthew freely alters the details of individual stories, embellishes, abridges, and summarizes the narrative, and in 4:22 through 13:53 rearranges the order of the materials derived from Mark.

The exact order of Mark 1:1-20 is followed in Matt. 3:1–4:22.

Thereafter the content of Mark 1:21–3:6 is summarized in Matt.
4:23-25; and the stories, except for 1:23-28 and 1:35-38, which are
omitted, are postponed to later contexts. Matthew's redistribution of
the materials of Mark 1:22–5:43 is as follows:

> Mark 1:29-34=Matt. 8:14-17
> Mark 1:40-45=Matt. 8:1-4
> Mark 2:1-12=Matt. 9:1-8
> Mark 2:23-28=Matt. 12:1-8
> Mark 3:1-6=Matt. 12:9-14
> Mark 3:7-12=Matt. 12:15-21
> Mark 3:31-35=Matt. 12:46-50
> Mark 4:35–5:20=Matt. 8:23-34
> Mark 5:22-43=Matt. 9:18-26

This manipulation of the order of the materials does not appear
to have been due to the possession of other narrative sources or to
a primary interest in the narrative as such. It seems rather to be
explained by a concern for the effective presentation of five great
masses of teaching material—chapters 5-7; 10; 13; 18; 23-25—which
have been systematically arranged by the evangelist into formal
discourses.[45] Although the situation that fits the first discourse corresponds to Mark 3:7-12, the discourse is actually bracketed between verses 21 and 22 of Mark 1, and the narrative of Mark 1:21–
3:6 is summarized in Matt. 4:23-25.[46] The stories composing this
section of Mark's narrative are postponed and in combination with
other materials constitute the introductions of the next two discourses, as follows: For the second discourse, chapter 10,

> Matt. 8:1-4=Mark 1:40-45
> Matt. 8:14-17=Mark 1:29-34
> Matt. 8:23-34=Mark 4:35–5:20

[45] Each discourse closes with a formula that serves to introduce the succeeding phase of the narrative background: 7:28; 11:1; 13:53; 19:1; 26:1.

[46] Mark's description of the impression created by Jesus' preaching in the
Capernaum synagogue (1:22) is used in Matthew (7:28-29) to describe the effect
of the Sermon on the Mount. By contrast with Mark's emphasis on Jesus'
ministry in the synagogues, Matthew refers to it incidentally in such summaries
as 4:23 and 9:35. Not until 12:9-14, which is part of the narrative preamble to
the discourse on the spiritual obtuseness of the leaders of the Jewish church
(chap. 13), is a story with a synagogue setting given in any detail. This probably
reflects the author's desire to distinguish the church from the synagogue.

Matt. 9:1-8=Mark 2:1-12
Matt. 9:18-26=Mark 5:22-43

For the third discourse, chapter 13,

Matt. 11 does not draw on Mark
Matt. 12:1-8=Mark 2:23-28
Matt. 12:9-14=Mark 3:1-6
Matt. 12:15-21=Mark 3:7-12
Matt. 12:46-50=Mark 3:31-35

In Matt. 13:54 the Marcan order is again resumed at Mark 6:1 and is thereafter followed. Except for characteristic retouching and embellishment the narrative background for the discourses of Matt. 18 and 23-25 is almost exclusively Marcan, and the materials retain their original ordering.

Rather clearly the function of narrative in Matthew is to focus attention on the teaching sections. This concentration of attention on Jesus' message discloses the evangelist's distinctive point of view and supplies the best clue for an analysis of the Gospel in terms of its message. The evident concern of the Gospel is to present Jesus as a teacher to whom, because of his unique relation to God, the ultimate revelation of truth was made.[47] Since Jesus' words are a report of that revelation, obedience to his message is man's supreme duty and the condition of God's approval on the Day of Judgment.[48] World evangelization consists in teaching all men everywhere to obey all the things Jesus "commanded."[49] By his arrangement and extensive report of Jesus' message the evangelist undertook to give the Christian revelation explicit relevance for the problems confronting the church of his times.

In addition to a preamble[50] and an epilogue,[51] the message of the Gospel falls into five grand divisions: 3:1-7:29; 8:1-10:42;

[47] 11:27-30.

[48] The imminence of the final judgment is constantly stressed, and the apocalyptic coloring of the traditional materials is everywhere heightened. Eschatological sanctions of reward and punishment supply the incentives for obedience to Jesus' teaching in each of the great discourses. The climax of the Gospel is the final discourse on the Judgment of the Son of Man. The hardships Christians endure and the heroic ideals by which they are called to live do not exceed their strength because of the nearness of the end and the gloriousness of their rewards in the Kingdom.

[49] 28:19-20.   [50] Chaps. 1-2.   [51] Chaps. 26-28.

11:1–13:58; 14:1–18:35; 19:1–25:46. The principal feature of each division is the formal discourse it embodies. Each discourse is introduced by a collection of stories, mostly drawn from Mark and editorially arranged to contribute to the exposition of the theme of the discourse.[52] Narrative and discourse complement each other in this presentation of Jesus' message for the church.

For this evangelist the words of Jesus are an authoritative revelation by which godly men will order their lives. Their authority inheres in the uniqueness of Jesus' relation to God. An exposition of the basis of that relationship is therefore a natural preface to the presentation of the message. The presentation of Jesus in the preamble as Son of David and Son of Man has that function.[53]

Having thus accredited Jesus, the author proceeds immediately to his elaborate presentation of the righteousness required for approval in the judgment at which Jesus as Messiah will determine the eternal destinies of men.[54] A narrative introduction [55] sketching the ministry and message of John the Baptist and the inauguration of Jesus' own ministry represents the multitudes who listened to them both as the nucleus of the Christian church. This narrative supplies a dramatic background for the Sermon on the Mount.[56] Not until 12:9-13 does Matthew tell a story detailing Jesus' activity in a synagogue service. The sequel to the story is that "the Pharisees left the synagogue and consulted about him, with a view to putting him to death." [57] Those who hear the first Matthaean discourse are the multitudes who have broken with the synagogue and implicitly constitute the Christian church.

The Sermon on the Mount, then, has the character of an authoritative guide in Christian living for new converts. Jewish legalism is shown to be hopelessly defective; and Christianity, stated in terms of normative teaching, is urged in its stead. By comparison with Moses and John the Baptist and the many others through whom God has previously spoken, Jesus as the Son, in the words of a younger Roman contemporary of the evangelist, "is entitled to as much more honor . . . as the builder of a house" by comparison with "the house he builds"; he is the "son set over the house of God," and the listening group who obey the Son's commands "are

---

[52] This is the view set forth by Bacon in *Studies in Matthew*. It is regarded as basically sound and is adopted as the principle in accordance with which the message of the Gospel can best be stated.

[53] 1:1–2:23.   [54] 3:1–7:29.   [55] 3:1–4:25.   [56] 5:1–7:29.   [57] 12:14.

that house." [58] The teaching emphases of the Sermon on the Mount are: (1) a Christian decalogue,[59] (2) Christ's commandments as a fulfillment of the law of Moses,[60] (3) the spirituality of Christian worship,[61] (4) righteousness as the Christian's only care,[62] (5) the family character of the Christian community,[63] (6) the parental character of God as the warrant for Christian prayer,[64] and (7) the adequacy and authority of Jesus' message as a revelation of God's will.[65]

But discipleship to Christ inherently involves a missionary obligation. The continuation of Jesus' saving ministry in deed and in word is understood to be the essence of that obligation. Accordingly the evangelist makes the next phase of his exposition a portrayal of the Christian missionary, his resources, incentives, and methods.[66] Ten miracle stories constitute the major portion of the narrative section. These stories serve a twofold function. They illustrate Jesus' triumphant faith, and they suggest the availability to disciples of the resources by which Jesus performed his mighty deeds.[67] The two nonmiraculous stories of the series [68] illustrate Jesus' requirement of unequivocal obedience as the condition of sharing his spiritual effectiveness. The connection between these stories and the commissioning of the Twelve as the first missionaries is established by the account of Jesus' pity for the bewildered multitudes.[69] They are said to have reminded him of "sheep that have no shepherd" and of an abundant harvest with no laborers to gather it.

The instructions given the Twelve function as the evangelist's interpretation of the spirit and task of Christian missions.[70] Jesus' own spiritual effectiveness is to be the continuing experience, not merely the fond memory, of the missionary. The awe of the multitude "who praised God for giving such power to men" expresses this confidence.[71] The experience of the Twelve illustrates God's collaboration with missionaries. Their commission involves the extension of the ministry of Jesus.[72] Their responsibility is to "the lost sheep of Israel's house." [73] Self-interest is never to affect their decisions.[74] Persecution and suffering will be their lot.[75] Who-

[58] Heb. 1:1-3; 3:3-6.   [59] 5:1-16.   [60] 5:17-48.   [61] 6:1-18.
[62] 6:19-34.   [63] 7:1-6.   [64] 7:7-12.   [65] 7:13-28.
[66] 8:1–10:42.   [67] 8:1–9:38.   [68] 8:19-22; 9:9-17.   [69] 9:34-38.
[70] 10:1-42.   [71] 9:8.   [72] 10:1-5.   [73] 10:6-7.
[74] 10:8-15.   [75] 10:16-39.

ever assists them "will have the same reward as a prophet."[76]

The narrative and discourse sections create assurance of the availability to missionaries of the divine guidance and support on which Jesus depended. Because of this, courage and utter fidelity should characterize the missionary. Not only so, but the coming of the Son of Man is imminent, and all who have in any way helped teach men to observe "the commands" of Christ will be gloriously rewarded.

The Christian community as Jesus' spiritual family is the evangelist's next theme.[77] Jesus' deeds and words were enigmatic to his formally religious Jewish contemporaries. His beneficence and wisdom actually appeared evil in origin to them. Where they saw only mystery, however, the spiritually endowed discovered the true credentials of messiahship and became disciples of Jesus. The entire series of stories composing the narrative portion of this section illustrates the hopeless and culpable blindness of the leaders and members of the Jewish church.[78] But a "remnant" had seeing eyes and hearing ears; and when the Pharisees plotted Jesus' death, these were loyal to him and became his spiritual family, the nucleus of the church of the future.[79]

The seven parables composing the body of the discourse of chapter 13 show the cleavage Jesus' message creates between the spiritually alive and the spiritually dead. Faith expresses itself in vital response to his teaching, and this response is shown to involve the principle of divine judgment. The parable of the dragnet [80] is the seventh of the series of parables and the climax of the discourse. As construed, it suggests a sifting of the membership of the Christian church analogous to the sifting of national Israel which Jesus' historical ministry precipitated. The visible church will thereby be differentiated from the spiritual church. False teachers among Christian leaders are denounced as spiritual descendants of the scribes and Pharisees. Jesus' spiritual family, the true church, are those who obey the spiritual intent of his message.

Matthew alone of the four Gospels speaks of the church as such. A distinctly ecclesiastical interest, which appears most clearly in the additions this evangelist makes to the narrative and discourse materials taken over from Mark, permeates the Gospel in its en-

[76] 10:40-42.   [77] 11:1-13:58.   [78] 11:1-12:50.
[79] 12:15-21, 46-50.   [80] 13:47-50.

tirety. This interest is specifically developed in the account of the origin and function of the church in 14:1–18:35. The church is regarded as having had its spiritual origin in the faith Peter voiced in his confession at Caesarea Philippi.[81] This faith was shared, however, by the Twelve,[82] who typify the Christian community. Thus the authority and responsibility delegated by Jesus to Peter[83] actually belongs to the church, whose faith Peter expressed.[84]

In the narrative phase of the development of his theme[85] the evangelist follows the order and largely reproduces the contents of Mark 6:14–9:32.[86] His distinctive emphases appear in his four significant additions to Mark's story, all of them giving prominence to Peter: (1) At Mark 6:50 he adds the story of Peter's effort to walk on the water.[87] Although the disciples at first think they see a "ghost," Peter ventures to brave the storm at Jesus' command. When he wavers, Jesus rescues him, whereupon the disciples confess Jesus as "certainly God's Son." Here is implicitly the faith of the church in the risen Lord, who will always be in the midst of believers, and who will visibly return to inaugurate his eternal Kingdom. (2) To Peter rather than to the disciples in general[88] Jesus explains the distinction between tradition and the essentials of the Law. There is a careful avoidance of the radical generalization of Mark 7:19b, "So he declared all food clean." The evangelist makes spiritual newness the distinguishing mark of Christian living. He nevertheless vests in the designated leaders of the church the authority to distinguish between primary and secondary values. (3) At Mark 8:29 he expands the account of the confession of Peter and stresses its crucial importance for the church.[89] The reference to the "gates of hell" expresses the church's faith in the risen Christ who had overcome the "powers of death" and can guarantee the church's triumph. The "keys of the Kingdom of Heaven" given to Peter and through him to the church, whose faith he expresses, symbolize the divinely conferred prerogative to declare commands obsolete or obligatory. Thus the church may at one and the same time denounce antinomianism and by the authorization of the glorified Christ formulate the Christian message afresh. (4) At Mark 9:32 instead of reporting Jesus' address upon arrival at

[81] 16:17.   [82] 14:33.   [83] 16:19.   [84] 18:18-20.
[85] 14:1–17:27.   [86] Omitting only Mark 8:22-26; cf. Matt. 15:31.
[87] 14:28-31.   [88] 15:15; cf. Mark 7:17.   [89] 16:17 ff.

Capernaum [90] he first interjects the story of the temple tax.[91] The net effect of the story is to dissociate the church from the synagogue and to show the thoroughly conciliatory attitude of the church toward the Roman government.

The discourse of 18:1-35 is an adaptation of Mark 9:33-50. There is a studied omission of Mark 9:38-40 as too latitudinarian for sound church administration. The admonition in 18:10 regarding the "children" whose "angels" have continual access to God sounds the dominant note of the entire discourse. There follows the parable of the lost sheep,[92] directions for the settlement of disputes between Christians,[93] the affirmation of the authority of the church,[94] and the teaching on the forgiveness of sins.[95] For none of the discourse beyond 18:10 is there a Marcan parallel.

As with the narrative introduction, the clue to the evangelist's emphasis in the discourse is found in Peter's question in 18:21. Peter is the great exemplar of the church's faith, and the authority delegated to him [96] belongs to the church as a disciplinary institution.[97] The "children who believe" [98] are not literally children but immature and wayward members of the Christian community. To Peter, then, and to future leaders who take him as their example, directions are given for properly dealing with the increasingly miscellaneous membership of the church. They must be solicitous for the inexperienced and the weak,[99] like good shepherds, going in search "for the one that is astray," [100] exercising authority over disputing church members,[101] magnifying the worth of persons by dealing redemptively with sinners.[102]

In each of the earlier discourses eschatological sanctions have served as incentives to obedience. The constant stress on the imminence of judgment functioned to discourage unsound teaching and to enforce types of teaching approved by the church. The reality of the author's personal concern with eschatology is indicated by the consistency with which he heightens the apocalyptic coloring of traditional materials by comparison with their use in the other Gospels. The elaborate development of the theme of judgment in 19:1-25:46 is therefore the logical climax of this Gospel.

[90] Cf. Mark 9:33-50.
[91] 17:24-27.
[92] 18:12-14; cf. 15:4-7.
[93] 18:15-17.
[94] 18:18-20.
[95] 18:21-35.
[96] 16:19.
[97] 18:18-20.
[98] 18:6, 10, 14.
[99] 18:1-9.
[100] 18:10-14.
[101] 18:15-20.
[102] 18:21-35.

Throughout 19:1–22:46 the evangelist relies almost entirely on the narrative of Mark 10:1–12:37.[103] Jesus' message is described as implicit in the Mosaic commandments, which he sought to enforce in their inner intent.[104] Jewish leaders misjudged Jesus because they misunderstood Moses.[105] Because Moses was in essential agreement with Jesus, they confounded themselves when they tried to entrap him.[106] Thus the author builds a background for the terrible denunciation of the scribes and Pharisees,[107] for the interpretation of the destruction of Jerusalem as a premonitory sign of the nearness of the judgment,[108] and for the exposition of the conditions of divine approval at this judgment.[109]

Matthew follows Mark's account of the Passion and Resurrection with no variations in order and with relatively few variations in content.[110] The evangelist makes certain additions[111] of which the general effect is to fix responsibility for the Crucifixion exclusively on the Jews, both leaders and people, and to extend the guilt of this deed to posterity. In line with this severe attitude toward the Jews he makes all question of Jesus' resurrection the outgrowth of Jewish calumny. The climax of the epilogue is the commission to the disciples to "make disciples of all heathen, . . . and teach them to observe all the commands" of Jesus in preparation for the end of the age.

[103] The principal additions are 20:1-16 (at Mark 10:31); 21:14-16 (at Mark 11:18); 21:28-32 (at Mark 11:33); 21:43-45 (at Mark 12:11); 22:1-14 (at Mark 12:12). The net effect of these additions is to accentuate the impression of the spiritual incapacity of Jewish religious leaders.

[104] 19:1–20:28.   [105] 20:29–22:14.   [106] 22:15-46.   [107] 23:1-36.

[108] 23:37–24:44.   [109] 24:45–25-46.   [110] 26:1–28:20.

[111] 26:52-53 (at Mark 14:47); 27:3-11 (at Mark 15:1); 29:19 (at Mark 15:10); 27:52-53 (at Mark 15:38); 27:62-66 (at Mark 15:47); 28:2-4 (at Mark 16:2). At 26:56 there is an omission of Mark 14:51.

XII

LUKE-ACTS

UNIFORMITY of vocabulary and numerous stylistic affinities establish with certainty the common authorship of the Gospel and the Acts. Allusions in their two prefaces make the latter the sequel to the former. That the two volumes were a literary unit and not two separate works by the same author, though less universally conceded,[1] represents an increasingly impressive consensus of opinion.

The contents of the books make them best understood as integral parts of a larger whole, conceived and executed as such. The purview of the preface to the Gospel exceeds the limits of that volume as definitely as the introduction to the Acts presupposes it. The account of "the movement which has developed among us" is merely begun in the Gospel and requires the continuation given in the Acts. That the two were originally planned to complement each other appears from the preface to the Acts: "In my first volume, Theophilus, I dealt with all that Jesus did and taught from the beginning until the day when . . . he . . . was taken up to heaven."[2] At the precise juncture here indicated a second phase of the account of the rise and expansion of Christianity begins, and to this the second volume is devoted. That the two volumes are halves of the treatment of a common theme is further illustrated by such details as the prospect in Luke 9:51 of Jesus' being "taken up to heaven" and the account of the event in Acts 1:9-11, and the promise of enduement with "power from on high" in Luke 24:49 and the story in Acts 2:1-4 of the bestowal of the Spirit.

The separation of the two volumes and their consequent treat-

---

[1] Streeter views the Acts as the sequel to the Gospel but regards it as doubtful that "when Luke wrote the Gospel he already anticipated a sequel" (*The Four Gospels*, p. 533).

[2] Acts 1:1-2. Josephus *Against Apion* II. 1 supplies a perfect parallel in the preface to the second volume of his two-volume treatise: "In the first volume, most honored Epaphroditus, I have demonstrated our antiquity and confirmed the truth of what I have said from the writings of the Phenicians, and Chaldeans, and Egyptians. . . . I shall now therefore begin a confutation of the remaining authors who have written anything against us."

ment as distinct works constitute one of the misfortunes of the history of early Christian literature. An understanding of the origin of the separation helps justify the modern treatment of the two volumes as a single work. There were many later imitations of the Acts but no contemporary parallel. By contrast, there were many gospels. Early in the second century the four canonical Gospels were published under the title "The Gospel." The incorporation of Luke as a unit in "The Gospel" was probably the beginning of its dissociation from Acts. Then, or at some subsequent time, the second volume of Luke's work was given the title "The Acts of the Apostles." The title does not describe the contents of the book itself but more accurately corresponds to the implications of the order of books in most ancient manuscripts, where the Acts is followed by the epistles of James, Peter, John, Jude, and Paul.

What the original title of the two-volume work was is a matter of conjecture. It probably did not embody any of the elements of titles familiarly associated with the books. The hyphenated compound "Luke-Acts" here used as a title has the value of emphasizing the unity of the work but has no better claim to originality than the more usual titles. No third volume was contemplated. The author's purpose was accomplished in tracing the course of the Christian movement from Jerusalem to Rome.

Authorship.—The author of Luke-Acts seems not to have read any of Paul's letters.[3] Yet all Christian writings of the thirty years following the appearance of Luke-Acts show convincing evidences of literary dependence on a collection of Paul's letters in which Ephesians was included.[4] These facts create the probability that the publication of Luke-Acts supplied the incentive for the collection and publication of Paul's letters. Ephesians, as the catholicizing preface to the collected letters, stands as the earliest witness for the circulation of Luke-Acts. Within the same decade Revelation[5] and the Fourth Gospel[6] made use of the Gospel half of the work.

---

[3] McNeile, *Introduction*, p. 86; Harnack, *Chronologie*, I, 249.

[4] Goodspeed, *Formation of the New Testament*, pp. 20-32; *New Solutions of New Testament Problems*, pp 11-20; *The Meaning of Ephesians; New Chapters in New Testament Study*, pp. 22-49. See also my *Paul Becomes a Literary Influence*, p. 1.

[5] Charles, *The Revelation of St. John*, I, lxvi. The most significant parallels are: Rev. 1:3 (cf. Luke 11:28); 3:5 (cf. Luke 12:8); 11:6 (cf. Luke 4:25); 18:24 (cf. Luke 11:50).

[6] See pp. 98-99.

The original Didache, also representing the turn of the century, reflects a point of view that in all probability was influenced by the letter of "the apostles and elders" which according to Acts 15:22-29 was sent to the non-Jewish Christians "in Antioch, Syria, and Cilicia." [7]

Papias relates no tradition of the origin of Luke-Acts comparable with his references to Mark and Matthew.[8] Marcion knew the Gospel and included it in his canon, but he appears not to have discussed its authorship.[9] Justin knew the Gospel and frequently conflated its version of Jesus' teaching with the usually preferred Matthaean version.[10] Justin's pupil Tatian included the Gospel in his *Diatessaron*. The Muratorian fragment describes the Gospel and the Acts as "compiled in his own name in order by Luke the physician," who had been Paul's companion. Irenaeus, Tertullian, and Clement of Alexandria so refer to both volumes; and from the close of the second century onward the tradition of their Lukan authorship is generally accepted.

The tradition of Lukan authorship may have had its only basis in inference from references to Luke in Col. 4:14, Philem. 24, II Tim. 4:11 and the "we" sections of the Acts.[11] Just as possibly, however,

---

[7] There are possible traces of indebtedness to Luke 6:28, 30, 32 in Did. 1:3, 5. Very probably, however, Matthew was the only Gospel used. In Acts 15:22-29 "the apostles and elders" exercised the "power to bind and loose" ascribed to Peter in Matt. 16:19 and to the whole apostolic group in Matt. 18:18 when they decided what requirements of the Law were obligatory for non-Jewish Christians. The suggestion of Streeter that the Didache was in effect "an amplification of, if not almost a commentary upon, the epistle . . . sent out by that Council to the churches of Syria" (*The Primitive Church,* p. 41) is thoroughly sound. This view makes the Didache in its earliest form a witness for the circulation of the Acts.

[8] Euseb. *Hist.* III. 39. 15-16. F. C. Grant doubts that Papias knew Luke-Acts (*The Earliest Gospel,* pp. 52-53). As an illustration of the case for an acquaintance with the four Gospels on the part of Papias see R. M. Grant's article, "Papias and the Gospels," *Anglican Theological Review,* April, 1943, pp. 218-22.

[9] Iren. *Her.* I. 27. 2; III. 11. 7; III. 14. 3. Tertullian says, "Marcion . . . ascribes no author to his Gospel" (*Against Marcion* IV. 2).

[10] There are thirty-seven instances in the *Apology* and the *Dialogue* where there can be no doubt of Justin's use of the Gospel. Resemblances in the following parallels, which are in no instance conclusive, suggest his possible familiarity with the Acts: *Apol.* 49:5 (cf. Acts 13:27, 48); 50:12 (cf. Acts 1:8-10); *Appendix* 10:6 (cf. Acts 17:23); *Dial.* 20:3 (cf. Acts 10:14); 39:4 (cf. Acts 26:25); 60:1 (cf. Acts 7:30 ff.) : 68:5 (cf. Acts 2:30); 118:1 (cf. Acts 10:42).

[11] Cadbury, *The Making of Luke-Acts,* p. 356.

Luke was known during the second century to have written the books, and the tradition grew out of that knowledge. The work exemplifies the techniques of Greek historiography and would more naturally be published under the name of its author than anonymously.[12]

However the tradition arose, it finds convincing support in the natural meaning of the data supplied by Paul's letters and the Acts. According to Col. 4:14 and Philem. 24 Luke was one of Paul's companions during an imprisonment which was more probably at Rome than elsewhere. The use of the first person plural in Acts 16:10-18; 20:5-16; 21:1-18; and 27:1–28:16 suggests that extracts from a travel journal kept by a participant in the respective situations have been incorporated in the larger work. The keeper of this journal was with Paul in Macedonia, traveled with him to Syria, and was his companion on the journey to Rome and during his imprisonment there. The author of Luke-Acts either drew on the diary kept by this person or was himself Paul's companion. If the diarist was the author of Luke-Acts, he was more probably Luke than any other of Paul's associates, in view of Paul's direct testimony regarding Luke's association with him.

The problem of the authorship of Luke-Acts is, then, the problem whether or not the person who wrote the "we" sections was responsible for the finished work. The author of Acts conceivably, of course, used the diary of another as one of his sources. The "we" sections, however, are so entirely of a piece with the larger work as to make it extremely difficult to differentiate their author from the author of the whole work. The same qualities of diction and thought characterize these sections and the work in its entirety. Their style, vocabulary, and emphases are indistinguishable. If there were two authors, the one responsible for the completed work has more successfully assimilated this particular source to his style than he did in his use of materials drawn from Mark's Gospel. The persistence of Marcan qualities in the latter materials argues against the view that in the "we" sections the author of Luke-Acts was adapting another's journal.

If, as seems probable, the diarist was also the author of Luke-Acts, interesting light is shed on his procedure. He appears to have accumulated his materials over an extended period with no thought,

[12] Dibelius, *A Fresh Approach to the New Testament*, p. 64.

originally, of putting them to the use he found for them ultimately
in his monumental two-volume work. Possession of such materials,
however, enabled him to respond to a situation confronting the
church such as Luke-Acts was so admirably designed to meet. The
diary, of which the original scope can only be surmised, dated more
than two decades earlier than Luke-Acts and bore a relationship
to the second half of that work somewhat analogous to that of
Proto-Luke to the Gospel.[13]

There are four principal objections to the identification of Luke
as the author of Luke-Acts: (1) The author of Luke-Acts was unacquainted with Paul's letters. The speeches in the Acts show
little if any traces of such teaching as these letters contain. The
same thing can be said of Mark, also a companion of Paul, and can
constitute no objection in the first instance not equally relevant in
the second. Paul's letters were not published at the time Mark and
Luke-Acts were written and never enjoyed any general circulation
except as a published corpus.[14] Luke knew Paul as a missionary
leader rather than as a writer of letters. His nonuse of Paul's letters
is entirely understandable and is no argument against his authorship of Luke-Acts. (2) There are divergences in representation of
fact between Paul's letters and the Acts. These appear principally
in the accounts of the relations between Peter and Paul and
Paul's visits to Jerusalem. Here again the problem is more apparent
than real. That the atmosphere of conflict in Gal. 2:6-14 is entirely
absent from the Acts is due to the author's irenic purpose rather
than to his lack of acquaintance with the facts. The account Acts
gives of these heroes of an older generation is precisely what would
be expected of a writer so motivated and writing a quarter of a
century after both men were dead. The other phase of the problem
is automatically solved if Galatians is regarded as the earliest of
Paul's letters and if the visits to Jerusalem of Gal. 1:18 and 2:10
are viewed as corresponding respectively to those of Acts 9:23-30
and 11:30; 12:25.[15] (3) Luke is never named in either of the two
volumes. Silence, however, can have no significance not also attached to the equivalent silence of Mark's Gospel. So pretentious
a work as Luke-Acts was hardly published anonymously. The second-
century tradition of Lukan authorship may have arisen from an

[13] See p. 111.   [14] See my *Paul Becomes a Literary Influence.*
[15] See pp. 25-26.

identification of the author at the time the work was published. (4) The prefatory statement in Luke 1:4, which covers both volumes, seems to distinguish the author from "the original eyewitnesses." It can be construed as denying any personal association with Paul on his part. Such an understanding of the preface is possible but the probabilities are against it. The reference is probably to the oral sources for the first volume and to testimony drawn from the many written sources employed and in no way rules out the kind of acquaintance with phases of Paul's career implied in the "we" sections of the Acts.

The First Readers.—Both volumes of Luke-Acts are addressed to Theophilus. This does not clearly identify him or indicate the nature of his relationship to the author. Possibly he was a person whose support was sought or a person who was already assisting with the publication and circulation of the work. Again, he may have been a personal friend of the author or a person whose status and character would serve to emphasize and illustrate the contents of the writing. Conceivably the dedication may have been purely formal, a literary device with no relevance to the contents or the audience of the publication. The prefaces to the volumes contain the available data about Theophilus, and conclusions are largely inferences from these data considered in the light of the contents of the work as a whole.

Theophilus was a common name. In the present instance it more probably designates a real person than the personification of the ideal Christian suggested to some by the literal meaning, "beloved of God." "Your Excellency" does not necessarily require that he was a Roman official, but it suggests he was.[16] To regard him as a Roman official helps give meaning to such efforts to integrate Christianity in Roman life as the synchronizing of important Christian events with the Roman calendar, the exoneration of Pilate of responsibility for Jesus' death, the dismissal of charges against Paul by Gallio, and the emphasis on Paul's Roman citizenship.

The possible relationships of Theophilus to the author and to the Christian movement are implicit in the author's statement of purpose, "that you may be reliably informed about the things you have been taught." Theophilus may have been a Christian who had received the elemental instructions given a catechumen and was

[16] Felix is so addressed in Acts 23:26 and 24:3, and Festus in Acts 26:25.

ready for more advanced instruction.[17] The language, however, does not require this meaning. The verb involved [18] is used in Acts 18:25 to denote instruction given new converts, but in Acts 21:21, 24 it describes false information about Paul given by his enemies. Something of the latter meaning is probably present here. This probability is increased by the use of "to know reliably" in Acts 21:34 and 22:30 to describe official investigation by a Roman military commander.[19]

As will be seen in the discussion of the date of Luke-Acts, there are striking affinities with such writings of the last decade of the first century as Ephesians, Hebrews, and Revelation. If Luke-Acts belongs to that decade and reflects the incipient stages of the same crisis as Revelation, the likelihood is greatly accentuated that Theophilus was a Roman provincial official who, like many others of his class, regarded Christianity as a subversive, politically dangerous movement.

Whether Theophilus was a convert or a hostile Roman official, Luke-Acts was hardly written for the exclusive attention of any individual. Gentile Christians who had not known the original leaders of the movement would have their faith sustained by such an account of the providential extension of the Christian movement and its establishment in the principal cities of the empire. Their sense of security would be strengthened by the assurance this account afforded of the political innocuousness of the movement. By the same warrant Roman officials whose views had been distorted by misrepresentations would be "reliably informed" and so have their suspicions disarmed.

Date.—If Luke-Acts shows evidence of literary dependence on the *Antiquities* of Josephus, the *terminus a quo* for reckoning the date becomes A.D. 93. The possibility of such indebtedness is suggested by the historical allusions contained in Luke 3:1-2 and Acts 5:36-38. In the first of these passages the ministry of John the Baptist is said to have begun "in the fifteenth year of the reign of the Emperor Tiberius, . . . *while . . . Lysanias was governor of Abilene.*" In speak-

---

[17] Cf. I Cor. 3:2; Heb. 5:11-6:4.

[18] Κατηχήθης from κατηχέω is neutral in meaning. It ordinarily connotes the giving of oral instruction.

[19] Γνῶναι τὸ ἀσφαλές. Cf. Luke 1:4: ἵνα ἐπιγνῷς . . . τὴν ἀσφάλειαν. See the article by H. J. Cadbury, "The Purpose Expressed in Luke's Preface," *The Expositor*, XXI (1921), 431-41.

ing of the area designated by Claudius as the kingdom of Agrippa, one of the districts listed by Josephus is "Abila of Lysanias." Referring later to the same matter he says Claudius "bestowed upon Agrippa, the tetrarchy of Philip and Batanea, and added thereto Trachonitis, *with Abila; which last had been the tetrarchy of Lysanias.*"[20] Apparently Josephus does not speak of Lysanias as the living ruler of the territory but merely associates the district with the name of Lysanias, who once ruled it. Conceivably Luke's statement involves an erroneous inference from the words of Josephus; but more probably, if it is anything more than a purely formal allusion, it refers to a different Lysanias.

In Acts 5:36-38 there is a reference to the insurrectionists Theudas and Judas of Galilee, both of whom, with their followers, were destroyed. Josephus tells of the beheading of Theudas during the procuratorship of Fadus (44-46) and describes him as "a certain magician" who "persuaded a great part of the people to take their effects with them and follow him to the river Jordan."[21] He tells further how Alexander, successor to Fadus as procurator of Judea (46-48), slew "the sons of Judas of Galilee," and he identifies Judas as "that Judas who caused the people to revolt."

In both instances the construction placed on the historical events is such as to make the differences as impressive as the agreements. Luke is easier to understand if ignorance rather than acquaintance with Josephus is predicated. The incidents and persons involved in the allusions were known in popular report and illustrated the emphases of the evangelist without reference to the accuracy of his historical identification of them. The allusions tend to refute rather than support any suggestion of literary dependence on Josephus.

Other data, however, do clearly establish a starting point for reckoning the date of Luke-Acts: (1) The controversies so vividly reflected in Paul's letters have lost their vitality, and Paul himself is dead. There is no adequate explanation of Paul's valedictory to the Ephesian elders other than the consciousness that Paul was now a figure of a relatively remote past.[22] (2) Events of the Jewish War (66-70) and especially the destruction of Jerusalem are his-

---

[20] *Antiquities* XIX. v. 1; XX. vii. 1.   [21] *Antiquities* XX. v. 1-2.

[22] Acts 20:17-38. Note especially vss. 26 and 38. Actually letters written by Paul during the period indicated in Acts 28:30 express his expectation of again visiting the Macedonian and Asian churches (cf. Phil. 1:21-26; 2:24; Philem. 22), which would surely have involved the renewal of his contacts with Ephesus.

torical recollections in Luke-Acts,[23] and these events are sufficiently remote for them to have lost the vivid significance they contained for Mark and Matthew.[24] (3) The author of Luke was clearly dependent on Mark's Gospel.[25] The *terminus ad quem* is fixed with a fair degree of accuracy by the author's lack of acquaintance with Paul's collected letters and by the use of Luke-Acts by the author of the Fourth Gospel.[26] The period within which Luke-Acts was written can thus be broadly defined as 70-95. Qualities common to Christian writings of the last decade of the first century [27] which tend to identify Luke-Acts with that decade are interest in Christian hymnody,[28] an awareness of the existence of heretical sects,[29] an anti-Baptist bias,[30] an exaggerated reverence for the apostles,[31] the assumption of a relatively elaborate church organization,[32] an atmosphere of persecution.[33]

The general character of the story of Luke-Acts confirms these more detailed indications of an approximate date of 85-95. The story is appropriate for times when the original leaders had passed away and living Christians possessed only a hazy idea of Christian beginnings. Christianity had established itself in the principal cities of the empire. It had so definitely differentiated itself from actual Judaism as to make it desirable to represent itself as the "ideal Judaism" in order to secure the legal privileges accorded Judaism as a tolerated religion. The movement had, moreover, grown sufficiently to cause Roman officials to suspect it of being politically dangerous. Ignorance of Paul's letters in contrast with the consistently abundant use of those letters as a collection in the Chris-

---

[23] Luke 19:43-44; 21:10-24.

[24] Luke omits the parenthetical exhortation of Mark 13:14 and Matt. 24:15, "The reader must take note of this."

[25] See pp. 100-9.   [26] See pp. 98-99.

[27] Such as Ephesians, Revelation, Hebrews, First Peter, the Fourth Gospel, and First Clement.

[28] Luke 1:42-55, 68-79; 2:14, 29-32; Eph. 5:14; Rev. 19:1 ff., 6 ff.; etc.

[29] Acts 20:30; Eph. 4:3-6, 14; Rev. 2:6, 15; I Clem. 39:1; I John 2:22, 26; 4:1; II John 7.

[30] Acts 18:4-5; John 1:19-36; 4:1.

[31] Acts 2:14, 43; 4:33-35; 5:3, 19; 8:1, 14; 10:26; 11:1; Eph. 2:20; 3:5; 4:11; Rev. 21:14; Heb. 2:3; I Clem. 42:1; 44:1.

[32] Acts 6:6; 11:30; 14:23; 15:2, 6, 22; 20:17; Heb. 2:3; I Pet. 5:1 ff.; I Clem. 40:2-5; 44:1-6.

[33] Luke 1:4; 23:2-23; Acts 18:12 ff.; 22:29; 24:22, 27; 25:10; 26:32; Heb. 10:32 ff.; 12:3; Rev. 1:9; 7:14; 18:24; I Pet. 2:13-17; 3:16-17; 4:7-19.

tian writings of the last decade of the first century indicate that Luke-Acts appeared shortly before the publication of the letters.

Place of Composition.—Antioch, Rome, and Ephesus are the chief possibilities as places where Luke-Acts may have been written. In the same context in which he describes Luke and Acts as "inspired books" and as examples of the art of "healing souls" Eusebius specifically designates Luke as the author and goes on to describe him as "by race an Antiochene and by profession a physician." [34] Eusebius may have thought Luke did his writing at Antioch, but he fails to make a statement to that effect. The important role of Antioch in the account of the expansion of Christianity in Acts [35] strengthens the case for Antioch. However, Matthew was rather certainly written at Antioch, and there are no indications of interdependence between Luke-Acts and Matthew. They use certain sources in common, but they use them quite differently. Their atmosphere and respective points of view are, furthermore, so different as to make it difficult to conceive of them as addressed to the same reading public.[36]

On the basis of three principal considerations B. H. Streeter has urged Rome as the place of composition: (1) Regarding it as the purpose of Acts "to trace the transition of Christianity from a sect of Judaism into a world religion," he thinks the narrative itself implies a Roman origin. (2) The letter of Clement to the Corinthians admittedly shows no knowledge of Luke's Gospel, but he thinks an acquaintance with Acts is reflected.[37] He accounts

---

[34] *Hist.* III. 4. 6.

[35] Acts 11:19, 22-30; 13:1-3; 14:26-15:3; 15:22, 30-35.

[36] This difference of atmosphere and point of view must not be overemphasized in its decisiveness. The Fourth Gospel and Revelation differ as radically but were both written at Ephesus.

[37] The parallels that constitute the evidence for Clement's use of Acts are: I Clem. 2:1 (cf. Acts 20:35); 5:6-7 (cf. Acts 1:8); 18:1 (cf. Acts 13:25). In no instance are these parallels convincing. The first instance involves the variant use of a saying the evidently proverbial character of which obviates any necessity of predicating literary derivation. Clement differs from Acts in not attributing the saying to Jesus and in the abbreviated form of the saying he employs. The description of Paul in I Clem. 5:6 as having been "a herald both in the East and in the West" similarly is a matter of popular report rather than of indebtedness to Acts 1:8. Clement's description in this context of Paul's sufferings more readily brings to mind Paul's own catalogue in II Cor. 11:23 ff. than the accounts of Paul's experiences in Acts. In the third case both writers have conflated I Sam. 13:14 and Ps. 88:21, conceivably in independence of one another or in common dependence on current practice. Even if it were granted as certain

for a lack of acquaintance with the Gospel on the supposition that the two volumes were two separate works written at an interval of a decade or more. (3) He accurately describes Acts as "the first of the Apologies." Because its portrayal of Christianity would have been useful to the Roman Christian community during Domitian's persecution, he thinks Acts must have been written at Rome.[38]

Other evidence favors Ephesus as the place where Luke-Acts was written. The prominence of Ephesus in the Acts account of Paul's career, especially his valedictory to the Ephesians elders, points strongly to Ephesus.[39] The Fourth Gospel and Revelation, both of them Ephesian writings, show literary dependence on Luke's Gospel.[40] If Luke-Acts was a single work, planned and executed as such, acquaintance with Luke would implicitly involve acquaintance with Acts. The many interests common to Acts and other books written at Ephesus tend to establish the Ephesian origin of Acts. Streeter is correct in describing Acts as "the first of the Apologies," but he would be more completely accurate if he so described Luke-Acts in its entirety. He errs in thinking the persecution situation which determined the apologetic character of the work required Rome as its adequate explanation. In view of the Ephesian origin of Revelation, Ephesus easily equals Rome as the probable location for such a writing as Luke-Acts. The heroic picture of Paul in Acts probably suggested the collection and publication of his letters. Ephesians, written as a preface to the published letters, was known to Clement of Rome.[41] Ephesians is thus an earlier witness for Acts than Clement of Rome. The publication of Paul's letters at Ephesus becomes, then, the earliest evidence for the existence of Luke-Acts, antedating both the Fourth Gospel and Revelation and rather conclusively fixing Ephesus as the place where Luke-Acts was written.

Occasion and Purpose.—According to the author's own statement of purpose, he proposed "to write a connected account" of the

that Clement knew Acts, the case for the Roman origin of Acts would not thereby be established. Clement knew Paul's letters as a published collection, and Ephesus was assuredly the place where Paul's letters in their published form appeared.

[38] *The Four Gospels,* pp. 531-39.   [39] Acts 18:19-22, 24—20:1, 17-38.

[40] See pp. 98-99, 164.

[41] Goodspeed, *The Meaning of Ephesians;* see also my *Paul Becomes a Literary Influence,* pp. 97, 103.

development of the Christian movement "from the beginning" in order that his reading public might be "reliably informed." To this end, he first described the ministry and message of Jesus in their Palestinian setting. In a second volume he gave an account of Jesus' continuing leadership in the person of the Spirit. Christ as the Spirit guided the Christian movement in its transition from a sect within Judaism to its character as a religion whose values and appeal were for all men.

When the evangelist said he wrote for the purpose of "reliably" informing his readers, he was not claiming superiority for his narrative primarily in terms of historical accuracy. He was doubtless critical of the miscellaneous and fragmentary character of his documentary sources, but he achieved a poor result if his object was solely to replace them with a historically adequate account of Christian beginnings.[42] More probably he wrote to allay suspicion and outright hostility. These had their origin in rumor and malicious misrepresentation. To put Christianity in its true light, therefore, the author of Luke-Acts described the life and message of Jesus and showed how he remained the determining influence in the Christian movement through the person of the Spirit.

This understanding of the author's intention does not necesssarily reduce the materials out of which the narrative was woven to fiction. Rather, essentially historical materials were articulated into a literary whole whose primary function was apologetic. Streeter's characterization of Acts as "really the first of the Apologies"[43] is thus an entirely accurate description of Luke-Acts in its entirety.

The circumstances under which Luke wrote are less clear than could be desired. The contents of his two volumes, however, implicitly reflect the critical character of the situation confronting the church. The special needs of this situation controlled the author's selection of materials from traditional sources, determined the point of view from which they were articulated, and supplied the incentive for their publication.

In the earliest explicit reference to Christianity in secular literature the Roman historian Tacitus (ca. 52–ca. 117), in describing the Neronian persecution, identifies Christians as having derived their name from Christ, who "had been put to death in the reign

---

[42] Scott, *Literature of the New Testament*, p. 77.
[43] *The Four Gospels*, p. 539.

of Tiberius by the procurator Pontius Pilate." Continuing, Tacitus notes that the execution of the founder of the movement did not accomplish its suppression, since "the deadly superstition, having been checked for a while, began to break out again, not only throughout Judea, where this mischief first arose, but also at Rome." [44] Paul and Mark dealt in their respective ways with the problem which Jesus' execution created for Christian faith itself. Luke, apparently, felt under the necessity of dealing with the political implications inherent in such a view of the event as Tacitus recorded. His method was to represent Jesus as a teacher of moral and religious truth and not a conspirator. Roman authorities themselves regarded him the victim of Jewish prejudices rather than a criminal. Christianity, instead of being politically dangerous, was Judaism as God had originally conceived it—the true religion for all mankind.

Essentially the same situation seems to form the background of Luke-Acts, Hebrews, Revelation, and First Peter. Christianity was in trouble with civil authority. The demand for supreme loyalty to Christ had aroused the suspicion of disloyalty or of a qualified loyalty to the emperor on the part of Christians. In such a situation the author of Luke-Acts undertook to demonstrate the groundlessness of the suspicions of outsiders and to fortify the confidence of Christians by giving to both a worthy conception of the movement that had originated in Palestine under the leadership of Jesus and had now under the guidance of the divine Spirit and with God's blessing established itself in the principal cities of the empire.

Message.—The Lukan account of the career of Jesus is in general agreement with the sequence of Mark's story. Following a prefatory narrative of the birth and childhood of Jesus in chapters 1 and 2, for which Mark has no parallel, the stages of the narrative are:

> Period of preparation—3:1-4:11; cf. Mark 1:2-13
> Ministry in eastern Galilee—4:12-9:17; cf. Mark 1:14-7:23
> Ministry in northern Galilee—9:18-50; cf. Mark 7:24-9:50
> Journey toward Jerusalem—9:51-19:28; cf. Mark 10:1-50
> Passion Week—19:29-23:56; cf. Mark 11:1-15:47
> Resurrection of Jesus—23:57-24:10; cf. Mark 16:1-8
> Postresurrection events—24:11-53; for which Mark in its best
> textual form has no parallel

[44] *Annals* XV, xliv.

Luke, however, was not entirely dependent on Mark for this sequence but would have told his story substantially as he did if he had never read Mark. He apparently employed Marcan materials to enrich his own account, the basic content of which, including a narrative framework whose stages were essentially those of Mark, he possessed in independence of Mark. This agreement between the two narratives makes it highly probable that Luke 1:3, instead of involving a claim to superiority in the matter of "order," is actually an affirmation of the adequacy of the author's selection and arrangement of his data for the accomplishment of his purpose. In his use of sections from Mark, Luke alters the details less freely than does Matthew, but Mark appears to have been a supplementary and not the primary narrative source.

A more detailed examination of Luke's narrative makes this relation to Mark clear:

1:1–2:52—Luke's account of Jesus' birth and childhood. There is no equivalent in Mark.

3:1–4:30—The order of events is in essential agreement with Mark 1:2-20, but the materials evidently represent a non-Marcan source which Luke preferred to Mark. Luke's account of Jesus' rejection at Nazareth (4:16-30) appears at a juncture in his narrative that would correspond to Mark 1:15. Mark has an account of the incident in 6:1-6a. Luke has an account of the call of the first disciples which he prefers to Mark 1:16-20, and which he locates differently in his account (5:1-11).

4:31–6:19—The order and materials are largely those of Mark 1:21–3:19. Non-Marcan additions are limited to 5:1-11 and 6:14-16. The only deviation from Marcan order is a reversal of the items of Mark 3:7-19a (cf. Luke 6:17-19; 6:12-16).

6:20–8:3—A wholly non-Marcan block of materials.

8:4–9:50—A narrative of the events of Jesus' Galilean ministry, of which Mark 4:1–9:40 is also an account. Of Mark's materials Luke makes no use of 4:26-29; 6:47–8:26 (except that the items of 8:11-21 appear in reverse order and differently located in Luke 12:54-56; 11:53–12:1), and 9:9-13. In the matter of order: Luke 8:4-18 follows Mark 4:1-25; Luke 8:19-21 interjects the story of Jesus' relatives which Mark gave earlier in 3:31-35; Luke 8:22–9:17 follows Mark 4:35–6:46; Luke 9:18-50 follows Mark 8:27–9:40. At a later point (13:18-21), Luke introduces a non-Marcan version of the parable of the mustard seed and pairs it as in Matthew with the parable of the leaven rather than with the parable of the fruit-bearing earth (Mark 4:26-29), which he omits.

9:51–19:28—A non-Marcan block of materials, within which there are
the following parallels: 17:1-2 (cf. Mark 9:42-48); 18:15-43 (cf. Mark
10:13-34, 46-50). The scene of Mark 10:1-45 is Perea, whereas that of the
entire section in Luke is undesignated until Jesus finally arrives at
Jericho.

19:29–23:56—An amalgamation of Mark 11:1–15:47 with a non-Marcan
account of Passion Week. There are a considerable number of Marcan
details that Luke does not use, such as: Mark 11:11-14, 20-25; 12:28-34
(cf. Luke 10:27); 14:3-9 (cf. Luke 7:36 ff.); 14:38*b*-42; 14:49*b*-51;
14:55-61; 15:16-20. Peculiarly Lukan details are: Luke 19:39-41; 21:24;
21:34, 37-38; 22:28-29; 22:31; 22:35-38; 22:43-44; 23:4-16; 23:27-32; 23:
39-43. More frequently than otherwise in this area materials from Marcan
and non-Marcan sources cannot be differentiated with complete certainty.

24:1-12—A non-Marcan account of the Resurrection in which certain
details correspond to those found in Mark 16:1-8.

24:13-53—An account of the postresurrection events peculiar to Luke.

Had Mark not been available as a source, the author of Luke
could have written a complete Gospel somewhat longer than Mark
and comprised at the minimum of the following Lukan sections: 1:1–
4:30; 5:1-11; 6:14-16; 6:20–8:3; 9:51–18:14; 19:1-27; 19:37-44; 21:18,
34-36; 22:14–24:53. Not improbably he had composed a gospel of
approximately these proportions which he reworked and enriched
with contributions from Mark when that work came into his possession. Lukan passages largely taken over from Mark in block are:

Luke 4:31-44=Mark 1:21-39
Luke 5:12–6:19=Mark 1:40–3:19*a*
Luke 8:4–9:50=Mark 4:1–6:45; 8:27–9:41
Luke 18:15-43=Mark 10:13-52
Luke 19:28-36=Mark 11:1-11
Luke 19:45–21:33=Mark 11:15–13:37
Luke 21:37–22:13=Mark 14:1-16

Luke's reading of Mark may also have suggested the use of other
materials, gathered originally with no such end in view,[45] in the
composition of Acts. His nonuse of Mark 6:47–8:26, itself a sort of
story of the Greek mission, was probably due to the suggestion he

[45]Goodspeed, *Introduction*, p. 199.

derived from it to devote a full half of his expanded publication to tracing the extension of the Christian movement, under the leadership of Christ as the Spirit, throughout the empire.

The literary methods employed by the author in his first volume were probably his methods throughout.[46] The objective tests by which those methods have been identified in the case of the Gospel, however, are lacking for Acts. For much of the second volume, especially its latter half, Luke had his own fund of experiences on which to draw. Elsewhere he made use of oral tradition, independent stories and sayings, and the cycles of materials already reduced to writing in localities where they were treasured. As in the Gospel, "order" in Acts signifies the planned treatment of a theme rather than an exhaustive or chronological account of the development of a movement.

Six summaries mark the stages of the development of the theme implicit in Acts 1:8. They are 6:7; 9:31; 12:24; 16:5; 19:20; and 28:31. The note of triumph is common to them all. With convincingly cumulative effect they describe the irresistible spread of the Christian movement, as by divine arrangement and immediate guidance, throughout the world. The initial phases of the story of Christianity's triumphal march are descriptions of the dynamic growth of the movement in Jerusalem (1:9–6:7) and Palestine (6:8–9:31). There follow accounts of its extension in ever-enlarging circles to Antioch (9:32–12:24), Asia Minor (12:25–16:5), southeastern Europe (16:6–19:20), and Rome (19:21–28:31).

The message of both volumes is built about three major emphases. In the first place, Christianity is the true Judaism and as such is inherently entitled to the legal recognition accorded nominal Judaism. That Christianity has this character is shown by the fidelity of the first Christians and their principal leaders to the services of the synagogue and temple, their reverence for the requirements of Scripture, and the superiority of their insight into the true import of Scripture.[47] Consequently Jewish misunderstanding of Christianity is actually a misunderstanding of Judaism as God conceived

---

[46] Harnack, *The Acts of the Apostles*. Harnack's careful analysis of the sources of Acts remains a stimulating guide. For a briefer account see Foakes-Jackson and Lake, *The Beginnings of Christianity*, I, v. 4-7.

[47] Luke 2:21-24, 27-32, 39-41; 5:14; 17:14; 21:37; 24:25-27, 44-47; Acts 2:46; 3:1; 5:30-31; 13:15; 15:15-17; 17:3; 18:19; 21:20, 26; 22:3 ff,

it.[48] This misunderstanding explains why the Jews rejected Jesus and persecuted his followers. What has currently passed for Judaism is instead a perversion of it. Therefore the recognition and privileges accorded Judaism under Roman law ought to be transferred to Christianity.

Christianity can also be shown to have been from the outset an indigenous and not an alien movement within the empire.[49] It has always been responsive to the needs of Roman life,[50] and has never condoned politically dangerous methods of action.[51] Specifically, neither Jesus nor any of his followers were ever found guilty of revolutionary tendencies or actions. Their accusers, who were regularly the Jews, used such charges to divert suspicion from themselves, where, according to subsequent events, it rightly belonged. Not only was nothing wrong found with Jesus in this regard,[52] but his principal followers were regularly exonerated whenever arraigned in Roman courts.[53] Paul, though sent to Rome a prisoner, went because of his own appeal, not after conviction as a criminal but as an innocent man falsely accused and seeking acquittal before the highest tribunal in the empire.[54] By contrast, the Jews, whose malice and blindness were responsible for most anti-Christian accusations,[55] have a record by no means so clear. Claudius expelled them in fairly recent times from Rome, and Roman provincial officials quite generally regard them as trouble makers.[56] It is no mere coincidence that "the high priests and the leading members

[48] Luke 2:34-35, 38, 47; 3:8, 9; 4:22-30; 5:21; 6:2-11; 7:30-35; 8:19-21; 10:23-37; 11: 31-54; 13:15-17, 33-35; 16:14; 18:11; 19:42-44, 47-48; 20:9-18, 42; Acts 1:16, 20; 2:16-38; 3:13 ff.; 4:11; 6:11; 8:3, 35; 10:43; 13:17 ff., 47; 14:3, 19; 15:15-22; 17:2-5; 18:5-6, 28; 19:8 ff.; 28:23-28.

[49] Luke 2:1-3; 3:1-2; Acts 18:2, 12; 28:7.

[50] Luke 3:12, 14; 5:27-32; 7:2-9; 15:1; 17:18; 19:2, 10; Acts 6:1; 8:4, 27 ff.; 9:34; 10:1-48; 11:1-26; 13:46-48; 16:12, 33; 17:22-34; 20:21; 28:7-9, 28.

[51] Luke 4:5-8; 20:20-26; 22:38, 50-53; Acts 18:14; 21:38 ff.; 22:25-29.

[52] Luke 23:1-4, 9, 12, 15, 20, 22, 24, 47; Acts 3:13.

[53] Acts 5:17 ff.; 13:28; 16:32-40; 17:9; 18:12 ff.; 19:35-41; 22:26-30; 24:23, 27; 28:18. In a single instance worthy of mention a judge who misjudged an apostle (Acts 12:1-23) was himself shortly afterward "struck down" by an angel and "was eaten by worms and died." Paul remembered having been "beaten three times by the Romans" (II Cor. 11:25), but no such reminiscence is recorded in Acts. Rather Paul's Roman citizenship is repeatedly emphasized as securing for him the considerate treatment to which the author feels all Christians are entitled.

[54] Acts 25:10-11, 21; 26:30-32; 28:16-20, 30-31.

[55] Luke 23:2; Acts 5:17; 18:12.   [56] Acts 18:2, 16-17.

of the Council and the people" called for the release of Barabbas, "who had been put in prison for riot and murder," in preference to Jesus,[57] who was personally blameless and who had approved of Pilate's severity toward those who employed insurrectionary techniques.[58] Moreover, they who contrived Jesus' death had as their accomplice not a man who had broken with Jesus from worthy motives but one who had come under the control of Satan.[59] That Jesus' accusers were themselves in league with Satan has been historically established by God's repudiation of them in the destruction of their city.[60]

The divine character of Christianity and its enjoyment of God's guidance and protection as such constitute the final emphases in the message of Luke-Acts. They who oppose the movement align themselves against the purposes and power of the heavenly order.[61] Supernaturalistic manifestations have characterized its entire history, and these are proof of God's involvement in the life and program of the church.[62] The miracles and God's immediate guidance of Christian leaders in all crises illustrate God's activity in and concern for the success of the entire enterprise.[63] More explicitly, the events of Christian history and the potency of the gospel message find their only adequate explanation in the activity of the holy Spirit.[64] In this spiritual quality Jesus' ministry and the accomplishments of Christian leaders are complementary. Christian missionaries therefore represent no purely human undertaking, but are God's own agents.[65] The story of Christianity's past is the surest clue to its future. Its spread throughout the world is due to its divinely appointed world mission.[66] God is the guarantor of its success, and Rome will not wish to be found in the tragic plight of the Jews, "actually . . . fighting God."

[57] Luke 23:19, 25; Acts 3:15.   [58] Luke 13:1-4.   [59] Luke 22:3, 22.

[60] Luke 21:20-28; 23:28-31.   [61] Acts 5:39; 12:2, 23.

[62] Luke 1:20-37; 2:9-15; 3:22, 38; 9:28-36; 24:2-5, 15-32, 35, 36; Acts 1:9-11; 4:31; 5:19; 8:26; 9:4 ff.; 10:3-19; 12:6-11; 16:9, 26; 18:9; 27:23-24.

[63] Luke 4:32-37, 41; 5:8-10, 17; 7:15-17, 22; 8:25, 28, 37, 46, 56; 11:15 ff.; Acts 2:43; 3:6 ff., 16; 4:10; 5:3, 9, 14-16; 6:8; 8:6; 9:34-35, 41; 12:23; 13:12; 14:3, 8-11; 19:11 ff.; 20:10-12; 28:3-6, 9.

[64] Luke 1:35, 42, 67, 80; 2:27; 3:16, 22; 4:1, 14; 11:13; 12:10; Acts 1:5, 8, 16; 2:4, 39; 4:8, 25, 31; 5:3, 9, 32; 6:3, 5; 7:55; 8:16; 9:17, 31; 10:19, 44; 11:12, 28; 13:2, 52; 15:28; 16:6; 19:2 ff., 21; 20:22; 21:4, 11.

[65] Luke 3:2; 9:1, 13-17, 40, 44; 10:1, 16-20; Acts 5:20; 6:3, 5, 10; 8:18.

[66] Luke 3:23-38; 10:30-37; 17:16-18; 24:47; Acts 1:8; 2:4, 6, 8-11; 4:28.

XIII

THE EPISTLE TO THE EPHESIANS

Authorship.—Paul's letters appear to have had no circulation singly outside the localities to which they were originally sent. They came to the attention of the church generally as a published collection. Evidence for their existence usually involves literary reminiscences of from five to nine of the letters and in certain notable instances the full ten-letter corpus. Evidence for the existence and circulation of Ephesians is coextensive with indications of the circulation of Paul's collected letters. Ephesians was clearly a member, and an extremely popular member, of that original corpus. There are no instances down to the beginning of the fourth quarter of the second century where the evidence for an acquaintance with any of Paul's letters does not involve evidence of approximately the same extent and clarity for a literary knowledge of Ephesians.

There was a period of initial popularity for the newly published Pauline letter collection extending from the appearance of Luke-Acts through approximately the first quarter of the second century. There followed, with the emergence of the heretical sects, a quarter of a century when Paul fell into disrepute and his letters into consequent disuse. This eclipse of Paul ended around the middle of the second century. His restoration to prominence as the exemplar and protagonist of orthodoxy was, from the standpoint of the history of early Christian literature, the most important achievement of the latter half of the second century. Throughout this three quarters of a century and more, Ephesians shared the fortunes of the other letters.

The Revelation of John is the earliest witness for the appearance of Paul's published letters. That an apocalypse should have as its introduction a corpus of letters to seven churches, itself with an epistolary preface addressed to the whole church, finds its most reasonable explanation in the predication of an acquaintance with the original form of the published letters of Paul. Those letters had been addressed to seven churches, and when published were prefaced by a general epistle directing the collection to the attention of the church everywhere. Aside from this monumental datum, Revelation reflects a knowledge of the ten letters of the group. Of the ten, Ephesians is most extensively used. The case is identical with the Fourth Gospel, the Ephesian contemporary of Revelation, except for the failure of any reminiscence of Philemon. In such other writings of this early period as First Peter, Hebrews, First Clement, the Johannine epistles, the epistles of Ignatius and Polycarp, all of which show an acquaintance with a majority of Paul's letters, Ephesians rarely falls lower than third in a listing based on the frequency and clearness of the literary reminiscences.[1]

During the period when Paul's letters fell into general disuse in orthodox circles, specific evidence for literary indebtedness to them rarely rises above the level of possibility. Where it exists at all, however, Ephesians is regularly one of the letters possibly known.[2] With the gradual restoration of the letters to currency in the church Ephesians shared the recovery of popularity, although Romans was thereafter the most widely used. The chief witnesses here are Second Peter, the writings of Justin, and the Pastorals. In order of influence as reflected in these writings Ephesians occupies respectively second, third, and fourth place.[3]

The definite ascription of Ephesians to Paul begins with the

[1] First Peter, Hebrews, and First Clement each reflect the influence of eight of the letters, all traces of acquaintance for Philippians and Philemon being lacking in First Peter, and for Second Thessalonians and Philemon in Hebrews and First Clement. Listed on a basis of frequency and clarity of literary reminiscence, Ephesians is second only to Romans in the instance of First Peter; stands third in the case of Hebrews, where the order is First Corinthians, Romans, Ephesians; and is fifth in the case of First Clement, where indebtedness is heaviest to the Corinthian letters and Romans, and to Galatians, Ephesians, Philippians and Colossians in that order of probability and extent. Philemon alone has no echo in the Johannine epistles and in that of Polycarp, where the order of importance is respectively Romans, the Corinthian letters, and Ephesians, and First Corinthians, Philippians, and Ephesians. In the epistles of Ignatius where all ten of the letters are reflected, the order of influence is First Corinthians, Romans, and Ephesians. The data for these conclusions are displayed in detail in my *Paul Becomes a Literary Influence*.

[2] On the basis of its possible influence on the several writings in this category its order is as follows: for James, Rom., I Cor., Gal., Eph.; for Jude, Rom., I Cor., Gal., Eph.; for Hermas, Eph., I Cor., I Thess., Rom., Phil.; for Barnabas, Eph., Rom., I and II Cor., I and II Thess., Col.; for the Didache, I Cor., Rom., II Thess., Eph., I Thess., Col.

[3] For Second Peter the order is Rom., Eph., II Cor., Gal., I Thess.; for the writings of Justin, Rom., Gal., Eph., Col., I Cor., II Thess.; for the Pastorals, Rom., I Cor., Phil., Eph., Col., II Thess., Philem., Gal., I Thess.

earliest references to its authorship. Marcion attributed it to Paul and included it in his Pauline canon under the title of Laodiceans. He listed it between Second Thessalonians and Colossians as the seventh letter. Conceivably Marcion exchanged its order with Galatians, which he placed first. He probably gave it the title Laodiceans as an inference from Col. 4:16, since there was no place name in its address. Irenaeus quotes Eph. 5:30 as the words of "the blessed Paul . . . in his letter to the Ephesians." [4] In the Muratorian canon it is known as Ephesians and is listed between Second Corinthians and Philippians as the third of Paul's letters. Thereafter it is regularly known as Ephesians and, until modern times, is regularly regarded as having been written by Paul.

Much in the epistle itself lends support to this external testimony regarding authorship. Paul is twice explicitly named as the author,[5] and other allusions suggest that Ephesians, Colossians, and Philemon were written under identical circumstances and were dispatched by the same messenger.[6] The author's ideas and phraseology bear undeniably strong resemblances to Paul's authentic letters. Such a combination of external and internal evidence would be conclusive were it not for other data in the epistle which argue convincingly for pseudonymity.

Paul habitually wrote to local Christian communities, but Ephesians is by every test an encyclical letter. The *Textus Receptus* has "at Ephesus" as a place name in the address of the epistle and is followed in this reading by our Authorized and Revised versions. The weight of manuscript evidence, however, is against the phrase, and such of the fathers as Origen, Basil, and Jerome did not regard it as original. The text familiar to Marcion evidently lacked it, else he would not have called it Laodiceans. The address fits the body of the epistle better when it is read, "To God's people who are steadfast in Christ Jesus." The encyclical character of Ephesians makes its identification with the period of Paul's career extremely difficult and lends probability to its location in the last decade of the first century.

The literary indebtedness of Ephesians to the other nine letters generally attributed to Paul makes its authenticity unlikely. Variety and originality of expression rather than repetitiousness characterize those letters. The different character of Ephesians in this respect

[4] *Her.* V. 2. 2.   [5] 1:1; 3:1.   [6] 4:1; 6:21; cf. Col. 4:7, 18; Philem. 1.

definitely sets it apart. Its derivative character is especially clear by comparison with Colossians, which it so largely incorporates, but the influence of all nine of the letters is observable in its imagery and language. This becomes doubly impressive when the author's own distinctive emphases, themselves essentially un-Pauline, are nevertheless expressed in forms of speech borrowed from Paul's genuine letters. The author apparently restricted himself to materials found in Paul's letters even though he addressed his message to a post-Pauline situation. The relationship of Ephesians to those letters has its best analogy in the Fourth Gospel. Ephesians and the Fourth Gospel are both expositions of selected Pauline insights for the needs of a later situation in the church.

As its literary dependence on Paul's letters suggests, the historical situation reflected in the epistle is more nearly that of the last decade of the century than that of the period of Paul's missionary career. The author is as definitely non-Jewish [7] as his reading public.[8] Moreover, author and readers have no personal knowledge of one another.[9] The author's written message is the only basis of acquaintance between himself and his readers.[10] The apostles are idealized as in Luke-Acts and Revelation, and Paul is implicitly numbered among them.[11] In contrast with Paul, for whom Christ alone was the foundation of the church and, as the Spirit, the agent of revelation, the apostles are here regarded as the "foundation," [12] and the church is itself viewed as the channel of revelation.[13] The epistle furthermore exhibits an awareness of the existence of heretical sects [14] and a sense of their menace to the unity of the church [15] hardly reconcilable with Paul's outlook. Such data suggest rather clearly the situation around the close of the century.[16]

These characteristics within the epistle itself radically reduce if they do not eliminate the probability of Pauline authorship. They lend plausibility, however, to the suggestion that Onesimus collected Paul's letters and in his name wrote Ephesians as a sort of prefatory exposition of their substance to commend them to the entire church.[17] This identification of the author explains the heavy

---

[7] 2:3; cf. Gal. 2:15; II Cor. 11:22; Phil. 3:4.   [8] 2:2, 11.

[9] 1:15; 3:2; 4:21.   [10] 3:2-3; 6:18-20.

[11] 3:1-12; cf. Acts 15:6, 22; Rev. 18:20; 21:14.

[12] 2:20-22; cf. I Cor. 3:11; II Cor. 3:17.   [13] 3:10.   [14] 4:14.

[15] 4:3-6.   [16] Cf. Acts 20:30; Rev. 2:6, 15; John 10:1, 8-10; 17:20-23.

[17] Goodspeed, *Introduction*, p. 239.

indebtedness of Ephesians to Colossians and the inclusion of Philemon among Paul's published letters. Nor was there another associate of Paul who would more appropriately acknowledge his profound personal indebtedness by writing in the apostle's name. If
the Onesimus of whom Paul wrote so affectionately in Philemon
was later the bishop of the Ephesian church whom Ignatius described as "a man of inexpressible love" and a stalwart opponent of
heresy,[18] he fits the data of Ephesians doubly well, and the ascription of the epistle to him becomes an invaluable aid in its
interpretation.

   The First Readers.—There was no place name in the original
address of Ephesians. Nor does the sense of the address require
the designation of a local community.[19] It is entirely intelligible
when read, "To God's people who are steadfast in Christ Jesus."[20]
The title "To the Ephesians" may be a reminiscence of the fact that
the epistle was written at Ephesus in connection with the publication of Paul's letters there. The collector of the letters, however,
had no reason for giving the epistle this or any other title. Not
until the time of Irenaeus was the epistle known as Ephesians. The
designation conceivably originated as an editorial conjecture based
on the location of Tychicus at Ephesus in the recently published
Pastoral epistles.[21]

   The address harmonizes with the encyclical character of the
epistle. Neither allusions nor personal greetings suggest a local
group among whom the author might once have lived and worked.
Author and readers appear rather to have been personally unknown
to each other.[22] The closing mention of Tychicus[23] is an isolated
variation from the rule of indefiniteness and serves to emphasize
rather than alter the impression that the readers were Christians in

---

[18] Ign. Eph. 1:3; 2:1-2; 6:2. There is nothing chronologically impossible in this
identification. If Onesimus was in his twenties when Paul wrote Philemon, he
would be approaching sixty when our epistle was written and would be in his
early seventies when Ignatius referred to him.

[19] For McNeile the destination of Ephesians is an enigma of which the true
solution "has yet to be found." This is due to the fact that while he recognizes
the catholic character of the epistle he finds the address without a place name
"next to impossible." He suggests an amanuensis might have left a blank space in
the address for the insertion of each locality to which a copy went (*Introduction*,
pp. 163-65). Scott shares this view (*Literature of the New Testament*, p. 179).
There is no evidence to support these surmises.

[20] Cf. Rom. 8:28.   [21] II Tim. 4:12; cf. Eph. 6:21.
[22] 1:15; 3:2; 4:21.   [23] 6:21-22.

general. It sounds very much like the similar references to Timothy in Heb. 13:23 and to Silvanus and Mark in I Pet. 5:12. In all probability the allusion was part of the literary disguise.

The reading public contemplated in the epistle was entirely Greek. Both author and audience were non-Jewish.[24] That there were once Jewish Christians is taken for granted: chronologically they had been "the first to believe in Christ." [25] But they now belong to a relatively remote past and are viewed objectively as a group with whom the contemporary Christian community sustains no living contacts. The conclusion to which these data rather clearly point is that Ephesians was an encyclical epistle designed for publication and for general circulation among Gentile Christians, who at this time almost entirely composed the membership of the church.

Date.—Those who think of Ephesians as having been written by Paul usually locate it during the period of his Roman imprisonment [26] and regard its date as identical with that of Colossians and Philemon.[27] When, however, the data of the epistle are viewed as making its authenticity incredible, its literary relationships become the decisive clue to the date.

There are no traces of acquaintance with Paul's letters in Mark, Matthew, or Luke-Acts. After Luke-Acts and for a quarter of a century or more, however, Christian writings are saturated with literary reminiscences of a collection of the letters in which Ephesians was included. Ephesians itself creates the impression of having been built out of materials from Luke-Acts and Paul's letters. In turn Ephesians was used by the authors of Revelation, First Peter, Hebrews, the Fourth Gospel, First Clement, and the epistles of Ignatius and Polycarp. These literary connections suggest a date of about 95. Such a date coincides with the historical allusions of the letter and is further confirmed by the agreement in tone with Luke-Acts, Revelation, First Peter, and the Fourth Gospel.

Place of Composition.—Those who attribute Ephesians to Paul usually make Rome the place of its origin. On the basis of precisely the same data, Ephesians, Colossians, and Philemon are all three located at Rome. A different view of the authorship of the epistle makes Ephesus its natural location. The traces of its early

[24] 1:13; 2:1-3; 3:1.   [25] 1:11-12.   [26] 3:1; 4:1; 6:20.
[27] 6:21; cf. Col. 4:7; Philem. 13.

circulation in Asia Minor as a member of the published collection
of Paul's letters constitute the evidence. Revelation, the Fourth
Gospel, the epistles of Ignatius, and the epistle of Polycarp to the
Philippians are the principal witnesses. The evidence they supply
points with a high degree of probability to Ephesus. Ephesus was
pre-eminent among the centers of early Christian life for its interest
in the creation and conservation of a body of Christian literature,
and the understanding of Ephesians as a preface to the earliest significant venture in Christian publication points to that city as its
most intelligible setting.

Occasion and Purpose.—Adolf Jülicher hesitated to date this
epistle in the last decade of the first century because, as he put the
matter, "no clear hypothesis of the circumstances under which a
Paulus redivivus might have composed the Epistle to the Ephesians
has ever been provided." He therefore found it "impossible to see
what purpose he could have served." [28] The difficulty of visualizing
a situation and defining a purpose for Ephesians has continued to
create confusion for those who undertake to interpret the epistle
within the framework of traditional opinion.[29] Light on problems
customarily dismissed as enigmatic depends on the resolution of this
difficulty.

Viewed as having been inspired by the publication of Luke-Acts
and addressed to a similarly situated reading public, Ephesians supplies the data needed for an accurate reconstruction of the situation
out of which it came. Its author, an Asian Christian, very probably
Onesimus, already possessed Colossians and Philemon. With these
letters in hand and with an initial sense of deep personal indebtedness to Paul he was stimulated by a reading of Luke-Acts to undertake the collection and publication of Paul's letters. That he thus
came by the suggestion is borne out by the irenic motivation common to Acts and Ephesians, by the vivid awareness in the two
writings of the indebtedness of Gentile Christianity to Paul, and
by the essential similarity of the picture of Paul in Ephesians as "an

[28] *Introduction*, pp. 146-47.

[29] E. F. Scott, for instance, views the epistle as having the character of "a
private meditation" reduced to writing by the author primarily "for his own
satisfaction." The writer sees heretical teaching as endangering the entire church
and as heading up in a particular locality. For this local group, of whose
members Paul had no personal knowledge and for whose identification no
sufficient data are now available, Paul composed Ephesians. (*The Epistles of
Paul to the Colossians, to Philemon, and to the Ephesians*, p. 123.)

envoy, and in prison" for the sake of the "heathen" to the representation in Acts." [30]

But Ephesians was neither a formal essay nor a "private meditation." It was addressed to the practical needs of a church-wide situation. It was as definitely related to contemporary circumstances as any of Paul's letters had been, differing in that its public was the church in its entirety. It was, as Moffatt has aptly said, "a manifesto of Paul's mind upon the situation," a "tract for the times." [31] Divisive influences were at work. Heretical sects were multiplying. By the side of these sectarian leaders the author of Acts had set the heroic figure of Paul, carefully emphasizing the conciliatory quality of his spirit to the practical elimination of the controversial note present in Paul's own letters. With a similarly irenic objective the author of Ephesians took the further step of publishing Paul's letters, thereby making it possible for the apostle to speak again for himself.[32] For Paul thus to speak to the entire church would, in the opinion of the author of Ephesians, emphasize the inferiority of the sectarian interpretations of the gospel. He must have seen, too, that such an impressive and inherently valuable literary statement of the Christian message would inevitably become a bond of unity, a sort of embryonic canon of Christian scripture.

But Paul's letters were entirely informal and local in character. Their relevance for Christians living a generation after they were written needed to be shown. The author of Ephesians undertook to do this. No other understanding of his purpose better corresponds to the contents of the epistle itself. For the needs of a later time he summarized Paul's essential message, carefully using Paul's own imagery and language wherever possible. In this way he illustrated how Christians might continue to derive stimulation from a series of messages to local Christian groups of an earlier generation.

This conception of the purpose of Ephesians explains its heavy indebtedness to Colossians and at the same time its elimination of the controversial tone of that letter. It makes entirely understandable the retention of Philemon in the published collection of Paul's letters. It illuminates the author's self-imposed restriction to the use of the imagery and phraseology of Luke-Acts and Paul's nine letters in writing a message distinctly his own to the church of his day.

[30] 3:1; 4:1; 6:20; cf. Acts 20:24-25; 28:20, 30-31.
[31] *Introduction*, p. 388.   [32] 3:4.

It provides the "clear hypothesis of the circumstances" for which Jülicher sought "under which a Paulus redivivus might have composed" an encyclical epistle in Paul's name, and it proposes reasonable solutions for the crucial problems of the epistle instead of dismissing them as enigmatic. That Ephesians was written to serve as a preface for Paul's published letters is therefore the most probable explanation of its purpose.[33] Its intention was to commend the letters to the entire church and thereby counteract sectarianism and promote Christian unity.

Message.—The prominence of exhortation in Ephesians supplies the clue for an understanding of its message. The theological emphases of the epistle reflect practical rather than theoretical interests. This note of urgent entreaty appears in the prayer that God will grant the readers "the Spirit of wisdom and revelation" so that they "may know what the hope is to which he calls" them.[34] It is present in the author's reminder of their former estranged and hopeless condition,[35] and in the insistence that they read Paul's letters for insight into "the secret of the Christ . . . that through union with Christ Jesus the heathen are fellow-heirs with the Jews."[36] It finds expression in the author's unceasing prayer that they may be "filled with the very fulness of God,"[37] and in the culminating series of exhortations that they "live lives worthy of the summons" they have received, being zealous "to maintain the unity of the Spirit through the tie of peace."[38]

The effort of the writer was to communicate to his readers a measure of the ardor and religious appreciation which a reading of Paul's letters had aroused in him. Greek Christians of the third and fourth generations needed to have their eyes opened to the grandeur of their faith and to the immeasurable worth of their privileges as Christians. The author summarizes the cardinal truths of Christianity for them, refers them to Paul's letters for an adequate exposition of these truths, and earnestly pleads for personal fidelity to them.[39] He describes Christian salvation as the fulfillment of God's "generous purpose," and as accomplished by means of "his surprisingly great power." God's mercy rather than man's merit is its explanation. The immediate results of salvation are

[33] Goodspeed, *The Meaning of Ephesians*, pp. 3-75.   [34] 1:17-18.
[35] 2:11-12.   [36] 3:1-6.   [37] 3:14-19.   [38] 4:1-6:20.
[39] 1:3-2:22.

newness of spiritual energy for the believer and the experience of direct guidance from Christ as head of the Christian community. These immediate blessings implicitly involve a sharing of Christ's heavenly exaltation. In fact the same "surpassingly great" power exerted by God "in raising Christ from the dead, and seating him at his right hand in heaven" becomes the resource of everyone who exercises faith. This is the basis of the worth of Christian salvation.

Divisiveness, whether due to racism or sectarianism, stands condemned by the impartiality of the love of Christ.[40] Christ's love implied the universalization of the heritage of the Jews. Paul's letters clearly taught the abolition of all special privilege. That "the heathen are fellow-heirs with the Jews, belong to the same body and share the promise with them" is the distinctive and timeless message contained in Paul's letters.[41] Because every local "family" or church "takes its name" from the Father and is strengthened by his Spirit, the church universal ought to be an indissoluble unity based on the common access to God enjoyed by each local group.[42]

By an effective and indissoluble unity within the church, and by the manifestation of a new quality of life by individual believers, Christians will demonstrate their appreciation of the worth of Christian salvation and will so commend its worth as to destroy the appeal of heretical teaching.[43] Paul's suffering in the interest of Greek Christianity ought to give weight to what he said about Christian unity. No heretical teacher can match his record of unselfish service.[44] Paul emphasized this unity by making it clear that the "one hope that belongs to the summons" Christians receive implies "one body." Christian unity roots in Christ's headship of this "body" whose every "ligament" ought to be so "adjusted and united" as to assure harmonious functioning. Christian unity leaves abundant room for diversity of endowment and activity, but it leaves no place for divisiveness.

They who "have been taught what Christ means" know that "union with him" involves the transformation of the whole life of the individual.[45] Converted Gentiles must lay aside the habits of the "old self" and "adopt a new attitude of mind." They must "put on a new self which has been created in likeness to God, with all the uprightness and holiness that belong to the truth." They must

---

[40] 3:1-21.   [41] 3:1-13.   [42] 3:14-21.   [43] 4:1-6:20.
[44] 4:1-16.   [45] 4:17-5:2.

"lead loving lives" with the love of Christ as the criterion and in this way "follow God's example, like his dear children." The governing principle in Christian living is "reverence to Christ."[46] Christians must therefore live as "children of light" and exemplify the "perfect goodness" which alone "pleases the Lord." They can have no relations with those heretical teachers whose "worthless arguments" minimize the moral seriousness of fleshly indulgence.

Returning to the theme of unity, the author likens the relationship between Christ and the church to an ideal marriage.[47] Christ loves the church, and the church in turn must obey him as Lord and keep its members loyal to him alone. A disruption of the unity of the church is equivalent to infidelity to Christ as sole Lord of its life. Christian eduation must safeguard the future unity of the church by providing youth "with Christian training and instruction." [48] Nor must the master-slave relationship be permitted to obscure the basic unity inherent in Christian faith.[49] Instead, slaves and masters must regulate their relations in the light of their common accountability to their heavenly Master, who "will show no partiality." Christian faith requires believers to join with Christ in warfare against "the devil's stratagems." [50] Believers must therefore be spiritually armed. They must share the "mighty strength" of the Lord, because their common enemies are the "spirit-forces of evil on high."

[46] 5:3-21.   [47] 5:22-33.   [48] 6:1-4.   [49] 6:5-9.   [50] 6:10-20.

XIV

THE EPISTLE TO THE HEBREWS

Authorship.—Hebrews was favorably known in the western half of
the church from the time of Clement of Rome onward, even though
it did not achieve canonical status until late in the fourth century.
The First Epistle of Clement to the Corinthians was probably inspired by the challenge of the author of Hebrews that the Roman
church "ought to be teaching others." [1] Similarly, it was probably
the purpose of the Shepherd of Hermas to soften the rigorous position of Hebrews that "it is impossible to arouse people to a fresh
repentance when they have once for all come into the light." [2] The
author of the Shepherd insisted on the possibility of at least one
such repentance. Justin also clearly knew Hebrews,[3] but like the
other earliest witnesses he says nothing of its authorship. The
omission of the epistle from Marcion's canon more probably indicates rejection of its Pauline authorship than lack of acquaintance
with the epistle.

Hebrews was generally known in the West around A.D. 200. It was
not, however, regarded as a letter of Paul. For that reason, pre-
sumbly, it was not treated as canonical. That view of its authorship
explains its omission from the Muratorian canon. It explains the
attitude of Irenaeus [4] and Gaius,[5] both of whom knew the epistle,
but neither of whom thought Paul wrote it. Tertullian described the

[1] Heb. 5:12. Bacon says that Hebrews is "used in forty-seven places by
Clement" (*Introduction*, p. 147; cf. Leipoldt, *Geschichte des neutestamentlichen
Kanons*, I, 188, 219). Passages that reflect literary acquaintance are: I Clem.
9:3-4 (cf. Heb. 11:5-7); 12:1 ff. (cf. Heb. 11:31); 17:1 (cf. Heb. 11:37); 19:2 (cf.
Heb. 12:1); 21:9 (cf. Heb. 4:12); 27:2 (cf. Heb. 6:18); 36:1 (cf. Heb. 2:18; 3:1);
36:2 (cf. Heb. 1:3-4); 43:1 (cf. Heb. 3:2-5).

[2] Heb. 6:4-8; cf. Herm. Mand. IV. iii. 1-7. Other passages that reflect acquaintance with Hebrews are: Vis. II. ii. 7 (cf. Heb. 11:33); Vis. II. iii. 2 (cf.
Heb. 3:13); Vis. III. vii. 2 (cf. Heb. 3:13); Vis. IV. ii. 4; Sim. IX. xiii. 7 (cf. Heb.
11:33); Sim. IX. ii. 2 (cf. Heb. 10:19-20).

[3] *Apol.* 12:9 (cf. Heb. 3:1); *Dial* 13:1 (cf. Heb. 9:13-14); 19:3 (cf. Heb. 11:15);
19:4 (cf. Heb. 5:6; 6:20; 7:1-2); 46:3; 56:1 (cf. Heb. 3:5); 67:9 (cf. Heb. 12:21);
96:1 (cf. Heb. 7:17, 24); 113:5 (cf. Heb. 5:6, 10); 121:2 (cf. Heb. 4:12-13).

[4] Euseb. *Hist.* V. 26. 3.   [5] Euseb. *Hist.* VI. 20. 3.

author as a comrade of the apostle and identified him as Barnabas.[6]

In contrast with this attitude of the West, the Alexandrian fathers and the eastern half of the church in general attributed Hebrews to Paul and from the outset included it in their New Testament canon. Clement of Alexandria represents Pantaenus as saying Paul wrote Hebrews but refrained from using his name because of "modesty" and "to give due deference to the Lord," who had designated him an "apostle of the gentiles."[7] Clement himself shared this view. He thought the nonuse of Paul's name was due to the apostle's knowledge that the Jews "had conceived a prejudice against him and were suspicious of him," and so "he very wisely did not repel them at the beginning by putting his name."[8] Clement was aware of the evident differences in the literary style of Hebrews and the other letters of Paul, but he accounted for it on the supposition that Paul wrote the epistle in Hebrew and Luke translated it into Greek. Origen subscribed to the tradition of "the men of old time" that Paul wrote Hebrews, but he attributed the diction of the epistle to an amanuensis whose identity God alone knew.[9] Eusebius, although aware of the attitude of the West, included Hebrews in his own fourteen-letter Pauline corpus;[10] and Athanasius, without taking the trouble to mention differences of opinion, listed Hebrews as one of the fourteen letters of Paul.[11]

Late in the fourth century ecclesiastical considerations rather than a fresh appraisal of historical evidence brought about an agreement between the East and the West. Hebrews and Revelation, which were respectively popular in these divisions of the church, were as a result both accorded canonical status. Hilary of Poitiers (367) was the first western leader to champion Paul's authorship of Hebrews.[12] He had lived as an exile in the East and had there come to regard Hebrews as written by Paul and as canonical. Priscillian and Rufinus were western contemporaries of Hilary who also accepted Hebrews as one of the fourteen letters of Paul.

Jerome and Augustine exercised a decisive influence on opinion in the West. Jerome was aware of the history of opinion regarding Hebrews in both sections of the church. While using great caution

---

[6] *On Modesty* XX. 3.

[7] Euseb. *Hist.* VI. 14. 4.

[8] Euseb. *Hist.* VI. 14. 3.

[9] Euseb. *Hist.* VI. 25. 11-13.

[10] *Hist.* III. 3. 5; VI. 20. 3.

[11] *Festal Letter* XXXIX. 5.

[12] *On the Trinity* IV. 11.

in his citations of the epistle, he implicitly treats it as a letter of Paul and has no doubt whatsoever of its right to be included in the New Testament.[13] Augustine is similarly conscious of the denial of the Pauline authorship of Hebrews, but he lists the epistle among those assigned to Paul [14] and entertains no doubt of its canonicity. The Councils of Carthage in 397 and 419 respectively reflect the transition in opinion brought about by Jerome and Augustine. In 397 Hebrews was differentiated from the thirteen letters of Paul. In 419, however, the Pauline corpus is described as consisting of fourteen letters.

The epistle itself tends to substantiate the early judgment in the West regarding its authorship. In its extant form it is anonymous rather than pseudepigraphic, although the mention of Timothy [15] conceivably means that Paul was originally described as the author. This is rendered less probable, however, by the author's differentiation of himself from the first hearers of the gospel message.[16] His admission of dependence on those who heard the Lord for acquaintance with what was "proclaimed by the Lord himself" represents a religious position which Luther, Erasmus, and Calvin rightly regarded as irreconcilable with Paul's explicit insistence that "the good news" he preached came to him directly "through a revelation of Jesus Christ." [17] Not only does the author's statement indicate a radically different religious point of view from Paul's, but it seems to describe him as belonging to the second or third generation of Christians.

The epistle is distinguished from Paul's letters also by its style. The author consciously strives for rhetorical effect, and his Greek style is polished and definitely literary. Energy rather than smoothness characterizes Paul's writing. Hebrews also lacks the miscellaneous and informal quality of Paul's letters. It is by comparison a systematic and elaborately worked out treatment of a single theme.

More important than the matter of style is the absence from Hebrews of the great Pauline conceptions of justification by faith, mystical union with Christ, and dying and rising with Christ. There are only the faintest traces [18] of Paul's pervasive emphasis on personally possessing the Spirit. Faith is the watchword of He-

---

[13] *On Illustrious Men* V; *Epistles* 53:8; 129:3.

[14] *Christian Doctrine* II. 8; *City of God* XVI. 22.   [15] 13:23.   [16] 2:3.

[17] Gal. 1:10-12.   [18] 6:4; 10:29.

brews and of Paul's letters, but its meaning in Hebrews is hardly Pauline. The conception of salvation, too, is almost wholly future —a matter of going to heaven, something to be realized at the end of the earthly existence—whereas Paul thought of the believer as assured of future salvation because in the immediate present he is "in Christ."

The First Readers.—Hebrews lacks any such specific address as regularly appears at the opening of Paul's letters. It probably never had an address. Instead the epistle opens with a statement of the theme of which the body of the writing is a systematic exposition. The author, nevertheless, clearly had in mind a local church group whose members he had long known and with whom he sustained the warmest personal relations. He addresses them as directly and intimately as a preacher would his audience,[19] and his personal allusions constitute natural elements in a homily.[20] The organization and style of Hebrews give it a definitely sermonic character. The epistolary conclusion[21] suggests that the author's message would more appropriately have been orally delivered but was reduced to written form and dispatched as an epistle because of the exigencies of the author's circumstances.

The intention of the title "To the Hebrews" was to designate the first readers as Jewish Christians, probably members of the Jerusalem church, who were conceived to be in danger of relapsing from Christianity into Judaism. However, this title is not earlier than the third century. Instead of shedding light on the identity of the original readers, it creates confusion because it reflects a serious misunderstanding of the author's purpose. The title probably originated as an inference from the apparent importance of Judaism in the argument of the epistle and was prefixed to the epistle in Alexandria, where the writing was accepted as Pauline and canonical nearly two centuries earlier than in the West.

Insuperable difficulties prevent an identification of the Jerusalem church or any other Jewish Christian group as the original recipients of Hebrews. The relevant data locate the epistle in the closing decade of the first century, and the Jerusalem church passed out of existence as a result of the Jewish War (66-70). Nor does the description of the recipients as not having taught others and

[19] 3:1, 12; 5:11; 6:9; 12:4; 13:7, 17.
[20] 5:11; 6:9-12; 10:32-39; 12:4-8, 14; 13:1-9, 17-19.　　　　[21] 13:20-25.

themselves needing to be taught "the very elements of Christian truth" [22] fit the Jerusalem church. Furthermore, the author derived his only knowledge of Judaism from reading the Septuagint version of the Pentateuch. He conceived of it as consisting in the Levitical ritual system and centering about the wilderness tabernacle, whereas the only actual Judaism into which a Jewish Christian of the first century could relapse consisted in the way of life set forth in the Law as interpreted through the synagogue. In that sense, therefore, Hebrews becomes a thoroughly un-Jewish book and can have had no relevancy for Christians who were being tempted to abandon Christianity for Judaism. Its message possessed effectiveness for Hellenistic Christians whose Bible was the Greek Old Testament and whose knowledge of Judaism was, like the author's entirely literary. They were tempted to become apathetic and purely nominal in their Christianity rather than to abandon Christianity for Judaism.

The very slender threads of evidence contributing to an identification of the character and geographical location of the group for whom Hebrews was written suggest the recipients were a relatively small and highly homogeneous non-Jewish circle within the Roman church, whose members were either accredited leaders or else persons in preparation for such leadership. The use of Hebrews by the authors of First Clement and the Shepherd, both of them representatives of Roman Christianity, indicates a Roman destination for the epistle. This is strengthened by the final greeting, "The brothers from Italy wish to be remembered to you." [23] Apparently Italian Christians with the writer outside Italy joined in greetings to their Roman friends.[24]

The systematic and elaborate treatment of a single theme which constitutes the content of Hebrews can hardly have been intended, however, for the entire membership of the Roman church. It would have been appropriate for a small group of leaders whose interests were specialized. That the recipients of the epistle were such a group is indicated by the emphasis on the qualifications and responsibilities of leaders running throughout the document.[25]

Date.—Eusebius interpreted Clement of Rome's frequent use of Hebrews as showing "the treatise was no recent thing," and so as

[22] 5:12.   [23] 13:24.

[24] Cf. Ign. Magn. 15:1: "The Ephesians greet you from Smyrna, where also I am writing you." See also Scott, *The Epistle to the Hebrews,* pp. 10-15.

[25] 3:16; 4:8, 11; 5:12, 14; 6:1, 10; 13:5, 7, 9, 17, 24.

helping to establish its Pauline authorship.[26] Actually Clement's familiarity with the epistle does nothing more than establish A.D. 96 as a *terminus ad quem* for it. Other data indicate "the treatise" was a very "recent thing" when Clement knew it. Most decisive of such data is the author's clear acquaintance with Paul's published letters, of which only Second Thessalonians and Philemon appear to have been unused.[27]

Other data favorable to some such date as 95 for the epistle are: (1) The readers belonged to a generation who had received their Christianity by tradition.[28] (2) They were mature Christians whose experience, in some instances, reached back to Nero's time.[29] (3) The "great struggle with persecution" associated with the "early days" [30] is rather clearly a reminiscence of the Neronian persecution. (4) References to immediately impending suffering [31] are sufficiently like those in Revelation and First Peter to suggest a location for Hebrews within the period of Domitian's attack on the church.

Place of Composition.—The greeting with which Hebrews closes [32] indicates the author was for the time being somewhere outside Italy, whence he and other Italian Christians who shared his exile sent greetings to their Roman associates. Evidence for a more specific identification of the place where Hebrews was written is not available. Its early popularity in Alexandria does not mean it necessarily originated there. Its heavy indebtedness to Paul's published letters might be interpreted as pointing to Ephesus, but this is not necessarily the case. Where outside Italy the epistle was written must remain a matter of conjecture.

Occasion and Purpose.—The author of Hebrews calls what he has "briefly" written a "word of exhortation." [33] In keeping with this description, the tone of fervent appeal characterizes the entire epistle. The alternation of doctrinal discussion with pleas for the readers to be governed by its practical implications [34] illustrates the author's definitely practical purpose. He wanted believers who faced concrete and pressing problems to find in religious faith resources for triumphant living.

[26] *Hist.* III. 38. 1-2.

[27] See my *Paul Becomes a Literary Influence*, p. 88.

[28] 2:3.   [29] 5:12; 6:4-7; 10:32.   [30] 10:32-34.

[31] 10:36; 11:35-39; 12:1-11; 13:7.   [32] 13:24.   [33] 13:22.

[34] 2:1-4; 3:1, 12-15; 4:1-3; 4:11-16; 5:11–6:14; 10:19-36; 12:1–13:17.

The group addressed had received Christianity as an inheritance. Their original leaders had mostly passed away, and these readers belonged to the third generation of believers.[35] They knew by report what their predecessors had undergone at the hands of Nero,[36] but they were unprepared for similar experiences of suffering themselves. Domitian's onslaught accordingly made them wonder if their religion was actually worth the hardships it brought upon them.[37] Instead of a relapse from Christianity into the legalism or ritualism of Judaism, the danger threatening to overwhelm them was utter discouragement. Their Christianity was becoming purely nominal. Their frame of mind resembled the mood of the first readers of Revelation.[38]

In earlier crises Christians had been sustained by the confident expectation of the imminent return of Jesus. Toward the close of the first century, and throughout the second, disappointment at the delay of the Parousia became a serious problem. Skepticism regarding it contributed to a loss of morale among the readers of Hebrews.[39] The sufferings they endured caused them to look critically at a religious heritage they had taken for granted. Discovering the traditional ideology of apocalypticism had become outmoded, they found themselves with no adequate intellectual warrant for their faith. They consequently tended to lose heart when identification with the Christian movement subjected them to severe penalties.

The absent teacher of this group undertook to quicken their consciences and renew their fervor by stimulating them to think profoundly about the real foundation of Christian faith. Traditional statements had lost their relevancy. Apocalypticism no longer provided a sound ideology. This teacher felt that the despondency of his readers would give place to courage if he could make them think discerningly about Christ as a person. Instead of specifically rejecting apocalypticism, he pushed its conceptions from the center to the circumference of the circle of vital Christian interests. The soundness of Christianity consisted not in its eschatological expectations but in its effectiveness for securing access to God for men. Christianity's incomparable asset in the personality of Christ gave it this effectiveness.[40] Accordingly the author of Hebrews

[35] 2:3; 13:7.   [36] 10:32-36; cf. Tacitus *Annals* XV. 44.   [37] 12:4-13.
[38] Rev. 2:4; 3:15-17.   [39] 9:28; 10:35-37; cf. II. Pet. 3:3-14.
[40] 8:1; 9:11; 13:8-16.

presents an inspiring Christology as the credential of the surpassing worth of the gospel and the cure for waning religious ardor.

Message.—The message of Hebrews is set in a framework the constituent elements of which were derived from different cultural backgrounds. From the apocalyptic tradition of primitive Christianity the author has retained the conception of history in terms of two ages between which a divine judgment intervenes.[41] He constantly adapts that view, however, to the definitely more congenial Platonic doctrine of two worlds that exist concurrently.[42] He thinks of the visible order as a shadowy copy of the unseen and eternal world of reality. In their quest for access to God men must turn from material creation and acclimate themselves in this higher world. They must follow the pathway pioneered by Christ when "he went once for all through that greater, more perfect tent of worship not made by human hands nor a part of our material creation" into the heavenly sanctuary as the condition of appearing "in the very presence of God." [43] The new age of primitive Christian expectation is understood to be a manifestation on earth of the order of heaven, but men may immediately begin to live the life of "the new order." Salvation, in fact, is interpreted primarily as the achievement of meaningful fellowship with God by means of a present commitment to Christ. Those who "anchor" their souls in the ideal world, "where Jesus has gone ahead of us," [44] possess the endurance and courage needed to meet earthly sufferings victoriously. The Christianity of Hebrews, then, consists in man's identification of himself through Christ with the eternal and unseen heavenly order and his consequent achievement of freedom from the fears that haunt the shadow world of time and sense.

The description of the provisions of the Levitical ritual as "only copied from the originals in heaven," and of "the heavenly originals" as requiring "far better sacrifices than these," [45] illustrates the religious implications of the author's world view and at the same time lays a foundation for the thesis of Hebrews that Christianity represents finality in religion. Christianity possesses the character of finality because it brings to perfect fruition all earlier endeavors to establish fellowship between men and God. Until the

[41] 2:14-15; 6:2, 5; 10:25, 27, 31.
[42] 4:9-14; 7:1-4, 10; 8:2; 9:11-14; 10:23-25.   [43] 9:11, 24.
[44] 6:17-20.   [45] 9:23; cf. 10:1-5.

coming of Christ [46] and his qualification of himself to serve men as the true high priest [47] Judaism had provided the surest path to God. To establish the final character of Christianity, therefore, the author of Hebrews felt he had only to demonstrate its superiority to Judaism. He treats the Law as consisting in observances of the Levitical ritual. Logically, then, he shows that Christ as God's son stands closer to God than the angels,[48] by whom Moses received the Law. He is, moreover, greater than Moses,[49] who inaugurated the Law. Finally, as "the high priest of the better system under which" Christians live, he belongs to a priesthood superior in kind to Aaronic priesthood.[50]

The author's interest in his thesis is entirely practical. His object is to make discouraged Christians proud of their faith. He thinks he can accomplish this by showing them the final character of the Christian revelation. He will by this means demonstrate Christianity's great worth. People who are religiously inclined at all will want to avail themselves of God's surest revelation of truth. They must also see how justly they deserve condemnation if they neglect the obligations implicit in this revelation.[51] The author's method of elaborating his position may seem a bit fanciful. The soundness of the position itself, however, is clear. With splendid clarity he sees that religious authority resides in "the man who wields it," and that "the priesthood which can bring us nearer to God must be one of inherent character and personality." [52]

Worship is for the author of Hebrews the essence of religion. Real access to God is the criterion by which he estimates the value of Christianity.[53] Before Christ came exceptional individuals enjoyed fellowship with God in a limited degree. Christ, however, brought within the reach of all men the privilege hitherto enjoyed by the exceptional and specially favored person. He accomplished this in several ways. He clothed faith with sanity and certainty by an intelligible and winsome revelation of God. He pioneered the pathway to God himself by fully exploring and adequately exemplifying the meaning of faith in his earthly life. By his sacrifice of himself he dealt adequately and decisively with sin for the first

---

[46] 1:1-5.   [47] 2:8-11; 5:7-10.   [48] 1:4-14; 2:5-18.   [49] 3:1-6.
[50] 3:14–10:18.
[51] 1:1-4; 2:1-3; 3:12, 19; 4:1, 12; 6:4-8; 10:26-30; 12:18-25.
[52] Scott, *The Epistle to the Hebrews*, p. 208.   [53] 10:19-22.

time in human history and in so doing obviated the most difficult obstacle to fellowship with God.[54] The supreme service Christ rendered men consisted in the reality he gave to the loftiest aspirations of ordinary men. He penetrated the veil of appearances hitherto obscuring God and pioneered a pathway by which any man can follow him into the very presence of God.[55]

Man's individual appropriation of the blessings made available by Christ depends on his exercise of faith. As defined by the author of Hebrews, faith consists basically in viewing as actual those realities of the spiritual order which cannot be comprehended by the senses.[56] It is both intellectual and moral.[57] It involves the conviction of the real existence of the ideal world. Just as definitely, faith enables men to adjust themselves to the spiritual order and in the midst of earthly existence conform their lives to the heavenly pattern. It expresses a preference for the spiritual order behind the shifting earthly scene. It endows human life with unwonted moral strength and makes heroic achievement possible for ordinary people. Men of faith are described as having "once for all come into the light and had a taste of the gift from heaven, and shared in the holy Spirit and felt the goodness of the word of God and the strong influences of the coming age." [58] The fearlessness and perseverance of such people grow out of the fact that like Moses they constantly see "him who is unseen." [59] The faith principle antedates Christianity. It is as old as Abraham. Faith is the vital principle which unites living men with "the men of old." Christian faith is distinctive because Christians have Jesus as their "leader and example in faith" and because he has now "taken his seat at the right hand of the throne of God." [60]

[54] 1:3; 2:11, 18; 7:26-27; 9:11-16, 26-28; 10:1-11; 13:8-13.
[55] 4:14; 6:19-20; 7:26-28; 9:24-25; 13:10.   [56] 11:1-2.
[57] 11:6.   [58] 6:4-6.   [59] 11:13-16, 27.   [60] 12:1-2.

XV

.THE REVELATION OF JOHN

Authorship.--The Revelation of John was intended in the first instance for public reading in the seven Asian churches mentioned in
the address. Its promises and predictions were, however, implicitly
intended for Christians everywhere. The author clearly expected a
wide circulation for his message. That there was a fairly widespread use of the writing is implied in Irenaeus' reference to the
"ancient and genuine copies" of it.[1] This is further borne out by
the statement of Eusebius that the Montanists used "testimonies
drawn from the Apocalypse of John." [2]

Except, however, for the highly probable reflection in First Peter
of literary acquaintance with Revelation,[3] no explicit evidence for
its circulation exists until the middle of the second century. Literary
parallels in the writings of the Apostolic Fathers consist of ideas
and imagery equally characteristic of other writings or so remote as
to have practically no evidential value.[4]

Andrew, bishop of Caesarea in Cappadocia in the fifth or early
sixth century, wrote a commentary on Revelation in which he represented Papias as regarding it an inspired writing. He says nothing
of Papias' judgment concerning its authorship. Eusebius, however,
who argues against the tradition of its authorship by John the
apostle, fails to quote Papias against the tradition, a fact which may
imply Papias' agreement with it. No extant statement of Papias
corroborates Andrew's allusion. In view of Papias' known interests,

---

[1] Irenaeus says that "all ancient and genuine copies" of Revelation read the
number of "the animal" (13:18) as "666" rather than "616" (*Her.* V. 30. 1; cf.
Euseb. *Hist.* V. 8. 5).

[2] *Hist.* V. 18. 14.

[3] The "Babylon" of I Pet. 5:13 is rather clearly suggested by the allusion of
Rev. 17:5, 9. The soundest understanding of the purpose of First Peter is that
it was written to disavow for Roman Christianity the bitterness of Rev. 18:6, 20.
The specific warning that no Christian should suffer as a "revolutionist" (I Pet.
4:16) suggests the mood Revelation implicity encouraged.

[4] I Clem. 34:3 (cf. Rev. 22:12; Isa. 40:10; 62:11; Prov. 24:12) ; Ign. Philad. 6:1
(cf. Rev. 3:12) ; Barn. 6:13 (cf. Rev. 21:5; Isa. 43:19) ; 7:9 (cf. Rev. 1:7, 13; Zech.
12:10) ; 21:3 (cf. Rev. 22:10, 12; Isa. 40:10).

however, Andrew's representation of his view of Revelation involves no improbability. Papias is therefore regarded as the earliest explicit witness for the circulation of Revelation.

The epistle of the churches of Vienne and Lyons, preserved in large part by Eusebius,[5] contains numerous echoes of the language of Revelation, but without specific mention of the book or reference to its authorship. At one point, however, where there is a free quotation of Rev. 22:11, the introductory formula used is, "That the Scripture might be fulfilled."[6] This indicates a circulation for Revelation in Gaul and a recognition of it as authoritative around the middle of the second century. Eusebius represents Theophilus of Antioch and Melito of Sardis, both of them belonging to the last quarter of the second century, as acquainted with Revelation and valuing it highly. He says Theophilus used "testimonies from the Apocalypse of John" in his *Against the Heresy of Hermogenes*.[7] Among the sixteen books attributed to Melito, one, according to Eusebius, was on Revelation.[8]

The tradition of the authorship of Revelation by John the apostle begins with the earliest explicit mention of the book. Justin refers to Revelation by name and says John, its author, was "one of the apostles of Christ."[9] Irenaeus makes frequent use of the book, assumes Christians generally knew and valued it, and himself clearly regarded John the apostle as its author.[10] Similarly, Clement of Alexandria, Tertullian, and Origen assume general acquaintance with it and regard it as the work of John the apostle. Thus, from the middle of the second century onward, the tradition exists that the John of Revelation was one of the Twelve. Nor is there record of a comparable tradition favoring an author other than the apostle.

Dissent from this identification of the author was more frequently on doctrinal than historical grounds. The Alogi rejected apostolic authorship for Revelation as a phase of their opposition to Montanism. Similarly Gaius, a Roman presbyter during the last quarter of the second century, rejected the authority and apostolic authorship of the book. In his attack on Proclus, a Montanist leader, Gaius suggested Cerinthus wrote the book and falsely attributed

[5] *Hist.* V. 1–2.   [6] *Hist.* V. 1. 58.   [7] *Hist.* IV. 24.

[8] *Hist.* IV. 26. 2.   [9] *Dial.* 81:4; cf. Euseb. *Hist.* IV. 18. 8.

[10] *Her.* II. 22. 5; III. 3. 4; IV. 20. 11; IV. 30. 4; V. 26. 1; Euseb. *Hist.* III. 23. 3; IV. 14. 6; V. 8. 4; V. 24. 16.

it to John.[11] The Muratorian fragment, which reflects Roman opinion about 200, describes the Fourth Gospel as written by John, "one of the disciples," but fails so to identify the John of Revelation. If anti-Montanist bias caused the author of this ancient list to mention Revelation in the same context with the Apocalypse of Peter and the Shepherd, his silence about John's identify may be a tacit denial that he was the apostle.

In the middle of the third century Dionysius of Alexandria, a vigorous opponent of millenarianism, denied that the John of Revelation was the apostle. He regarded the Fourth Gospel and the First Epistle of John as having been written by the apostle and argued on linguistic and stylistic grounds that Revelation could not have been from the same hand. He described the author as "a holy and inspired person" but denied he was John the apostle. He saw in John Mark a possible identification of the author of Revelation, but he did not urge it. Because he knew "there were two tombs at Ephesus, and that each of the two is said to be John's," Dionysius concluded there was a John "among those that were in Asia" other than John the apostle. He credited the latter with the authorship of the Fourth Gospel and First Epistle of John, and thought this other John probably wrote Revelation.[12]

Eusebius, who preserves the argument of Dionysius so fully, and who was evidently influenced by Dionysius, regarded a second John known as "the Elder" as author of the writing.[13] Rejection of apostolic authorship and authority thereafter became increasingly frequent in the East, with the result that Revelation did not find a place in the Peshitto and the earliest forms of the Egyptian and Armenian versions of the New Testament. Greek manuscripts of the book, moreover, became rare by the beginning of the fifth century.

No data in the book itself warrant the identification of its author with any particular one of the several Johns of the early church. He is described simply as the "slave" of Jesus Christ and the "brother and companion" of his readers in the persecution that afflicted all Asian Christians.[14] His acquaintance with the past of each of the groups addressed and his knowledge of their existing circumstances [15]

[11] Euseb. *Hist.* II. 25. 6; III. 28. 2.
[13] *Hist.* III. 25. 2, 4; III. 39. 5-7, 14.
[15] 2:2-5, 13, 19, 21; 3:10.

[12] Euseb. *Hist.* VII. 25.
[14] 1:1, 4, 9; 22:8.

show him to have been an Asian Christian of standing and wide experience. Of the types of leadership recognized in the early church,[16] that of the "prophet" best suits him,[17] and he specifically calls his book a "prophecy."[18] While he never seeks to create a hearing for his message on the basis of official status, he clearly speaks with the confidence of a man who was conscious of his role as the bearer of a divine message.[19]

Nothing in Revelation requires acquaintance with the historical Jesus on the part of the author. There is, indeed, an absence of such personal reminiscences as would be expected had he been one of the Twelve. He speaks of the apostles objectively as though he was not of their number and accords them reverence which rather definitely marks him as a member of a later generation. They appear to have belonged to the heavenly throng of martyred heroes,[20] and he views them with a veneration they would not have felt for one another.[21] These data make it extremely improbable that the author of Revelation was John the apostle.

The identity of the author of Revelation will probably continue to be a matter of varying judgments, as during the first four centuries of Christian history. He was indisputably, however, a Christian prophet of Asia with a timely and compelling message whose inspiration was thoroughly real. He spoke in his own name, which for his contemporaries carried the weight his purposes required, however enigmatic subsequent centuries have found it. Whatever the variety of his sources, the personality of a single author gives unity to the book.

The First Readers.—"The seven churches of Asia," explicitly designated as "Ephesus, Smyrna, Pergamum, Thyatira, Sardis, Philadelphia, and Laodicea," were the immediate public to which Revelation was directed. The individual messages to these churches in the second and third chapters indicate the author's intimate acquaintance with local needs. Those needs caused him to write. His sense of identification with his readers[22] and his closeness to their circumstances constantly come to the surface.[23] Those concrete and immediate circumstances rather than a cycle of events destined

[16] I Cor. 12:28; 14:32; Acts 15:32; Eph. 3:5; 4:11; Rev. 16:6; 18:20.

[17] 1:1, 11, 19; 10:11; 22:6, 8-9, 16.   [18] 1:3; 22:7, 10, 18-19.

[19] 1:1-3:22; 22:8-21.   [20] 18:20.   [21] 21:14.   [22] 1:9; 22:9.

[23] 2:2-5, 13, 19, 21, 3:10.

to extend through successive centuries presaged the eschatological program "very soon" to be inaugurated.[24]

The blessing pronounced on "the man who reads" the book and on those "who hear it read" shows the book was designed in the first instance for public reading in the churches addressed.[25] This does not mean it was intended exclusively for the local groups named. The conditions forming the immediate background of Revelation were by no means restricted to Asia, as Hebrews, First Clement, and First Peter plainly show. In view of the precarious status of Christians generally, therefore, the address of the prophecy to "seven" churches means the prophet intended his message for Christians everywhere. He was thoroughly acquainted with Paul's published letters, and he wrote in Ephesus, where interest in the creation of a body of Christian literature definitely existed. He probably himself wrote for publication and not merely to ensure the public reading of an emergency message to the seven local churches named in the address.

Date.—According to Irenaeus, the Revelation "was seen . . . toward the end of Domitian's reign." [26] Domitian's reign extended from the year 81 until he was killed on September 18, 96.[27] This makes 95 an approximately accurate date on the basis of Irenaeus' testimony.

The historical situation reflected in the book and its evident literary dependence on Paul's published letters support the accuracy of the tradition reflected in the statement of Irenaeus. Certain allusions in the writing might appear to establish an earlier date.[28] These, however, belong to sources incorporated without an adjustment of their details and are only indirectly relevant for the determination of the date of Revelation. The stage of the development of emperor worship implied, the character of the persecution to which Christians are being subjected, the expectation of Nero's return, and the spiritual condition of the Asian churches are the distinguishing characteristics of the situation reflected in Revelation. Since the

[24] 1:1; 2:16; 3:11, 20; 14:15; 22:6-7, 10, 12, 17, 20.   [25] 1:3; 22:18.

[26] *Her.* V. 30. 3; Euseb. *Hist.* III. 18. 3; V. 8. 6.   [27] Pliny *Letters* IX. 13.

[28] The implications of 11:1, 8 are that the temple still stands and that the destruction of Jerusalem has not been accomplished. The reference to the temporary safety of Christians who escaped from Jerusalem (12:14-16) points to the reign of Vespasian. Similarly, Vespasian is probably the sixth of the "seven kings" of 17:10, counting from Augustus and excluding Galba, Otho, and Vitellius—the "one" who "is reigning."

time of Julius Caesar heads of the Roman state had been theo-
retically entitled to divine honors. The worship of Augustus was
authorized by the Senate and after his death spread to Asia. Caligula
(37-41) demanded that his statues be everywhere worshiped. But
not until the time of Domitian did an emperor take a really serious view of his divinity, and previous to his reign there existed no
such provisions as appear in Rev. 13:4, 8, 11-18 for the general
worship of the emperor with parallel penalties for refusal to do so.

When Christianity became known as a religious movement distinct from Judaism, it automatically assumed the status of a *religio
illicita,* since Rome did not accord legal recognition to new religions.
This does not mean, however, that systematic measures were at
once taken to suppress the movement, and Christians do not appear
to have been prosecuted for belonging to an unlawful religion
earlier than the reign of Trajan (98-117).[29] Membership in the
church did, however, become a sufficient ground for suspicion of
individuals as lawbreakers. Punishment meted out to persons under
such suspicion would vary with the seriousness with which provincial authorities conceived of the menace they constituted to the
public safety and welfare. Nero's persecution was limited to the
city of Rome and was designed to dispel popular suspicion that the
emperor was himself responsible for the burning of the city. To
"stifle scandal," says Tacitus, Nero "substituted as culprits, and
punished with the utmost refinements of cruelty, a class of men
loathed for their vices, whom the crowd styled Christians."[30] By
contrast, the persecution of Domitian, though short,[31] extended to
the provinces and employed banishment or expropriation of pos-
sessions or even death in the punishment of individuals who refused
to accord the emperor divine honors.[32] This persecution probably
supplied the precedents for the procedures mentioned in the correspondence between Pliny and Trajan.[33] It was not the systematic

---

[29] Pliny *Letters* X. 96-97; Tertullian *Apology* V.   [30] *Annals* XV. 44.

[31] Euseb. *Hist.* III. 20. 1-7; Tertullian *Apology* V.

[32] Rev. 1:9; 2:10, 13; 6:10; 18:24; cf. I Pet. 1:6; 2:11; 3:14-17; 4:12-17; 5:9;
Heb. 10:32-36; 12:4; 13:3; I Clem. 1:1; Dio Cassius *Roman History* LXVII. 14. 2.

[33] Pliny *Letters* X. 96-97. Pliny as provincial governor of Bithynia-Pontus wrote
the emperor that since he had never been present "at any trials of the Christians" he was "unacquainted with the method and limits to be observed either
in examining or punishing them." He wanted to know "whether the mere
profession of Christianity, albeit without the crimes associated therewith," was

enforcement of a statute making membership in the church a crime, but the punishment of recalcitrant individuals under the general authority all Roman magistrates possessed to suppress tendencies dangerous to the general welfare.

Shortly after Nero's death the fanciful report became current that he was not dead but had fled to Parthia, whence he would return backed by Parthian armies to punish his enemies.[34] The popular expectation of Nero's return took a variety of forms, certain of which are reflected in Revelation. Between 69 and 88 three "pretenders" to the role of the returning Nero appeared, and they are probably the explanations of the references of Rev. 6:2; 9:13-21; 16:12-14. In chapters 13 and 17 the myth takes the distinctive form of "the animal" that will "come up out of the abyss" but will "go to destruction." This imagery involves the blending of the figures of the returning Nero and of the Antichrist. The "eighth king," who is at the same time "one of the seven," [35] evidently postdates the pretenders of 69-88 and is best identified as Domitian.

Finally, the deterioration of the spiritual condition of such great Asian churches as Ephesus,[36] Sardis,[37] and Laodicea [38] suggests the lapse of a relatively long time since the period of Paul's missionary activity. Spiritual inertia had apparently supplanted the original

---

punishable. Pending advice from Trajan, he says his procedure had been to question accused persons to discover if they were Christians. Those who "confessed" were threatened with execution and were given an opportunity to renounce their faith. If they "persevered," his practice was to order them executed on the ground that their "contumacy and inflexible obstinacy deserved chastisement." Trajan replied that Pliny's method had been "extremely proper." He suggested, however, that "no search should be made for these people" and no anonymous accusations used against them as evidence. Persons who were suspected or who had confessed were to be acquitted if they would worship the Roman gods. Persons properly found guilty and refusing to repent, however, "must be punished." The emperor made it clear that his counsel was not given under any "general rule . . . which can be applied as the fixed standard in all cases of this nature" but rather applied to the use of the general authority with which every governor was clothed.

[34] Sibylline Oracles V. 137-54. H. C. O. Lanchester, who writes the article on "The Sibylline Oracles" in Charles, ed., The Apocrypha and Pseudepigrapha of the Old Testament, thinks the completed Sibylline Oracles belonged to the reign of Hadrian and was completed prior to 130, but that lines 111-78, in which the reference to Nero's flight from Rome occurs, should be dated 71-74 (II, 373, 400). This dating would tend to confirm the judgment that the conceptions of Rev. 13; 17 are a development of the time of Domitian. Juvenal says that in Domitian Rome beheld "a baldpate Nero rise to curse mankind" (Satires IV. 37-38; cf. Martial Epigrams XI. 33).

[35] 17:8-12.   [36] 2:4-6.   [37] 3:1-3.   [38] 3:14-18.

fervor of Asian Christians. A date of approximately 95 for Revelation makes this understandable. Too, the development of heretical movements of impressive proportions whose doctrines were sufficiently well known to require no detailed exposition points rather definitely to the close of the first century.[39]

Revelation is usually assumed to sustain no relationships to other New Testament writings that shed light on its date.[40] The literary data of the writing itself, however, suggest that Revelation was the earliest witness to Paul's published letters. The publication of those letters is the surest *terminus a quo* for the date of Revelation. The author of the Muratorian canon, although misconceiving the order of the relationship, sensed the reality of the literary parallel between the Pauline letter collection and the letter collection with which Revelation opens.[41] The introduction of an apocalypse with a corpus of letters to seven churches, itself prefaced by a general letter,[42] becomes intelligible only when Paul's letters to seven churches, published with our Ephesians as a catholicizing preface, are seen as the literary precedent.

Beyond this general resemblance, numerous allusions and parallels throughout Revelation reflect a probable literary indebtedness to all letters in the original Pauline letter collection except Philemon. Ephesians appears to have been most frequently used.[43] If, as is probably the case, First Peter was written in the name of the Roman church to disavow the bitterness of Revelation, the publication of Paul's letters and the writing of First Peter become the *termini* for reckoning the date of Revelation, which coincides with other evidence pointing to an approximate date of 95.

Place of Composition.—The author says he "found" himself "on the island called Patmos, for uttering God's message and testifying to Jesus," and that "on the Lord's day" he "fell into a trance" and was supernaturally directed to write an account of his visions and "send it to the seven churches." [44] Patmos was a thinly populated, rocky island about fifty square miles in area, located in the Aegean

---

[39] 2:6, 14, 15, 24.

[40] Moffatt, *Introduction*, p. 507; Jülicher, *Introduction*, p. 282.

[41] Reversing the true order of the dependence, the author of the Muratorian canon says, "The blessed Apostle Paul himself, following the order of his predecessor John, writes only by name to seven churches."

[42] 1:4-20. Goodspeed, *New Solutions of New Testament Problems*, p. 7.

[43] See my *Paul Becomes a Literary Influnece*, pp. 41-51.   [44] 1:9-11.

Sea to the southwest of Miletus. The island seems to have been a favorite place for the banishment of undesirables.[45] The author of Revelation appears to have been so regarded because of his activities as a leader among Asian Christians. His reference to the scene of his visions conforms to the practice of apocalyptic writers in making the circumstances under which revelations had come to them vividly real to their readers.

Presumably, when the term of his banishment was finished, this Asian prophet returned to the scene of his ministry and resumed his labors among the churches to whom he addressed Revelation. The writing of this book was a phase of the resumption of his ministry. He wrote, not so much because he was geographically separated from his reading public, but because writing had become an effective method of preaching and gave the prophet's message a wider hearing. Patmos, therefore, though the scene of the visions, was not necessarily the place where the written account of them was composed.[46] The communities addressed were in the vicinity of Ephesus. Ephesus, as the chief of these communities and as the greatest center of literary activity during the first century of Christian history, is the most likely place for him to have committed his message to writing. Acquaintance with Paul's collected letters, which were published at Ephesus, strengthens the case for Ephesus as the place where Revelation was written. Finally, Eusebius, after quoting Irenaeus on the date of Revelation,[47] indirectly suggests Ephesus as the place of its origin in his statement, "John also took up his abode once more at Ephesus after his exile on the island." [48]

Occasion and Purpose.—Two and a half centuries earlier than the crisis reflected in Revelation a Jewish prophet had denied the claims of Antiochus Epiphanes to divine honors and in the book of Daniel had repudiated the claim of the political sovereign to final authority. In a similar situation and spirit the Asian prophet who wrote Revelation affirmed the supremacy of the lordship of Christ against the blasphemous demands of Domitian.

The milder attitudes of earlier Roman emperors [49] gave place

---

[45] Pliny *Natural History* IV. 12. 23; Tertullian *On the Prescription of Heretics* XXXVI.

[46] 1:9.   [47] *Hist.* III. 18. 3.   [48] *Hist.* III. 20. 8-9.

[49] Tacitus records that Tiberius refused "to be consecrated in the image of the deity through all the provinces" because to do so would be "vanity and arrogance" and would reduce to mockery "the honor paid Augustus." He felt

under Domitian to an identification of worship of the emperor with loyalty to the empire. Christians refused to conform to the demands of the state cult. This brought the church under suspicion and resulted in the punishment of nonconforming individuals. A profound appreciation of the seriousness of the issues involved moved the author of Revelation to plead with his fellow sufferers to make no compromises for the sake of immunity from suffering. Christ alone was their Lord, and worship of "the Beast" would be the equivalent of degrading Christ from the place belonging exclusively to him.

Like other apocalypses Revelation was designed to bolster the morale of people whose actual and prospective sufferings made earthly compensations inadequate as incentives for endurance. They had seen many of their number subjected to dire penalties. Such terrifying displays of ruthlessness were designed to frighten them into conformity. The author of Revelation had himself suffered for his faith. As their "brother and companion in the distress" he undertook to stimulate the fortitude of his readers by arousing their religious loyalty. His purposes were immediate and practical. He had no thought of forecasting the course of a continuing world order nor of shedding light on speculative theological problems. He used inherited theology and traditional materials to move his own generation to heroic fidelity in a sharp, relatively brief crisis.

This Christian prophet thought the return of Jesus to judge the world was near. During the relatively short interim prior to this glorious event Christians ought gladly to endure whatever hardships an earthly despot could inflict. Martyrdom might itself become the prelude to a doubly abundant participation in the blessings of the messianic age. The prophet realistically believed the glowing promises he held out to those whose endurance did not fail. He expected the eschatological Kingdom might be inaugurated momentarily. Its blessings would make present difficulties inconsequential.

The author of Revelation was keenly aware of two aspects of the church's need. Christians needed to develop a more vivid awareness of the peril in which the church stood. They needed also a

---

that for emperors generally to permit their deification would empty the conception of any real meaning and give such acts the character of "experiments in flattery" (*Annals* IV. 37-38; cf. Suetonius *Tiberius* 26). Claudius similarly discouraged proposals so to honor him in Alexandria (H. I. Bell, *Jews and Christians in Egypt* [London: Oxford University Press, 1924], p. 28).

profounder comprehension of the bases of Christian hope. The prophet addressed his message to both phases of this need. Though clearly sensing the unprecedented seriousness of Domitian's affirmation of the ultimate character of political authority, he insisted with utmost vigor that the peril of the church was only partly outward. For him the spiritual deterioration pictured in chapters 2 and 3 constituted a threat the seriousness of which was comparable to the demands of "the Beast." Nowhere does he show himself more truly a prophet than in his predication of survival in persecution on a renewal of spiritual health. He urged that hope hinged on the fidelity of Christians to their victorious and exalted Lord, who had himself endured suffering, conquered death, been elevated to God's right hand in heaven, and would shortly return to judge the world and inaugurate the messianic Kingdom.

Message.—Apocalyptic eschatology supplies the philosophy of history in a majority of the books of the New Testament. Revelation alone, however, makes the denouement of history its principal theme. Apocalypse was one of the popular literary forms of postexilic Jewish prophecy. Its principal qualities are illustrated in such writings as Daniel and Enoch. These features were taken over by the first Christians and adapted to their own ends. Christians were, in the first instance, Jews whose Messiah had made a preliminary appearance on earth and was momentarily expected to come a second time to consummate his redemptive mission.

The author of Revelation conceived of the future in terms of the imagery of traditional apocalypticism, modifying it only insofar as his Christian inheritance required. He thought the end was imminent,[50] and yet his multiplication of series of premonitory calamities and his introduction of the conception of a millennial kingdom antecedent to the final judgment [51] suggest that the delay of the Parousia was problematical both to him and to his readers.[52] His primary stress was therefore on the certainty of divine intervention and the eternity of the messianic Kingdom by comparison with the transitoriness of the dominion of Rome.

[50] 1:1, 3; 3:11; 10:6; 22:6-7, 10, 12, 20.   [51] 20:4.

[52] The delay of Jesus' expected return became an acute problem for Christians generally toward the close of the first century and continued in varying degrees of reality to be so. The authors of Hebrews, First Peter, the Fourth Gospel along with the prophet of Revelation make their respective approaches to the problem, each in his own way. They are one in their testimony to the reality of the problem. Cf. II Pet. 3:3-4.

The "seals" of chapter 6, the "trumpets" of chapters 8 and 9, and the "bowls" of chapter 16 are pictorial representations of the trials intended to prepare the world for the Messiah's final activities. They consist of natural calamities raised to an incalculable degree of intensity and divinely designed to move the responsive to repentance, to test the fidelity of the saints, to punish the obdurately evil. The Christian community itself can claim no immunity from this ordeal of suffering but can be strengthened by the assurance of final deliverance and everlasting blessedness.

In the instances of earlier Jewish apocalypses, Egypt, Assyria, Syria had severally been conceived as attempting to thwart the purposes of God and therefore destined to experience visitations of his wrath. For the author of Revelation, Rome has challenged the divine authority, and its annihilation will be the principal event presaging the glorious deliverance of "those who are written in the Lamb's book of life." The nearness of that event is one of the prophet's absorbing interests.

Domitian, pictured as a sort of blending of returning Nero and the demonic Antichrist, is viewed as the incarnation of cosmic evil and the great antagonist of Christ. The bitterness of his onslaught against God's people reflects the imminence of his overthrow and the chaining of Satan in hell for a thousand years, during which period the martyred saints are to be "restored to life" and reign as Christ's associates. Following this thousand years, Satan is expected to be released. He will again revolt against God's authority but will be defeated and cast finally into hell. Thereafter follow the general resurrection, the judgment, and the assignment of eternal destinies.

The focus of attention throughout is the ultimately happy condition of those "who are invited to the marriage supper of the Lamb." Their sorrow and pain will have ended,[53] and they will be associated with God and Christ in their rule of the world.[54] As the supreme reward of their fidelity they will be given "the crown of life" and permitted to drink "without cost from the spring of the water of life." Their dwelling place will be the heavenly city, in whose principal street flows "a river of living water, clear as crystal," which issues "from the throne of God and of the Lamb."[55]

[53] 7:15-17; 21:3-4; 22:3-4.   [54] 3:12, 21; 5:10; 19:7-9; 21:7; 22:4.
[55] 2:7, 10, 17; 3:5; 7:17; 13:8; 17:8; 20:12, 15; 21:6, 27; 22:1-2, 14, 17, 19.

XVI

THE FIRST EPISTLE OF PETER

Authorship.—According to the address of the epistle, the author expected it to circulate widely. He wanted it read wherever Revelation was known and its influence felt. This ambition, judging by available evidence, was only partially realized. In the immediate situation, however, the popularity of First Peter compares favorably with that of its rival publication.

Parallels in language and thought suggest but do not establish acquaintance with First Peter by the author of First Clement.[1] According to Eusebius, Polycarp in his letter to the Philippians "employed certain testimonies taken from the former epistle of Peter." [2] Although there are no formal quotations of First Peter in Polycarp's letter, the literary data do clearly support the idea of indebtedness on Polycarp's part.[3] The epistle was probably known to the author of James,[4] and the phrasing of certain passages in the epistle from Lyons and Vienne suggests the possibility of acquaintance with First Peter.[5] Eusebius says Papias "used testimonies drawn from the former epistle of John, and likewise that of Peter," [6] but he preserves no statement of Papias to illustrate his position, and the characterization of the epistle as Petrine is probably his own. There is no mention of First Peter nor any convincing evidence of acquaintance with it in the letters of Ignatius, Barnabas, the Didache, Second Clement, and the writings of Justin.

---

[1] I Clem. 7:2, 4 (cf. I Pet. 1:18-19); 30:1-2 (cf. I Pet. 2:1; 5:5); 59:2 (cf. I Pet. 2:9, 15); 49:5 (cf. I Pet. 4:8; Jas. 5:20; Prov. 10:12).

[2] *Hist.* IV. 14. 9.

[3] Polyc. Phil. 1:3 (cf. I Pet. 1:8); 2:1 (cf. I Pet. 1:13, 21; Ps. 2:11); 5:3 (cf. I Pet. 2:11; 5:17); 10:2 (cf. I Pet. 2:12; 5:5); 8:1-2 (cf. I Pet. 2:21; 4:16; Isa. 53:9); 2:2 (cf. I Pet. 3:9); 7:2; 11:4 (cf. I Pet. 4:7).

[4] Jas. 1:18 (cf. I Pet. 1:3, 23); 1:21 (cf. I Pet. 2:1-2); 4:1 (cf. I Pet. 2:11); 5:19 (cf. I Pet. 2:25); 3:13 (cf. I Pet. 3:15-16); 1:12 (cf. I Pet. 5:4); 4:10 (cf. I Pet. 5:6); 4:7 (cf. I Pet. 5:9).

[5] The influence of 5:6-8 may appear in the epistle from Lyons and Vienne as Eusebius preserves it (*Hist.* V. 1 25; V. 2. 5-6).

[6] *Hist.* III. 39. 17.

The Muratorian canon makes no mention of the epistle, although it lists the Apocalypse of Peter as canonical.

The earliest reference to the epistle as by Peter occurs in II Pet. 3:1. On this basis Adolf Harnack concluded that the author of Second Peter transformed a homily into an epistle by the addition of 1:1-2 and 5:12-14 and for the first time associated it with the name of Peter.[7] This, however, involves a complete misconception of the character of First Peter as an encyclical[8] and the relationship of pseudonymity to its original purpose. The next witness who attributes the epistle to Peter and the first to quote it formally under the apostle's name is Irenaeus.[9] Thereafter it is so quoted by Tertullian, Origen, and Clement of Alexandria. Eusebius says First Peter was frequently used by "the elders of olden time . . . as a work beyond dispute,"[10] and he himself listed it among the "acknowledged writings."[11]

The literature with which First Peter shows acquaintance is also significant for a discussion of its authorship. The author had a thorough knowledge of Paul's letters in their published form and used them extensively. His indebtedness to them is so evident that he could more easily be identified as Paul than Peter if the possibilities were restricted to these two. Like the author of the Fourth Gospel, he used the materials of Paul's letters selectively for the enforcement of emphases of his own. The only Pauline letters of which no trace is discoverable in First Peter are Philippians and Philemon. Heaviest indebtedness is to Romans and Ephesians;[12] but acquaintance with Second Corinthians and Galatians is highly probable, and with First Corinthians, Colossians, and the two Thessalonian letters possible.[13]

With almost equal certainty the author of First Peter knew He-

---

[7] *Chronologie*, I, 464.

[8] There are indications of the epistolary character of the writing throughout: 1:3, 13, 22; 2:1, 11, 13, 18; 3:1, 8, 13; 4:12; 5:1-5, 9. Furthermore, the style of 1:1-2 and 5:12-14 more nearly approximates that of First Peter than that of Second Peter.

[9] *Her.* IV. 9. 2 and V. 7. 2 quote I Pet. 1:8; and IV. 16. 5 quotes I Pet. 2:16.

[10] *Hist.* III. 3. 1.   [11] *Hist.* III. 25. 2.

[12] Moffatt recognizes the necessity of interpreting the resemblances between Ephesians and First Peter in terms of literary relationship. His strange espousal of the authenticity of the latter, however, requires that he posit indebtedness on the part of Ephesians. (*Introduction*, p. 337.)

[13] See my *Paul Becomes a Literary Influence*, pp. 51-69.

brews [14] and, like Clement of Rome, wrote in response to the challenge of Hebrews that the Roman church become a teacher of other churches.[15] The inclusion of greetings to the Asian churches from their "sister-church in Babylon" strongly suggests acquaintance with Revelation.[16] Very probably the author wrote to disavow in the name of the Roman church the essentially revolutionary attitude of the author of Revelation toward the empire. The reference to Mark in 5:12-14 in the same context in which Silvanus is mentioned as Peter's amanuensis suggests an acquaintance with the tradition that Mark's Gospel was in reality Peter's and, inferentially, an acquaintance with the Gospel itself. The officialized picture of Peter [17] conceivably reflects the points of view of Matt. 16:18-19, but it more probably expresses simply the type of interest in church offices apparent in I Clem. 40–41. Agreements between First Peter and the Petrine speeches in Acts may denote literary dependence of the epistle, but the parallels are not in themselves convincing.[18]

If Peter were not named in the address, the epistle would contain no suggestion of his connection with it. The data of the epistle raise difficult obstacles to its acceptance as the work of Peter. The vocabulary and the Greek style in which it is written are definitely literary. This fact, coupled with the author's use of the Septuagint version of the Old Testament, can hardly be reconciled with Petrine authorship. The introduction of Silvanus as Peter's amanuensis is an implicit confession of the contradiction involved in the ascription of such a writing to Peter.[19] The author appears never to have visited the localities mentioned in the address. He had no such inti-

---

[14] 1:2 (cf. Heb. 12:24); 2:2 (cf. Heb. 5:12-13); 2:5 (cf. Heb. 3:6); 2:25 (cf. Heb. 5:2); 3:9 (cf. Heb. 12:17); 3:11 (cf. Heb. 12:14); 3:18 (cf. Heb. 7:27); 3:21 (cf. Heb. 9:24); 4:11 (cf. Heb. 13:21); 4:14 (cf. Heb. 11:26; 13:13); 5:3, 10-12 (cf. Heb. 13:20-22).

[15] Heb. 5:12; Ign. Rom. 3:1. This is the view of Goodspeed (*Introduction*, pp. 265-69).

[16] 5:13; cf. Rev. 14:8; 16:19; 17:5, 9; 18:2, 10, 21.

[17] In 1:1 and 5:1 Peter is in turn described as an apostle, an elder, and a witness; cf. Acts 1:8, 22; 5:32; 10:39.

[18] Moffatt, *Introduction*, p. 335. Typical parallels are: 1:17 (cf. Acts 10:34); 1:22 (cf. Acts 15:9); 2:4 (cf. Acts 4:11); 4:13, 16 (cf Acts 5:41).

[19] In Gal. 6:11; II Thess, 3:17; and Col. 4:18 there are indications that Paul employed amanuenses. Mark (Col. 4:10; Philem. 24) and Sylvanus (I Thess. 1:1; II Thess. 1:1; II Cor. 1:19; cf. Acts 15:22) were traditionally known as Paul's co-workers. Their introduction in I Pet. 5:12-13 is better understood as a literary device to create verisimilitude than as a historical explanation of the Pauline tone of the epistle and the literary quality of its Greek.

mate knowledge of the circumstances of his readers as Paul's letters reflect. This impression of remoteness which the epistle itself creates coincides with the nonexistence of any early tradition that Peter contributed to the establishment and development of the Asian churches.[20] Nor would Paul's reference to Peter in Galatians encourage the development of such a tradition or create the expectation that Peter would within slightly more than a decade write an encyclical letter to churches where Paul had labored. The encyclical character of First Peter tends automatically to locate it outside the limits of Peter's lifetime and in the time area of Ephesians and Revelation.

According to the tradition that makes Peter in some sense responsible for Mark's Gospel, Peter's preaching at approximately the period when he supposedly wrote our epistle consisted largely in reminiscences of Jesus' words and deeds.[21] That he would have written a letter completely lacking in any references to Jesus' life and message is simply incredible. The essential soundness of the tradition of Mark's indebtedness to Peter's preaching leaves little warrant for the suggestion that in writing his epistle at the very time of Mark's collaboration with him at Rome Peter could assume a general knowledge of Jesus' life that would make any reference to its principal events unnecessary.[22]

The references to persecution in First Peter do not have the mistreatment of Christians under Nero as their background. Christians "all over the world" are described as "having the same experience of suffering" as the addressees of the epistle.[23] This suffering is, moreover, specifically represented as due to their being known as Christians.[24] Such allusions are best satisfied by conditions that existed under Domitian. They find their clearest parallels in Hebrews and Revelation and add force to other points of contact with those writings which tend to locate First Peter outside the chronological limits of Peter's lifetime.[25]

[20] Eusebius traces to Origen a tradition that Peter "preached in Pontus and Galatia and Bithynia, in Cappadocia and Asia to those Jews who were of the Dispersion" (Hist. III. 1. 2), but the coincidence of the statement with the language of I Pet. 1:1 suggests this was entirely an inference from the address of the epistle.

[21] Euseb. Hist. III. 39. 15; cf. Acts 10:35-43.

[22] Moffatt, Introduction, p. 334.   [23] 5:9.   [24] 4:16.

[25] The three writings were addressed to readers who were being persecuted because they were Christians (Heb. 10:32-36; 11:35-38; 13:3; Rev. 1:9; 2:10 ff.;

Parallels in ideas and language between Romans, Ephesians, and First Peter admittedly require explanation in terms of literary relationship of some description. Advocates of Petrine authorship suggest that Peter read Romans while at Rome. The author of Ephesians, "a Paulinist, imbued with his master's spirit," was indebted both to Paul's letters and to First Peter.[26] This explanation, however, fails to take account of the literary contacts between First Peter and Paul's other letters. It also disregards the fact that acquaintance with Paul's letters from the outset involved a published collection to which Ephesians belonged. Indebtedness in the present instance is therefore best understood as reflecting literary dependence on Paul's published letters on the part of the author of First Peter.

According to these data, First Peter was probably pseudonymous. The author's reasons for writing pseudonymously are understandable and were approved by the literary ethics of antiquity. A Roman Christian, more concerned for the effectiveness of his message than the perpetuation of his name, wrote this epistle to a circle of Asian churches in the name of Peter at a time when writing in Peter's name had become more or less equivalent to writing in the name of the Roman church.

The implicit reference to Peter's martyrdom in 5:1-2 [27] was calculated to give effectiveness to the message of the epistle. It finds an analogy in the claim of the author of Revelation that his message is really the message of Jesus. It gives the epistle a more or less testamentary character and has the effect of affirming Peter's approval of the author's message.

With complete accuracy A. H. McNeile describes pseudonymity as "a device mostly adopted when a writer has a specific purpose for which he borrows the authority of a greater name." Finding no such purpose in First Peter, he insists on its authenticity.[28]

6:9 ff.; I Pet. 1:6; 2:11; 3:14-17; 4:12-17; 5:9). In view of such mistreatment and the temptations inherent in it, the constant note common to the three writings is a hortatory combination of warning and encouragement (Heb. 2:1-3; 3:14; 4:14; 6:4-8; 10:26-31, 39; Rev. 2:4 ff.; I Pet. 1:14, 19; 4:17-19; 5:7-9). In some crisis, best identified as the reign of Domitian, when believers tended to lose sight of compelling Christian goals, the authors of these three books, each in his own way, pointed to Christ as the true clue to history and the sound basis for Christian hope.

[26] Moffatt, *Introduction*, pp. 382, 388.   [27] Cf. II. Pet. 1:13-15.

[28] *Introduction*, p. 207; cf. Scott, *Literature of the New Testament*, p. 221.

The predication of a situation in which pseudonymity was advantageous, however, supplies the most fruitful clue for the interpretation of the epistle. Its author used Pauline materials as if he had been writing in Paul's name. Ephesians, so thoroughly known by our writer, offered a suggestive precedent. But it had pre-empted the use of Paul's name. Addressing his words to a circle of churches already stirred by the message of Revelation, the author of First Peter needed the authority of an impressive name as an aid in counteracting the essentially vindictive and revolutionary spirit of the earlier writing. The tradition of Peter's activity at Rome was well established by the close of the first century and appears to have been essentially sound. First Peter is a part of that tradition. Writing in the name of the Roman church,[29] which had known persecution before Domitian came on the scene, and convinced of the basic soundness of Paul's attitude toward civil authority and toward mistreatment of any sort, the author of First Peter undertook to urge conciliation in place of revolution [30] by reaffirming certain phases of Paul's message under the authority of the name of Peter.

The First Readers.—The epistle is addressed "to those who are scattered as foreigners over Pontus, Galatia, Cappadocia, Asia, and Bithynia." They are further described as having been "chosen and predestined by the consecration of the Spirit to be obedient to Jesus Christ, and to be sprinkled with his blood." [31] References to their "heathen" background [32] show they were racially non-Jewish. They are, nevertheless, regarded as the true Israel.[33] They are suffering because they are citizens of a heavenly Kingdom and therefore "foreigners" from the point of view of the existing world order. They are to be kept loyal to their heavenly pattern of life by their consciousness of having been "born anew to a life of hope through Jesus Christ's resurrection . . . , and to an imperishable, unsullied, and unfading inheritance, . . . a salvation that is now ready to be disclosed at the last time." [34]

The area in which these Christians lived includes the territory covered in the address of Revelation and extends beyond it to the adjacent provinces. The inclusiveness of this address probably reflects the purpose of First Peter to checkmate the influence of

Revelation by championing in the name of Peter a point of view which readers would find corroborated in Paul's recently published letters.

Date.—The literary *termini* of the period within which First Peter properly belongs are the publication of Paul's letters and Polycarp's letter to the Philippians. The author clearly knew Paul's collected letters, especially Ephesians, and his own epistle was known to Polycarp. First Peter should therefore be assigned to the general period 95-117, which locates it in the reign of either Domitian or Trajan.

Supplemental data confirm these limits and suggest a narrower definition within them: (1) The author knew Hebrews, Revelation, and possibly Luke-Acts. (2) His emphasis on the respect due elders as church officials and the character of his reference to Peter's martyrdom suggest he was a contemporary of the author of First Clement and that a common situation constituted the background of both writers.[35] (3) The encyclical character of the epistle points to the turn of the first century. Its general indebtedness to Ephesians and Revelation suggests that its encyclical address found its literary precedents in those writings, and the character of its teaching emphases tends to locate it within the same decade. (4) The type of persecution which the epistle reflects relates it to the background common to Luke-Acts, Hebrews, and Revelation.[36] That its victims were the Christian communities "all over the world," [37] whose members suffered because they were Christians, proves conclusively that First Peter referred to a situation definitely more serious than the Neronian excesses involved.[38]

Trajan was the first Roman emperor to equate Christianity with criminality.[39] The description of the sufferings of Christians as due to their identification as Christians tends to locate First Peter

[35] In First Peter the office of elder appears to have become a lucrative one, so much so that the motives of its occupants are suspected and it has become necessary to urge respect for the office despite the unworthiness of some individual officials. Paul never refers to the office of elder. The earliest such references are found in Acts 11:30; 14:23 (cf. 15:6, 23; 16:4; 20:17). First Clement shares First Peter's concern about respect for elders and refers to Peter's martrydom and reward (5:4) in a way that closely corresponds to I Pet. 5:1-2 (cf. II Pet. 1:13-15; Acts 20:17-38).

[36] 1:6-7; 4:12-14; 5:9.   [37] 5:9.   [38] 4:12-14.

[39] Case, *The Social Triumph of the Ancient Church,* pp. 166-75; Riddle, *Early Christian Life,* pp. 144-53.

in Trajan's reign. Christianity, however, had never been legally recognized, and identification with it had for some years been sufficient to create popular and official suspicion of individuals.[40] The details of the persecution described in the epistle do not necessarily require the times of Trajan, and their correspondence with those of Hebrews and Revelation tends to favor identification with the circumstances of the closing years of the reign of Domitian. Accordingly a date of 95-100 is regarded as best satisfying the relevant data.

Place of Composition.—All relevant data favor Rome as the place where First Peter was written. On the basis of tradition which he traces to Papias and Clement of Alexandria, Eusebius interprets "Babylon" of 5:13 as a metaphorical reference to Rome and says the epistle was "composed at Rome." [41] The reference to Mark in 5:13*b* is an implicit indication of acquaintance with the tradition of Peter's primary responsibility for Mark's Gospel, and the publication of the epistle in Peter's name was the equivalent of claiming for it the authority of the Roman church.[42] The author's acquaintance with Hebrews and the similarity of certain of his interests to those of First Clement are supplementary evidences in favor of Rome. The silence of the Muratorian canon regarding First Peter and Hebrews argues for the Roman origin of both. It almost certainly signifies a knowledge that neither of these epistles could lay any sound claim to apostolic authorship.

Occasion and Purpose.—The variety of data which the epistle itself supplies constitutes the only sound basis for a reconstruction of the situation to which its message was directed. Gentile Christians,[43] who were under severe pressure from an unsympathetic society and from the state,[44] were the reading public. Their circumstances were essentially those of the readers of Luke-Acts, Hebrews, and Revelation. The epistle is an encyclical written in the name of Peter—

---

[40] Tacitus says that Nero sought to divert suspicion from himself in connection with the burning of Rome by fixing the blame on the Christians. He accounts for the fact that they were his easy victims on the ground that they were generally "loathed for their vices." (*Annals* XV. 44.) It was unquestionably that they were Christians, however, that marked them for unpopularity and so enabled Nero to use them for his purposes with a considerable degree of approval. Cf. Luke 6:22; 21:17; Acts 5:41; 11:26.

[41] *Hist.* II. 15. 2; cf. Rev. 14:8; 16:19; 17:5; 18:2, 10, 21.   [42] *Ibid.*

[43] 1:14, 18; 2:9; 4:3.   [44] 1:6; 2:12; 3:14-17; 4:7, 12-17, 19; 5:9, 10.

which in effect meant in the name of the Roman church [45]—but its substance and language are so impressively Pauline as to leave no doubt of literary indebtedness to Paul's published letters. The addressees were the Christian communities of Pontus, Galatia, Cappadocia, Asia, and Bithynia, which evidently include the area covered in the address of Revelation. These churches owed their Christianity ultimately to the missionary labors of Paul, and they had quite recently been made aware of this indebtedness by the appearance of Luke-Acts and the publication of Paul's letters. Literary indebtedness to Hebrews and Revelation also sheds light on the occasion and purpose of the epistle.

The meaning of these data is implicit in the author's assurance and warning that church members need not be ashamed "if a man suffers for being a Christian," but that under no circumstances must one of them suffer "as a murderer or thief or criminal or revolutionist." [46] The author of Luke-Acts had undertaken to show Roman authorities the political inoffensiveness of Christianity. Whether justified or not, political officials suspected the church of encouraging subversive tendencies. Certainly the identification of Rome as an agent of Satan by the author of Revelation and his joy at the prospect of its utter destruction [47] were implicitly revolutionary sentiments and could be understood as aligning the church with forces aiming at the overthrow of the state. In any event, here was an extreme departure from the point of view of Paul's letters. [48]

The plea of First Peter that Christians disavow revolutionary techniques makes the epistle a logical sequel to and, very probably, a conscious refutation of the sentiments voiced in Revelation. Its author accredits his message and demonstrates the genuineness of his confidence in the effectiveness of Christian love by speaking in the name of the "sister-church in Babylon," where Christians had earlier suffered and where they were at the time suffering as severely as in Asia. [49] He interprets undeserved suffering as offering an opportunity to demonstrate a superior quality of life. Victory for Christianity could in his estimation be achieved only by exemplifying the distinctly Christian virtues. Such living, he thought, would arouse the respect of the perpetrators of injustice. He exhorted

[45] 5:13.   [46] 4:16.   [47] Rev. 18:6, 20.
[48] Rom. 13:1-7; cf. I Pet. 2:13-17; 3:13.   [49] Heb. 13:7; I Clem. 5.

the church, therefore, to take persecution as a challenge to exalt and not compromise the ideal of life of which Christ had been the exemplar.

Message.—The emphases of First Peter were the direct outgrowth of the emergency out of which it came. The author was undertaking to help his readers understand their undeserved suffering and to portray the spirit in which they as Christians should meet it. His objectives were immediate and entirely practical.

The epistle draws a clear distinction between "being abused for the sake of Christ" and the deserved penalties inflicted upon the "murderer or thief or criminal or revolutionist." [50] No man need be ashamed if he suffers "for being a Christian," but the discredit is very real when he has to endure "being beaten for doing wrong." [51] Suffering worthily met in the course of living in the spirit of Christ actually becomes a blessing because it results in a deepening consciousness of fellowship with Christ and a consequent and ever-increasing spiritual joy.[52]

The explanation of their sufferings is that "the life of hope" into which the risen Christ has caused them "to be born anew" has constituted the Christian community "the chosen race, . . . the consecrated nation." This has caused the heathen to regard and treat them as "aliens and exiles." [53] Such being the case, Christians should accept the situation as a challenging opportunity to exemplify the quality of the new life opened to them by Christ. By so doing they will effectively refute "the ignorant charges of foolish people" which have brought them under suspicion.[54] Their behavior will moreover exert a saving influence on their enemies and will demonstrate that Christian salvation involves sharing the redemptive mission of Christ himself. More effectually than by words they will thus "declare the virtues of him" by whom they were "called . . . out of darkness into his wonderful light." [55]

However much the situation may tempt them to declare a moratorium on love and adopt the spirit of violence and vindictiveness, Christians must see that the times require of them a consistent manifestation of good will. They will best meet "the test of fire" currently being applied, not by becoming embittered and resorting to the methods of revolutionaries, but by entrusting their souls

[50] 4:14-16.   [51] 2:20.   [52] 3:13-18.   [53] 2:9-12.
[54] 2:15.   [55] 2:9.

"to a Creator who is faithful" and steadfastly continuing "to do what is right."[56] They can become the associates of a world-conquering Christ only by their audacious employment of the resources which Christ himself commended as efficacious.[57]

On three bases this Christian teacher feels that Christians will find abundant justification for living as he has counseled: (1) Their suffering will be short-lived, because "the end of all things is near."[58] (2) The experience of Jesus, who, though innocent, met suffering with patience and turned it into opportunity, illuminates the way for Christians and discloses the compensations of which they may be assured.[59] (3) The vast worth of the salvation which they now partially enjoy, and which they will enjoy in its fullness in heaven, amply justifies the costs currently being exacted. Kept safely for them in heaven, beyond the vicissitudes of temporal existence, Christians possess "an imperishable, unsullied, and unfading inheritance."[60]

[56] 4:12, 19.   [57] 4:13.   [58] 4:7; 5:10.   [59] 1:10-12; 2:23-24; 5:1.
[60] 1:4-5, 10-12; 3:21-22; 5:8-11.

XVII

THE GOSPEL OF JOHN

Authorship.—There are no clear traces of acquaintance with the Fourth Gospel on the part of Clement of Rome, Polycarp, Barnabas, or Hermas.[1] There are, however, passages in the letters of Ignatius that suggest indebtedness.[2] These allusions may of course represent no more than an employment of similar ideas, and it has to be remembered that Ignatius' dependence is much more basically on Paul's published letters than on the Fourth Gospel. Perhaps, however, the predication of a knowledge of the Fourth Gospel by Ignatius provides the soundest explanation of the language and allusions that are found in his letters.[3] There are strong but not entirely convincing reasons for supposing that acquaintance with the Fourth Gospel is reflected in the Longer Ending of Mark.[4] Papias presumably also knew the Fourth Gospel. His report of the elder's disparagement of Mark for its lack of "order"[5] and of Matthew's Greek Gospel as a translation from the Hebrew original by an unknown interpreter[6] conceivably reflects his estimation of the su-

[1] There is only the barest possibility of an echo of John 12:28 and 17:3 in I Clem. 43:6. Polycarp apparently preferred oral tradition to written gospels, but if he knew a written gospel it was Matthew. For the possibility of his acquaintance with the Fourth Gospel the following passages provide a slender basis: Polyc. Phil. 5:2 (cf. John 5:21; 6:44); 10:1 (cf. John 13:34; 15:12, 17); 12:3 (cf. John 15:16). Barnabas knew and used Matthew, but not any of the other Gospels. The merest possibility in 6:3 of an unconscious conflation of John 6:51, 58 and Isa. 28:16 provides no sufficient basis for a modification of the judgment that Barnabas shows acquaintance with no Gospel except Matthew.

[2] Ign. Eph. 5:2 (cf. John 6:33); Magn. 7:1 (cf. John 5:19, 30; 8:28; 10:30); Rom. 7:2 (cf. John 4:10-11, 14; 7:38); 7:3 (cf. John 6:33); Philad. 7:1 (cf. John 3:8; 8:14); 9:1 (cf. John 10:7, 9); Smyrn. 1:2 (cf. John 20:25).

[3] Moffatt, *Introduction*, p. 579.

[4] The Longer Ending of Mark (16:9-20) follows the Lukan account of the post-resurrection appearances of Jesus except that in vs. 9 there seems to be a preference for John 20:11-18 (cf. Matt. 28:9-11). So think Sanday, *The Criticism of the Fourth Gospel*, p. 241; and Bacon, *The Fourth Gospel in Research and Debate*, p. 213-16. For a somewhat different interpretation of the data see Streeter, *The Four Gospels*, pp. 351-60.

[5] Euseb. *Hist.* III. 39. 15.

[6] Euseb. *Hist.* III. 39. 16. Harnack, *Origin of the New Testament*, p. 72, note 2.

periority of the Fourth Gospel. In his interpretation of John 14:2 Irenaeus may also be depending on the similar exegesis of the passage by Papias.[7]

Much more certainly than the witnesses thus far cited, Justin was acquainted with the Fourth Gospel. In *Apol.* 61:4-5 he clearly quotes John 3:3-4, introducing the quotation with the formula "Christ said." [8] By comparison with his heavy indebtedness to Matthew, Mark, and Luke, his use of John is meager and indefinite, but it is sufficient to establish his acquaintance with it. Justin says nothing of the authorship of the Gospel, and he rather clearly thinks of it as less authoritative than the older Gospels. This attitude on his part assumes additional significance because he thought John the apostle was the author of Revelation.[9]

Irenaeus knew all four of the canonical Gospels and explicitly assigned the authorship of the Fourth Gospel to "John, the disciple of the Lord, who also had leaned upon his breast," who, he says, published the Gospel "during his residence at Ephesus in Asia." [10] Equally specific is the assertion of the Muratorian canon that "the fourth of the gospels is John's, one of the disciples." John is furthermore said to have written at the urging of "his fellow-disciples and bishops" and in accordance with a revelation to Andrew, "one of the Apostles, that John was to write all things in his own name, and they were all to certify." Matching these statements representing opinion in the West around the close of the second century, Eusebius quotes Clement of Alexandria as having said, "John, . . . conscious that the outward facts had been set forth in the Gospels, was urged on by his disciples, and, divinely moved by the Spirit, composed a spiritual Gospel." [11]

Prior to the testimony of Irenaeus, the Muratorian writer, and Clement of Alexandria, there apparently existed no advocacy of

---

[7] *Her.* V. 36. 2. Irenaeus interprets John 14:2 as indicating the gradations of heavenly rewards, and in support of his exegesis says: "The presbyters, the disciples of the apostles, affirm that this is the gradation and arrangement of those who are saved, and that they advance through steps of this nature." The presbyters on whose authority he depends were probably known to him through Papias. So Moffatt, *Introduction*, p. 577, and McNeile, *Introdutcion*, p. 307.

[8] Other passages from Justin that strengthen the case for acquaintance are: *Apol.* 23:2 (cf. John 1:13-14) ; 35:6 (cf. John 19:13) ; *Dial.* 25:1 (cf. John 8:39) ; 88:7 (cf. John 1:20, 23) ; 110:1 (cf. John 7:27) ; 135:5 (cf. John 1:13) ; 136:3 (cf. John 5:46-47).

[9] *Dial.* 81:4; cf. Euseb. *Hist.* IV. 18. 8.

[10] *Her.* III. 1. 1; cf. Euseb. *Hist.* V. 8. 3-4.   [11] *Hist.* VI. 14. 7.

John's authorship of this Gospel. Not only so, but around the close of the second century, when the first affirmations of apostolic authorship appear, there was dissent on the part of equally orthodox leaders in the church, as is illustrated in Hippolytus' defense of Johannine authorship against the objections of the presbyter Gaius. Again, the elaborateness of the statement of the Muratorian canon about the Fourth Gospel and the First Epistle of John suggests the controversial atmosphere in which Hippolytus wrote. The statement may be more apologetic than historical in character.

The earliest testimony to the apostolic authorship of the Fourth Gospel identifies Ephesus as the place of its publication. The tradition of Johannine authorship is thus bound up with the tradition of John's residence in old age at Ephesus, which means that the validity of the one is rather decisively affected by whether or not the other can be established. It is precisely the weakness of the case for John's residence at Ephesus that constitutes a well-nigh insuperable obstacle to an assignment of the Gospel to him.

As in the matter of authorship, the testimony of Irenaeus is the primary source for evidence of John's residence at Ephesus. However, Irenaeus claims Polycarp as authority for what he says about the matter; and this, if established beyond a peradventure, would be practically the equivalent of demonstration. Irenaeus says that he himself, in "early manhood," saw Polycarp, whom he describes as one "who not only was instructed by Apostles and held intercourse with many who had seen the Lord, but also received in Asia his appointment from Apostles as bishop of the church at Smyrna." [12] In the same context Irenaeus describes the Ephesian church as "a true witness of the tradition of the Apostles" on the ground that it was "founded by Paul" and had "John remaining among them permanently until the times of Trajan." Again, in refuting the idea that Jesus' public ministry was only one year in length, Irenaeus refers to the testimony of "the elders," whom he describes as "those who were conversant in Asia with John, the disciple of the Lord"; and he concludes with the statement that John resided at Ephesus "up to the time of Trajan." [13]

---

[12] *Her.* III. 3. 4; cf. Euseb. *Hist.* IV. 14. 3-8. Irenaeus does not claim himself to have heard Polycarp tell how "John, the disciple of the Lord, when at Ephesus," refused to bathe in the same house with Cerinthus; but he says "there are those who have heard him."

[13] *Her.* II. 22. 5.

Irenaeus' most significant testimony is contained in his letter to Florinus.[14] Florinus, it appears, was in danger of "being dragged . . . into the error of Valentinus." Irenaeus wrote to counsel him, and to enforce his advice he reminds Florinus that "he himself had reached back to the first succession from the Apostles," meaning thereby "the elders before us, who also were disciples of the Apostles." He then specifically reminds Florinus of his own association with Polycarp, "that blessed and apostolic elder," as follows: "When I was still a boy I saw thee in lower Asia in the company of Polycarp." He says his memories of Polycarp are especially vivid because they were childhood memories, and he counts as one of the surest of them his recollection of how Polycarp "would tell of his intercourse with John and with the others who had seen the Lord."

Polycrates, "who was bishop of the community at Ephesus," and who about 195 wrote a letter to "Victor, bishop of the Romans," tends to corroborate what Irenaeus said. In his letter Polycrates mentions "John, and together with him Philip the apostle and his daughters." [15] Of Philip and "his daughters" he says: "Philip, one of the twelve apostles, . . . has fallen asleep in Hierapolis, as have also two daughters who grew old in virginity, and his other daughter who lived in the Holy Spirit . . . rests at Ephesus." In this context he adds: "John too, who leaned back on the Lord's breast, who was . . . both martyr and teacher, . . . has fallen asleep at Ephesus."

This tradition of the disciple John's residence at Ephesus rests on highly questionable foundations. Its chief proponents belong to the close of the second century and were almost certainly confused regarding the facts they interpret. Witnesses, furthermore, are entirely lacking at the time and place where they would normally have been most vocal.

Irenaeus describes Papias as "a hearer of John and a companion of Polycarp, a man of primitive times"; [16] and Eusebius, who regards Papias as "evidently . . . a man of exceedingly small intelligence" because of his millennialism,[17] points out Irenaeus' heavy indebtedness to Papias.[18] Eusebius, furthermore, emphasizes Irenaeus' confusion about Papias' acquaintance with John by saying

---

[14] Euseb. *Hist.* V. 20. 4-8. Eusebius describes the letter as a "most charming note" and says it was appended to Irenaeus' lost treatise *De Ogdoade.*

[15] Euseb. *Hist.* III. 31. 2-4; V. 24. 2-4.

[16] *Her.* V. 33. 4; cf. Euseb. *Hist.* III. 39. 1.

[17] *Hist.* III. 39. 13.   [18] *Ibid.*

on Papias' own authority that the latter "was in no sense a hearer and eye-witness of the holy apostles" but instead learned "the things pertaining to the faith from those who were their pupils." [19] To make Papias' status explicitly clear, Eusebius then quotes him at some length [20] to show his habit of inquiring of every "follower of the elders" about the Lord's disciples. Papias' personal acquaintance was with a certain "John the elder," to be carefully distinguished from the disciple John. He concludes with the judgment that Papias' observation that "two persons in Asia have borne the same name," John, is corroborated by the fact that "there were two tombs at Ephesus, each of which is still to this day said to be John's."

According to Irenaeus' own statements, his acquaintance with Polycarp belonged to his childhood and early youth. He was confused and inaccurate, in Eusebius' judgment, regarding Papias' relationship to John the disciple. He also confused James the son of Zebedee with James the head of the Jerusalem church. He could therefore have been inaccurate in his understanding of Polycarp's allusions to John of Ephesus. Such misunderstanding may be explained and in a measure justified by Papias' twofold use of the phrase "disciples of the Lord." He so described Andrew, Peter, Philip, Thomas, James, John, and Matthew. He carefully distinguished them, however, from men like Aristion and John the elder, to whom he also applied the title "disciples of the Lord." [21]

Polycrates, like Irenaeus, appears to have been capable of confusing historical personalities whose names were the same. A notable instance was his inaccurate designation of Philip the deacon as "Philip, one of the apostles." [22] It does not follow from this that Polycrates necessarily confused the two Johns, but the possibility is thereby established.

Neither Ignatius nor Polycarp show the slightest awareness of John the disciple's ever residing at Ephesus, nor do they connect his name with the Fourth Gospel. Their silence is significant because they represent the locality and time at which a gospel known to have been written by the last of the disciples would have enjoyed great authority. Not only are they silent about John, but they are emphatic and explicit in their exaltation of Paul. Ignatius

[19] *Hist.* III. 39. 2.
[21] Euseb. *Hist.* III. 39. 4.
[20] *Hist.* III. 39. 3-7.
[22] Euseb. *Hist.* III. 31. 3-5.

describes Ephesian Christians as "ever of one mind with the Apostles," [23] but he evidently regards Paul as having given expression to that "mind." Paul is the only apostle he ever mentions by name.[24] Though Polycarp neither mentions John nor shows acquaintance with the Fourth Gospel, he exhibits a thorough knowledge of Paul's published letters, and he thinks of the letters as embodying Paul's message to the churches everywhere.[25]

Significantly, also, the author of Luke-Acts knows no more of the disciple John's residence at Ephesus than did Ignatius and Polycarp. Writing his great two-volume work at Ephesus during the last decade of the first century, he would surely have been aware of the presence in the Christian community of the aged John and would almost as surely have counted his influence of equal value with Paul's in counteracting "perversions of the truth" by heretical teachers. Instead, those whom "the holy Spirit has made . . . guardians and . . . shepherds of the church of God" are counseled solely in the name of Paul.[26]

Not only is there complete silence about John's having lived at Ephesus on the part of persons and at the time when clear expression of an awareness of his presence there would normally have been expected, but there is an early and persistent tradition that John the disciple was executed at the time of the martyrdom of James. James was executed about A.D. 44 during the reign of Herod Agrippa I.[27] The normal implication of the report of Jesus' prophecy of the martyrdom of James and John [28] is that at the time Mark's Gospel was written the deaths of these disciples had actually occurred. This probability is strengthened by Papias' statement that "John the divine and James his brother were killed by the Jews," [29]

[23] Ign. Eph. 11:2.   [24] Ign. Eph. 12:2.

[25] Adolf Harnack, "Patristische Miscellen," *Texte und Untersuchungen zur Geschichte der altchristlichen Litteratur* (Leipzig: J. C. Hinrichs, 1900) , XX, ii, 89.

[26] Acts 20:18-35.   [27] Acts 12: 2.   [28] Mark 10:39; Matt. 20:23.

[29] The De Boor fragment of the seventh- or eighth-century Oxford manuscript refers to the fifth-century *Chronicle* of Philip of Side as recording Papias' saying that "John the divine and James his brother were killed by the Jews." The ninth-century Coislin manuscript of Georgius Hamartolus attributes essentially the same statement to Papias and then refers to the prophecy of Mark 10:39 as being fulfilled in the martyrdoms of the two brothers. With Papias' statement in mind or else referring to the same tradition, Aphraates (344) in a homily on "Persecution" lists the early martyrs and then, evidently intending to include James and John, says, "And James and John walked in the footsteps of their Master Christ."

and by the commemoration on the same date in a fifth-century Syriac church calendar of the martyrdoms of James and John.

When the testimony of the Gospel itself concerning its author is sought, it becomes necessary at once to distinguish between the hand that wrote the body of the Gospel and the editor or editors responsible for chapter 21. The Gospel originally ended with 20:31, and someone other than its author affirmed the reliability of what he had written as a means of commending the Fourth Gospel to a reading public already familiar with and more favorably inclined toward gospels such as Matthew, Mark, and Luke.[30] In his reference to "this disciple who testifies to these things and who wrote them down," the editor clearly means "the disciple" who in verse 20 he has said was "very dear to Jesus" and who at the supper "leaned back on Jesus' breast." It is he who in the judgment of the author of chapter 21 wrote the Gospel in its entirety. He does not, however, give this disciple a name. He may intentionally have left his identity obscure.[31]

The closest approach to an identification of the author in the body of the Gospel appears in 19:35, where a connection of some sort between the author and an eye-witness is affirmed. The eye-witness is clearly the beloved disciple of verses 26-27, whom Jesus observed standing near the cross, and to whom he committed his mother. No identification of this disciple as the author of the Gospel is made. His testimony is merely used to corroborate what the author had written. The close verbal correspondence between 19:35b and 21:24 and the fact that the sense of the context does not suffer if 19:35-37 is omitted suggest the possibility that the passage originated as an interpolation by the author of chapter 21.

The author of the Gospel nowhere claims to have been an apostle, and the weight of evidence supplied by the Gospel indicates that he was not. He was demonstrably dependent on such

[30] John 21:24. It is not unlikely that the editor who added this final chapter was also responsible for the publication of the fourfold Gospel collection and that in 21:25 he refers to that corpus in its entirety rather than to the Fourth Gospel individually. (Goodspeed, *Formation of the New Testament*, pp. 34-37; *New Chapters in New Testament Study*, p. 40.)

[31] The mention of Nathanael, who does not appear in the Synoptics, and "two other disciples" who are never named along with "the sons of Zebedee" as having been with Jesus by the seaside (21:2) makes it impossible to be sure just who the "beloved disciple" was. He may have been a purely ideal figure typifying profound spiritual insight with reference to Jesus' earthly ministry.

secondary sources as the Synoptic Gospels, which is hardly comprehensible for one who was an eye-witness and participant in the events discussed. It is equally unlikely that one of the Twelve, especially in extreme old age, would so radically have recast primitive Christian conceptions and forms of expression into the Hellenistic molds so naturally employed in this Gospel. Furthermore, the apparent remoteness of the author from the actual conditions of Jesus' earthly life tells against his having had personal knowledge of them. His vital interests, the trends of his thought, his employment of Hellenistic rather than Jewish literary forms, his nonuse or thoroughgoing transformation of the inherited apocalypticism of early Christianity, the objective way in which he habitually speaks of "the Jews" combine to show that the author was much more probably Greek than Jew.

However unsound it may be, some account must be given of the probable origin of the tradition of Johannine authorship. The data for such a tradition are fairly clear. Rev. 1:9 and 22:9 leave no doubt that there was an influential leader in the Ephesian Christian community by the name of John during the last decade of the first century. To this John, however, the apostles were figures belonging to a venerable past.[32] He thought of himself as a prophet and not as an apostle. Papias also knew an Asian elder named John. He specifically differentiates that John from the apostle of the same name, but at the same time he designates Aristion and John the elder as in some sense "disciples of the Lord."[33] Finally, the author of Second and Third John, who was also the author of First John but probably not the author of the Fourth Gospel, introduces himself simply as "the Elder." He was not necessarily John the elder whom Papias knew. That elder's known sympathy with millennialism suggests his authorship of Revelation rather than the Fourth Gospel, and certainly the hand that wrote one did not write the other.[34] There were many elders in Asia, and John was a common name. Identifications of one with the other are hardly warranted.[35]

---

[32] Rev. 18:20; 21:4. [33] Euseb. *Hist*. III. 39. 4.

[34] Dionysius of Alexandria in the third century showed that the differences between the Fourth Gospel and Revelation are such that they cannot be attributed to the same author (Euseb. *Hist*. VII. 25. 1-27).

[35] The assignment of the Fourth Gospel to John begins relatively late and has poor warrant in either external or internal evidence. It is somewhat analogous to the traditional designation of Paul as the author of Hebrews. As was the case

Toward the close of the second century, when apostolic authority became a safeguard for traditional Christian teaching against heretical and sectarian tendencies, apostolicity became a necessary credential of books included in the developing Christian canon of Scripture.[36] This is illustrated by the eagerness of the author of the Muratorian canon to find an apostolic connection of some sort for each of the books he lists. Such an interest could easily have been a contributory cause of the confusion of the Johns of Ephesus.

Irenaeus and the author of the Muratorian canon were contemporaries and were equally influenced by the apostolizing tendency. This is of crucial importance, since Irenaeus' statement to Florinus was apparently the source of all subsequent identifications of John the apostle with Ephesus and his designation as the author of the Fourth Gospel. The tradition of John's residence at Ephesus in his old age and his authorship of the Fourth Gospel more probably arose from this tendency to demand apostolic authority as a condition of canonicity than from a critical appraisal of available historical data.

The First Readers.—The Fourth Gospel became extremely useful to the church as a whole during the second century. By its employment of the vocabulary and ideology of Hellenism for the restatement of the gospel story and the interpretation of Christian experience it tremendously facilitated the expansion of the Christian movement in the Greco-Roman world. The author of the twenty-first chapter rather than he who wrote the body of the Gospel, however, had this broader public consciously in mind. The church as a whole became the reading public for this Gospel when, during the first half of the second century, it appeared as a member of the fourfold Gospel corpus, published as "The Gospel."

The public visualized by the evangelist was a relatively small and definitely local Ephesian group. If not a definite group in the organized sense they were a cultivated minority within the Ephesian church. The book at the outset was probably too "modernistic" for Ephesian Christians in general and made its appeal to the more cultured members and leaders of the local Christian community.[37]

with Hebrews in the West, it is probable that hesitancy to accept the Fourth Gospel was originally due to knowledge on the part of Ephesian contemporaries that its author was one of their own number and not an apostle.

[36] Harnack, *Origin of the New Testament*, p. 56.

[37] Streeter so conceives of the first readers (*The Four Gospels*, pp. 370, 479).

It was designed for and welcomed by Hellenistic Christians who on the one hand were perplexed by the apocalypticism of early Christian tradition and on the other were as definitely repelled by the crudities of the sacramentarianism of the mystery cults. The Fourth Gospel met the needs of such people by spiritualizing the expectation of the visible return of Jesus and, by its doctrine of the Spirit, conserving the values of the mystery cults and Gnosticism without sacrificing the footing in history emphasized in the earlier tradition.

A sound evidential basis for some such conception of the first readers exists in the use which the author makes of materials from the Synoptic Gospels. Each of the Gospels was originally written for a local group. They had the entire church as a reading public only when published together as "The Gospel." In the instance of no one of the four did the author intend to supplement the sources on which he had drawn. Each evangelist wrote an account of the life and message of Jesus which in his own estimation supplied an adequate interpretation of the meaning of Christianity for the public he had in mind. The Fourth Gospel was written from this point of view. The author's own statement of purpose in 20:31 was in principle an accurate description of the motivation of each of our evangelists.

This evangelist knew and drew upon Mark, Matthew, and Luke-Acts, but he found none of them suitable for the needs of his own immediate public. He accordingly wrote a Gospel which he thought would conserve their values and take their places. With his Gospel in hand the readers he visualized would have no need for any other work of its type. The omission, supplementation, thoroughgoing metamorphosis, and chronological rearrangement of Synoptic materials in the Fourth Gospel provide an accurate basis, therefore, for conceiving of those for whom the author formulated his message.[38]

The first readers of this Gospel were a cultured but nonetheless vitally religious group. Salvation was much more definitely their concern than philosophy. They coveted the satisfactions promised initiates of the mystery cults, but they found "knowing" God by means of obedience to Christ definitely more effective than the formulae of these cults. Their specifically religious interest was

[38] E. C. Colwell's extremely illuminating employment of the creative use of the Synoptics by the author of the Fourth Gospel as a basis for defining the public of the latter (*John Defends the Gospel,* pp. 127-51) is adopted here as essentially sound.

paralleled by an equally serious concern for a definition of the
Christian message in authoritative terms and for the development
of the church, which by its unity, catholicity, and leadership would
be qualified to conserve and properly interpret the revelation of
truth by Jesus. This pronounced ecclesiastical bent of the original
audience of the Gospel implicitly heralded the trend which by
the end of another century developed into Catholic Christianity.[39]

The audience envisioned by this evangelist was for only a short
period his reading public. In not much more than a quarter of a
century some member of this smaller group saw the values of the
Fourth Gospel for the entire church. By combining the four Gospels, each hitherto local in its popularity, and publishing the massive
fourfold corpus as "The Gospel," this prophetic editor gave the
Synoptics and along with them his favorite Fourth Gospel a
church-wide reading public.

Date.—The literary dependence of the Fourth Gospel on the
Synoptics and on Paul's published letters is sufficiently certain to be
treated as an assumption. This makes 95-100 the *terminus a quo*
for the determination of its date. Traces of acquaintance with the
Gospel in the literature of the first half of the second century
serve to establish the *terminus ad quem*. A knowledge of it on the
part of the author of the Longer Ending of Mark, Ignatius, Papias,
and Justin shows that the Gospel enjoyed a circulation during the
first quarter of the century and makes 115 an approximately accurate
terminal date.

Conceivably also the evangelist shared the definitely counter-
revolutionary concern of the author of First Peter.[40] Both writers
probably desired to reduce the inflammatory influence of the re-
recently published Revelation. Such an interest tends to locate the
Fourth Gospel in the same general time area with these other
writings and to make 95-115 the probable period of its origin.[41]

Place of Composition.—The literature with which the author of
the Fourth Gospel was most indubitably acquainted was Ephesian

[39] *Ibid.*   [40] *Ibid.*, pp. 102-9.

[41] A fair consensus of scholarly opinion favors such a date. See McNeile, *Introduction*, p. 275; Moffatt, *Introduction*, p. 581; Scott, *Literature of the New Testament*, p. 235; Jülicher, *Introduction*, p. 396. If John 5:43 necessarily involved a
reference to Bar Kochba as a messianic pretender, the Fourth Gospel would
belong to the reign of Hadrian, and 135 would become the starting point for
reckoning its date. Such an interpretation is no more required in this case,
however, than in the instance of II Thess. 2:3.

in origin.[42] Similarly, the literature in which the earliest possible traces of indebtedness to the Gospel appear belonged to the Ephesian circle of influence. The first specific testimony regarding the Gospel also tends to locate it at Ephesus.[43] Interests common to the Gospel and the Ignatian letters, such as concern for church unity and opposition to Docetism, constitute supplemental evidence favorable to Ephesus. However great the uncertainty about the identity of the author, there is little doubt on anyone's part that the Fourth Gospel was written at Ephesus.

Occasion and Purpose.—The history and circumstances of the church at the time the Fourth Gospel was written supply the clue to the author's purpose. The Christian movement was approximately three quarters of a century old. The leaders of the first generation were all gone. Christianity had ceased to be a movement within Judaism, and the Jewish-Christian element within the church had become a diminishing minority. Major success had attended Christianity in the Greco-Roman world, and the increasing majority of the membership of the church was Gentile. Hellenism rather than Judaism supplied the cultural framework for thought and experience, so that the need for a statement of the Christian message in terms of Greek thought was urgent.

In addition to this general situation there were specific circumstances and problems that engaged the author's attention and helped mold his purpose. He had not been the first to sense the importance of utilizing the conceptions of Hellenism for the exposition of Christianity. Gnosticism represented an effort to restate the gospel message in terms of Greek thought, but it sacrificed certain basic values because of its essentially aristocratic character and its readiness to dissociate Christianity from its historical origins. Again, the world to which Christian leaders addressed their message was already profoundly religious, and the relatively new movement was viewed as an unwelcome competitor by Hellenistic Judaism, the followers of John the Baptist, and the mystery cults. Not only so, but the church had not achieved legal recognition and, with however little justification, had come under the suspicion of civil

---

[42] Luke-Acts and Paul's letters in their published form. For a discussion of the importance of Ephesus in the history of early Christian literature see Goodspeed, *New Chapters in New Testament Study*, pp. 22-49.

[43] The Acts of John; Iren. *Her.* III. 3. 4 (cf. Euseb. *Hist.* V. 8. 4) ; Tertullian *Against Marcion* III. 14; IV. 5; V. 16; Latin preface to the Vulgate text of John.

authorities as potentially seditious. In the presence of these problems and tendencies there began to develop within the church an awareness of the inadequacy of its essentially atomistic organization. There was a growing sense of the necessity for the church to become more closely knit and ecumenical in character. The Christian message needed authoritative formulation, and Christian leadership needed to be officialized. The emergence of Catholic Christianity was implicit in this awareness.

As other writings of the same time and locality show, and as the limited use of the Fourth Gospel indicates, the approach of this evangelist had the appearance of novelty and even radicalism. It made its first appeal to a cultivated minority within the Ephesian community rather than to Christians in general. With keen insight, however, the author rightly read the signs of the times, and his formulation of the Christian message increasingly voiced the mind of the church.

According to the author's own statement in 20:31, religion rather than biography in any systematic sense was his concern. In his basic intention to create devotion to Christ his motivation was essentially the same as that of his predecessors. Their formulations of the Christian message, however, did not satisfy him. The distinctiveness of his handling of their materials grew rather directly out of his religious experience and the completeness with which that experience dictated his exposition of religion. He wrote to stimulate faith in Jesus as the condition of sharing the divine "life" he incarnated and could impart to surrendered lives. He desired to emphasize the reality of the knowledge of God which grew out of inner spiritual fellowship with Christ. Like Paul he felt himself at no disadvantage in his acquaintance with Christ by comparison with those who had followed him in Galilee and Judea. He and his contemporaries could, in his estimation, know Jesus more profoundly than the first disciples had been able to do. He wrote to awaken the sense of this possibility in his readers and in this way contribute to the realization of their quest for eternal life. Contributory to this larger aim was the evangelist's interest in promoting church unity, dignifying church leadership, counteracting the charges of Judaism, winning the followers of John the Baptist to collaboration rather than competition, and showing the deficiencies of Gnosticism while at the same time giving sounder Christian content to certain of its conceptions.

Message.—The materials with which the Fourth Evangelist worked were drawn almost exclusively from the Synoptics. He added practically nothing to those materials as such, but with them as a basis he created a distinctively new superstructure of meaning. By omitting, rearranging, radically transforming these traditional materials, he reshaped the account of the career and message of Jesus into an exposition of the meaning of Christianity in terms of the needs of his Hellenistic public. The net effect of the reconstruction was conservation rather than innovation. It established for Greek Christianity a wholesome appreciation of the vital relationship between the historical Jesus and the Christ of faith.

The message of the author is developed in discourse materials interwoven with selected narratives or appended to them in extensive blocks. The teaching sections are interpretations of the inner meaning of the incidents and events composing the narrative. The truth seen through the lens of historical fact is clearly the primary concern of the evangelist. The story of John the Baptist and Jesus is an evangelistic plea for Baptists to become Christians. John was himself the forerunner of Jesus and not a competitor. He knew his mission was completed when he had identified Jesus as "God's lamb."[44] The account of the call of the first disciples delineates the stages of the development of "belief."[45] The wedding at Cana symbolizes Jesus' mission to change the quality of human life and establish a spiritually new order of life among men.[46] Jesus' Judean ministry supplies a frame for the exposition of the mystery and necessity of regeneration.[47] Similarly, Jesus' activity in Samaria shows that God draws to himself through Christ spiritual children from every racial group.[48] The irrelevance of time and space to the continuing effectiveness of Jesus as humanity's deliverer is the point of the two stories at 4:53–5:47. Told with the feast of Purim as their setting, they suggest that the gifts Christ bestows express divine generosity and are alone worth possessing. The miracles of 6:1-21 supply a background of power for the elaborate discourse of verses 22-71 on Jesus as the bread of life. Christ relives his life in the believer who mystically feeds on him. The discussions of chapter 7 emphasize the availability of a "knowledge" superior to that achieved in the processes of formal education. The story of the restoration of sight to a man "who had

[44] 1:19-37.   [45] 1:38-51.   [46] 2:1-11.   [47] 2:12-3:36.   [48] 4:1-42.

been blind from his birth" [49] is a peg on which to hang an elaborate discourse on Jesus as the "Light of the World." [50] The theme in chapter 10 is the Christian leader as shepherd. The story of the raising of Lazarus supplies the dramatic basis for the role of Jesus as the giver of life. He is himself "Resurrection and Life," and eternal life becomes the blessing of those who believe in him. The "supper discourses" embody a conception of the church as the community of believers in whose midst the Spirit continues the work of Christ.[51] The passion story unfolds as a prearranged program of every phase of which Jesus was completely aware and at every turn of which he was completely the Master.[52]

The evangelist had no intention of producing a new story of Jesus. He rather undertook by the use of allegory to bring to light the hidden spiritual depths of the old and familiar story. His interest in history is its significance for faith, and his constant effort is to explore the inner meaning of what actually transpired. By contrast with the numerous incidents and emphases of the Synoptics, a few incidents are elaborately developed in the Fourth Gospel for the dramatic exposition of a correspondingly limited number of great ideas such as incarnation, revelation, regeneration, belief, life. These ideas are not separable from one another, and all derive their meaning from the central significance of the personality of Christ.

The feature of the Gospel that gives unity to its emphases and controls all its details is its portrait of Jesus. Everything Jesus said and did shows he was God's "only-begotten" Son. The qualities of the divine order of existence were apparent in his words and deeds, and through his humanity men constantly beheld God's "glory." He is, in fact, an essentially divine being, "abounding in blessing and truth," who "lived for awhile" among men, and whose earthly career was a phase of his larger and eternal service. The divinity of his humanity accounts for the difficulty his immediate family and nation had in understanding him.[53] It gives proper meaning both to his profound knowledge of human life [54] and his aloofness from men.[55] Because of it he was the Master in his knowledge of [56] and

[49] 9:1-7.   [50] 8:1-9:41.   [51] 13:1-17:26.   [52] 18:1-20:31.

[53] 2:3-5, 18-20; 3:11; 7:5, 11, 15; 8:27.   [54] 1:42, 47-49; 2:24-25; 4:18, 29.

[55] 2:4, 24; 3:31; 4:27, 32; 5:17; 7:10, 16.

[56] 1:50-51; 4:18; 4:53; 5:42; 6:15, 61, 64, 70; 11:15, 23; 13:1, 3.

control over whatever transpired about him.[57] At the same time the humanity of the Logos-Christ was no mere appearance. His flesh-and-blood character was as thoroughly real as his Logos character. He grew weary from a journey, grieved at the death of a friend, was indignant at false charges, obeyed the laws of nature, functioned within the limitations imposed by time and space. A wholly super-natural Christ would have been a Gnostic Christ and would have supplied no foundation for the evangelist's conviction that salvation is by incarnation.

The dominant importance which Jesus as a person occupies in the Fourth Gospel and the categories employed in his portraiture express the evangelist's conviction that Jesus was the bearer of a new and final revelation of God. This revelation was inherent in and inseparable from his personality. He is himself "the bread that gives life," [58] "the light of the world," [59] "the door of the sheepfold," [60] "the good shepherd," [61] "Resurrection and Life," [62] "Way and Truth and Life," [63] "the true vine." [64] To have seen Jesus, therefore, is to have seen "the Father." [65] The only real judg-ment consists in the attraction or repulsion men experience in the presence of Jesus. Salvation is achieved through sharing the life he imparts.

This sharing of Jesus' life is the central religious conception of the Gospel. The evangelist's supreme concern is that "men believe that Jesus is the Christ, the Son of God" and thus "have life as his followers." [66] This "life" the possession of which means salvation is different in kind from ordinary life. It is the essence of God's own being. Its possession by men requires, therefore, a radical change in human nature. To illustrate and effect this transforma-tion the Logos-Christ joined the human race.

"Belief" and "knowledge" are crucial prerequisites for persons who are to "have life" as Jesus' followers. To know "the only true God" whose "messenger" Jesus is [67] and to believe that "Jesus is the Christ" [68] are conditions men must meet. This knowledge and belief, however, grow out of profound meditation on Jesus' words and complete obedience to his will.[69] They are also vital conse-

---

[57] 2:7-8, 15-19; 7:1-11, 30, 33; 8:20; 10:18; 11:8-11; 14:2, 22; 16:5, 7, 22-28; 19:11, 17, 26-30.

[58] 6:35.	[59] 8:12.	[60] 10:8.	[61] 10:14.	[62] 11:25.
[63] 14:6.	[64] 15:1.	[65] 14:9.	[66] 20:31.	[67] 17:3.
[68] 20:31.	[69] 7:17.			

quences of God's own redemptive approach to men's spirits. They who become believers do so because the Father "draws" them.[70] This initiative of God lies at the basis of the whole vital process the further stages of which are moral obedience, knowledge, and belief. The remaking of human nature is distinctly a supernatural achievement. God himself brings it about. It is as mysterious as the wind,[71] whose effects are observable and whose power is indisputable but whose course lies beyond human control and understanding. They who are "born over again from above" are thereby enabled to recognize Jesus in his true character and so to share the "life" he imparts. When the prerequisites for receiving this "life" have been met, the reborn man keeps himself spiritually vital by meditation on Jesus' spoken message,[72] by feeding on Christ as "the living bread that has come down out of heaven," [73] and by the maintenance of a continuous, mystical union with Christ, best illustrated in the dependent relationship of "branches" to the "vine." [74] The Christian community, which is typified in the upperroom fellowship,[75] and the establishment of which was the principal concern and crowning achievement of Jesus' earthly career, supplies the environment within which these vital processes are all sustained.[76]

[70] 6:44; 12:32.   [71] 3:8.   [72] 5:24; 6:63, 68; 8:31; 15:7; 17:8.
[73] 6:35, 53-58. This has to do, presumably, with participation in the observance of the Eucharist.
[74] 15:1-16.   [75] 17:1-26.   [76] 14:15-21, 25-31.

XVIII

THE EPISTLES OF JOHN

Authorship.—The earliest traces of probable literary acquaintance with the Johannine epistles appear in Polycarp's letter to the Philippians and in a statement of Papias preserved by Eusebius.[1] In a situation substantially analogous to that reflected in II John 10-11, and in language probably reminiscent of II John 7 and I John 4:2, Polycarp warns his readers: "For everyone who does not confess that Jesus Christ has come in the flesh is an anti-Christ." [2] Eusebius says Papias "used testimonies drawn from the former epistle of John." [3] There is also probably an echo of the language of III John 12 in the immediately preceding quotation from Papias where Eusebius reports him as saying that he delights in "those who recall the commandments given by the Lord to faith and reaching us from the truth itself." [4]

Irenaeus is the first definitely to quote the Johannine epistles.[5] In urging avoidance of the Gnostics and in refutation of the Gnostic contention that "Jesus was one, and Christ another," Irenaeus says, "His disciple in his epistle . . . commands us to avoid them." In specifying what this command is Irenaeus quotes II John 7-8 and then, as though from the same epistle, I John 4:1-2. Evidently the "epistle" as viewed by Irenaeus included both First and Second John and it was probably his designation for the three-letter corpus. Irenaeus clearly regarded John the apostle as the author. Similarly, though he makes no use of the two shorter epistles, Tertullian

---

[1] Parallels involving coincidences of language with First Clement, Hermas, and the letters of Ignatius are unconvincing: I Clem. 49:5; 50:3 (cf. I John 4:18; I Cor. 13:4-7) ; Herm. Mand. III. I (cf. I John 2:27) ; Ign. Eph. 7:2 (cf. I John 4:2) ; 18:2 (cf. I John 5:6) ; Smyrn. 6:2 (cf. I John 3:17) ; 7:1 (cf. I John 3:14) .

[2] Polyc. Phil. 7:1.

[3] *Hist.* III. 39. 47. "The former epistle of John" is probably the designation of Eusebius rather than Papias. It nevertheless implies that Papias knew the corpus of Johannine epistles.

[4] *Hist.* III. 39. 3. "The truth itself" is the phrase to be noted.

[5] *Her.* III. 16. 8.

242

quotes I John 1:7 as "from the Epistle also of John." [6] Quoting I John 1:1-4 as the statement of John "in his Epistle," the Muratorian canon, the author of which was a contemporary of Irenaeus and Tertullian, later lists along with Jude as epistles accepted in the Catholic Church "the two bearing the name of John." This latter allusion may refer to the two shorter epistles, First John having been mentioned earlier in the context with the Gospel.[7] More probably the reference is to the Johannine letter corpus as composed of two epistles. Whether the Muratorian writer referred to all three or to only two of the epistles, and whether or not his two-letter corpus contained Third John, he explicitly designates John the apostle as the author of the Gospel and the epistles.

Clement of Alexandria knew more than one of these epistles and probably knew the three of them. He actually quotes only First John, which he calls "the longer epistle." [8] This "longer epistle" he attributes to John the apostle. Origen, like Clement, quotes only First John, but he clearly knows the three epistles. He is the first to suggest the possibility that different hands wrote the longer and the two shorter epistles. According to Origen, John "who leaned on Jesus' breast . . . left one Gospel," and "he also left an epistle of a very few lines." Continuing he mentions Second and Third John but adds that "not all pronounce them to be genuine." [9] Probably reflecting an awareness of such a judgment in certain sections of the church, Eusebius lists First John among the "undisputed" writings and describes it as by the author of the Fourth Gospel, but adds, "The remaining two are disputed." [10] He thinks that John the elder, whom he says Papias clearly distinguished from the apostle, wrote Second and Third John and Revelation.

The subsequent history of opinion regarding Second and Third John is a phase of the story of the development of the seven-letter Catholic corpus. Except in Syria, where all seven letters were not included in the Syriac New Testament until the recension of Philoxenus in A.D. 500, the Catholic corpus was completed during the fourth century. Athanasius included all seven in the New Testament

[6] On Modesty XIX. In the succeeding context he quotes I John 1:5-6, 8-9; 2:1-2; 3:3-10; 5:16.

[7] Gregory, Canon and Text of the New Testament, pp. 131-32; Moffatt, Introduction, p. 479.

[8] Miscellanies II. 15. 66.   [9] Commentary on John V. 3.

[10] Hist. III. 25. 17-18; III. 39. 5-6.

list of his thirty-ninth *Festal Letter* in 367. Under the influence of Augustine and Jerome the seven Catholic epistles were established in the canon of the western church.[11]

The Johannine epistles are anonymous. The author of the two shorter ones designates himself simply as "the Elder." They supply no data to warrant his identification with the elder named John. Nor do the data of the epistles supply any basis for a differentiation of the author of First John from the author of Second and Third John. On the contrary, the vocabulary, style, and interests of the three epistles make their common authorship a matter of practical certainty.

The similar data do not clearly establish the common authorship of the epistles and the Fourth Gospel. Resemblances and differences in language, style, and thought are here about equally impressive; and scholars differ in their judgments, depending largely on whether they elect to emphasize the coincidences or the variations.[12] The consideration that weighs decisively against identity of authorship is the lack of originality in the epistles. Their author manifests no such creative ability in handling the emphases for which he is indebted to the Gospel as the author of the Gospel demonstrated in his handling of materials from Paul's letters and the Synoptic Gospels. He presupposes the message of the Gospel and undertakes merely to recall and emphasize it, contributing nothing new himself so far as the substance of the message goes.[13] He much more nearly resembles the editor who appended the twenty-first chapter to the Gospel than the author who wrote the Gospel itself.

The authors of the Gospel and the epistles are also distinguished by the very different use they make of Paul's published letters. The Gospel reflects acquaintance with all letters of the original Pauline collection except Philemon, and its clearest and heaviest indebtedness is to Ephesians. Although the author of the epistles probably knew Paul's letters, the evidence for it never rises to the level of certainty. Except for the possibility that the reference to the church in Second John as "the chosen lady" is a reminiscence of the de-

[11] Jerome regarded the apostle as the author of First John, and the Elder as the author of Second and Third John (*On Illustrious Men* IX; XVIII).

[12] For elaborate lists of these agreements and differences see Brooke, *The Johannine Epistles*, pp. xi-xvii; Charles, *The Revelation of St. John*, pp. xxxiv-xxxvi.

[13] I John 2:7, 21, 26; 3:11; II John 5.

scription of the church as the bride of Christ,[14] the epistles show no specific literary indebtedness to Ephesians. This nonuse of Paul's letters serves to emphasize the degree of the author's dependence on the Fourth Gospel. The case is somewhat analogous to the completeness with which Paul's letters satisfy the literary indebtedness of Ephesians.

The three epistles were probably written originally as a corpus, as were the letters to seven churches in Rev. 1:4–3:14 and the Pastorals. They were not separate messages on different occasions.[15] References to the epistles by Irenaeus and the Muratorian author lend themselves best to such an understanding of the matter. This probability is strengthened by the fact that the two shorter letters alone supply a clue to the kind of situation which could explain such a manifesto as First John. Dissociation of the shorter letters from the longer came when the significance of their original arrangement had been forgotten and when the designation of the author of the shorter letters as "the Elder" created difficulties for those who desired to attribute First John to the apostle.

In any event, and whatever his name, the author of the epistles was an effective and widely influential leader. He was sufficiently well known to require no more explicit designation than the two shorter letters supply. He speaks with the assurance that his authority will be recognized and his counsel treated with respect. He writes as one whose official responsibility requires him to travel from church to church and keep local leaders true to normative Christian teaching. He thinks of his work as "God's service." Associated with him are other traveling teachers for whom he urges cooperation and financial support commensurate with the dignity and importance of their duties.[16]

The First Readers.—The first epistle lacks allusions that identify it with a particular locality. It has neither address nor closing salutations. It is an epistle in only the most general sense.[17] It is characterized throughout, however, by the affectionate concern of an experienced pastor giving written counsel to constituents on matters of widespread interest.[18] Those for whom the epistle is

---

[14] Eph. 5:25 ff.   [15] Goodspeed, *Introduction*, pp. 318-23.
[16] I John 1:1-5; 2:1, 12 ff., 26; 4:6, 14; II John 12; III John 5-8, 10, 13.
[17] I John 1:4; 2:1, 7-8, 12-13, 26; 5:13.
[18] 2:1, 7, 12, 18; 3:13; 4:1; 7, 11.

written are Christians of long standing who do not owe their conversion to the writer but are in some sense subject to his official oversight.[19]

Second John is addressed to a church, described as "the chosen lady and her children." No data in the letter make the identification of a particular church possible. The author nevertheless had a local community rather than the church at large in mind. This church has apparently been disturbed by itinerant teachers whose message is at variance with the positions of traditional Christianity. The Elder feels not only that Christian hospitality does not require entertainment for heretical missionaries but that it is the duty of Christians to deny them entertainment lest they collaborate in the dissemination of error.[20]

Third John is addressed to Gaius, who is four times described as the "dear friend" of the Elder. The second person singular is used throughout the letter, which serves to emphasize its personal character. The letter supplies no clue to Gaius' place of residence, but it does indicate that he was a member of the church to which Second John was directed.[21] In that church Gaius apparently supports the point of view of the Elder and extends hospitality to his emissaries in contrast with Diotrephes, who has maliciously accused the Elder, refused to welcome his representatives, and interfered with those who wished to welcome them.

The data of the two shorter letters give point to the longer member of the corpus and create the impression that the three were originally dispatched together. The Elder preferred to "talk face to face" with Gaius [22] and with the members of his church.[23] Because of the immediate impossibility of so doing he prepared an orthodox Christological statement, First John, and with Second and Third John as cover letters sent it, presumably, by Demetrius.[24] He expected this statement to be read first to Gaius' church and then to other churches his representatives would visit.[25]

The tradition which early connected the authorship of these epistles with the Johns of Ephesus implicitly suggests that they were intended for a church or a group of churches in the Ephesian circle of influence.[26] The issues involved in them are those dis-

[19] 2:7; II John 5.   [20] II John 10-11.   [21] III John 9.   [22] III John 13.
[23] II John 12.   [24] III John 12.   [25] III John 5-8.
[26] Augustine wrote ten homilies on First John, in the title of which it is designated as "The Epistle of John to the Parthians." This may mean that

cussed by such men as Ignatius and Polycarp. The available evidence locates them in Asia Minor and suggests that the first readers were members of churches in the general vicinity of Ephesus.

Date.—The author's dependence on the Fourth Gospel and his probable acquaintance with Paul's published letters establish the *terminus a quo* for the date of the epistles. The probable acquaintance of Polycarp and Papias with the epistles locates them in the first quarter of the second century. Ignatius [27] and Polycarp [28] were, like the author of First John, concerned with the refutation of Docetism. The development of church life and organization reflected in the epistles may mean that their author was an older contemporary of Ignatius. The letters of Ignatius reflect a situation in which the local church might accept counsel from outsiders but was not under any necessity of so doing and was independent of the supervision of leaders other than those of its own choosing. An elder with the functions which the elder of the Johannine epistles appears to take for granted had no place in the church as Ignatius knew it. Conceivably the Elder and his associates represented an older type of organization. Diotrephes conceivably opposed them because he favored complete autonomy for the local congregation.[29] This possibility, with such other data as are relevant, makes a date of about 110 for the Johannine epistles approximately accurate.

Place of Composition.—Indications of the place of composition are entirely lacking in the letters themselves. The only relevant evidence is that which suggests Asia Minor as the destination. This may mean the epistles were written at Ephesus.

Occasion and Purpose.—Because it was generally assumed that matter was intrinsically evil and that God could therefore have at most only an indirect relationship with material creation, Hellenistic Christians, especially in Asia Minor, had difficulty in expressing their Christian faith in the categories of Greek intellectualism. The effort so to express the meaning of Christianity was neces-

---

Augustine thought the epistle was sent to Rome (cf. I Pet. 5:13; Euseb. *Hist.* II. 15. 2). However, Augustine never explains or comments on this title, and there is no suggestion of a Roman destination for the epistle in early tradition.

[27] *Trall.* 10; Smyrn. 2; 4:2; 5:2.   [28] Polyc. Phil. 7:1.

[29] Adolf Harnack, *"Über den dritten Johannesbrief," Texte und Untersuchungen zur Geschichte der altchristlichen Litteratur* (Leipzig: J. C. Hinrichs, 1897), XV, 21-27.

sary in the interest of intelligibility. The missionary impulse required it. It gave rise, however, especially in the definition of the significance of Christ for faith, to theories which endangered fundamental positions of historic Christianity. That the Jesus who had lived a human life, been tempted, suffered, and died, was the divine Son of God, was the fundamental conviction of Christian orthodoxy. This conviction presented grave difficulties for Hellenistic Christians.

Paul had dealt with a phase of the problem in his letter to the Colossians. There God's remoteness was the problem. According to Gnostic theory, access to God was through a gradation or series of intermediary qualities or beings. Christ was the member of the series in contact with material creation, a sort of bottom rung in a spiritual ladder from earth to heaven. He thereby lost his uniqueness and adequacy. The moral values involved in his earthly life were correspondingly undermined. In refutation of this mistaken view Paul represented Christ as the "likeness of the unseen God, born before every creature," the agent through whom "everything in heaven and on earth, the seen and the unseen, angelic thrones, dominions, principalities, authorities" came into existence. This made him Master of the whole created order. For the Fourth Evangelist, writing at Ephesus a decade or more earlier than the Johannine epistles, the reality of Christ's humanity had been called in question. For that reason he made his thesis the great assertion of John 1:14: "So the Word became flesh and blood and lived for a while among us, abounding in blessing and truth, and we saw the honor God had given him, such honor as an only son receives from his father."

The Johannine epistles appear to have been written to affirm the inseparability of Christ and Jesus. For the author a sound basis for fellowship with God and Christian morality involved the assumption "Jesus Christ has come in human form." [30] A serious crisis in the circle of Asian churches for whose supervision the Elder was responsible caused him to write. Itinerant preachers whose views were Docetic were militantly active. They had denied "the coming of Jesus Christ in human form." [31] The Elder denounces these

[30] I John 2:22; 3:23; 4:2, 5; 5:1, 10, 12, 20.

[31] II John 7. Of similar Christians Ignatius says they affirmed Christ's suffering was "only a semblance," and he retorts, "It is they who are merely a semblance" (Trall. 10) —hence the term "Docetists."

teachers as "impostors," insists they are actually agents of the Antichrist, and forbids them entertainment in the homes of Christians.[32]

The Elder found it impossible to visit the churches affected by
the propaganda of the Docetist teachers. It would have been his
preference to talk with the members of every church "face to face."
In lieu of that he sent to represent him a group of teachers for
whose doctrinal soundness he could confidently vouch and of whose
morality he was certain. They were men like Demetrius. For them
the Elder desired hospitable entertainment in local communities
and financial support as they traveled from community to community.[33] To supply these "brothers" with proper credentials he
wrote brief letters to Gaius and to the local church of which he
was a member. In addition he prepared a manifesto of his own
Christology for public reading in churches his representatives visited. By criteria established in this statement Asian Christians were
to judge the soundness of the preaching of all itinerant missionaries.
This was the function of First John.

The aggressive evangelistic activity of the Docetists, or "Seem-
ists," caused the Elder to write. The refutation of heresy, however,
was only secondarily his purpose. His concern with sound doctrinal
teaching lay in its relevance to Christian ethics and vital religious
experience. For him a correct Christology established a sound basis
for obedience to the law of God defined as Christian love,[34] and
such obedience resulted in a satisfying fellowship with God.[35] He
reminded his readers that the Christian revelation of truth had
come by the medium of a life historically lived and not by speculative thought. Jesus was therefore the irrefutable fact to which
speculation must adjust itself. The experience of earlier generations
of believers had been that men found fellowship with God through
Christ.[36] Conceptions of Jesus calculated to reduce his significance
for faith should be rejected as unsound. The traditional view that
the pre-existent Son of God actually joined the human race in
Jesus, and that Jesus was for that reason uniquely qualified to reveal
God and guide men into fellowship with him, best explained past
Christian experience. It continued to be the only sound basis for
Christian certainty.[37] The Elder's desire for Asian Christians to re-

[32] II John 7-11.   [33] III John 5-8.   [34] 2:20-23; 4:2-3; 5:5.
[35] 3:22-24; 5:2-4.   [36] 2:13-14, 20-21, 27; 3:5, 14; 4:4, 16; 5:18-20.
[37] 1:1-3; 2:24; 4:14; 5:6, 11, 20.

main unconfused regarding the nature and basis of religious certainty moved him to write as he did.[38]

Message.—The Elder saw apathy as a more serious threat than heresy to the spiritual health of the Asian churches. The tendency to welcome false and destructive ideas was the consequence of the nominal character of their Christianity. Their faith was more inheritance than discovery. It was theory and not an inner certainty determining the course of the lives of believers.

For the Elder, religion meant the experience of fellowship with God. Jesus was the great exemplar of this fellowship. With his assistance men could also have this experience.[39] The deficiency of the faith of the Asian churches was not a lack of acquaintance with the content of the Christian message. It was a failure inwardly to apprehend the experience described in that message. They needed to reproduce and not merely discuss Christian experience. They possessed only the knowledge a teacher could impart. They needed their lives quickened by the indwelling Spirit.[40]

Depending on whether or not men meet the conditions for fellowship with God, the Elder classifies them as belonging to one or the other of two categories: light or darkness, truth or falsehood, righteousness or sin, God or the world.[41] The tests by which men may be sure of their status are of crucial importance and are emphasized by frequent reiterations.[42]

The false bases of Docetic knowledge constitute the focus of attention in the Elder's formulation of his message. Over against them he emphasizes the true conditions for knowing God and maintaining "union" with him. These conditions are both ethical and theological. They involve obedience to God's commandments, the inner principle of which is Christian love,[43] and the recognition and affirmation of the reality of the incarnation of Christ in Jesus.[44] Neither emphasis takes precedence over the other. They are inseparable except for the purposes of discussion. There can be no minimizing of the reality of sin, and a mysticism which is not morally conditioned is counterfeit. Immorality and spirituality

---

[38] 2:3, 5; 3:16, 19, 24; 4:2, 6, 13; 5:2.

[39] 1:3; 2:23-25, 28; 3:6, 24; 4:13-14; 5:10-12, 20.   [40] 2:26-27; 4:2, 13; 5:6.

[41] 1:5-7; 2:9-11, 15-17; 3:10, 14; 4:4-6; 5:19.

[42] 2:3, 5; 3:16, 19, 24; 4:2, 6, 13; 5:2.   [43] 2:3-6; 3:4, 10-12, 22; 4:12, 21.

[44] 2:22; 4:2; 5:1, 5, 10.

are irreconcilable, and esoteric knowledge can never have precedence over the insights of love. Because these positions are inherent in the historical life of Jesus, the acknowledgment that "Jesus Christ has come in human form" is indispensable to fellowship with God. To live a life of Christlike obedience and to affirm the reality of the humanity of Jesus Christ are thus halves of a single whole. Like twin pillars they support vital communion with God.[45] The way in which these emphases alternate in First John illustrates their complementary character:

FELLOWSHIP CONDITIONED ON OBEDIENCE	FELLOWSHIP CONDITIONED ON SOUND CHRISTOLOGY
1:5–2:17	2:18-27
2:28–3:24	4:1-6
4:7-21	5:1-12

The two great falsehoods with which the Docetists have confused Asian Christians are (1) their claim to "have fellowship with him," although living "in darkness";[46] and (2) their denial that "Jesus is the Christ." [47] The Elder first formulates his own statement of the sound bases of fellowship with God in the form of refutations of these falsehoods.[48] He insists (1) that they who enjoy "union" with Christ "must live just as he lived," [49] and (2) that only he who "acknowledges the Son has the Father." [50]

He next proceeds to show that these two bases of a real knowledge of God are halves of a single whole. He reiterates the conviction already stated that the true marks of the children of God are that they "love one another" [51] and acknowledge "that Jesus Christ has come in human form." [52] He then specifically relates these emphases by combining them as God's command that men "are to believe in his Son Jesus Christ, and love one another," [53] thus making belief and righteousness inseparable.

Finally he makes a fourfold reiteration of each of his two great affirmations of the necessity of moral obedience and correct belief,[54] alternating them as though they were warp and woof of a closely woven fabric:

[45] 3:23-24.   [46] 1:6.   [47] 2:22.   [48] 1:5–2:17; 2:18-27.
[49] 2:6.   [50] 2:23.   [51] 2:28–3:22.   [52] 4:1-6.
[53] 3:23-24.   [54] 4:7–5:12.

OBEDIENCE TO THE DICTATES OF LOVE	A SOUND VIEW OF CHRIST
4:7-8	4:9-10
4:11-13	4:14-16
4:17-21	5:1
5:2-4	5:5-12

The Elder's logic is simple. God is love. Therefore the surest mark of fellowship with God is for men to love one another. God has given a convincing historical demonstration of his character in "sending his Son as an atoning sacrifice for our sins." [55] It follows from this that "God keeps in union with him and he with God" who acknowledges that "Jesus Christ is the Son of God." [56] Only so can men "know and believe in the love God has" for them.[57]

[55] 4:10.   [56] 4:15.   [57] 4:16.

XIX

.THE EPISTLE OF JAMES

Authorship.—The <u>address of the epistle "to the twelve tribes that</u> <u>are scattered over the world" suggests its author expected his</u> <u>published message to be widely read.</u> The absence of any mention of the tract or any convincing evidence of literary acquaintance with it earlier than Origen, however, indicates a limitation of its circulation to the locality where it originated for approximately a century.

On the basis of a limited number of parallels involving resemblances in expression and idea to First Clement[1] and a considerably more extensive series of such coincidences with Hermas,[2] acquaintance with James by the authors of those writings can be defended. The ideas and forms of expression in which these similarities consist, however, did not necessarily originate with James. Moreover, the author of James was conceivably acquainted with First Clement and Hermas. The use of widely current paraenetic materials by the three authors in complete independence of one another is probably the soundest explanation of the correspondences. An even less substantial basis exists for the claim for an acquaintance with James by Ignatius,[3] Polycarp,[4] Justin,[5] Second Clement,[6] and Irenaeus.[7] There are no traces of such knowledge in Barnabas, the Didache, the Muratorian canon, and the writings of Tertullian and Cyprian.

[1] I Clem. 10:1 (cf. Jas. 2:23); 12:2 (cf. Jas. 2:25); 30:2 (cf. Jas. 4:6).

[2] Vis. III. ii. 2 (cf. Jas. 4:8); III. ix. 6 (cf. Jas. 5:4); Mand. II. 2 (cf. Jas. 4:11; 3:8); III. 1 (cf. Jas. 4:5); IX. 1, 6 (cf. Jas. 1:4-8); IX. 2 (cf. Jas. 5:11); IX. 11 (cf. Jas. 1:17; 3:15); XI. 5 (cf. Jas. 3:15); XII. ii. 4 (cf. Jas. 4:7) XII. vi. 3 (cf. Jas. 4:12); Sim. 1. 8 (cf. Jas. 1:27); IX. xxiii. 2-4 (cf. Jas. 4:11-12). For more elaborate lists for First Clement and Hermas see Mayor, *The Epistle of St. James,* pp. lvii ff.

[3] Ign. Eph. 5:3; cf. Jas. 4:6.   [4] Polyc. Phil. 12:3; cf. Jas. 1:4.

[5] *Dial.* 16:4 (cf. Jas. 5:6); 100:5 (cf. Jas. 1:15).

[6] II Clem. 6:3, 5 (cf. Jas. 4:4); 15:1 (cf. Jas. 5:16); 16:4 (cf. Jas. 5:20); 20:2-4 (cf. Jas. 5:7-10).

[7] *Her.* IV. 16. 2 (cf. Jas. 2:23; IV. 34. 4 (cf. Jas. 1:25); V. 1. 1 (cf. Jas. 1:22).

The earliest explicit reference to the epistle was made by Origen.[8]
He quoted it frequently and regarded James the brother of the
Lord, whom he also described as an "apostle," as its author. Origen
was aware of the debatable status of James in certain areas of the
church, but for him it was canonical. Hippolytus, a Roman contemporary and acquaintance of Origen, may also have known
James; but if so his acquaintance was not thorough, for in his
possible quotation of Jas. 1:1 he alludes to it as "the saying of
Jude." [9]

Origen, apparently, popularized James in Alexandria, and its
recognition was thence extended throughout the Greek-speaking
church in the East. There from the time of Origen onward it was
generally accepted as canonical and as having been written by
James the brother of Jesus. Eusebius' references to its doubtful
status [10] more probably described his awareness of opinion in the
Syrian and western divisions of the church than his own judgment
or that of his eastern contemporaries.

Through western leaders who were acquainted with the favorable
attitude toward the epistle in the East, James became known to
the Latin church. Toward the close of the fourth century it increasingly came to be regarded as scripture. Hilary of Poitiers was
the first western leader to quote the epistle as by "the apostle
James." [11] Jerome included it in his Vulgate version of the New
Testament and quoted it frequently in his other writings. Augustine, whose New Testament canon was identical with Jerome's,
was the first African father to make use of James, and his point of

[8] *Commentary on John* XIX. 23; etc. In *Hist.* VI. 14. 1 Eusebius says that in
the *Hypotyposeis* Clement of Alexandria gave concise explanations of "all of
the Canonical Scriptures, not passing over even the disputed writings," and he
explains that by the latter he means "the Epistle of Jude and the remaining
Catholic Epistles, and the Epistle of Barnabas, and the Apocalypse known as
Peter's." In view of Clement's relationship to Origen, it becomes possible on the
basis of Eusebius' statement to credit a knowledge of James to Clement, but the
matter remains uncertain since there is no passage from Clement himself to
substantiate it.

[9] Goodspeed, *History of Early Christian Literature*, p. 238. Neither James nor
Jude was included in Hippolytus' New Testament, the three Catholics enjoying
that status being First Peter and First and Second John.

[10] *Hist.* II. 23. 24-25; III. 25. 3.

[11] *On the Trinity* IV. 8. This treatise was written by Hilary in 356-58, when he
was an exile in Asia Minor. He quotes Jas. 1:17 and Mal. 3:6 in the same context as though the one had the same kind of authority as the other.

view was reflected in the approval of the epistle as canonical by the councils of Hippo in 393 and Carthage in 397 and 419.

Similarly, in such centers of Syrian Christianity as Antioch and Edessa, where the influence of Alexandria was felt, James achieved recognition by the first quarter of the fifth century. Its translation into Syriac was probably for inclusion in the Peshitto, in which the three catholic epistles were James, First John, and First Peter. In contrast with the general acceptance of James following its canonization in the West, the epistle continued to occupy a doubtful status in areas of the Syrian church unaffected by Greek influences.

That James was unknown to the church outside the locality where it originated until the time of Origen and was thereafter tardily and hesitatingly accepted in the West and in Syria make its authorship by James of Jerusalem extremely unlikely. Apostolicity early became a credential of canonicity. Skepticism about the authorship of this epistle from the outset probably explains the slowness with which it won a place in the New Testament. Jerome, whose influence was largely responsible for its inclusion in the canon in the West, knew the tradition of its pseudonymity. In his personal judgment James the Lord's brother wrote the epistle. He nevertheless felt obligated to report that it was thought "by some to have been published by someone else under his name, and gradually, as time went on, to have gained authority." [12]

Origen's judgment that the epistle was written by James the brother of Jesus may have been his own inference from the allusions of Paul's letters and Acts.[13] It may, on the other hand, have been tradition. In either event it probably represents the impression the author desired to create. His designation of himself in the superscription as "James, a slave of God and of the Lord Jesus Christ" is best understood as originally the conscious assignment of authorship to a revered figure of the relatively remote past in whose spirit the actual author addressed his own contemporaries. The epistle was probably in its inception pseudonymous. In accordance with currently legitimate literary practice the author wrote in the name of James, the Lord's brother and first head of the Jerusalem church. The names of Paul, Peter, and John were pre-empted by their

[12] On Illustrious Men II.

[13] Gal. 1:19; 2:9, 12; Acts 15:13 ff.; 21:18 ff.; cf. Jas. 2:14-26.

association with letters in circulation in the church. Confronted with a misuse of Paul's teaching to excuse moral lethargy,[14] this Christian teacher decided to write a letter of correction in the name of James of Jerusalem, an entirely understandable procedure.

The data of the epistle support this view of the author's intention. Koinê Greek was the language he customarily used. His varied and adequate vocabulary, excellent Greek style, and effective adaptation of the diatribe form combine to indicate that he was a Greek Christian "teacher."[15] The public he addressed was composed of Greek rather than Jewish Christians. Certainly the specific issues with which James of Jerusalem is represented as concerned in Galatians and Acts do not emerge at all in this epistle. Nor is Paul attacked on grounds which originally aroused the antagonism of conservative Jewish Christians. The impression made by the epistle is that author and audience knew Paul exclusively from his letters. The issue was a misuse of Pauline formulae to justify inertia.

The First Readers.—The address of the epistle describes the first readers as "the twelve tribes that are scattered over the world." It is needlessly literalistic to interpret this as meaning either Jews or Christians of Jewish origin. Jewish tribal divisions had vanished centuries before the Christian era, and "the twelve tribes" of this address have only the symbolic character of those enumerated in Rev. 7:4-8. Nothing in the epistle suggests readers of Jewish origin. The sins condemned are more characteristically human than Jewish and were familiar in Hellenistic society. The "faultless law that makes men free"[16] refers to the Christian principle of love rather than the Mosaic system. There is nowhere any hint of an awareness of antagonistic groupings of Jewish and Gentile Christians comparable to the time of Paul and the Jerusalem "pillars." The address is a symbolic designation of Christendom as the true Israel.[17] Christians are "the people of God in their dispersion." The messianic Kingdom is their true home. Pending its coming they are aliens in the existing world order.

---

[14] The "senseless" man of Jas. 2:20 represents essentially the type of problem which the "ignorant, unsteadfast people" who like him "twist to their own ruin" the teaching of Paul (II Pet. 3:16) constituted for a contemporaneous Christian leader.

[15] 3:1.   [16] 1:25; cf. Barn. 2:6; Just. *Dial.* 12:3.

[17] Cf. Gal. 3:7-9; 6:16; Rom. 4:16; 9:6-8; Matt. 3:9; 12:46-50; Acts 10:34-37; Eph. 1:1; Rev. 7:4-17; 21:10-15; I Pet. 1:1.

The contents of James make it unimaginable that it was written for delivery by messenger to a particular circle of readers. It is clearly a treatise designed for publication. The epistolary address was a literary device familiar in Greek usage from the fourth and third centuries B.C. onward. It implies no such intercourse between author and readers as Paul's letters reflect. The epistle is actually a tract prepared for circulation among Christians in general. Its public was the church in its totality—"the people of God in their dispersion."

Date.—Although extremely difficult to establish because of their allusive and indirect character, the literary connections of James supply almost the only clue to its date.[18] The epistle contains no direct quotations of earlier Christian writings. The author, however, appears to have known Paul's published letters. The data establish the strong probability of the author's acquaintance with Romans, First Corinthians, Galatians, and Ephesians.[19] The probability of acquaintance with these letters is increased by the author's concern with the current misinterpretation of Pauline conceptions, popularized by the widespread circulation of his letters. The epistle makes no such explicit reference to Paul's letters as appears in II Pet. 3:18. The concern with a misuse of Paul's teaching which is common to two epistles may indicate both belonged to the same general period of 125-50.

[18] Conclusions from the relevant data as frequently reflect the point of view of the interpreter as the decisiveness of the data. The author of James clearly knew the Septuagint. Instances of his formulae of citation of it are 2:8, 11, 23; 4:5. For indications of possible acquaintance with First Clement and Hermas see footnotes 1, 2. Parallels that might point to acquaintance with Hebrews—such as 2:25 and Heb. 11:31, etc.—have the same quality of indecisiveness as for Clement and Hermas. The author conceivably knew Matthew and Luke: 1:13 (cf. Matt. 6:13); 1:22 (cf. Matt. 7:24; Luke 6:46); 4:11 (cf. Matt. 7:1; Luke 6:37); 5:12 (cf. Matt. 5:34 ff.); 2:5 (cf. Luke 6:20); 3:1 (cf. Luke 12:48); 4:4 (cf. Luke 16:13); 4:17 (cf. Luke 12:47). Clearly such parallels do not necessitate literary indebtedness for their explanation. They may, however, indicate that the epistle was written in a locality where the interests were those that inspired the development of the written accounts of Jesus' teaching on which the Synoptic Gospels drew. The probability that 1:1 is a universalization of I Pet. 1:1 suggests an indebtedness of the one to the other. This probability is somewhat strengthened by parallels involving verbal coincidences, such as: 1:25 (cf. I Pet. 1:12); 1:27 (cf. I Pet. 1:19); 3:13 (cf. I Pet 3:2, 4); 3:17 (cf. I Pet. 1:22); and by other parallels that involve resemblances in thought, such as 1:12 (cf. I Pet. 5:4); 1:18 (cf. I Pet. 1:23); 1:21 (cf. I Pet. 2:1-2); 4:1 (cf. I Pet. 2:11); 4:10 (cf. I Pet. 5:6).

[19] See my *Paul Becomes a Literary Influence,* pp. 186-96; Moffatt, *Introduction,* p. 466.

The publication of Paul's letters in about 95 is the *terminus a quo* for estimating the date of James. Between 95 and the use of the epistle by Origen, the only datum significant for its narrower location is the type of its concern with Paul's teaching. Paul's letters enjoyed a period of tremendous popularity immediately following their publication. During the second quarter of the second century, however, probably due to the espousal of Paul by heretical groups, this popularity waned. Mention of Paul disappears, and evidence of acquaintance with his letters becomes extremely meager. James apparently belongs to this period. His criticism is not so much of Paul's teaching as of those "ignorant, unsteadfast people" denounced in II Pet. 3:16, who "twist to their own ruin" the Pauline doctrine of faith. After 150 Paul recovered his standing in orthodox Christian circles, and by the time the Pastoral epistles were written—and partly, at least, due to their influence—Paul became the champion of orthodoxy.

Origen's judgment that James was written by the Lord's brother indicates his judgment of its antiquity. He could hardly have entertained this view of it had it been written later than 150. A date, then, of about 125 best corresponds with the data of the epistle itself and the tradition about it.

Place of Composition.—The author's primary concern with the "good life" [20] and his conception of Christianity as "the faultless law" [21] in accordance with which the "good life" might be achieved create a general resemblance to Matthew and Didache 1–6 that suggests Syrian Antioch as the place where the epistle was possibly written.[22] On the basis of some sort of literary connection between James and such Roman writings as Hebrews, First Clement, Hermas, and First Peter, the epistle could have been written at Rome. The nonuse of James in the West and in Syria, however, and the tardiness with which it was finally included in the New Testaments of those sections of the church argue against either a Roman or an Antiochan origin.

Origen was the first Christian father to refer to James. Perhaps he found it at Caesarea and brought it with him to Alexandria. It may well have been written at Caesarea and enjoyed a purely local circulation there until Origen's appreciation of it gained for it a wider currency. Its origin at Caesarea would supply as good a setting

[20] 3:13.   [21] 1:25.   [22] Goodspeed, *Introduction*, p. 295.

as Antioch for the affinities the epistle seems to have with the tradition of Jesus' teaching incorporated in the written sources on which Matthew and Luke drew. The earlier acceptance of James in the Greek church would also favor Caesarea as the probable place of its composition.

Occasion and Purpose.—James is a published sermon. The intention of its author was to call the church to repentance for what he took to be the alarmingly prevalent laxity which justified moral inertia by an identification of assent with saving faith. He scathingly denounces a conception of faith in which creedal orthodoxy becomes important for its own sake. If faith is effective, it must involve commitment to "the faultless law that makes men free," with the result that the individual actually and specifically "obeys and acts upon it." [23] Insofar as the epistle has a discoverable theme it is this insistence that piety be morally energetic and socially fruitful. The 54 imperatives in its 108 verses supply the surest clue to its purpose.

The data of the epistle do not identify it with a definite situation. The author's message seems to have been formulated with reference to the general needs of the church as he had himself observed them. He proposed to quicken the conscience of the Christian community generally on issues which he felt were inadequately treated in popular preaching and on which Christians were both timorous and insensitive. He desired to extend the suspicion he himself felt of a piety that threatened to become too exclusively devotional and creedal. He thought piety should magnify the homely virtues and the commonplace social obligations. It was his purpose not so much to extend the knowledge of truth as to make familiar truth imperative.

Message.—Instead of being merely a series of moralistic exhortations wholly lacking in unity, James is a homily whose general theme is "The Uprightness God Wishes." [24] The method of the preacher's exposition is concrete illustration, and his message has the kind of coherence that the Sermon on the Mount possesses. The illustrations require no particular sequence for their effectiveness. Each sheds it own light on the general theme more or less as the illustrations in the series of Matt. 5:21-48 display the character of the righteousness which in Matt. 5:20 is made prerequisite to

[23] 1:25.   [24] 1:20.

admission to the Kingdom. The transition from one illustration to another is marked by the recurrent salutation "my brothers," the nine occurrences of which denote the natural divisions of the thought of the epistle. Each of these divisions sketches some quality which belongs to the nature of Christian piety.[25]

The good life is conceived in definitely religious terms. Its expressions are phases of man's duty to God and issue in the enjoyment of God's approval. Because God's approval alone matters, "the uprightness God wishes" necessarily should be man's "greatest care." [26] God and the world are incompatible objects of human devotion, and "the friendship of the world" inevitably comes to involve "enmity with God." [27] Christian "uprightness" is viewed as originating in a deeply religious humility that disposes men to obey God's "message" as having "power" to save their souls.[28] A merely academic assent which results from "listening" to Christian preaching is inadequate. What is required is a hunger and thirst which demand for their satisfaction an actual appropriation of Christian truth.

James makes distinctly Christian conduct the index to the reality of such an appropriation of truth. He insists on the necessary correspondence between perception and performance. He brands as counterfeit an exclusively devotional or intellectualistic piety.[29] Goodness is for him the truest spirituality.[30] Because God is "the Father" and the standards by which men will ultimately be judged root in his character,[31] it is definitely "a religious observance . . . to look after orphans and widows in their trouble." [32]

Although differing from the Pauline and Johannine view that "the uprightness God wishes" originates in regeneration, James clearly sees that man achieves the good life only by God's constant assistance. By prayer,[33] under the guidance of the Spirit residing in his heart,[34] the believer finds himself enabled to obey "the faultless law that makes men free." [35] By so living he keeps himself in readiness for "the coming of the Lord." [36]

[25] 1:2-18 endurance; 1:19-27 obedience; 2:1-13 impartiality; 2:14-26 integrity; 3:1–4:10 discipline; 4:1–5:6 humility; 5:7-11 patience; 5:12-18 prayerfulness; 5:19-20 redemptive love.

[26] Cf. Matt. 6:33.   [27] 4:4; cf. Matt. 6:24.   [28] 1:21-22.   [29] 2:14-26.

[30] 3:13.   [31] 1:20; 4:12; 5:10; cf. Matt. 25:31-46.   [32] 1:27.

[33] 1:5; 5:13.   [34] 4:5.   [35] 1:22, 25.   [36] 1:12; 2:13; 5:7-11.

XX

THE EPISTLE OF JUDE

Authorship.—The earliest clear evidence of acquaintance with Jude is its incorporation in Second Peter.[1] The author of the latter epistle makes no formal reference to Jude but is nevertheless unmistakably indebted to it. The Muratorian canon includes Jude among the generally accepted writings of the church, but it notes the differences of judgment about its authorship.[2] The epistle was known to Tertullian and his readers as an apostolic writing the author of which was Jude.[3] Clement of Alexandria quotes the epistle specifically as by Jude;[4] and Eusebius says that in the *Outlines,* along with his "explanations of all the canonical Scriptures," Clement also commented on "the disputed writings," meaning thereby "the Epistle of Jude and the remaining Catholic Epistles, and the Epistle of Barnabas, and the Apocalypse known as Peter's."[5] Origen also refers to the epistle as by Jude, who he thinks was the Judas listed in the Gospels as a brother of Jesus.[6] Origen

[1] Earlier possible traces of acquaintance with Jude are unconvincing. The wording of the doxologies of I Clem. 20:12; 65:2 resembles that of Jude 25 (cf. Ecclus. 18:5), but it more probably represents liturgical usage than literary indebtedness. Similarly, the reference to the defilement of the body in Herm. Sim. V, 7, 2 and Jude 8 requires no predication of literary indebtedness for its explanation. Polycarp's exhortation "to build yourselves up into the faith given you." (Poly. Phil. 3:2) is a possible reminiscence of Jude 20, but as probably reflects the increasingly common conception of Christianity as authoritative teaching.

[2] The Muratorian statement is: "The Epistle of Jude no doubt, and the two bearing the name of John, are accepted in the Catholic Church."

[3] With Jude 14-15 in mind as support for his own argument for the scriptural status of Enoch, Tertullian urges that, in addition to the considerations already adduced, Enoch possesses "a testimony in the Apostle Jude" (*On the Apparel of Women* I. 3).

[4] *The Instructor* III. 8 formally quotes Jude 5-6; *Miscellanies* III. 2 makes specific use of Jude 8-16; cf. Eusebius, who says that Clement in his *Miscellanies* "made use of testimonies from the disputed writings," among which he lists Jude along with Wisdom of Solomon, Sirach, Hebrews, and the epistles of Barnabas and Clement (*Hist.* VI. 13. 6).

[5] *Hist.* VI. 14. 1.　　　　　　　　　　[6] Mark 6:3; Matt. 13:55.

also refers to him as "the Apostle Jude." [7] On the ground that few of "the ancients" mentioned it, Eusebius says Jude like James "is considered spurious." [8] However, he lists it among the "disputed" as distinguished from the "spurious" writings.[9] Athanasius lists Jude last in the full corpus of seven Catholic epistles included in his New Testament.[10] Jerome likewise knew Jude as one of the seven Catholic epistles and regarded it as by "Jude the brother of James." On the basis of its antiquity and the general use made of it in the church he says "it has gained authority and is reckoned among the Holy Scriptures." He refers to no dispute about its authorship, but says some reject it because it "quotes from the apocryphal book of Enoch." [11]

The epistle designates its author as "Jude, a slave of Christ Jesus, and the brother of James." Possibly the latter phrase was added by a later hand on the basis of inference from the gospel lists of the brothers of Jesus and as a means of giving apostolic authority to the message of an otherwise unknown writer.[12] More probably the author so described himself as a way of accrediting his message. On this understanding of the matter Jude like Second Peter was written pseudonymously.[13]

Indications of the author's outlook supplied by the epistle make his preference for pseudonymity entirely understandable. He was a man who "believed passionately in a creed," [14] who conceived of Christianity in terms of strict orthodoxy,[15] to whom the apostles were the venerated figures of an authoritative past.[16] He made no effort to refute heresy by demonstrating its unsoundness by argument. Instead he proposed to destroy the influence of sectarian leaders by denunciation. In authoritarian fashion he undertook to

[7] *Commentary on Matthew* X. 17; XVII. 30; *On First Principles* III. 2. 1.

[8] *Hist.* II. 23. 24-25.   [9] *Hist.* III. 25. 3.

[10] *Festal Letter* XXXIX. 5.   [11] *On Illustrious Men* IV.

[12] Harnack, *Chronologie*, I, 468; Goodspeed, *Introduction*, p. 348.

[13] The Judas of the gospel lists probably died before A.D. 70. According to the story of Hegesippus (Euseb. *Hist.* III. 20. 1-2) the grandsons of Jude were arraigned by Domitian as the surviving kinsmen of Jesus. When, however, he saw their poverty and their humble appearance, he ordered them released as harmless. They were mature men at the time, and Eusebius adds the note that they lived thereafter "until the time of Trajan." Their father was dead at the time of their arrest, which probably means that their grandfather died much earlier.

[14] Bigg, *The Epistles of St. Peter and St. Jude,* p. 325.

[15] Vss. 3, 20.   [16] Vs. 17.

overwhelm those who "make light of authority" [17] by showing that their teaching and behavior represented nonconformity with the authoritative teaching of both Scripture and of "the apostles of our Lord Jesus Christ." [18] Such a leader would normally seek to give his message the weight inherent in the name of a man long dead and with whose memory was associated the kind of veneration befitting a brother of the traditional head of the Jerusalem church.

The First Readers.—Jude is addressed to "those who have been called, who are dear to God the Father and have been kept through union with Jesus Christ." The address is as definitely encyclical as are those of Ephesians and Second Peter. So conservative a critic as Charles Bigg, who contends for the authenticity of both Jude and Second Peter, recognizes the indefiniteness of the superscription and concludes that "Jude may have been addressed to almost any community in which Greek was spoken." [19] Actually its message was for Christians wherever the threat of schism existed and wherever the ideals and moral practices of Docetism endangered traditional teaching and standards.

There is no early tradition indicating opinion as to the section of Christendom to which the first readers belonged. The false teaching condemned has the general character of that denounced in the Johannine and Ignatian epistles. Asia Minor therefore may have been the area for which Jude was intended. As probably, however, Christendom in general constituted the public for which the author wrote.

Date.—Its incorporation in Second Peter fixes the *terminus ad quem* for establishing the date of Jude. Veneration for the apostles such as appears in this epistle is characteristic of Christian writings from the closing decade of the first century onward.[20] The Fourth Gospel and the Johannine epistles represent the earliest orthodox rejoinders to the propaganda of Docetism. The first extant writings that are favorable to Docetism belong to the second quarter of the second century.[21] The creedal conception of Christianity and the

---

[17] Vs. 8.

[18] The increasing tendency of Christians of the second century to exalt the authority of apostolic teaching is illustrated in such writings as Barnabas, the Didache, Second Peter, and the Pastorals. Jude reflects this trend and is probably marked thereby as belonging to the first quarter of the second century.

[19] *Op. cit.*, p. 321.   [20] Eph. 2:20; 3:5; Rev. 18:20; 21:14.

[21] The Gospel of Peter and the Acts of John.

tendency to make the words of the apostles co-ordinate with the authority of Scripture suggest the general period from which Barnabas, the earliest form of the Didache, and Second Peter came. It is the period of "maturing Christianity." [22] A date of about 125 probably best satisfies such data as the epistle supplies.

Place of Composition.—The incorporation of Jude in Second Peter, which was almost certainly written at Rome, and its recognition as canonical in the West before Second Peter and James were so recognized [23] argue strongly for the Roman origin of Jude. The hostility of its author to men who "make light of authority" and who "create division" [24] may also be taken to typify the characteristically Roman attitude. The vigor of his antipathy for heretical teaching makes him a natural predecessor for Irenaeus.[25] Rome is probably the likeliest place at which to locate such a polemical pamphlet as Jude.

Occasion and Purpose.—The author of Jude says he was "just on the point of writing" a pastoral letter "about our common salvation" when a crisis of some description required him to defer that enterprise and instead "write and appeal" to Christians generally "to come to the defense of the faith that has once for all been intrusted to God's people." [26] He describes this crisis as having been created by certain persons who "sneaked" into the church and were using their membership as camouflage for the popularization of practices and ideas alien to the original character of Christianity. Their propaganda had achieved success beyond the realization of the leadership of the church, and the discovery of the proportions of the movement had shocked the author of Jude. He conceives of it as actually jeopardizing the foundation of Christian faith and life. All else must therefore wait while he expresses his concern to all who will read what he writes.

He assumes the familiarity of his readers with the content both of "the faith" and the heretical teaching threatening it. He therefore makes no effort to give an exposition of either. He rather seeks to arouse orthodox Christians to a sense of the seriousness of the menace represented in heretical teaching by denouncing the proponents of the teaching. Their antinomian attitudes, the divisive-

---

[22] Riddle, *Early Christian Life,* pp. 217-31.

[23] As expressed in the judgments of Tertullian and the author of the Muratorian canon.

[24] Vss. 8, 19.   [25] *Against Heresies.*   [26] Vs. 3.

ness they have introduced into the Christian fellowship, their gross immorality belie their lofty pretensions to spiritual superiority. Abandonment of the standard beliefs of traditional Christianity, he feels, naturally produce the results exemplified by these "godless persons." Therefore in the interest of Christian unity and sound morality he writes to challenge all who may read his tract to defend "the faith that has once for all been intrusted to God's people."

Message.—"The faith" to the defense of which the author of Jude calls his readers was not the attitude of trustfulness and corresponding self-surrender. It was rather a body of teaching that derived its authority from its agreement with the content of Scripture and the words of the apostles. It had the finality of revelation and constituted the only secure foundation for Christian morality. It was subject neither to criticism nor to alteration. Men must believe it and be governed by its implications.

The author's attention is devoted chiefly to the antinomian teachers, whom he accuses of proposing substitutes for the accepted Christian ideology. Their immorality is the natural corollary of their heresy. They are a threat to the spiritual health of the church because they disown Jesus Christ as the "only Master and Lord." [27]

The body of the epistle [28] is devoted to a delineation of the evil characteristics of these heretical leaders and illustrations from Scripture showing the certainty and the terrible character of their doom. Their unbelief and their immorality subject them to penalties corresponding to those inflicted on (1) those people who, having been brought safely out of Egypt, nevertheless "did not believe," (2) "the angels who neglected their responsibilities," (3) "Sodom and Gomorrah and the neighboring towns which like them indulged in immorality," (4) Cain, (5) Balaam, (6) Korah. This emphasis on the certainty and awful character of punishment for unfaithfulness has the sound of the Epistle to the Hebrews,[29] also a product of Roman Christianity.

Toward the close of his appeal,[30] almost as something he was about to overlook in his indignation and haste, the author refers to the way orthodox Christians should behave in the crisis. He urges them to regard the traditional Christian message as final and un-

[27] Vs. 4.   [28] Vss. 5-19.
[29] Heb. 2:2-3; 3:12-19; 4:1, 6, 11-13; 6:4-8; 10:26-31; 12:15-17, 25-28.
[30] Vss. 20-23.

alterable. They ought also to "pray in the holy Spirit," who inspired the apostolic message. The Parousia is an element in that message and so is to be patiently awaited. They must pity Christians confused by heretical teaching and try to save them, "snatching them out of the fire" destined for those who have misled them. On those who are committed to the positions of the heretics they will look "with pity mixed with fear, loathing even the clothes their animal nature has stained."

XXI

THE SECOND EPISTLE OF PETER

Authorship.—Jerome witnesses both to the popularity of Peter's name in the Christian literature of the first two centuries and to the pseudepigraphic character of the majority of the books written about him and in his name. Writings which he says are "rejected as apocryphal" are "his Acts, . . . his Gospel, . . . his Preaching, . . . his Revelation, . . . his Judgment." He views Mark's Gospel as really Peter's, and in his opinion Peter "wrote two epistles which are called Catholic." On the basis of differences in the style of the two Petrine letters, however, he says Second Peter "is considered by many not to have been by him." [1] For Jerome himself these differences were sufficiently accounted for on the supposition of Peter's employment of different amanuenses.[2]

In the earliest certain allusion to Second Peter, Origen says Peter "left only one epistle of acknowledged genuineness." He knows a second epistle ostensibly by Peter. Without trying to account for or explain away the current skepticism about its authenticity he simply says of it, "This is doubtful." [3]

The New Testament of Eusebius contained all seven of the Catholic epistles. There is the clear recognition, however, that the canonical status of several of these epistles was the outgrowth of their having been "read in public in most churches" rather than certainty of their apostolic authorship.[4] He says only one of the Petrine epistles is recognized "as genuine and acknowledged by the elders of olden time." Second Peter was studied, however, "along with the other Scriptures," although the tradition about it was that "it is not canonical." [5] When Eusebius classified the books of the New Testament according to the prevailing judgment in the church, he described Second Peter along with James, Jude, and

---

[1] *On Illustrious Men* I.

[2] *Letters* LIII. 9 (*To Paulinus*); CXX. 11 (*To Hedibia*).

[3] *Commentary on John* V. 3.   [4] *Hist.* II. 23. 25.

[5] *Hist.* III. 3. 1, 4.

Second and Third John as "disputed, nevertheless familiar to the majority." [6]

Doubt of its authenticity rather than complete lack of acquaintance with Second Peter may explain the attitude of Irenaeus. The instances of his formal quotation of things "said by Peter" are all passages from First Peter.[7] The first of these he introduces with the formula, "Peter says in his epistle," as though he recognizes only one epistle as by Peter. Representatives of opinion in the western church contemporaneous with Irenaeus, such as the author of the Muratorian canon, Tertullian, and Cyprian, show no acquaintance with the epistle.

Clement of Alexandria represents a comparable period in the East. His extant writings contain no quotations of Second Peter and no passages necessarily reflecting literary acquaintance with it. Eusebius, however, says that in the *Outlines* Clement gave "concise explanations of all the canonical Scriptures," including such "disputed" writings as "Jude and the remaining Catholic Epistles, and the Epistle of Barnabas, and the Apocalypse known as Peter's" [8] According to this statement Clement knew and commented on Second Peter. This was probably the case, although direct corroboration from the extant remains of Clement's writings is lacking.

Athanasius [9] and Augustine,[10] both of whom decisively influenced the determination of the canon for the entire church, recognized Second Peter as canonical and said nothing of any dubiousness regarding its authenticity. Similarly, the epistle was recognized as canonical by the third Council of Carthage in 397. That doubts about its Petrine authorship continued to exist in the church is of course made clear by Jerome.

The epistle itself explicitly and insistently claims to have been written by Peter the apostle. The author describes himself in the superscription as "Simon Peter, a slave and apostle of Jesus Christ." This claim is supported in the body of the epistle by the author's application to himself of Jesus' prediction of Peter's martyrdom,[11]

---

[6] *Hist.* III. 25. 3.

[7] *Her.* IV. 9. 2 (cf. I Pet. 1:8) ; IV. 16. 5 (cf. I Pet. 2:16) ; V. 7. 2 (cf. I Pet. 1:8). In V. 23. 2 and 27. 3 Irenaeus adapts Ps. 90:4 as in II Pet. 3:8 but makes a different application of the passage. This may show acquaintance with the epistle on the part of Irenaeus, but not necessarily so.

[8] *Hist.* VI. 14. 1.   [9] *Festal Letter* XXXIX. 5.

[10] *On Christian Doctrine* II. (8) 13.   [11] 1:14; cf. John 21:18-19.

his representation of himself as having been with Jesus "on that sacred mountain" on the occasion of the Transfiguration,[12] and his implicit reference to First Peter as having been written by himself.[13]

This zeal of the epistle for its own authenticity is entirely understandable in terms of the author's purpose, but creates doubt rather than confidence about the fact itself. The differences in language and style from First Peter are too radical to be explained by the employment of different amanuenses.[14] Although Peter probably had nothing to do with writing either epistle, a sounder case can be made for the earlier than for the later of them. Other data in the epistle which definitely locate it well into the second century and thereby remove the possibility of Petrine authorship are: (1) the incorporation of Jude as its second chapter; (2) the author's classification of himself and his readers as belonging to a generation acquainted with the founding fathers only by tradition; [15] (3) the designation of Paul's collected letters as Scripture; [16] (4) reference to the use of Paul's letters by heretics.[17]

These data illustrate the relatively late date of Second Peter. Like other writers of pseudepigraphic works of the second century [18] the author used Peter's name to commend his message because he felt Peter would so have expressed himself had he faced the problems confronting the church. In this sense the author of Second Peter felt he had a right to speak in Peter's name. For him Peter was the true representative of Christianity in its original and authoritative form. This made it appropriate to condemn heresy by his authority.

The First Readers.—The superscription of the epistle designates the first readers as "those who through the uprightness of our God and Savior Jesus Christ have been given a faith as privileged as ours." [19] They are further identified as having been also the recipients of First Peter [20] and as belonging to a public for whom Paul's letters enjoyed the status of scripture.[21] There are no indications in the epistle that the author had a local church or a particular group of churches in mind. Nor did a relationship of

---

[12] 1:17-18; cf. Matt. 17:5; Mark 9:7; Luke 9:35.   [13] 3:1.

[14] Moffatt, *The General Epistles*, p. 174.   [15] 3:2, 4.   [16] 3:16.   [17] *Ibid.*

[18] Gospel of Peter, Acts of Peter, Teaching of Peter, and Preaching of Peter.

[19] 1:1.   [20] 3:1.   [21] 3:16.

genuinely personal acquaintance exist between author and readers.[22] Heretical trends such as the epistle condemned affected the church generally and were not confined to any given locality.

The writer's message was intended for Christendom in its entirety. The first readers were those Christians to whose attention this little homily happened to come. The meager use made of it in early Christian literature and the hesitancy with which it was admitted to the canon suggest it enjoyed a limited popularity and a correspondingly restricted circulation.

Date.—The considerable body of Christian literature with which Second Peter shows acquaintance and the historical situation implicit in the allusions it contains point rather clearly to a date around the middle of the second century. The author knew Mark's Gospel as substantially Peter's,[23] and he assumed a general familiarity on the part of his readers with the Synoptic account of the Transfiguration.[24] The probability that he knew the four Gospels as a published corpus is suggested by the reference to Jesus' prophecy of Peter's martyrdom as told in the editorial appendix to the Fourth Gospel.[25] The representation of Paul as Peter's "dear brother" more nearly corresponds to the irenic picture in Acts than to that reflected in Paul's own letters.[26] Not only were Paul's letters known as a published collection, but for this author and his public they had the status of scripture.[27] The attitude of severity toward "backsliders" may reflect a knowledge of the similar judgment expressed

[22] Moffatt describes as simply "literary drapery" statements that appear to presuppose such acquaintance, as 1:12, 16; 3:1-2, 8, 14, 17 (*Introduction*, p. 368).

[23] 1:15; cf. I Pet. 5:13; Euseb. *Hist.* III. 39. 15.

[24] 1:17; cf. Matt. 17:5; Mark 9:7; Luke 9:35.

[25] 1:14; cf. John 21:18-19. The publication of the Gospel corpus was probably the occasion that inspired the writing of John 21.

[26] 3:15; cf. Gal. 1:16-18; 2:6-14; I Cor. 1:12; 3:22; 9:5.

[27] The heretics who according to 3:16 misused Paul's letters were probably the followers of Marcion. The author's own attitude toward Paul and his letters seems to represent a position intermediate between those reflected in the writings of Justin and in the *Acts of the Scillitan Martyrs.* Justin says it was the practice of Christians to read the Gospel along with the "writings of the prophets" in their Sunday services (*Apol.* 67:3). He knew Paul's letters, but he refrains from mentioning his name, and he tells of no such formal use of the letters in the churches. The Numidian Christian questioned by the proconsul is said in the *Acts of the Scillitan Martyrs* to have replied that Paul's letters were kept in the church "strong box" along with the "holy books." Presumably they were themselves counted among the "holy books."

in Hebrews.[28] Acquaintance with First Peter [29] and with Jude [30] is of course unmistakable.

Place of Composition.—There are no decisive indications in Second Peter of the place of its origin. The relevant data of the book suggest Rome. Its abhorrence of heterodoxy is typically Roman. Peter and Paul were traditionally supposed to have labored together at Rome, "preaching . . . and laying the foundations of the Church," and they were thought to have died as martyrs at Rome during the reign of Nero.[31] The references in the epistle to Peter's martyrdom [32] and to his having collaborated with Paul in instructing the churches by means of letters [33] strongly suggest a Roman setting.

The ostensibly prophetic reference to Mark's Gospel as the depository of Peter's message and as written to enable the church after the apostle's death to recall the things he had taught [34] also links the epistle with Rome. First Peter was certainly a Roman document, and the present author's insistence on the Petrine authorship of both epistles [35] tends to identify them with the Roman Christian community. The popularity of Jude at Rome as evidenced by its inclusion in the Muratorian canon was probably responsible for its incorporation as the second chapter of Second Peter. This also probably indicates Rome as the place where the latter originated.

Occasion and Purpose.—The situation that inspired the writing of this epistle is described as having been foreseen by Peter. As there had been "false prophets . . . among the people" in Old Testament times, so now, as Peter knew would be the case when he and the other apostles were all gone, there are "false teachers" within the church, "who . . . introduce destructive sects and deny the Master who has bought them." [36] Incensed by the propaganda of

[28] 2:20-21; cf. Heb. 6:4-8; 10:26-31.   [29] 3:1.   [30] Chap. 2.

[31] Iren. *Her.* III. 1. 1; Tertullian *Scorpiace* XV; cf. I Clement 5:3-7; 6:1; Ign. Rom. 4:3; the Muratorian canon.

[32] 1:14.   [33] 3:1, 15.

[34] 1:15; cf. Iren. *Her.* III. 1. 1; Euseb. *Hist.* II. 15. 2; III. 39. 15.

[35] 1:1, 14, 17, 18; 3:1, 15.

[36] 2:1. For earlier references to the appearance of heretical sects, see Acts 20:29; Eph. 2:20; 4:14, 21; 5:6-8; Rev. 2:2, 6, 9, 13-15, 20; 3:3, 8-11. The reference in Second Peter is best satisfied as having to do with the activities of Marcion.

these "false teachers," our author, himself an ardent advocate of orthodoxy for whom Peter typified the apostolic faith in its purest form, says that he wrote to arouse his readers "to remember the things foretold by the holy prophets, and the command of the Lord and Savior" through the apostles.[37] The epistle is in effect a manifesto of orthodoxy directed against heretical teachers who had abandoned the message of the founders of Christianity and had as a natural result also abandoned Christian morality.[38]

The incorporation of Jude to serve as the author's own denunciation of these "false teachers" indicates the similarity of the purposes of the two writings. Both were written in advocacy of a strict and uncompromising orthodoxy. In the instance of each, variation from the traditional Christian message in itself constituted heresy and deserved severe condemnation. The authorities by which contemporary teaching was to be adjudged sound or heretical were the books of the Old Testament, understood to be prophetic of the Christian revelation, and the emphases of the traditional Christian message, which was assumed to be Christ's message through the apostles.[39] As in the Johannine epistles, Jude, and the Pastorals, orthodoxy and morality are associated as cause and effect. The abandonment of traditional teaching and traditional ethics is viewed as a certain sign of the nearness of "the last hour." [40]

The specific indictments drawn against the "false teachers" are their ridicule of the expectation of the Second Coming [41] and their misinterpretation of the Pauline doctrine of freedom to sanction antinomianism.[42] These attitudes are both treated as typifying the heretical spirit of irreverence for and disbelief in the fundamentals of traditional Christian faith. The increasingly prevalent disbelief in the Parousia was in part due to the passage of time but was probably more largely the outcome of the impact of Gnostic teaching which created skepticism about the historical foundations of Christianity. The concern of Second Peter for a revival of the confidence of earlier generations in the Second Coming was essentially a concern for the reaffirmation of the validity of the traditional as against the heretical understanding of the content of the

---

[37] 3:2.   [38] 3:3, 11-13.   [39] 1:12-21; 2:21; 3:16.
[40] I John 2:18-29; 4:1-3; II John 7; III John 9; Jude 4-18; I Tim. 1:6, 7, 19; 4:1, 7; 6:3-5, 20-21; II Tim. 1:13, 14; 2:14-19, 23-25; 3:1, 13-17; 4:3-5; Titus 1:10-12; 3:9-11.
[41] 3:3-7.   [42] 3:16.

Christian message. A realistic expectation of the return of Jesus had been a vital phase of the earliest faith. For the author of Second Peter it typified that faith. Accordingly a revival of the faith of earlier days would involve the resuscitation of adventist expectancy. Primary concern, however, is for orthodox Christian teaching, of which adventism was a traditional symbol.

Message.—The author's basic position is developed at the outset. His message is fundamentally a plea for fidelity to "old-fashioned" Christianity. Readers of the epistle are urged to commit themselves to the conception of the gospel message that came to them through established tradition. This traditional faith of the church deserves reverence rather than the ridicule heaped upon it by "false teachers," the net effect of whose activities has been the introduction of "destructive sects" into the church.[43]

Instead of being naïve and outmoded, orthodox Christianity embodies "every requisite for life and piety," and supplies authoritative guidance for those whose sincere desire is to "escape the corrupting influences that exist in the world through passion, and come to share in the divine nature." [44] The twofold basis which it discloses for an "understanding of our Lord Jesus Christ" is moral fitness and historical evidence in contrast with the purely human speculations of the heretics.[45]

They who supplement faith "with goodness, . . . knowledge, . . . self-control, . . . steadfastness, . . . piety, . . . a spirit of brotherhood, and . . . love" will be "neither idle nor unproductive" in the matter of religious "understanding." [46] Spiritual blindness or nearsightedness is the fruitage of a faith empty of such moral meaning.[47] This moral emphasis of Christianity has a solid footing in history as well as in experience. The tradition about Jesus rests on "eyewitness" testimony and not on "fictitious stories," as the heretics claim.[48] Too, the historical revelation of truth through Jesus Christ is made doubly certain because it represents fulfillment of the inspired insights of Scripture.[49]

False teachers within the church, who "introduce destructive sects and deny the Master who has bought them," had their prototypes in the "false prophets" of Old Testament times and will bring upon themselves an equally certain "swift destruction." [50] People

[43] 2:1.   [44] 1:3, 4.   [45] 1:20.   [46] 1:5, 6, 9.
[47] 1:9.   [48] 1:12-18.   [49] 1:19-21.   [50] 2:1.

who "follow their immoral ways and . . . cause the true way to be maligned" will share their destruction. They should be forewarned by the way in which God has dealt with wrongdoers in the past. Jude's characterization and vigorous condemnation of heretical teachers is taken over and in chapter 2 of Second Peter applied to the "false teachers" who are denounced.[51]

As in Jude,[52] the appearance of these "mockers . . . going where their passions lead" means for the author of Second Peter the nearness of "the last days." He urges this upon his readers as an additional and urgent reason for so living as to be found by Christ "unstained and irreproachable."[53] The heretical point of view specifically attributed to these "mockers" is disbelief in the Parousia. The ground of their disbelief appears to have been an elapse of time sufficiently long since the first generation of Christians "fell asleep" to constitute prima facie evidence of the illusoriness of the expectation of Christ's return to inaugurate the Kingdom. The "one fact" which the author of Second Peter is sure the heretical teachers overlook is that "with the Lord one day is like a thousand years and a thousand years are like one day."[54] Actually this passage of time is more properly regarded as illustrating God's patience. Orthodox Christians welcome it as affording an opportunity to live "holy and pious lives," never wavering in their well-warranted expectation of "new heavens and a new earth, where righteousness will prevail."[55]

[51] 2:3-18; cf. Jude 4-16.   [52] Jude 18.   [53] 3:3, 14.   [54] 3:8.
[55] 3:12-13.

XXII

THE EPISTLES TO TIMOTHY AND TITUS

Authorship.—From the closing decades of the second century until modern times the tradition was that Paul wrote the epistles to Timothy and Titus. Irenaeus is the first witness who shows an indisputably clear acquaintance with the epistles, and he ascribes them to Paul.[1] These epistles appear never to have circulated except as members of a thirteen-letter corpus of Paul's letters. Prior to the middle of the second century, however, the Pauline letter collection was composed of only ten members. Marcion's canon contained ten letters only, and his failure to include the Pastorals was more probably due to lack of acquaintance with them than to dislike for their teaching, however great that might have been.[2] Had the epistles been written before the middle of the century, Marcion would have known them. Justin's nonuse of them greatly strengthens the likelihood that they were written around 160 or later.

The one Christian writer of the first half of the second century who is seriously held by modern scholars to have known the Pastorals is Polycarp, Bishop of Smyrna, who in about 115 wrote an epistle to the Philippians.[3] Unquestionably Polycarp wrote under the conscious influence of Paul, whom he knew through his published letters, but it is debatable whether the collection of Paul's letters with which he was familiar was composed of thirteen members or only ten.[4] The probabilities favor the latter, but the possi-

[1] *Her.* I. 16. 3; II. 14. 7; III. 3. 4; IV. 16. 3.

[2] Tertullian charged Marcion with inconsistency in including a personal letter like Philemon in his *Apostolicon* and excluding "the two epistles to Timothy and the one to Titus." He thinks their exclusion was due to Marcion's intention "to carry out his interpolating process even to the number of St. Paul's epistles" (*Against Marcion* V. 21). Jerome shares the view that Marcion knew and deliberately rejected the Pastorals (*Preface to Titus*).

[3] Goodspeed, *History of Early Christian Literature,* p. 25.

[4] Passages in Polycarp's epistle that supposedly show indebtedness to the Pastorals are: 4:1 (cf. I Tim. 6:7, 10); 4:3 (cf. I Tim. 5:5); 5:2 (cf. I Tim. 3:8-11; II Tim. 2:12); 9:2 (cf. II Tim. 4:10); 12:3 (cf. I Tim. 2:1).

bility of the former must be allowed in view of the impressive array of scholars who interpret the data of Polycarp's Epistle to the Philippians as showing literary indebtedness to the Pastorals.[5] However, the entire series of parallels would seem to be sufficiently explained as the independent use by the two writers of widely current paraenetic materials. Or, if it is judged that the resemblances require explanation in terms of literary indebtedness, it becomes entirely reasonable and probable that the author of the Pastorals knew Polycarp's Epistle to the Philippians.[6] This is especially true in view of the admitted presence of allusions in First Timothy and Titus belonging to the atmosphere of the middle of the second century. Instead of regarding such allusions as interpolations, as Harnack has done,[7] they are better understood to indicate the period when the epistles in their entirety originated, which means that Polycarp could not have known them at the time he wrote his epistle.

From the time of Irenaeus, however, the Pastorals were consistently ascribed to Paul. The author of the Muratorian canon says Paul wrote these epistles to Timothy and Titus "from personal inclination and attachment," but that they are nonetheless "to be in honor . . . with the Catholic Church for the ordering of the ecclesiastical

[5] Representatives of this view are: Harnack, *Chronologie,* I, 481; *Die Briefsammlung des Apostels Paulus* (Leipzig: J. C. Hinrichs, 1926) , p. 72; Leipoldt, *Geschichte des neutestamentlichen Kanons,* I, 189; Jülicher, *Introduction,* p. 180; Moffatt, *Introduction,* p. 416; McNeile, *Introduction,* p. 312; Scott, *Literature of the New Testament,* p. 194; *The Pastoral Epistles,* p. xxiii. Harnack's understanding of the data represents and probably influenced the conclusions drawn by all members of this group. Although it is his judgment that the entire series of parallels listed in note 4 are best explained as representing literary indebtedness on the part of Polycarp, he admits that a common use of paraenetic materials might account for such instances of resemblance as are represented in Polyc. Phil. 4:1 and I Tim. 6:7, 10; Polyc. Phil. 4:3 and I Tim. 5:5; Polyc. Phil. 5:2 and I Tim. 3:8-11. He insists, however, that literary indebtedness alone can explain the coincidences between Polyc. Phil. 5:2 and II Tim. 2:12; Polyc. Phil. 9:2 and II Tim. 4:10; Polyc. Phil. 12:3 and I Tim. 2:1. It does not occur to him that, granting the necessity of explaining the resemblances in terms of literary indebtedness, the author of the Pastorals was as probably acquainted with Polycarp's epistle as was Polycarp with the Pastorals. Harnack agrees that there are elements in the Pastorals definitely later than Polycarp's epistle. He says that I Tim. 5:17-22 cannot be dated earlier than 130, that I Tim. 3:1-13 and Titus 1:7-9 breathe the atmosphere of the middle of the second century, and that I Tim. 6:20 sounds like an explicit reference to Marcion's *Antitheses;* but he insists that these passages are interpolations and that the Pastorals in their original form should be dated 90-110, thereby making Polycarp's acquaintance with them possible.

[6] Goodspeed, *Introduction,* p. 344.   [7] See note 5 above.

mode of life." Tertullian[8] and Clement of Alexandria[9] quote them as by Paul, and Athanasius[10] and Jerome[11] include them in their lists of Paul's letters. Except for the lateness of indications of acquaintance with the Pastorals, the external evidence is consistently favorable to Paul's authorship of them.

The point of view disclosed in these epistles and the style common to the three of them establish the identity of their authorship. If Paul wrote one of them, he wrote them all. There is no evidence of a plurality of authors. Nor are there convincing indications that the author had in view the needs of a variety of situations. Instead of being three distinct communications, the Pastorals were probably a single epistle whose threefold form was a literary artifice contributing to the purpose of the author.

The author clearly intended to represent the epistles as in some sense Paul's. He might have meant to make Paul their ostensible author. Perhaps he intended to suggest no more than that the epistles were written in the spirit of the letters known in their published form for fifty years as Paul's and so glaringly misused by heretical leaders.[12] Some such intention is involved in the designation of Paul as author in the superscription of each of the three epistles. The same is the case with certain passages in Second Timothy and Titus which appear to be autobiographical and intimately circumstantial.[13]

Precisely these allusions, however, create the initial difficulty with the idea that Paul was really the author. Persons who had been so closely associated with Paul as Timothy and Titus would require no such formal assertions of his apostolic credentials and no such elaborate description of his responsibilities as a Christian leader as the superscriptions of the Pastorals supply.[14] Similarly, the passages apparently referring to situations in which Paul and his younger associates were participants involve irreconcilable contradictions in

[8] *On the Prescription of Heretics* VI; XXV; XXXIII; XXXVII; *Against Marcion* V. 21.

[9] *Miscellanies* II. 6, 11; III. 6, 18; IV. 3, 20; V. 1.

[10] *Festal Letter* XXXIX. 5.

[11] *On Illustrious Men* V.

[12] Cf. II Pet. 3:16.

[13] II Tim. 1:3-5, 15-18; 3:11; 4:6-21; Titus 1:5; 3:12-15. There are no passages of comparable character in First Timothy.

[14] I Tim. 1:1-2; II Tim. 1:1-2; Titus 1:1-4.

chronology.[15] The treatment of these passages as genuine bits from Paul's authentic correspondence editorially pieced together as in the sixteenth chapter of Romans offers for some a plausible explanation of their lack of homogeneity in their existing contexts. Ingenious efforts have been made to locate the fragments in the scheme of the apostle's career as it is known from his extant letters and the book of Acts.[16] At best this approach affords no basis for attributing the Pastorals to Paul. It merely predicates a use by the author of fragments from genuine Pauline letters. These fragments are more probably fiction of the same sort as the similarly concrete and circumstantial allusions found in an approximately contemporary apocryphal writing, the Acts of Paul.[17] The allusions function in both instances to create verisimilitude.

Other internal data whose cumulative effect is unfavorable to Paul's authorship of the Pastorals are: (1) The personal characteristics and interests of the author of the Pastorals are radically different from those reflected in Paul's unquestionably genuine letters. He is more definitely an ecclesiastic than a prophet. For him religion consists in an acceptance of a body of authoritative teaching. Sound morality is bound up with this attitude of acceptance.[18] By contrast, religion for Paul meant a transforming inner experience the consequence of which was personal competence to make moral decisions. Faith for the author of the Pastorals means fidelity to orthodox Christian doctrine. He accordingly meets error with denunciation rather than reasoned refutation. He undertakes no careful exposition of sound teaching. The originality of thought and the vigorous grasp of truth so characteristic of Paul are qualities absent from the Pastorals. (2) The eschatology of the Pastorals is formal and academic. The atmosphere of imminence and vivid

[15] This is especially true of II Tim. 4:6-21, which is the longest of the passages and the one for whose genuineness the best case can be made.

[16] See especially the elaborate exploration of the possibilities by P. N. Harrison, *The Problem of the Pastoral Epistles,* pp. 115-35. Moffatt reviews other similar efforts and regards them all as unconvincing beyond establishing, to his own satisfaction, the probability that "the author had some *reliquiae Paulinae* at his disposal" (*Introduction,* pp. 402-6).

[17] *Ca.* 160. See Goodspeed, *Introduction,* pp. 340-41.

[18] Favorite descriptions are: "the faith" (I Tim. 1:19; 3:9; 4:1, 6; 5:8; 6:10, 21; II Tim. 3:8; 4:7; Titus 1:13), "the truth" (I Tim. 3:15; 4:3; 6:5; II Tim. 2:15, 18; 3:8; 4:4; Titus 1:14), "the teaching" (I Tim. 4:13, 16; 6:1; II Tim. 3:10; Titus 2:10), "the deposit" (I Tim. 6:20; II Tim. 1:12, 14), "wholesome instruction" (I Tim. 1:10; 6:3; II Tim. 1:13; 4:3; Titus 1:9; 2:1).

expectancy regularly present in Paul's letters has disappeared.[19] The
author conceives of the leadership and program which the church
requires in terms of continuity rather than impending catastrophe.
(3) By comparison with Paul's letters the vocabulary of the Pastorals belongs not merely to a different author but to a different
century. It is the vocabulary of the Christian literature of the
middle of the second century.[20] Similarly, the style of the Pastorals
is characterized by smoothness and diffuseness instead of the colorful
ruggedness and fervid warmth of Paul's letters. (4) The stage of
institutional development within the Christian movement assumed
in the Pastorals cannot be associated with the period of Paul's life.
The discussion of church offices [21] and the implicit assumption of
the canonical status of at least some Christian writings [22] lie quite
evidently outside Paul's purview and belongs to the atmosphere of
the middle of the next century. (5) The central place which heresy
occupies in these epistles indicates the passing of the primitive
period of Christian history.[23] The problems considered resemble
those with which the authors of First John, Jude, and Second Peter
were concerned. The sectarian emphases which this orthodox
churchman combats in Paul's name are best identified with the
propaganda of the Marcionite and Gnostic sects, who also claimed
Paul as their principal authority. (6) There is no way whereby the
circumstances reflected in the Pastorals can be made to agree with
the representation of Paul's activities in his letters and in Acts.[24]
The assumption of the authenticity of these epistles admittedly requires the predication of a Roman imprisonment for Paul sub-

---

[19] I Tim. 6:15; II Tim. 1:12, 18; 3:1; 4:1-2; cf. I Thess. 4:13–5:3; II Thess.
2:1-12; I Cor. 7:26-32; 15:23-28, 52; 16:22; II Cor. 5:1-5; Rom. 8:23; Phil. 3:20-21;
Col. 3:4.

[20] Harrison, op. cit., pp. 68-84; Moffatt, Introduction, p. 406.

[21] I Tim. 3:1-13; 5:17-22; Titus 1:7-9. Harnack regarded these passages as not
earlier than A.D. 130 and as probably belonging to a period several decades
later (Chronologie, I, 481).

[22] I Tim. 5:18 quotes Luke 10:7 alongside Deut. 25:4 as scripture (cf. Just.
Apol. 67). The reference to "the books" and "the parchments" in II Tim.
4:13 is probably also a description of Christian writings as scripture. It has the
sound of the description which a Numidian Christian gave of the contents of
the church "strong box" in the Acts of the Scillitan Martyrs.

[23] I Tim. 1:3-7; 2:8; 4:7; 6:3-4, 20; II Tim. 2:14-19, 23-26; 3:8; 4:3-5; Titus
1:10, 13-14; 3:9-11. Earlier references to the emerging sects are: Acts 20:29-30;
Eph. 4:3-6, 14; Rev. 2:6, 15.

[24] See the thorough discussion by E. F. Scott, The Pastoral Epistles, pp. xvi-xxi.

sequent to that of Acts 28:15, 30-31. The supposed interim between imprisonments becomes the setting for the activities implied in the Pastorals. Eusebius [25] and Jerome [26] interpret the reference to Paul's "first appearance in court" in II Tim. 4:16 as implying acquittal in an earlier trial, followed by a period of freedom during which Paul preached the gospel "also in the West." The author of the Muratorian canon also mentions "the departure of Paul from town on his journey to Spain." Both he and Eusebius account for the description of only the first of Paul's Roman imprisonments in Acts on the ground that Luke did not go to Spain and it was Luke's purpose in Acts to trace "the course of the history" only "so long as he was present with Paul." This tradition had its origin more probably in speculation than in historical evidence.[27] It does, however, testify to an early recognition of the impossibility of locating the Pastorals in the scheme of Paul's life supplied by the recognized letters and Acts.

The First Readers.—According to the allusions contained in the epistles, First Timothy and Titus were written in the midst of a missionary campaign in the East during which Paul himself visited the churches in Macedonia, made stops at Troas, Corinth, Miletus, and Crete, and spent a winter at Nicopolis. Timothy and Titus were his principal assistants throughout this period.[28] When Second

---

[25] *Hist.* II. 22. 3-4, 6.   [26] *On Illustrious Men* V.

[27] Paul's distressing announcement to the Ephesian elders that "they would never see his face again" (Acts 20:38) suggests that so far as Luke knew Paul was not released from the imprisonment of Acts 28:15 ff. His omission of an explicit mention of Paul's fate was part of his effort to conciliate Roman civil authorities. This indefiniteness of Acts, coupled with Paul's own mention of his desire to visit Spain (Rom. 15:24) and the somewhat uncertain meaning of the allusion in I Clem. 5:7 (ἐπὶ τὸ τέρμα τῆς δύσεως), gave imagination a starting point for the creation of the tradition that Eusebius reported as history. The earliest formulation of the tradition, and probably the source of all subsequent versions of it, is that in the Acts of Peter III. 1-3 (see James, tr., *The Apocryphal New Testament*, pp. 304-6). The author of the Acts of Peter may have been indebted to II Tim. 4:16. Just as probably the indebtedness was on the side of the Pastorals. An acceptance of the tradition as history would, however, leave this phase of the problem of the Pastorals unsolved, since the tradition makes a place for the journey to Spain, and the Pastorals imply that the scene of Paul's activity was the East.

[28] According to First Timothy, Paul left Timothy at Ephesus and himself went on to visit the Macedonian churches (1:3). He expected soon to rejoin him (3:14), and he writes in order that Timothy may know how to proceed in the event Paul should be delayed beyond his expectations (3:15). According to Titus, Paul left Titus in Crete "to correct what defects there were, and to

Timothy was written, Paul was supposedly in prison at Rome, with only Luke as his companion, but with the early prospect of being joined by Timothy and Mark.[29] The frequency with which Timothy and Titus had been mentioned in Paul's authentic letters made them the appropriate addressees for the Pastorals.[30]

Timothy and Titus were hardly the real recipients of these epistles. The improbability here is as great as in the matter of authorship. The area in which Paul and his several associates are represented as working is in general that described in Acts and in Paul's genuine letters as the scene of their missionary activities. The Pastorals represent Paul as temporarily separated from Timothy and Titus [31] and writing for their guidance during this brief period. Detailed and formal instructions of the type contained in the Pastorals become unintelligible, therefore, when taken as literally intended for men of the Christian maturity of Timothy and Titus and for the guidance of churches to whom they and Paul were personally known.

The real public to whom these epistles were addressed was the leadership of the church in its entirety.[32] The epistles constituted a single encyclical address rather than a series of personal letters. The account which they give of Paul's widespread activity and his dispatch of trusted lieutenants to numerous stragetic centers is unmistakably a literary device for suggesting the church-wide importance of their message. It had the effect of bringing the Pastorals to the attention of ministers generally. Paul had been somewhat

---

appoint elders in each town" (1:5). He planned shortly to send Artemas or Tychicus to relieve Titus, whom he directs to join him at Nicopolis, where he has decided to "settle . . . for the winter" (3:12-13). Presumably he sent Titus to Dalmatia from Nicopolis (II Tim. 4:10).

[29] In Second Timothy, Paul is represented as being in prison at Rome, but as having recently visited Troas, Corinth, and Miletus (1:16-17; 4:13, 20-21). During this campaign that had just preceded his present imprisonment Paul had sent, to represent him where he was himself unable to go, Crescens to Galatia, Titus to Dalmatia, and Tychicus to Ephesus (4:10, 12).

[30] Timothy is mentioned thirteen times in Paul's letters: I Thess. 1:1; 3:2, 6; II Thess. 1:1; I Cor. 4:17; 16:10; II Cor. 1:1, 19; Rom. 16:21; Phil. 1:1; 2:19; Col. 1:1; Philem. 1. Paul refers to Titus eleven times: Gal. 2:1, 3; II Cor. 2:13; 7:6, 13, 14; 8:6, 16, 23; 12:18. By comparison, he mentions Silas only three times (I Thess. 1:1; II Thess. 1:1; II Cor. 1:19), Luke twice (Col. 4:14; Philem. 24), Mark twice (Col. 4:10; Philem. 24), and Barnabas five times (Gal. 2:1, 9, 13; I Cor. 9:6; Col. 4:10).

[31] I Tim. 3:14-15; Titus 1:5; II Tim. 4:9.

[32] I Tim. 2:8; II Tim. 4:22; Titus 3:15.

discredited in orthodox Christian circles because of his popularity with heretical sects. The author of the Pastorals disapproved this surrender of Paul to those who misunderstood him. Instead he thought the leadership of the church should claim him as the truest exponent of orthodoxy. Through Timothy and Titus as typical ministers the Pastorals commended Paul and his letters to the ministry of a later age.

Date.—As clearly as the Pastorals were the work of a single author, they belonged to a single occasion. There is no real basis in external or internal evidence for supposing that the epistles were separated by intervals of time. Tradition and the epistles themselves make possible an approximately accurate definition of the period out of which they came. The period they suggest lies well outside the span of Paul's historical career.

The tone and specific allusions of the epistles reflect a time when Christian practices and institutions were being standardized, when Christian beliefs were being formulated into creeds,[33] when a new sense of unity was developing among the scattered Christian communities. It was the period of transition into Catholic Christianity, but its atmosphere and problems were more nearly those of the third than of the fourth quarter of the second century.

Irenaeus is the earliest clear witness to the existence of the Pastorals.[34] No allusions in Christian literature before Irenaeus require explanation in terms of literary indebtedness to the epistles. Their author, however, appears to have known Marcion's *Antitheses* and to have been deeply concerned with the refutation of the principal positions taken by the great heretical leader.[35] An acquaintance with the *Antitheses* locates the Pastorals between 144, when Marcion was expelled by the Roman church, and 180. The emphases of the epistles confirm some such date and are most intelligible against the background of this period.

---

[33] The conception of Christian faith as a hallowed and authoritative tradition, to be accepted and defended, has already been discussed in some detail as a phase of the problem of authorship. Closely related qualities that appear in the epistles and that typify the mind of the neo-Catholic Church of the third quarter of the second century are: (1) the clergy in contradistinction from the laity are guardians of the truth (I Tim. 5:17-22); (2) Christian hymns are becoming affirmations of orthodoxy (I Tim. 3:14-16); (3) Christian faith is publicly confessed in standardized formulae (I Tim. 6:12; cf. 2:5; 3:16; II Tim. 2:8); (4) a canon of Christian scripture is emerging.

[34] See page 275.   [35] I Tim. 6:20.

The central problem with which the author deals is heresy and its refutation. His references to traitorous associates and to leaders who have proved weak and unworthy suggest the corruption of many church leaders by false teaching.[36] The instruments with which orthodox ministers are advised to combat error are those currently emerging as the bulwarks of an incipiently Catholic Christianity: a canon of scripture embodying revealed truth, a creedal summary of Christian beliefs widely agreed upon as fundamental, and an authoritative church whose clergy were qualified on the basis of specified standards. Paul, who had once been a blasphemer and a persecutor of the church,[37] and whose letters had more recently been canonized by the Marcionites,[38] was the ideal apostle in whose name effective remedies for heresy could be formulated.

This concern with heresy qualifies the counsel which the author gives on the variety of subjects with which he deals. His discussion of church offices and organization illustrates how definitely this and all other interests are made incidental to the larger issue created by the sects. The heresy and schism which threatened the effectiveness of the church belong to the period when Marcion and such Gnostics as Cerinthus, Cerdo, Valentinus, and Basilides were influencing the course of Christian thought.[39] The "worldly, empty phrases and contradictions of what they falsely call knowledge" against which Timothy is warned and by the profession of which "some people have made a failure of the faith" [40] are an unmistakably clear reference to heresy as represented in the Marcionite and Gnostic sects.[41]

The martyrological tone of the Pastorals is an additional datum indicative of the second half of the second century. It appears in

---

[36] I Tim. 1:3, 7, 20; 4:1; 6:3-6; II Tim. 1:15; 2:18, 20; 3:9, 13; 4:4, 9-11, 14, 17; Titus 1:11; 3:9-11.

[37] I Tim. 1:12-17.   [38] II. Pet. 3:15-16.

[39] Just. *Apol.* XXVI; LVIII.   [40] I Tim. 6:20.

[41] This is borne out by the more or less detailed references to the characteristics of these sects: antinomianism as the outgrowth of moral indifference bred by the notion of a superior "gnosis" (I Tim. 1:7-10; II Tim. 3:15-17); rejection of the Old Testament, which the Pastorals counter with an affirmation of its inspiration (II Tim. 3:16) and the exhortation that it be read publicly and in private (I Tim. 4:5, 13); asceticism that maintained that the true "gnostic" could disregard the demands of the body in such matters as exercise (I Tim. 4:8), marriage and foods (I Tim. 4:3-5; 5:22-23), and as already having achieved a degree of spirituality that destroyed the meaning of a future resurrection (II Tim. 2:18); a false emphasis on myths and genealogies (I Tim. 1:4); the denial of the oneness of God and of the adequacy of a single mediator between God and men (I Tim. 2:5-7).

such characteristic ways as the technical sense of terms like "confess" and "witness,"[42] the prominence of the figure of "fighting" in illustrations of the Christian life,[43] the martyrological use of the trial of Jesus,[44] the comparison of Jesus and the emperor,[45] the use of Paul to illustrate the spirit of the true martyr.[46] The allusions to the hardships suffered by Christians refer to the times of Antoninus Pius (138-61) and Marcus Aurelius (161-80) and mark the Pastorals as having the same general background as the letter of the churches of Lyons and Vienne,[47] the *Martyrdom of Polycarp,* the *Acts of the Scillitan Martyrs,* and the *Acts of Justin.*[48]

Place of Composition.—Paul is represented in First Timothy as having left Timothy at Ephesus and gone on a visit to the Macedonian churches.[49] It is his plan to rejoin Timothy at Ephesus at a relatively early date. Because of the possibility of delay he writes him this letter.[50] Taken at face value, this means First Timothy was written from some point in Macedonia. According to Titus, ostensibly the second of the Pastorals, Paul had left Titus in Crete and gone on to Nicopolis for the winter,[51] whence, presumably, he wrote the epistle to Titus. The allusions in Second Timothy locate Paul in prison at Rome, where he expected Timothy would shortly join him.[52]

As already indicated, these details are better regarded as belonging to the *mise en scène* than to history. Rome was probably the place where the three epistles were written. There the great sectarian leaders, Cerdo, Marcion, and Valentinus were active and influential. Irenaeus, the earliest witness to the existence of the Pastorals, also belonged to the Roman circle of influence. That he derived the title and introductory sentence of his work *Against Heresies* from First Timothy [53] suggests how intimately the Pastorals belonged to

---

[42] I Tim. 6:12; cf. *Acts of Justin* 4:6; 6:1.

[43] I Tim. 6:12; II Tim. 4:7; cf. *Acts of the Scillitan Martyrs* 17.

[44] I Tim. 6:13; cf. *Martyrdom of Polycarp* 1:1.

[45] I Tim. 6:15; cf. *Martyrdom of Polycarp* 9:3; *Acts of the Scillitan Martyrs* 2, 3, 6, 9.

[46] II Tim. 2:3; 3:10-12; 4:7-8.   [47] Euseb. *Hist.* V. 1-4.

[48] Riddle, *The Martyrs,* p. 156.

[49] 1:3.   [50] 3:14-15.   [51] 1:5; 3:12-13.   [52] 1:16-17; 4:13, 20-21.

[53] This writing is ordinarily known under the title *Against Heresies.* Eusebius (*Hist.* V. 7. 1) employs the fuller title, used also at times by Irenaeus, *A Refutation and Overthrow of Knowledge Falsely So Called,* which clearly reflects I Tim. 6:20. The opening sentence of the preface quotes I Tim. 1:4.

the spirit of the West during the second half of the second century. The earliest orthodox New Testament,[54] which included the Pastorals as letters of Paul, also expressed the sentiment of the Roman church, as did the Apostles' Creed, which was a formulation of essential Christian beliefs approximately contemporaneous in date with the Pastorals.[55]

Occasion and Purpose.—The data which the epistles themselves supply indicate that they were only secondarily concerned about church offices and order. Their author took for granted the ecclesiastical organization as it existed,[56] pleading neither for its perpetuation as such nor for its renovation. The relatively brief references to church order [57] show that the primary intention of the author is misconceived when the Pastorals are viewed as an early manual of discipline.

The vital concern of the author is indicated in his frequent summaries of orthodox teaching [58] and his recurrent denunciations of heresy.[59] For him normative Christian doctrine possessed the validity and authority of revelation and was to be accepted unquestioningly as the guide for Christian living. The life which was good according to Christian standards would normally be the outcome of orthodox beliefs. Sound morality therefore required orthodox ideology as an indispensable foundation. The church existed to guard Christian teaching as originally formulated by the apostles against contamination. The ordained ministry of the church there-

[54] The Muratorian canon.

[55] In the judgment of A. C. McGiffert the creed was framed at Rome for antiheretical purposes shortly after the middle of the second century. He views it in its entirety as "inspired by hostility to the views of Marcion" and as lacking no element essential to an "anti-Marcionite symbol." To him the literary evidence convincingly locates the creed in the third quarter of the second century "in the interval between the literary activity of Justin Martyr and that of Irenaeus." (*The Apostles' Creed*, pp. 82, 108, 170.)

[56] The system reflected is one in which "elders" function as an administrative board for the local church. They are formally ordained and are known interchangeably as "elders" and "bishops." In instances they are salaried officers who devote their full time to the work of the church. Qualified "elders" are the responsible teachers of the community. They are assisted by "deacons," whose qualifications and duties are less clearly defined, and by "widows," whose credentials and functions are described in detail, and who are paid for their work.

[57] I Tim. 3:1-13; 5:3-22; Titus 1:5-9.

[58] I Tim. 2:5-6; 3:16; 6:11-16; II Tim. 1:8-10; 2:11-14; Titus 2:11-14; 3:5-7.

[59] I Tim. 1:3-13, 19-20; 4:1-18; 6:3-5; II Tim. 2:16-26; 3:6-9; Titus 1:9-16; 3:9-11.

fore have had it as their primary responsibility to conserve and transmit the gospel message in its primitive purity.[60] Paul is represented as having insisted on the selection of church leaders who would guard and transmit the apostolic message with courageous fidelity. The menace of heretical teaching to the life of the church is described as having colored what Paul said on every particular subject.

The epistles contain no detailed description of the heretical teaching which they condemn. It apparently represented a blending of "Jewish fictions" and the "worldly, empty phrases and contradictions" of Gnosticism.[61] The indefiniteness of these references and the suggestion of a Jewish tinge in the unsound teaching served to create verisimilitude for the denunciation of Marcionism by Paul. A specific description of the heresy to be refuted would have made its condemnation by the apostle too anachronistic. The author might, with great appropriateness, have given his refutation the form of a positive exposition of Paul's conception of "knowledge" as one of the "endowments" of the Spirit.[62] As though taking the farewell address to the Ephesian elders at Miletus [63] as a model, he preferred to have Paul denounce the perversions of apostolic doctrine as though he foresaw they would arise to plague the church of later times.

These data, coupled with the twofold pseudonymity of the epistles, make the purpose of the Pastorals clear. The thing of utmost importance was the maintenance of traditional Christian teaching in a time of diversity of points of view. Believing that Christianity in its Pauline version was basically sound, however badly its reputation had suffered because of its espousal by Marcion, this writer determined to acquaint the church afresh with Paul's letters and to secure the inclusion of the ideas they contained in the developing creed of the Christian community. The inclusion of the Pastorals in the Pauline letter collection of the Muratorian canon suggests that the epistles were written as part of a gratifyingly successful effort to popularize Paul's letters in orthodox Christian circles.

Messsage.—The Pastoral epistles belong to that considerable body of literature produced by the orthodox leadership of the church

[60] II Tim. 1:14 (τὴν καλὴν παραθήκην φύλαξον) ; cf. I Tim. 6:20.
[61] I Tim. 1:4-10; 4:7, 8; 6:5, 20; II Tim. 2:18; 3:16-17; Titus 1:14.
[62] I Cor. 12:9; 13:2, 9, 12; 14:6; II Cor. 2:14; 4:6; 6:6; 11:6.
[63] Acts 20:18-35.

during the second half of the second century in support of traditional Christian teaching against all forms of heresy, especially
Marcionism. In some instances this literature took the form of a
detailed refutation of the principal positions advocated by heretical
teachers and a corresponding defense of orthodox doctrines which
those teachers opposed.[64] With equal or, perhaps, greater effectiveness orthodox leadership employed pseudepigraphy as a means of
representing the apostles or some particular one of them—especially
Paul, since he had been espoused by Marcion—as champions of
orthodoxy and opponents of heresy.[65] Usually the founding fathers
were described as seeing in the false teachers of their own
times the forerunners of the sectarian leaders who menaced the
faith and unity of the Christian community a century after. Not
infrequently a writing involved a combination of these techniques.
The message of the Pastorals is best understood when stated in
terms of the pattern of thought fairly common to the writings of
this general type and period.

Tertullian's *On the Prescription of Heretics* combines a systematic
refutation of Marcionism with an indirect use of the pseudepigraphic
principle. It represents in organization and emphasis the same
conception of Christianity that appears in the Pastorals and affords
a helpful guide for the interpretation of the message of the latter.
Four basic premises govern Tertullian's thought: (1) There is an
authoritative body of doctrine, a "rule of faith," which was "taught
by Christ" to the original disciples.[66] For the faith "deposited in the

[64] Justin *Apology* and *Dialogue with Trypho,* Irenaeus *Against Heresies,* Tertullian *On the Prescription of Heretics* and *Against Marcion.*

[65] The Epistle of the Apostles *(ca.* 150), Third Corinthians *(ca.* 160), the
Apostles' Creed (150-80), the Pastoral epistles (150-80).

[66] Chap. XIII. The affirmations composing the "rule" closely resemble those
of the Apostles' Creed and are evidently a positive statement of the traditional
Christian beliefs questioned by Marcion. They are: that there is only one God, who
created the world "through his own Word"; that this "Word" was also his "Son"
and was the agent of revelation to the patriarchs and the prophets; that "by the
Spirit and power of the Father" the Word "was made flesh" in the womb of the
virgin Mary, and, "being born of her, went forth as Jesus Christ"; that as Jesus
he taught those who followed him the content of faith and worked miracles;
that he was crucified and "rose again the third day"; that, "having ascended
into the heavens, he sat at the right hand of the Father"; that in his stead he
sent "the power of the Holy Ghost" to lead believers; that he "will come with
glory to take the saints to the enjoyment of everlasting life" and "to condemn
the wicked to everlasting fire," this assignment of destinies to follow upon the
resurrection of both saints and sinners and the "restoration of their flesh."

rule" he claimed the saving power attributed to "faith" in Luke
18:42.[67] The content of this authoritative statement or "rule" determined the limits of inquiry for Christians, investigation and discussion being disallowed save such as could proceed "without im-
pairing the rule of faith." [68] The only sound knowledge on this
basis was therefore "to know nothing in opposition to the rule." [69]
(2) The apostles to whom Christ delivered the faith taught it to
Paul, and between Paul and Peter and the rest of the apostles there
was complete agreement. Paul's letters show that he was not the
recipient of a superior or contradictory revelation of truth but
shared the faith taught by Christ and faithfully transmitted by his
original followers.[70] Not only so, but Paul reverenced the Old
Testament, found the gospel message implicit in it as those who
were apostles before him had done, and taught that the God of
the Old Testament, not another God, was revealed in Christ.
On Paul's authority, therefore, heretics who rejected the Old Testament forfeited the right to use any portion of Scripture in the
formulation of their teaching.[71] (3) Paul was the great anti-
Gnostic. His letters, and especially the Pastorals, implicitly condemned those very heretics who acclaimed him as the only true
apostle.[72] (4) The apostles faithfully transmitted to "apostolic
churches" the truth taught them by Christ. Those churches through
their properly selected and instructed leadership faithfully and
continuously guarded the purity of this message and dependably
passed it on to the churches of Christendom.[73]

[67] Chap. XIV.   [68] Chap. XII.   [69] Chap. XIV.
[70] Chaps. XX–XXV; cf. *Against Marcion* V. 1, 3, 6, 13, 18.

[71] Chaps. XVI; XXXVI; XXXVIII. Similarly in chap. 31 of the Epistle of
the Apostles the validity of the Old Testament and Paul's doctrinal agreement
with the other apostles are affirmed by having Jesus instruct the Twelve to
pass on to Paul, whose conversion he foresees, all that he has taught them and
especially that the Old Testament is implicitly a message about Christ. In Third
Corinthians (1:9-15; 3:9-10), in refutation of those who forbade Christians
to use the Old Testament, Paul is represented as teaching that God bestowed
a portion of the spirit of Christ on the prophets, with the result that their
message was a proclamation of "the true worship of God."

[72] Chap. XXXIII.

[73] Chaps. XXXVI; XLI–XLIII. Tertullian makes discipline an unfailing
"index" of doctrine and by contrasting the orderliness of the "apostolic
churches" with the chaos of heretical churches shows that the former are the
custodians of divine truth. He describes the conduct of members of heretical
churches as "frivolous, . . . worldly, . . . merely human, . . . without discipline,"
as suits their creed." Because their catechumens claim perfection without being

These emphases are the framework on which the message of the Pastorals hangs.[74] The employment of pseudepigraphy makes the exposition less systematic than it might otherwise be, but when clearly seen and evaluated as literary disguise it contributes to the effectiveness of the author's message.

The conception of faith as normative teaching is expressed in certain repeated characterizations.[75] It appears also in recurring reminders to Timothy and Titus as typical ministers that they are trustees of "instructions" apostolic in origin,[76] that those "instructions" authoritatively fixed the content of what they "must teach and preach," [77] that they are formulated in "trustworthy" sayings "entitled to the fullest acceptance," [78] that together they constitute an authoritative message which ultimately "comes from our Lord Jesus Christ" and may therefore be described as "God's message." [79] Disbelief of such a body of doctrine or dissent from particular items in it do not indicate a possession of true "knowledge" but mark a person as "conceited," "ignorant," and motivated by "a morbid craving for speculation." [80] Faith, thus conceived, is personally appropriated by being "comprehended," [81] the reality of "the comprehension of religious truth" being best demonstrated in its control of character and conduct.[82]

---

instructed, catechumens and full-fledged believers cannot be differentiated. Women perform all the functions of the ordained ministry, teaching, exorcism, healing, and even baptism. Ordination is carelessly administered, and novices frequently occupy responsible offices. Promotion is easy. Continuity is so lacking that "today one man is their bishop, tomorrow another." They even impose priestly functions on laymen. In the orthodox churches, however, the "fear of God" prevails, and there is "seriousness, an honorable and yet thoughtful diligence." Admission to the ministry is "well-considered," participation in the "communion" is "safely guarded," promotion is based on "good service." Modesty, devotion, and submission to authority characterize the conduct of church members, so that the church is united and God manifests himself in all things.

[74] Indebtedness is acknowledged to Martin Rist's study "Pseudepigraphic Refutations of Marcionism" (*The Journal of Religion*, XXII [1942], 39-62) for calling attention to the pattern of thought generally reflected in anti-Marcionite literature. I had reached similar conclusions regarding the purpose of the Pastorals in my study "The Significance of the Pastoral Epistles" (*Religion in the Making*, I [1941], 515-21).

[75] See note 18 above.   [76] I Tim. 1:18; II Tim. 2:2.

[77] I Tim. 4:11; 6:3; Titus 1:8; 2:1, 15; 3:8; II Tim. 2:14.

[78] I Tim. 1:15; 3:1; 4:9; Titus 1:12; 3:8; II Tim. 2:11.

[79] I Tim. 6:3, 4; II Tim. 2:9.   [80] I Tim. 6:4.   [81] Titus 1:1, 3.

[82] I Tim. 1:19-20; 2:8-15; 4:1-16; 6:3-10; Titus 1:10-16; 3:11; etc.

The content of faith is made specific in the recurrent summaries of sound teaching and the denunciations of heresy prominently featured in each of the epistles.[83] As in the Apostles' Creed and Tertullian's *On the Prescription of Heretics,* the beliefs affirmed are those rejected by Marcion. Instead of a series of deities, "there is but one God." He is the creator, the ruler of the universe, the God whom Paul's forefathers served, the God of the Old Testament. He is the "living God" in the sense that he "maintains all life" and is "the Savior of all men." It is he, too, who "in his own time" will judge the world through "our Lord Jesus Christ." [84] Between God and men there is "one intermediary, . . . the man Christ Jesus," [85] who was "descended from David," [86] but whose thoroughly real humanity constituted no barrier to the functioning of the Spirit through him.[87] His mission in the world was "to save sinners." [88] In the accomplishment of his redemptive mission he "made his great profession . . . before Pontius Pilate," [89] died sacrificially "as a ransom for all men," [90] was raised "from the dead," [91] was then "taken up into glory." [92] He sent the Spirit in his stead to renew men's spirits so that they might become "possessors of eternal life." [93] He will return as God's representative to judge the world and bestow immortality on those who until then "keep his command stainless and irreproachable." [94]

Pauline Christianity, thus summarized, becomes clearly an exposition of the traditional rather than a conflicting revelation of truth. It fully accords with "predictions made long ago" [95] and is substantially the faith "testified to at the proper times." [96] It originated with Jesus Christ, from whom Paul, like the other apos-

---

[83] These summaries of sound and heretical teaching appear at the beginning, in the main body, and at the conclusion of each epistle:

CHARACTERIZATIONS OF HERESY	SUMMARIES OF ORTHODOXY
I Tim. 1:3-13, 19-20	I Tim. 1:17; 2:5-6; 3:16
I Tim. 4:1-18; 6:3-5	I Tim. 6:11-16
Titus 1:10-16; 3:9-11	Titus 2:11-14; 3:5-7
II Tim. 2:14-26; 3:6-9; 4:3-4	II Tim. 1:8-10; 2:8, 11-13

[84] I Tim. 1:17; 2:5; 4:10; 6:13, 15-16; II Tim. 1:13; Titus 2:11-12; 3:5-6.
[85] I Tim. 2:6.   [86] II Tim. 2:8.   [87] I Tim. 3:16.   [88] I Tim. 1:15.
[89] I Tim. 6:13.   [90] I Tim. 2:6.   [91] II Tim. 2:8.   [92] I Tim. 3:16.
[93] Titus 3:4-7.   [94] I Tim. 6:14; II Tim. 2:11-13.   [95] I Tim. 1:18.
[96] I Tim. 2:6-7.

tles, received it.[97] It is the old-fashioned faith of Timothy's mother
and grandmother, and Paul is pleased because Timothy subscribes
to this ancestral faith [98] and will transmit it in uncorrupted form
to future generations.[99] It is implicitly the faith of the Old Testament,[100] and an exposition of the Old Testament in the light of
Christian revelation and experience is therefore fundamental to
Christian preaching and teaching.[101]

It is also a part of the message of the Pastorals to have Paul appear
as implicitly the great opponent of heresy. In this role he is made
to condemn unsound trends in his own times which in their fully
developed forms were later espoused by Marcion. This gives meaning to his prophecy of a time when men would "turn from listening
to the truth and wander off after fictions," rejecting the "wholesome instruction" of orthodox teachers for the vagaries of those
who "suit their whims and tickle their fancies." [102] The author's
use of pseudonymity required him to avoid an explicit identification
of the heretical teaching he so vigorously denounced.[103] But the
disguise is sufficiently transparent to leave no doubt that Marcionism was the menace against which he warned the church.[104]

For the author of the Pastorals, as for Tertullian, discipline was
an "index" of doctrine. Heresy has arisen because men aspire "to
be teachers of law" who "do not understand the words they use or
the matters they insist upon." [105] The disagreement of such people
with the "wholesome instruction which comes from our Lord
Jesus Christ" results from their being "conceited, ignorant" persons,
with a "morbid craving for speculations and arguments." The
fruit of their teaching is naturally "envy, quarreling, abuse, base
suspicions, and mutual irritation." [106]

By its careful discipline of those who preach and teach, however,
the "church of the living God" safeguards and faithfully transmits
"the truth," of which it is "the pillar and foundation." [107] Because
it is thus guarded and handed on as a "splendid trust," [108] Christian
doctrine continues to be identical with the statement of faith given
by Jesus Christ to the original Christians.[109] Successive generations

[97] I Tim. 6:3-4.   [98] II Tim. 1:5.   [99] II Tim. 2:2.
[100] II Tim. 3:14-17.   [101] I Tim. 4:5, 13.   [102] II Tim. 4:3-5.
[103] For the relevant passages see note 59 above.
[104] For a summary of Marcionite emphases see note 41 above.
[105] I Tim. 1:7.   [106] I Tim. 6:3-5.   [107] I Tim. 3:15.
[108] I Tim. 6:14, 20; II Tim. 1:14.   [109] II Tim. 1:3, 5, 13.

of ministers have made it their concern to commit the message to "trustworthy men" who were "capable of teaching others." [110] The traditional practice of the church has been never to "ordain anyone hastily." [111] Careful training "for the religious life" was from the outset the prerequisite to ordination, and ordination involved the assumption of responsibilities to which the minister would thereafter be wholly devoted.[112]

Because of the seriousness of their responsibility as teachers and preachers of the Christian message [113] "elders" must be men mature in Christian experience.[114] Their "assistants" must also first be "tested" and be permitted to serve only when there is "no fault to be found with them." [115] It violates apostolic tradition for women "to teach or domineer over men" and they are accordingly required "to keep quiet" in church.[116] "Widows," however, who can meet the requirements of age and character may be employed as church visitors, and when so employed are to be paid for their services.[117] The ministry of the church must be carefully disciplined because the message the preacher "shapes" is "God's message." [118]

[110] II Tim. 2:2.   [111] I Tim. 5:22.   [112] I Tim. 4:14-15.
[113] I Tim. 5:17.   [114] I Tim. 3:6.   [115] I Tim. 3:10.
[116] I Tim. 2:12.   [117] I Tim. 5:3-16.   [118] II Tim. 2:9, 15.

BIBLIOGRAPHY

Bacon, Benjamin W.: *The Beginnings of Gospel Story.* New Haven: Yale
University Press, 1920.

————: *The Fourth Gospel in Research and Debate.* New York: Moffatt,
Yard & Co., 1910.

————: *The Gospel of the Hellenists.* New York: Henry Holt & Co., 1933.

————: *An Introduction to the New Testament.* New York: The Macmillan Co., 1924.

————: *Studies in Matthew.* New York: Henry Holt & Co., 1930.

Barnett, Albert E.: *Paul Becomes a Literary Influence.* Chicago: University
of Chicago Press, 1941.

Bigg, Charles: *The Epistles of St. Peter and St. Jude.* New York: Charles
Scribner's Sons, 1901.

Branscomb, B. Harvie: *The Gospel of Mark.* New York: Harper & Bros.,
1937.

Brooke, A. E.: *The Johannine Epistles.* New York: Charles Scribner's Sons,
1912.

Burton, E. D.: *The Epistle to the Galatians.* New York: Charles Scribner's
Sons, 1920.

Cadbury, H. J.: *The Making of Luke-Acts.* New York: The Macmillan Co.,
1927.

Case, S. J.: *Experience with the Supernatural in Early Christian Times.*
New York: The Century Co., 1929.

————: *The Social Triumph of the Ancient Church.* New York: Harper &
Bros., 1933.

Charles, R. H.: *A Critical and Exegetical Commentary on the Revelation
of St. John.* New York: Charles Scribner's Sons, 1920.

————, ed.: *The Apocrypha and Pseudepigrapha of the Old Testament.*
Oxford: Clarendon Press, 1913.

Colwell, E. C.: *John Defends the Gospel.* Chicago: Willett, Clark & Co.,
1936.

Dibelius, Martin: *A Fresh Approach to the New Testament and Early
Christian Literature.* New York: Charles Scribner's Sons, 1936.

Dodd, C. H.: *The Epistle of Paul to the Romans.* New York: Harper &
Bros., 1932.

Easton, Burton Scott: *Christ in the Gospels*. New York: Charles Scribner's Sons, 1930.

————: *The Gospel According to St. Luke: A Critical and Exegetical Commentary*. New York: Charles Scribner's Sons, 1926.

Filson, Floyd V.: *Origins of the Gospels*. New York: Abingdon Press, 1938.

Foakes-Jackson, F. J., and Lake, Kirsopp: *The Beginnings of Christianity*. London: Macmillan & Co., 1920-33.

Frame, J. E.: *The Epistles of Paul to the Thessalonians*. New York: Charles Scribner's Sons, 1912.

Goodspeed, Edgar J.: *The Formation of the New Testament*. Chicago: University of Chicago Press. 1926.

————: *A History of Early Christian Literature*. Chicago: University of Chicago Press, 1942.

————: *An Introduction to the New Testament*. Chicago: University of Chicago Press, 1937.

————: *The Meaning of Ephesians*. Chicago: University of Chicago Press, 1933.

————: *New Chapters in New Testament Study*. New York: The Macmillan Co., 1937.

————: *New Solutions of New Testament Problems*. Chicago: University of Chicago Press, 1927.

Grant, Frederick C.: *The Earliest Gospel*. New York and Nashville: Abingdon-Cokesbury Press, 1943.

————: *The Growth of the Gospels*. New York: Abingdon Press, 1933.

Gregory, C. R.: *Canon and Text of the New Testament*. New York: Charles Scribner's Sons, 1907.

Harnack, Adolf: *The Acts of the Apostles*. Tr. J. R. Williams. London: Williams & Norgate, 1909.

————: *Die Chronologie der altchristlichen Litteratur bis Eusebius*. Leipzig: J. C. Hinrichs, 1897.

————: *The Origin of the New Testament*. Tr. J. R. Wilkinson. New York: The Macmillan Co., 1925.

Harrison, P. N.: *Polycarp's Two Epistles to the Philippians*. Cambridge: The University Press, 1936.

————: *The Problem of the Pastoral Epistles*. New York: Oxford University Press, 1922.

James, M. R., tr.: *The Apocryphal New Testament*. Oxford: Clarendon Press, 1924.

Jülicher, Adolf: *An Introduction to the New Testament*. Tr. Janet Penrose Ward. New York: G. P. Putnam's Sons, 1904.

Knox, John: *Marcion and the New Testament.* Chicago: University of Chicago Press, 1942.

———: *Philemon Among the Letters of Paul.* Chicago: University of Chicago Press, 1935.

Lake, Kirsopp: *The Earlier Epistles of St. Paul.* London: Rivingtons, 1914.

Leipoldt, Johannes: *Geschichte des neutestamentlichen Kanons.* Leipzig: J. C. Hinrichs, 1907.

McGiffert, A. C.: *The Apostles' Creed.* New York: Charles Scribner's Sons, 1902.

McNeile, A. H.: *An Introduction to the Study of the New Testament.* Oxford: Clarendon Press, 1927.

Mayor, J. B.: *The Epistle of St. James.* London: Macmillan & Co., 1892.

Moffatt, James: *The General Epistles.* New York: Harper & Bros., 1928.

———: *An Introduction to the Literature of the New Testament.* New York: Charles Scribner's Sons, 1927.

Rawlinson, A. E. J.: *The Gospel According to Mark.* London: Methuen & Co., 1927.

Richardson, Alan: *The Miracle-Stories of the Gospels.* London: Student Christian Movement Press, 1941.

Riddle, Donald W.: *Early Christian Life.* Chicago: Willett, Clark & Co., 1936.

———: *The Gospels: Their Origin and Growth.* Chicago: University of Chicago Press, 1939.

———: *The Martyrs: A Study in Social Control.* Chicago: University of Chicago Press, 1931.

Ropes, J. H.: *The Singular Problem of the Epistle to the Galatians.* Cambridge: Harvard University Press, 1929.

Sanday, William: *The Criticism of the Fourth Gospel.* New York: Charles Scribner's Sons, 1905.

Scott, E. F.: *The Epistle to the Hebrews.* New York: Charles Scribner's Sons, 1923.

———: *The Epistles of Paul to the Colossians, to Philemon, and to the Ephesians.* New York: Richard R. Smith, 1930.

———: *The Fourth Gospel: Its Purpose and Theology.* New York: Charles Scribner's Sons, 1907.

———: *The Literature of the New Testament.* New York: Columbia University Press, 1932.

———: *The Pastoral Epistles.* New York: Harper & Bros., 1937.

———: *The Validity of the Gospel Record.* New York: Charles Scribner's Sons, 1938.

Streeter, B. H.: *The Four Gospels: A Study of Origins.* New York: The Macmillan Co., 1925.

——: *The Primitive Church.* New York: The Macmillan Co., 1929.

Taylor, Vincent: *The Formation of the Gospel Tradition.* London: Macmillan & Co., 1935.

——: *The Gospels: A Short Introduction.* 4th ed. London: Epworth Press, 1938.

INDEXES

Index of Subjects and Persons

Achaicus, 47
Adventism, 37, 43, 198, 272-73
Alexander the Great, 35
Alexandrinus, codex, 64
Alogi, 203
Amiatinus, codex, 60
Amyntas, 23-24
Andrew, of Caesarea, 202-3
Antichrist, 40, 42, 60, 136, 208, 242, 249
Antiochus Epiphanes, 40, 210
Antinomianism, 29, 76, 160, 264-65, 272-73
Anti-Semitism, 149-51, 155, 159, 162
Antitheses, of Marcion, 276, 282
Antoninus Pius, 284
Antony, 23, 71
Aphraates, 230
Apollos, 55
Apologetic motive in Luke-Acts, 71-72, 168-69, 173-75, 179-80, 222
Apostles, Epistle of the, 287
Apostles' Creed, 285, 287, 290
Apostolicity, 233, 262-63, 267, 277, 288-89
Apphia, 87, 89
Aquila, 49-50
Aramaic, 129, 135, 147, 148
Archippus, 84, 86, 87-92
Aristides, 21
Ariston, the presbyter, 141
Armenian version, 141, 204
Athanasius, 193, 243, 262, 268, 277
Athenagoras, 21
Attalus of Pergamum, 22
Augustine, 193-94, 244, 246-47, 254, 268
Augustus, 23, 60, 206-7

Bacon, B. W., 95, 123, 142, 157, 192, 224
Barabbas, 180
Bar Kochba, 151, 235

Barnabas, 25, 26, 28, 134, 193, 281
Barnabas, Epistle of, 15, 21, 33, 59, 147, 182, 214, 225, 253, 261, 263, 264, 268
Basil, 183
Basilides, 283
Bauer, W., 69
Beast, 211, 212
Belief, 240-41, 289-92
Bell, H. I., 211
Bigg, C., 262, 263
Branscomb, B. H., 114, 137, 140
Brooke, A. E., 244
Brutus, 71
Bultmann, R., 118, 121
Burch, E. W., 142
Burton, E. D., 24

Cadbury, H. J., 165, 169
Cadoux, C. J., 27
Caligula, 207
Calvin, 194
Carthage, Councils of, 194, 255, 268
Case, S. J., 120, 222
Cassius, 71
Catholic Christianity, 235, 237, 270, 281-83
Credo, 283, 284
Cerinthus, 203, 283
Charles, R. H., 146, 164, 208, 244
Chloe, 47, 52, 55
Christology, 70, 80, 83-86, 139, 144-45, 157, 160, 190, 199-201, 212, 223-24, 238-41, 248-51, 265, 271, 290
Chrysostom, 135
Church, 157-61, 184, 190-91, 235, 241
Claudius, 28, 36, 170, 179, 211
Clement of Alexandria, 15, 33, 39, 61, 70, 79, 133, 150, 165, 193, 203, 215, 221, 226, 243, 261, 268, 277

297

Index of Sources in Early Noncanonical Writings